HESBAN

Series Editors

Lawrence T. Geraty
Øystein Sakala LaBianca

ANDREWS UNIVERSITY PRESS

in cooperation with the

INSTITUTE OF ARCHAEOLOGY
ANDREWS UNIVERSITY

BERRIEN SPRINGS, MICHIGAN

TELL HESBAN
AND VICINITY
IN THE IRON AGE

by

Paul J. Ray, Jr.

Managing Editor
Paul J. Ray, Jr.

Technical Assistants
Robert D. Bates
Stephanie C. Merling

HESBAN 6

Published with the financial assistance of the
National Endowment for the Humanities
and Andrews University

Illustrations, unless otherwise noted, are from the Horn Archaeological Museum (Heshbon Expedition archive).
Cover design by Paul J. Ray, Jr. Series cover design by Peter Erhard.

A joint publication of the
Institute of Archaeology
and Andrews University Press
Berrien Springs, Michigan 49104-1700

07 06 05 04 03 02 01   5 4 3 2 1

ISBN 0-943872-19-7
Library of Congress Control Number: 2001135198

ACKNOWLEDGMENTS

The publication of archaeological research is inconceivable without the encouragement, help and suggestions of many individuals. This volume was originally the product of a doctoral dissertation under the direction of Randall Younker, whose assistance was invaluable. The other committee members, all of whom made valuable suggestions and recommendations, were David Merling, Richard Davidson, Øystein LaBianca and Burton MacDonald.

Besides the able assistance received from each of the above individuals, the author wishes to acknowledge his indebtedness to Larry G. Herr, who has laid much of the groundwork for understanding the Iron Age at Tell Hesban. This includes his original assignation of the loci, which was adapted here for the most part; his introductory paper for an ASOR symposium (1979a); his work with Jim Sauer on the Iron Age pottery of Tell Hesban; his correspondence with the author regarding this aspect of the research; his comments on a draft of two chapters of the work when it was still in dissertation form; as well as the many insights into the Iron Age in central Transjordan gained from his numerous works cited throughout.

David Merling, as curator of the Horn Archaeological Museum, greatly assisted this project by opening up the museum archives, object collections and library for my use. Øystein LaBianca encouraged my use of his data on bones and seeds as well as other unpublished material from the original Heshbon Expedition. Ralph Hendrix, the former publications director of the Institute of Archaeology, allowed my access to the Heshbon photo archives.

I am further indebted to Robert Bates, who helped with the formatting of a number of the graphics and to Stephanie Merling, who proofread the manuscript in its final form.

The publication of this volume could not have been completed without the support of the Institute of Archaeology, the administration of Andrews University, and the encouragement of Andrews University Press.

Finally, special recognition must go to my wife Barbara, and our children Zechariah and Rebekah, whose encouragement and loving sacrifice of time that we might have spent together have made this work possible.

Paul J. Ray, Jr.
Andrews University
Berrien Springs, Michigan
August 2001

Table of Contents

List of Figures

List of Plates

List of Tables

Preface

Many of us associated with the Madaba Plains Project in Central Transjordan, and other scholars as well, have eagerly awaited Paul Ray's synthesis of the archaeological data from Hesban and Vicinity in the Iron Age. Yet, at the same time we have wondered, what could really be said about Iron Age Hesban, given that most of the settlement remains dating to this period had been swept by later occupants off the tall's summit onto its slopes and into its huge reservoir! This situation left very little in the way of stratified occupational layers from the Iron Age for the archaeologist to study. Indeed, some of us have wondered what could possibly be learned from an assemblage with so little promise!

In this volume, Paul Ray has provided a compelling example of how much CAN be learned, despite overwhelming limitations, when the scope of inquiry is properly framed. By undertaking a painstaking reevaluation of the stratigraphic evidence preserved in the records from the original Heshbon Expedition; by taking full advantage of information provided by various specialists on the pottery, objects, bones and seeds from Iron Age strata; by taking into account the findings of archaeological surveys in the region surrounding Hesban; by undertaking his own very focused archaeological probe on the tall; and by building on proposals by others regarding the meaning of all these finds in terms of changes over time in the everyday life at Hesban; Paul Ray has provided the archaeology of Transjordan with an example of the best practice in extracting valuable historical and cultural information from an assemblage consisting largely of secondary deposits and fills.

Another significant contribution of this volume is its account of how the archaeologists who dug at Hesban in the sixties and seventies evolved in what they saw to be their goals and objectives. Over the decade that the site was excavated, the Heshbon Expedition became increasingly concerned with anthropological questions as a complement to its original concerns with historical and biblical questions. And its methods changed accordingly, to the point that the expedition gained a reputation in Near Eastern archaeology circles as a leading "processual archaeology" dig! The volume is thus a good place to go to find out how the research agenda of the Madaba Plains Project originated.

Significantly, it is the findings of the Madaba Plains Project during the decades following the Heshbon Expedition which make Paul Ray's most controversial claim in this volume not only plausible, but compelling —namely his claim that the earliest settlement at Hesban appears to have been a small unfortified Reubenite village. This confirmation of the biblical story of the tribe of Reuben rebuilding Heshbon (Num 32:37) came, unfortunately, too late to cheer Siegfried S. Horn, who died in 1993—disappointed by not finding evidence of Israelite occupation at Iron Age Hesban. He would have been greatly buoyed on reading *Tell Hesban and Vicinity in the Iron Age*!

— Øystein S. LaBianca
Andrews University
Berrien Springs, Michigan
August 2001

Foreword

There is no question for those familiar with the Hesban project, that when Siegfried Horn initiated the Heshbon Expedition, he was hopeful of finding evidence to illuminate the biblical periods that correspond to the Late Bronze and Iron Ages. While the findings for those periods appeared quickly in the preliminary reports published in the *Andrews University Seminary Studies,* their final publication was delayed for a variety of reasons, one of which was to find a person with both the expertise and time to pull all the Iron Age findings together. Jim Sauer, of course, did the important initial analysis of the Iron Age pottery (regrettably, Jim's untimely death precluded his finishing that project in the manner that he hoped). Larry Herr also did important work on both the Iron Age stratigraphy and pottery of Hesban and was an indispensable guide in the latter follow up work. However, other commitments and responsibilities precluded him from doing the Iron Age volume for the Hesban Final Publication Series. While trying to identify which staff member could best work up the Iron Age period, Sten LaBianca and Larry Geraty pushed for the publication of other volumes in the Hesban series. As a result, excellent volumes on the Hesban Necropolis, the processes of sedentarization and nomadization in the region around Hesban, the Hesban Survey, its environmental context, its faunal remains, its historical context, and the finds from the Hellenistic and Roman periods have preceded the appearance of this Iron Age volume.

In the meantime, LaBianca was able to persuade Paul Ray, one of our doctoral students at Andrews University with considerable field experience, to undertake this task for his doctoral dissertation. Paul's work with Sten as the Field Archaeologist for later follow up work at Hesban during the late 90's made Paul especially well suited for this task. Because of my own experience as a field archaeologist in Jordan, I was asked to direct the dissertation. Colleagues, Øystein LaBianca and Dave Merling from the Institute of Archaeology and Richard Davidson from the Old Testament department at Andrews University worked with Paul as well. Larry Herr, although not a faculty member at Andrews, continued to provide excellent and critical input as well. Burton MacDonald, a veteran field archaeologist who has many years of experience working in Jordan served as an external examiner for the defense. After successfully defending the dissertation, Paul Ray has reworked and reformatted the dissertation so that it would be suitable for inclusion in the Hesban Final Publication Series.

In his Preface for this volume LaBianca notes how well Paul was able to reconstruct so much of Iron Age Hesban in spite of a lack of many stratified occupational layers from that period (there were some). Paul was also compelled to reconstruct some of the sections due to some loss of original materials in a transfer of museum materials at Andrews University. Thanks to the redundancy built into the Hesban recording system and the insights provided by the so-called "new archaeology," Paul Ray has done an admirable job of both restoring lost data and recreating the Iron Age period at Hesban. He has synthesized an incredible amount of data into a concise and readable report that will proudly take its place next to the other volumes of the Hesban series.

— Randall W. Younker, Director
  Institute of Archaeology
  Andrews University
  Berrien Springs, Michigan
  October 2001

Chapter One

INTRODUCTION

Chapter One

Introduction

Forces, both natural and manmade, constructive and destructive work over the centuries to form the complex phenomena of the Middle Eastern tell, thus making the process of unraveling its secrets a major challenge. The Iron Age remains at the site of Tell Hesban, located in what is today the Hashemite Kingdom of Jordan, have been the focus of this study.

Interpretation of the excavated material at Tell Hesban has been aided by comparison with cultural material excavated at sites within the immediate and more remote geographic contexts of the tell. These include the recent archaeological excavations at Tell el-ᶜUmeiri, Tell Jawa, and Tell Jalul. Surveys have also broadened the database in the immediate area. These include the survey of the hinterlands of Hesban, carried out while the site was being excavated (Ibach 1987) and newer surveys in the region initiated in the hinterlands of Tell el-ᶜUmeiri, Tell Jalul and again at Tell Hesban,[1] with the survey at Tell el-ᶜUmeiri now published in part (Boling 1989; Younker 1991a; Christopherson 1997b). In addition, data available from a much larger context such as the surveys in the Baqᶜah Valley, the Greater Amman area and the Dhiban Plateau as well as other surveys (Gordon and Villiers 1983; McGovern 1986; Gordon and Knauf 1987; Yassine, Ibrahim and Sauer 1988; Abu Dayyah et al. 1991; Ji and ᶜAttiyat 1997) have been drawn upon and these were further checked against the data presented in the *Jordan Antiquities Database and Information System* (Palumbo 1994), henceforth *JADIS*. With this evidence at hand, an attempt to reconstruct the everyday life (including such elements as settlement patterns, social organization, subsistence, and trade) of the communities that settled at Tell Hesban and vicinity throughout the Iron Age[2] has been made.

Beyond the interpretive task we have also included a chapter on the process by which the tell was investigated archaeologically during the five major seasons of excavation from 1968 through 1976. The goals, methods, presuppositions, and

strategies of those who produced the data whereby Hesban's history (and especially the Iron Age) can be reconstructed, have been revisited within the parameters of the times. Thus, the dynamic of the Hesban excavation has been set in its own context, and its unique contribution to the history of the discipline of archaeology in general and the paradigms of "Biblical Archaeology" and the "New Archaeology," in particular, have been evaluated.

Three separate components have thus been dealt with in this study. The first component involves the identification of the Iron Age stratigraphy of Tell Hesban whereby the excavated architectural and soil/debris layers have been delineated. The second, and broader component, is interpretive. It involves the reconstruction of the everyday life of the inhabitants of Iron Age Hesban and its environs. The third component is reflective and seeks to ascertain the unique niche of the Heshbon Expedition within the development of the "New" or "Processual Archaeology" by tracing the evolution of the Hesban methodology.

Site Location and Description

Tell Hesban (fig. 1.1) (map reference: 2267:1344) is located at 3148′ latitude north and 3548′ longitude east on a hill that rises 895 m above sea level in the middle of the central Jordanian Plateau. It is flanked by the Wadi el-Marbat on its east side and the Wadi Majar on its west side (cf. fig. 5.13). The former flows south towards Madaba and the latter also to the south before swinging back to the north where it runs into the Wadi Hesban and then progressively into the Wadi er-Rameh and the Wadi Kefrein, finally draining into the Jordan River to the west (Glueck 1946: 241; Younker 1994b: 55).

History of Investigation

Though some preliminary investigation had been initiated prior to the beginning of this study, a

Figure 1.1   Map of Jordan with Inset of Tell Hesban and Vicinity.

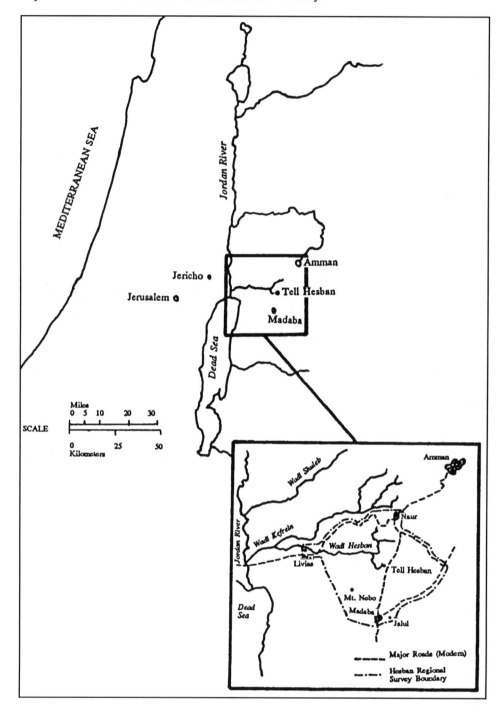

full study of the Iron Age site has yet to be fully addressed. The history of Heshbon from the literary sources (including the Iron Age) has been collected and discussed by Vyhmeister (1989a). In addition, each excavation season (1968, 1971, 1973, 1974, and 1976)[3] was followed by a full preliminary report (Boraas and Horn 1969b; 1973; 1975; Boraas and Geraty 1976; 1978), but no attempt at a synthesis of the Iron Age was possible at this time. The most complete study was an unpublished paper by Herr (1979a), but the nature of that paper, prepared for an ASOR Symposium (Herr 1979b), made this excellent work necessarily brief and thus incomplete. What has been said about the Iron Age remains in recent summary articles (Shea 1979; Geraty 1982: 699-702; 1992: 181-184; 1993: 626-630; 1997: 19-22; LaBianca 1989b: 261-69; Fisher 1994) has been based upon Herr's study.

A few preliminary remarks have also been made regarding the history of Hesban's evolving excavation methodology (Boraas 1994; Geraty 1994; LaBianca 1990; 1994a), but these have each focused on selective aspects and, thus, no attempt at a complete synthesis of the subject has yet been made.

In addition to the accounts of the Western explorers and travelers of the 19th and early 20th centuries who made comments about the tell and life in the region (collected by Vyhmeister 1989b), an attempt has been made by LaBianca (1989a; 1990), who uses the food systems concept, to present a model of cultural change. His conceptualization views the history of the occupation of the site in terms of four distinct cycles of intensification (sedentarization) and abatement (nomadization). However, as Falconer (1992: 761) has pointed out, LaBianca has not based his work on a detailed analysis of the archaeological material evidence nor has he provided broad enough controls.

Finally, recently the book entitled *Hesban After 25 Years* (Merling and Geraty 1994) appeared containing studies on nearly every aspect of the excavation of Tell Hesban. However, within the studies on the periodization of the tell, there was none to be found on the Iron Age, indicating the lacuna in this area even after a quarter of a century. The intent of this study is to fill that lacuna.

Limits of the Research

Due to the vast quantity of material that was

Table 1.1 Tell Hesban Strata.

Stratum	Dates
1	A.D. 1870-1976
2	A.D. 1400-1456
3	A.D. 1260-1400
4	A.D. 1200-1260
5	A.D. 750-969
6	A.D. 661-750
7	A.D. 614-661
8	A.D. 551-614
9	A.D. 408-551
10	A.D. 365-408
11	A.D. 284-365
12	A.D. 193-284
13	A.D. 130-193
14	63 B.C. - A.D. 130
15	198-63 B.C.
16	700-500/450 B.C.
17	925-700 B.C.
18	1050-925 B.C.
19	1100-1050 B.C.
20	1150-1100 B.C.
21	1225-1150 B.C.

excavated at Tell Hesban, the publishing of the stratified remains has logically been divided into archaeological/historical periods. A consensus has been reached in regard to the periodization of the tell (Storfjell 1983: 9), which until recently has been divided into 19 (now 21 cf. Table 1.1) strata with three gaps as follows: the Iron Age strata (21-16) followed by a gap in occupation; the Late Hellenistic-Roman period strata (15-11); the Byzantine period strata (10-7); the Early Islamic or Umayyad-Abbasid period strata (6-5) followed by another gap in occupation; the Middle Islamic or Ayyubid/Mamluk period strata (4-2) followed by one final gap in occupation and the Late Islamic or Ottoman/Modern (Stratum 1).

The present study has been limited to the Iron Age (strata 21-16). These strata are well defined. At the upper end is Stratum 21 which is the first Iron Age horizon to be positively identified. At the other end is the occupational gap between the Iron II/Persian and the Late Hellenistic periods.

The approximately 50 acres (20 hectares) of Tell Hesban (Herr 1993b: 36) have served as the limits for the descriptions of the architectural and soil/debris layers and their associated finds (fig. 1.2; pl. 1.1). Since the original survey team delim-

Figure 1.2   Plan of Tell Hesban with Excavation Areas.

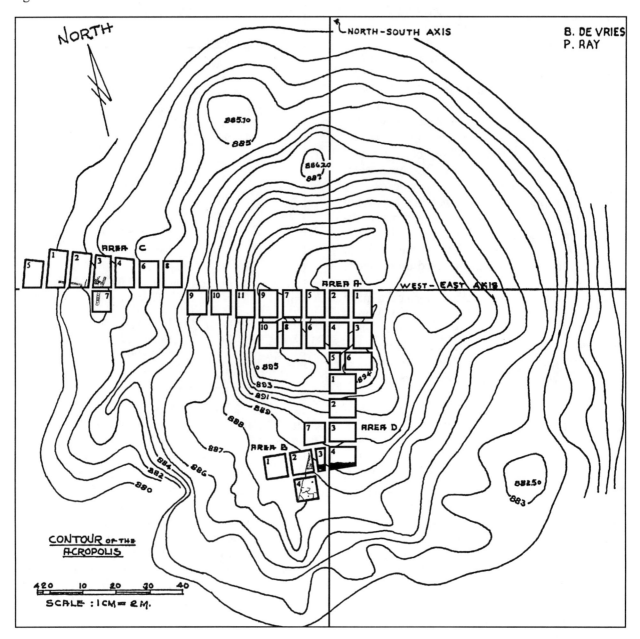

Plate 1.1 Aerial View of Tell Hesban (Courtesy Richard Cleave).

ited a radius of approximately 10 km around the tell as the project area, additional materials from this hinterland have also been considered. However, since there are indications that Tell Hesban was dominated from time to time throughout the Iron Age by various socio-political entities within the region, a somewhat wider area bounded by the Wadi Zerqa to the north and the Wadi Mujib on the south was also taken into account. Therefore, all the pertinent data from the tell, the survey area as well as central Transjordan as a whole, have served as the geographical limits for this study. However, for the sake of parallels, published material within the wider scope of greater Transjordan and Palestine has also been included.

The primary sources for the collection of data were the archives of the Heshbon Expedition which are housed in the Horn Archaeological Museum on the campus of Andrews University. Included among these are locus summary lists; field excavation notebooks, which contain the locus sheets, top plans, drawings, sketches, field supervisors notes, square supervisors notes and pottery readings; the photo archives, including photo lists, black and white photographs, negatives and slide transparen-

cies; architectural and section drawings; and object registries with field descriptions. In addition, there are data from the various specialists, which include information on ecology, fauna, flora, and ethnoarchaeology as well as regional survey data with information on other contemporary sites in the area. However, as with all projects, after 25 years, some of the records are missing (e.g., photographs and duplicated photo numbers, pages are sometimes misplaced and drawings lost).[4] Obviously, the present study has therefore been limited in terms of availability of evidence, which probably represents 99% of the data.

The actual collected remains, including the objects and the ceramic corpus, are yet another category of primary source material. The former are also housed at the Horn Archaeological Museum and have been dealt with in this study from the point of view of their contribution to an understanding of their stratigraphic context as well as their potential for reconstructing the everyday life of the inhabitants of Tell Hesban. Due to unfortunate circumstances, a complete ceramic volume, the background of which would have made this volume more useful and complete, has not yet been produced. Only the typologically significant sherds for each period are now slated to appear (Sauer and Herr forthcoming) with some of the remainder to be published in the period volumes of the Hesban series. Part of the ceramic material, including much of the Iron Age, is now housed in Canada in preparation for that volume, with the remainder located in the Horn Archaeological Museum. Due to this situation, only a selective sample of the more stratigraphically significant sherds from each stratum has been presented (chapter 3).

Due to the above limitations, the present work has utilized the preliminary field readings as recorded in the locus summaries, the corpus of Iron Age II/Persian period (Stratum 16) sherds from Area B of the 1968 Season published by Lugenbeal and Sauer (1972), a few others from the various subdivisions of the Iron Age that have also been published along with photographs but no line drawings (Sauer 1986; 1994), as well Sauer and Herr (forthcoming) on more recent developments on the work of the ceramic corpus as a basis for the stratigraphic conclusions presented herein. Although the final analysis of the corpus of Iron Age ceramics is not expected to yield major differences from the results presented here, one should still consider conclusions with respect to this material as tentative since its final analysis has yet to be completed.

Another source of data has been the secondary source material available from the published preliminary reports of the excavation in *Andrews University Seminary Studies* and elsewhere along with the final volumes already available in the *Hesban* series. Finally, for comparative purposes, various excavation reports on Iron Age sites from both Transjordan and Palestine have provided additional secondary source material for cultural and historical parallels.

Methodology

The purpose of this study has been to identify the Iron Age material evidence which was excavated at Tell Hesban, define it stratigraphically, and synthesize it diachronically. This research effort has sought to arrive at an understanding of this evidence by systematically collecting data and evaluating it through its relationship to past occurrences. The use of data obtained from the research of the scientific specialists on the Heshbon excavation team was used secondarily for the purpose of asking historical questions. Ethnoarchaeological research, with interviews functioning for the purpose of historical research, was also utilized.

In order to accomplish our objectives, the following steps were taken in cooperation with the guidelines established in Andrews University Heshbon Expedition (1977): (1) division of the loci by period; (2) ordering of the loci according to stratigraphic sequence within each square; (3) correlation of loci between squares; (4) division of correlated loci into strata;[5] (5) checking preliminary reports; (6) final write-up, stratum by stratum; and (7) preparation of site-wide stratum plans.

The results of the above procedure have been presented in the first part of the chapters (5 and 6) on specific strata as "Stratigraphy." In these chapters there is a description of each stratum, as far as possible, in terms of its idealized three stages: (c) construction/preparation; (b) use; and (a) destruction/abandonment. Other parts of these chapters consist of "Interpretation" of these strata and an overview which places them within their regional context during Iron Age I and II. In these sections, we not only seek to set each stratum in archaeological-historical perspective but also attempt to reconstruct the everyday life of the people who left these ancient remains. In order to accomplish the latter, other lines of evidence such as animal bones, carbonized seeds, ecological data, ethnoarchaeological findings, and regional survey data were taken into consideration. Bone data were used for making inferences about the subsistence economy (cf. Meadow 1983) during the various stages of the Iron Age. The use of carbonized seeds and other botanical remains have allowed us to make further assessments about subsistence strategies as well as interaction between nomads and pastoralists within the larger temporal framework of the study (Late Bronze Age through Early Persian periods). In addition, other ecological data such as lake level changes allowed us to make some suggestions about the ancient environment and its relationship to human activities. The ethnoarchaeological findings were used for insights into social organization as well as economic and technological aspects of society (cf. Kamp and Yoffee 1980; Glock 1983). Finally, the regional survey data functioned to bring relevant insights into settlement patterns and trading relationships.

Notes

[1]The data from the new Tell Hesban survey (see Christopherson 1997c for a general orientation) are not yet available and hence have not been included in this analysis. This is also the case for the new Khirbet el-Medeineh on the Wadi eth-Themed (Dearman) survey. The ᶜIraq el-Emir (Ji 1998) and the Dhiban Plateau (Ji and ᶜAttiyat 1997; Ji and Lee 1998) surveys have appeared only in preliminary form. Parts of the latter have been incorporated within.

[2]According to *JADIS*, there are 144 additional sites between the Wadis Zerqa and Mujib with unspecified Iron Age remains. This means that no differentiation (Iron Age I or II) was able to be made from the ceramics located at these sites. Although it is likely that the majority of these sites were occupied at some point during Iron Age II, they have not been included in the present study because their exact point of reference cannot be known for certain.

[3]The small-scale 1978 excavations carried out at the North Church (probe G.14; Lawlor 1980) contained remains from the Byzantine and later periods and had no bearing on the present study. They were therefore not included in this study.

[4]The section drawings had to be partially reconstructed from photos and field notes because the originals were lost when the Horn Museum changed locations on the campus of Andrews University before the final inked copies were completed. Fortunately, for the most part, the Iron Age loci were unaffected as most of them had been copied before the originals were lost.

[5]The so-called "Master Locus List" (incorporating steps 1-4 above) had already been developed during the early post-excavation phase of the Heshbon Expedition. This list was adapted here for the most part, with some modification due to later developments. Further revisions during the course of the current research were also made (see Appendix A for details).

Chapter Two

THE EVOLUTION OF THE ARCHAEOLOGICAL METHODOLOGY AT TELL HESBAN

Chapter Two

The Evolution of the Archaeological Methodology at Tell Hesban

The "State of the Art" in 1968

In order to say something meaningful about the history of the archaeological methodology used by the excavators of Tell Hesban, it is also necessary to trace, at least in a general way, the history of methodology of the discipline of Syro-Palestinian archaeology so that the former can be put into proper perspective.

A Short History of Archaeological Methodology in the Middle East between 1838 and 1970

The year 1968 came near the end of what Dever (1980a: 44) has called "the third archaeological revolution (1948-70)." It was during this time that archaeologists working in the Middle East began to realize the full potential of their discipline. It might also be called "the classificatory-historical period" to borrow a phrase from American archaeology (Willey and Sabloff 1974: 131; 1980). This period followed two pre-World War II "archaeological revolutions." The first (1838-1914) involved archaeology's initial encounter with tells or mounds, while the second (1918-1940) concentrated on shaping a scholarly discipline (Dever 1980a: 42-43).

The former (or "Classificatory-Descriptive Period") began in 1838 with the modern exploration of Palestine by Edward Robinson and Eli Smith, and also included explorations of Jerusalem by de Saulcy (1850 ff), Wilson (1865), Warren (1867), and Clermont-Ganneau (1869-71). It was also during this period that the Palestine Exploration Fund (1865), the Deutscher Palästina-Verein (1878), the École Biblique (1890), and the American Schools of Oriental Research (1900) were formed. It culminated with two major advances. Sir Flinders Petrie's knowledge of the distinctive objects of each period of dynastic Egypt

allowed him to use those same types of objects that he found in association with the local Palestinian pottery at Tell el-Hesi in 1890 to form a basic ceramic sequence for the Levant (Moorey 1991: 29). This was followed up by Bliss, who was not only able to refine that ceramic chronology, but also found that Tell el-Hesi was made up of super-imposed soil layers. He may already have had some vague inkling of this when he began excavations at the tell in 1891 in that he had worked at Meidum for a few months in 1890-91 with Petrie, who was somewhat influenced by Schliemann and Pitt-Rivers, the former of whom had originally observed this phenomenon at Troy (Aldred 1987: 23; Moorey 1991: 26, 29). Whatever the case may be, these two concepts (ceramic chronology and stratigraphy) were put together by Bliss at Tell el-Hesi (Blakely 1993: 111-112), thus, bringing about the first major breakthrough in Syro-Palestinian archaeology.

The other advance in methodology at this time was the introduction by Reisner of the "debris-layer" technique of stratigraphic excavation at Samaria. This consisted of the separation of the superimposed occupational layers of the tell with analysis of the disturbances of these layers. The aim was to reveal both the human and natural processes which produced the tell. The technique also noted the location of all artifacts by a detailed recording system with photographs, maps, architecture plans, and descriptions, with a registry of all artifacts and the location where they were found by elevation (Wright 1975: 109-110; Levy 1995: 46; Davis 1995: 44).

Unfortunately, the advances of Petrie, Bliss, and Reisner were initially ignored and the basic methodology of the day was to open up large sections for horizontal exposure with small supervisory staffs and large numbers of local laborers. Finds were recorded in a registry. Field recording was confined to the excavator's diary and consisted mostly of architecture. Sections, when drawn, were schematic, and publications consisted mainly of building plans and objects with descriptions (Toombs 1982: 90; cf. Bliss and Macalister 1902: 1-11), based on an interest in cultures (groups of assemblages representative of a particular time and place; cf. Renfrew and Bahn 1991: 98).

The latter (or "Classificatory-Historical Period: Chronology Phase") was dominated by two individuals. The first was Clarence Fisher, who was Reisner's architect at Samaria. Reisner, like Petrie, was an Egyptologist and soon returned to Egypt, leaving Fisher to carry on the debris-layer technique in Palestine. Since Fisher participated in nearly every major excavation up to World War II and was advisor to all ASOR-affiliated digs as well, the technique soon became known as the Reisner-Fisher method (Wright 1958a: 41; King 1987: 18-19). However, though Fisher claimed to be carrying on Reisner's methodology, his own method was actually fundamentally different. Viewing the tell site as a series of strata which were formed by the superimposition of the remains of architectural features that could be dated by careful excavation, he concentrated on the wide exposure of architecture, which he attempted to dig one stratum at a time, often working in arbitrary 30 cm levels, in order to clarify building phases. Instead of trenches, he dug in areas upon which he placed an arbitrary grid (Moorey 1991: 56; Davis 1995: 43-44).

The second leading figure of this period was W. F. Albright, who arrived in Palestine in 1919. He claims to have arrived as a skeptic of the accuracy of Israelite tradition, but that the artifactual evidence he encountered soon convinced him of the basic historicity of the Scriptures (Albright 1924: 5-6; 1933: 5-6; Davis 1993: 54-55). Other studies suggest that despite his training, the influence of his conservative past set him out on a programmatic enterprise against Wellhausenanism from the very beginning, much as Ernst Sellin had done earlier (King 1983: 46; Bunimovitz 1995a: 61), but scholarly and political considerations were the cause of his seemingly liberal/conservative alterations (Sasson 1993: 4-5; Long 1993: 36-42). His personal methodology, though seldom articulated, was a combination of empiricism (objective "realia") and positivism (Dever 1993b: 26-28). Although he was influenced by Fisher both in terms of excavation technique and pottery chronology, with his excavations at Tell Beit Mirsim, he moved beyond Petrie's sequence dating to develop a full-blown

pottery typology, which in some ways was a reaffirmation of the chronology of Bliss (cf. Albright 1938: 3; Blakely 1993: 114). While paying lip service to the Reisner-Fisher method (Albright 1938: 4), he actually took Fisher's modification of the excavation method and Reisner's recording system and added his ceramic typology for chronological control and, with it, influenced a whole generation of archaeologists. However, Albright, like Fisher, had only a limited comprehension of stratigraphy, and thus his understanding of the stratigraphy at Tell Beit Mirism was based on ceramics and his notions of biblical history. His section drawings for the site are schematic and in need of being redone (Dever 1993b: 31; Davis 1995: 44-45).

With the arrival of the British Mandate, Departments of Antiquities were developed in Palestine (1920) and Transjordan (1923). During this period, the most influential excavations were Tell Beit Mirism (1926-32) and Megiddo (1925-39). Archaeologists became interested in the prehistorical periods in addition to the Bronze and Iron Ages, the latter having the biggest impact on biblical studies. Glueck pioneered the first surface survey in Transjordan (1932-47) and the Jewish national school came into existence. In terms of methodology, excavations were still managed by a single archaeological director, though many times with an advisor and a growing number of supervisory personnel. The use of Fisher's method, where adhered to, necessitated a move away from the earlier dependence on untrained, unsupervised workmen, whose job it was to move dirt and hunt for objects (Bade 1934: 11-12, 51-53).

Notes on methodology, where they exist, include comments on mapping, topography of the site and its immediate environs, photography, pottery, and provision for publication (Grant 1931: 1-5). The diary system was still in vogue, but was more "scientific" than earlier (Toombs 1982: 91; cf. e.g., Grant 1931: 11-77). The emphasis on pottery typology not only shifted the interest from culture to chronology, with archaeological reports of the era reflecting the sequence and dating of cultures tied to the political history of the region (Toombs 1982: 90), but stratigraphy took a secondary role, the attention having been diverted away from the pioneering work of Reisner and onto Albright's modification of Fisher's method. Thus, there was a methodological stagnation in terms of stratigraphical excavation (Davis 1995: 45).

The Classificatory-Historical Period: Descriptive Phase

After World War II, there was a quick resumption of archaeological fieldwork. Among the more notable and trend-setting American and British excavations in Palestine at this time were those of Shechem (1956-73, Wright), Gezer (1964-74; Wright, Dever, Lance, and Seger) and Jericho (1952-58, Kenyon). The now significant Jewish national, or Israeli, school also initiated some new trends at Hazor (1955-58) and Masada (1963-65), both by Yadin. The Jordanian national school was in its infancy, with excavations at Irbid and Qweilbeh (1958-59, Dajani); Jerash (1959, Maᶜayeh); Samaria (1965-67, Zayadine); Amman (1966-67, Dajani; 1968-72, Zayadine with Dornemann), and Sahab (1969-75, Ibrahim) to name a few (Dever 1985: 38; Geraty and Willis 1986: 7-8), though none are notable for methodological advances. Among the foreign excavations in the country, the Heshbon Expedition was just getting under way (1968).

The major methodological breakthrough of the period came in the 1950s when Kathleen Kenyon introduced her "balk-debris-layer" method of stratigraphic excavation. She had learned this method from Mortimer Wheeler in the 1930s at the Roman-British town of Verulamium and had tested it somewhat at Samaria under Crowfoot (King 1987: 19). It came into its own, however, in her excavations at Jericho from 1952-58. Here, she dug in 5 x 5 meter squares with intervening 1 meter balks which were used to view the debris in section. The location of these squares was determined by a superimposed grid laid upon the site. In contrast to Reisner, who focused as much on the processes that produced a tell, whether human or natural, as disturbances (Davis 1995: 43-44), it would seem that Kenyon placed more emphasis on factors that disturb the normal layering of debris and sediment such as ground slope, fills, pits, foundation, and robber trenches (Davies 1988: 49-50) and had an inadequate awareness of what is known today as "site formation processes" (Bunimovitz 1995a: 63). This "new" technique (re)introduced the third dimension as well as the element of control into field archaeology. It also made it possible to separate the soil layers and the objects found within them with greater accuracy and to recognize the sub- phasing of the architecture more precisely (Dever 1980a: 44; 1985: 34). Kenyon's definitive

statement of her method appeared the same year (1952) that she began the excavation at Jericho. Though controversial, the results were superior, especially when reexcavating sites which had previously been dug under less sophisticated methods, a tendency among other archaeological digs at this time. Wright saw no difference between Kenyon's method and that of the method of "Reisner-Fisher" (King 1987: 19). Others have either suggested Pitt-Rivers as its originator (Toombs 1982: 90; cf. Renfrew and Bahn 1991: 29) or argue for its descent from him to Petrie and then to Wheeler and Kenyon (Moorey 1991: 27). Moorey, perhaps due to his British bias, has downplayed the role of Reisner considerably (1991: 36).

Wright combined the "Reisner-Fisher" method with the refinements of the Wheeler-Kenyon method at Shechem (King 1988: 25). This was mediated through Callaway, who was instrumental in bringing the method there (Mattingly 1995: 21-22). Wright also modeled his excavation somewhat on the organizational pattern of Yadin at Hazor (King 1987: 18). This combination of elements at Shechem became the basic excavation technique of nearly all American, British, and to some extent French excavations in Israel and Jordan during the 1960s. Besides the added control of digging in limited 5 x 5 meter squares, there was also a preference on these excavations to focus on sherd analysis. Sherds are ubiquitous and lend themselves to quantitative analysis (cf. e.g., D. Cole 1984: 1-7). The Israeli school, however, as it developed after 1948, emphasized architecture and large-scale exposure in contrast to the limited exposure of 5 x 5 meter squares. Through the influence of Immanuel Dunayevski, who pioneered this so-called "architecture method," buildings, floors, and artifacts were related to each other on the basis of architecture instead of debris layers (Levy 1995: 48). The Israelis also preferred to base their results on *in situ* whole ceramic forms as opposed to sherds and tended to work at sites which had not previously been dug (Dever 1980a: 45; 1985: 35). As a result of these methodological differences, there was a heated debate and a series of exchanges between the two schools, little of which actually ended up in print (Aharoni 1973a: 23*; Dever 1973: 1*-8*).

With the appearance of *Samaria-Sabaste III* in 1957, another methodological controversy arose in regard to Kenyon's interpretation of fill materials (Davies 1988: 50). Kenyon contended that the period in which a specific floor was laid should be dated by the fills beneath the floor. Yadin (1958: 34), however, argued that fills below a floor predate the floor and, thus, the material found within the fills should be dated to the period before the floors. In addition, Yadin took Wright to task for dating the temple at Shechem to MB IIC, since the temple and the fill below it were from the same period. Wright responded by arguing that while it is generally true that a building is later than the soil upon which it rests, in this case there was definite evidence that showed that the temple was built in the same period as the fill, since MB IIC deposits were sealed above the first floor level of the temple (Wright 1958b: 34). Wright then went on to redate Kenyon's pottery periods at Samaria (1959: 67-78), and to suggest that both Kenyon and Yadin had oversimplified the problem of fills (1962: 34-40).

Yet another major controversy, and one with far-reaching results, occurred in the late 1950's. Albright had little interest in theology in a formal sense, but because of what was seen as his conservative positions, he had earlier been accused of being a closet fundamentalist (Albright 1934: 28; Davis 1993: 55). However, it was his student G. E. Wright, now the leading American biblical archaeologist and at the same time also the leading spokesperson for the "neo-orthodox" biblical theology movement, who was to become the main figure of this new controversy. His only excavation experience before 1956 was with Albright at Beitin in 1934. Subsequent to that experience, he had made a reputation with a series of "armchair" review articles on earlier excavation reports. Theologically, he focused on the "acts of God" in history and advocated the position that participation in biblical faith meant that the primary datum for faith was history (Wright 1952: 126-27). This idea has an impact on archaeology because, with Albright, he saw archaeology as providing the primary data for history. With their emphasis on archaeology being an adjunct of biblical studies, and Wright's statements about archaeology being the means to shed light upon the Bible (Wright 1957: 17), a reaction arose against what appeared to be an "archaeology proves the Bible" position (Dever 1980b: 1-5; 1985: 53-61).

The balk-debris-layer method had brought about a more sophisticated excavation technique. Although there continued to be a major emphasis on ceramic typology, field reports became more and more descriptive with very little synthesis. A trend that facilitated this was the introduction in the late 1960s of the interdisciplinary approach to archaeology with an increasing number of specialists and, with this, a move away from the one-man archaeological "genius" of previous generations. The increase of excavation costs at this time and the demand for larger staffs and specialists in the coming years were to bring about a need for funds beyond the capabilities of one sponsoring institution, creating a move toward consortia of institutions and student volunteerism to supplement (in Jordan) if not replace (in Israel) the need for local laborers. Notwithstanding the various controversies, this was a period of broadening horizons and growth in the overall discipline (Dever 1985: 38-40).

The Heshbon Expedition in the Horn Years

The Heshbon Expedition went into the field in 1968 after a false start the previous year due to the Six-Day War (Trapped by Fighting in Jordan 1967, sec. 2; Marks 1967-68: 2; Boraas and Horn 1969a: 104; Horn 1994: 10-11). The site of Tell Hesban had been chosen by Siegfried Horn on the basis of a process of elimination of other sites which had either been of interest to him or had been suggested by archaeological colleagues as potential candidates, as well as a series of circumstances (tactical and otherwise) which made it a desirable place to excavate (Boraas and Horn 1969a: 102-3; Horn 1982: 1-4; 1994: 5-7). In addition, Horn liked the challenge of excavating a site in an area of Palestine that was less known and could contribute to the overall understanding of the Levant as well as the potential for finding inscriptional evidence, which had tended to be more productive in Transjordan (Horn 1994: 7-8). Financial support for three seasons of excavation had already been pledged in 1966 by the Archaeological Research Foundation, based in New York City (Horn 1994: 4; Geraty 1994: 40), of which the budget for the first season was in the neighborhood of $20,000 (Heshbon Expedition Archives). About the same time (1966), Horn commissioned a B.D. thesis on the history of Heshbon from the literary sources (Geraty and Running 1989: ix), which was published in abbreviated form (Vyhmeister 1968: 158-177) shortly before the excavation.

The 1968 Season

With the backing of ASOR and a permit from

Plate 2.1   Hesban 1968 Staff.

the Department of Antiquities of Jordan, the
Andrews University Heshbon Expedition took to
the field from July 15 to August 30, 1968. The
rather late starting date was due to the fact that
Boraas and one other key staff member were also
involved in the excavations at Shechem, which
were carried out in June and July (Boraas and Horn
1969a: 105, 111). Horn was the director of the
project, formulated its aims, and chose the areas to
be excavated. Roger Boraas, a colleague from
Horn's Shechem days, was the chief archaeologist.
It was his job to give instruction in methodology
and field techniques and to ensure that proper procedures and "scientific methods" were carried out
so that the aims of the project could be met (Boraas
and Horn 1969a: 107). The field technique was
that of the Wheeler-Kenyon method (Boraas and
Horn 1969a: 111) as adapted from the excavations
at Shechem as well as that used at Pella by Toombs
(Boraas 1968: 1, 3; 1994: 17). Boraas was a specialist in the method having been a student of
Toombs, who had learned it directly from Kenyon
at Jericho (Boraas 1994: 22, n. 9). He had also
worked at Shechem under Callaway, who had been
under Kenyon's tutelage at Jerusalem (Mattingly
1995: 21). Both Callaway and Toombs had also
studied with her in London in the 1961-62 academic year (Mattingly 1995: 17, 21).

The staff (pl. 2.1) consisted of 42 foreign
archaeologists, specialists, and students. They
were assisted by three representatives from the
Department of Antiquities of Jordan, several
archaeology students from the University of
Jordan, and around 115 local workmen (Boraas and
Horn 1969a: 105, 109-110). Boraas had sent written instructions to the staff six months prior to the
excavation.   This included suggested readings,
equipment to bring, and information on basic procedures (1968: 1-10). Whether due to budgetary
concerns or some other reason, there were no pre-
ordered locus sheets for the first season. Thus,
minute instructions for the makeshift ones, which
were to be made on the small notebooks to be pro-
cured locally at excavation time, were also given
(Boraas 1968: 3-7; 1994: 22, n. 11). These included information on basic items such as terminology
(and symbolic conventions), locus descriptions, the
recording of pottery, object readings, and photo
numbers, how to make top plans and section drawings, the interpretation section, and the duties of
square and area supervisors (Boraas 1968: 3-10;
Boraas and Horn 1969a: 112-115).   The field
recording described therein was an adaption of that
which was used on the excavations at Shechem,
Gezer, and Pella (Boraas and Horn 1969a: 111).

Four Areas (A-D) were opened on the tell.
These were supervised by two of Horn and
Boraas's colleagues from Shechem (Beegle and
Thompson), another, who had excavated at Dothan
(Van Elderen), and a graduate student at Harvard

University (Bird) (Horn 1994: 8-9). Two of these areas were chosen on the basis of already visible architecture and other surface features (A and D) which made them propitious to excavate. The hope of finding a defensive structure on the western edge of the mound led to the choice of Area C (Boraas and Horn 1969a: 116-17; Horn 1969a: 30-32; Boraas 1994: 15-17). These were arranged in such a way as to form north-south and east-west axes, which would produce a site-wide stratigraphic linkage (Boraas 1994: 17). The fourth area (B), actually one large square (B1), was opened as a preliminary sounding. This was done for the purpose of acting as a guide to the stratigraphy of the site (Boraas and Horn 1969a: 116; Horn 1969a: 30-31; Boraas 1984: 39-41; 1994: 16). The limited goal and funding for a three-season expedition, uncertainties about the depth of debris at the site, and the commitment to specialization all contributed to a strategy based on stratigraphic depth, rather than breadth of exposure (Boraas 1984: 42-44).

Besides the emphasis on the acropolis and its southern access route, the possible defensive installation on the west side of the tell, and the preliminary sounding mentioned above, the explicit aims of the first season also included the production of a contour map of the site. This was produced by Bert de Vries, the expedition's surveyor and architect.

Beyond the purely archaeological aims of the project, there was the hope that historical questions (e.g., evidence of Sihon the Amorite as well as that of the Israelites) would also be answered (Horn 1967: 1; Boraas and Horn 1969a: 99-102; Horn 1969a: 28-30; cf. Geraty 1994: 41). In fact, it was actually hoped that the excavation would produce evidence to support an early 15th-century B.C. date for the Exodus–a date supported by certain chronological statements in Scripture. However, except in the popular press (Shafer 1969: 12-14) and church periodicals (Horn 1969b: 4; 1969c: 67-68), this goal was not made explicit until some time after the excavations were over (Horn 1982: 5; cf. LaBianca 1990: xvii; 1994a: 25-26). In hindsight, the above-mentioned motivation for the original excavation of the site might be criticized as being in the style of traditional, "biblical archaeology," i.e., the search for biblical and historical connections (Dever 1993d: 127), nevertheless, this was common practice at the time.

Notwithstanding the more traditional approach, which focused on historical questions, there was already in the first season a commitment to specialization (Boraas 1984: 42-43; LaBianca 1990: xvii; 1994a: 26-28). This new trend had begun slightly earlier in 1966 with the introduction of a geologist (Rueben Bullard) to the excavation team at Gezer (Dever, Lance, and Wright 1970: 9; Dever 1985: 40; 1986: 1, n. 3). The first specialist to work at Hesban was the anthropologist Robert Little (Boraas and Horn 1969a: 103, 109; Little 1969: 232-39). Concurrently (1968), the Gezer excavations (Dever et al. 1974: 1) also sought the advice of an anthropological consultant (Evelyn Rattray). The earlier utilization of volunteer labor supplied by archaeology students under Bade, Albright, Kenyon, Wright, and others had been considerably expanded to include those without any previous training in archaeology by Yadin at Nahal Hever (1961) and Masada (1963-65) (Atkinson 1994: 68-70). The use of students was expanded even further into a field school at Gezer in 1966 (Dever, Lance, and Wright 1970: 9). At Hesban, where the use of volunteers was also the norm, Boraas was in charge of providing instruction (Boraas and Horn 1969a: 107, 112).

The recent political changes in the region made some equipment unavailable, and forced individuals and replacement equipment, which were coming by roundabout routes, to arrive late (Horn 1994: 12-13). Therefore, the 1968 season got off to a rough start. Nevertheless, through hard work and team spirit, the aims and goals of the first season were for the most part achieved. The results of the 1968 season included the discovery of three phases for both the Islamic and Byzantine periods as well as evidence for Roman period and Iron Age III (Persian period) remains. One of the more spectacular finds was a five-line ostracon dating to ca. 500 B.C. (Cross 1969: 228). Sherd evidence was also located for Iron Age II, Iron Age I, and Late Bronze Age (Boraas and Horn 1969b: 217-222). Though the sounding in Area B was laid out so as to avoid major architecture and to expedite rapid maximum stratigraphic penetration, an Islamic period lime kiln and what was then thought to be a two-phased Persian and Greco-Roman period wall bisecting the square were found.[1] Thus, bedrock was not reached by the end of the season (Beegle 1969: 119, 122-124; Horn 1969a: 34-35; Boraas 1984: 39-41). Although, no loci from the Late Bronze Age were found during the 1968 season, the recovery of several LB sherds from the deepest levels of the sounding in Area B suggested the possibility that material from the period of Sihon might be forthcoming in future seasons (Horn 1968-69: 2.4; 1969d: 6; 1969e: 146).

The commitment to a year of analysis and publication before returning to the field (Horn 1971-72: 1) allowed for the rather prompt and full publication of the preliminary report for the first season's work, as well as shorter reports in other journals (Horn 1969a: 26-41; 1969f: 395-98). The fact that Horn was also the editor of *Andrews University Seminary Studies* (begun in 1963) facilitated in providing an available medium for the preliminary report to appear in a timely fashion (Boraas 1988: 327). The preliminary report was also released as Volume 2 of the Andrews University Monograph Series and received favorable reviews in the *Palestine Exploration Quarterly* (Bennett 1972: 161) and *Syria* (Parrot 1971: 503-4).

The vast amount of sherd material which had been found in the Area B.1 sounding was in need of attention. Following the 1968 season, this material was worked on by James Sauer, who along with Ed Lugenbeal published 547 of these sherds (Lugenbeal and Sauer 1972: 21-69). Sauer dated them from the seventh to six centuries B.C., but would later reclassify them as Iron IIC/Persian. This was a major achievement in that this seventh-sixth century B.C. Ammonite pottery, which had previously been known only from several tombs in and around Amman, was now published from a stratigraphically controlled tell excavation (Horn 1971-72: 4).

The Heshbon Expedition was scheduled to go into the field for its second season in 1970, but was called off due to the Jordanian civil war (Van Elderen 1970-71: 2-4; 1970 Heshbon Expedition Abandoned 1970). The news release of its cancellation by Andrews University also noted that Horn was digging at Heshbon in order to "discover the exact date of the Exodus" (Heshbon Expedition Archives). Another phase of the civil war broke out in September of that year forcing the newly appointed director of ACOR (Murray Nichol) to abort his plans in the interest of the safety of his family. ACOR had been founded after the Six-Day War in 1967, because the new political boundaries created the need for an institution to facilitate the now isolated American excavations in Jordan. The directors for the first two years of ACOR's existence were Rudolph Dornemann and Bastiaan Van Elderen. Horn was asked to replace Nichol as the third director and began his duties in December of 1970 (Horn 1970-71: 2-4; Wright 1970-71: 2-3;

King 1983: 197-200). The second season was rescheduled to take place from July 15 to August 20, 1971, and hope was again raised that evidence "from the time of Moses" might be found (Americans to Dig for Bible City 1971, sec. 1).

The 1971 Season

The 1971 excavation season continued in all four areas (A-D) that had been worked in the previous season, with additional squares in each. With a slightly larger budget of about $20,500 (Heshbon Expedition Archives), the goals of the expedition were now expanded to include the excavation of tombs at Gourmeyet Hesban to the west (Area E) of the tell as well as another cemetery to its southwest (Area F). The specific aims for the season were to: locate the southern and western extremities of the Byzantine church in Area A; continue work in the Area B.1 sounding; clean out the Islamic period kiln which had been found in that square; extend the lateral exposure in Area B; attempt to find the city wall on a lower slope in Area C; join the structures in Area D to those in Area A; excavate the tombs which had recently been clandestinely pilfered; and to discover additional tombs and have aerial photographs taken (Boraas and Horn 1973: 6-8).

The staff for the 1971 season (pl. 2.2.) was slightly smaller than in 1968 with only 40 foreigners from the U.S., Canada, and Europe. Twenty were graduate students. There were also 11 Jordanians including the representatives from the Department of Antiquities and students from the University of Jordan, besides about 130 local workmen and a number of other local assistants (Horn 1972a: 15; Boraas and Horn 1973: 2, 4). In terms of continuity, only one of the four area supervisors from the previous season (Thompson in Area C) returned in 1971. Sauer, who had worked on the pottery from the sounding between seasons, became the expedition's ceramic specialist as well as the new supervisor for Area B. Lawrence Geraty, who was at that time a doctoral student at Harvard University and had been the associate Area supervisor with Phyllis Bird during the previous season, became the supervisor of Area D. Dorothea Harvey from Urbana College in Urbana, Ohio, was the Area A supervisor (Boraas and Horn 1973: 2-3). In addition, the newly opened excavations in the cemeteries (Areas E and F) were supervised by Douglas Waterhouse who had been asso-

Plate 2.2   Hesban 1971 Staff.

ciate supervisor with Thompson in Area C in the 1968 season. De Vries continued once again as the expedition's surveyor and architect (Boraas and Horn 1969a: 108; 1973: 3-4).

The excavation methodology was the same as the previous season (Boraas and Horn 1973: 6, n. 8), the only new addition in 1971 being the introduction of actual locus sheets to replace the 1968 makeshift ones.   The consecutively numbered pages consisted of a heading with fill-in areas for identifying the year, area, square, and locus number, followed by sections for "progress of excavation," locus description, the location of the locus in the square, identification of loci under and over the active locus, the dimensions of the locus and its levels on the first side of the sheet. On side two, there was room for details on associated pottery and objects, photograph descriptions, places to reference section and plan numbers, and space for a preliminary interpretation of the locus (Heshbon Expedition Archives).

In terms of specialists, Reuben Bullard, who had previously done geological work at Gezer as well as serving as a geological advisor to other excavations on the West Bank and Cyprus, joined the Heshbon Expedition in 1971 to do a geological survey of the tell and the surrounding region (Boraas and Horn 1973: 5; Bullard 1972: 129-141). Thus, geology was added to the anthropological work begun in the previous season. Unfortunately, Robert Little was able to participate for only a brief

period of time during the 1971 season, and he focused on the human skeletal material from two of the tombs. He was joined by his student, Øystein LaBianca, who assumed the responsibility for the bone material which was found (Boraas and Horn 1973: 4).

Little had set up a basic procedure for the collection and cleaning of bones during the previous season (Little 1969: 233-35). At that time, he had cleaned and registered 6,682 bones, some of which, for lack of time in the field, were shipped to the U.S. to be completed there (Little 1969: 235). LaBianca, then an undergraduate student at Andrews University, processed this material as part of a lab assignment for an anthropology class taught by Little. This lab work led to an invitation to work at Hesban. In preparation for his participation on the excavation he also carried out further informal research on faunal analysis (LaBianca 1995a: 5-6).

The results of the 1971 season included the classification of the Byzantine church founded on bedrock in Area A as a basilica-type structure. With the exception of one Roman period wall supporting the southern row of columns, the only earlier remains on the summit were ceramic. Thus, it was concluded that if any earlier occupation had existed on the eastern part of the summit, it had been destroyed by subsequent building and quarrying operations during the Roman period or later. In Area B, 16 archaeological strata dating from modern to Late Iron Age II were found along with further exposure of Wall B.1:17B in Square B.2. The city wall which had been expected in Area C remained elusive, though one wall (C.1:30) possibly dating to Late Iron II suggested the possibility that earlier architecture existed in this area. Excavation in Area D included the uncovering of another section of the Umayyad stone pavement which had been found the previous season, as well as the excavation of several cisterns, one of which had a 229,000 liter capacity. Ten tombs were excavated in the two cemeteries (E.2, E3, F.1, F.4-10), the highlight being the excavation of the Roman period "Rolling Stone" (F.1) and "Swinging Door" (F.5) Tombs (Boraas and Horn 1973: 8-14).

Other significant accomplishments from this season included the completion of the contour map of the tell and aerial photography. An important negative conclusion was that the tell did not contain remains earlier than the seventh-sixth century B.C. The excavators were led to this conlusion by Sauer's stratigraphic refinements of what appeared to be an "adequate comprehensive stratigraphic sequence," accounting for all the major stages of occupation of the tell excavated through the 1971 season, supplemented by extensive numismatic finds. This evidence seemed to indicate that Tell Hesban could not be identified with the Heshbon of Sihon in the time of Moses (Boraas and Horn 1973: 14-15). In order to make sure that potential Late Bronze Age evidence was not missed, the plans for the following season were to include soundings on the lower parts of the tell in order to see if the stratigraphical history there was the same as on the acropolis. A new survey component was also to be initiated in the territory surrounding Tell Hesban in order to search for another possible candidate for Sihon's Heshbon (Horn 1971-72: 4; Boraas and Horn 1973: 16). These two possibilities for locating OT Heshbon were also suggested in popular reports on the second season's work (Horn 1972d: 11), and in publications dealing with more academically related issues (Geraty 1972: 34-35).

The excavations at Tell Hesban, where both foreign and Jordanian archaeologists worked together and produced results of interest to both, were taken up with as much excitement in Jordan as they were in the West. In 1971, there were articles about Tell Hesban and the excavations being done there in the local Jordanian press (Know Your Country: Tell Hesban and the Archaeological Excavations, 1971) and the major tourist magazine (Hesban, 1971).

The preliminary results of the second season, including the specialist reports (Bullard 1972; LaBianca 1973a), were again published in a timely fashion in *Andrews University Seminary Studies*, with shorter summaries appearing in other journals (Horn 1972a: 15-22; 1972b: 422-26). The preliminary report was also published as volume 6 of the Andrews University Monograph Series with a favorable review in *Theologische Literaturzeitung* (Zobel 1979: 288).

Between the 1971 and 1973 seasons, the activities of two of the staff members would lead to important contributions that not only gave the Heshbon Expedition acclamation, but would point the way to new directions. The first was the publication of Sauer's monograph on the pottery of the 1971 season (Sauer 1973). The main contributions of this work, as pointed out by Rast (1974: 434-35), were the detailed sub-divisions for the late periods and their representative pottery. These later groupings were also praised as being, for the most part, independently dated by coins. However, others (Brower and Storfjell 1982: 1-6) have serious reservations on the value of dating by coins. The sampling of the pottery was from good stratigraphic contexts, adding to the understanding of the ceramic development of the later periods, and also demonstrating the importance of a site (Hesban) in Transjordan for filling in gaps in the knowledge of Middle Eastern ceramics. Finally, it was noted that the study laid the groundwork for all future work in the area. Tell Hesban was ultimately to become the type-site for the pottery sequence in central Transjordan for the Roman through the Islamic periods.

The second activity was by LaBianca, who, after the 1971 excavations, began the process of keypunching the data on the 5,867 bones found that season into the computer and using the resulting database analysis as the basis for his report (LaBianca 1973a: 135; 1995a: 8). His interest in zooarchaeology took him to Harvard University's Museum of Comparative Zoology as a special student in the 1972-73 academic year to study with Barbara Lawrence and Richard Meadow. While studying in the Department of Anthropology and working on a more in-depth analysis of the bones of the domestic animals from the 1971 season, he was introduced in a graduate seminar to the "new archaeology" movement (see below) which was the current focus in New World and British archaeology at the time. Its stress on the utilization of specialists in archaeology and other emphases (see below) provided him with the rationale to push for a much-expanded anthropological agenda, including ethnoarchaeology and taphonomical studies (LaBianca 1994a: 33-34; 1995a: 8-10) for what was intended to be the third and last season of the Heshbon Expedition (Horn 1971-72: 1).

About the same time (spring of 1973), Boraas, having already encountered the "new archaeology" through his reading of D. L. Clarke's *Analytical Archaeology*, visited the environmental archaeology laboratory at the Institute of Archaeology in London where he was introduced to the technique for studying ancient plant remains known as froth flotation (LaBianca 1994a: 32-33). Geraty, Herr, and Sauer, all doctoral students at Harvard at the time, were also becoming aware of the agenda of the "new archaeology" (LaBianca 1994a: 34). In addition, LaBianca submitted to Horn the expedition's first explicit research design. This dealt with the various aspects of the zooarchaeological remains and consisted of the nature and type of research, the nature of the data, the extent of the researcher's control over the data, the method of gathering and recording of data, the attributes of and the method of presentation of the raw data, as well as the handling of interrelationships among them (LaBianca 1973b: 1-5). That the time was ripe for this new direction to have an entering wedge into the Heshbon Expedition methodology seems to be reflected in a popular piece by Horn (1972c: 11-12) on archeological methodology, where both the subtitle of the article itself and a number of comments within reveal an acquaintance with some of the issues and trends of the "new archaeology."

The 1973 Season

The third season of excavations at Tell Hesban was conducted between June 20 and August 14, 1973. A larger budget of about $26,000 (Heshbon Expedition Archives) for this season provided for a larger staff (pl. 2.3) consisting of a 49-member foreign team from the U.S., Canada, Europe, Australia, and South Africa. About half were students, and ten were Jordanians including the representatives from the Department of Antiquities, and archaeology students from the University of Jordan. In addition, there were 130 local laborers (Boraas and Horn 1975: 101-102, 105). In terms of continuity of staff, Van Elderen was again the

supervisor of Area A as in 1968. Sauer, Thompson, and Geraty all returned, supervising Areas B-D respectively. Beegle, who had supervised the sounding in 1968, was also back, this time supervising the Area F cemetery excavations as well as the new probes (Area G), to be opened up on the lower part of the tell. Waterhouse also returned and was the supervisor, this time, of the new topographical survey team. Bert de Vries served again as the surveyor and architect for the expedition (Boraas and Horn 1975: 102-104). While LaBianca was the only specialist for the third season, his wife and several assistants under his direction expanded the anthropological work to include ethnoarchaeology and taphonomical components (LaBianca and LaBianca 1975: 235). There was also an attempt in at least one of the field reports to integrate the bone data (Sauer 1975a).

Since this season was originally intended to be the last (Horn 1973-74: 1; 1974: 151; Boraas: 1974a: 5), the aims for the campaign were directed toward the finishing up of the excavations (Boraas and Horn 1975: 105). Some of the squares were reduced in size in order to reach bedrock, at least along their main north-south or east-west axes and the north balks of the squares in Area B. Other problems such as the western dimensions of the Byzantine church on the acropolis, the location of the Esbus to Livias portion of the Roman road, and the search for additional tombs also received attention. In addition, a number of new probes were laid out on the lower slopes of the tell and a survey of other settlements in the immediate region was begun (Boraas and Horn 1975: 105-106). Both of these latter operations were done in order to explore the options for the location of Sihon's Heshbon. The excavation methodology was essentially the same as that of the previous seasons (Boraas and Horn 1975: 105, n. 3).

The end of the season, however, found the expedition with a number of unsolved problems, some of which had to do with some unexpected new features, which were brought to light for the first time during this season. The excavation of the church remained uncompleted, with its western edge still not exposed. The survey team was able to trace the course of the Roman road leading from Livias in the Jordan Valley toward Esbus by the location of a number of Roman mile stones, curb stones, subsurface roadbeds, guard-towers, and road stations. In addition, they visited and sherded 103 sites within a 10 km radius of the tell,[2] some of which had not

Plate 2.3 Hesban 1973 Staff.

been previously mentioned by earlier explorers. Several Roman and Byzantine tombs were discovered in the southwest cemetery (Area F) and four new probes (G.1-4) were opened on the lower slopes of the tell. One of these (Probe G.1) had a fill with Iron Age I sherds covering bedrock. Other significant features found during the 1973 season included a bath complex of the Ayyubid/Mamluk period, which obstructed the western edge of the basilica; an L-shaped wall (C.1:40/63), which appeared to be part of the defensive system of the town in the Early Roman period; and a defense wall (D.1:4) from the Late Hellenistic period surrounding the acropolis. Evidence from the Abbasid period (a stone-lined pit and foundation trench) was also exposed in a probe (B.6), with homogenous pottery from this period being isolated for the first time (Horn 1973-74: 1-4; Boraas and Horn 1975: 106-115).

By far the most exciting features found during the 1973 season were a defensive (possibly Iron II/Persian period) structure in Square C.3, a thick plastered floor in Square B.1, and a possible retaining wall in Square B.2. The latter consisted, up to that point, of eight courses of header-stretcher ashlar masonry. The floor and wall in Area B were parts of a structure, dating to Iron Age II, and interpreted as possibly being one of the reservoirs or pools mentioned in Song of Solomon 7:4. In addition, Iron Age I sherds were found in debris layers in Square C.1, and two other walls in Area B (Squares 2 and 3) also appeared to be Iron Age in

date, making this the earliest material found so far on the tell (Horn 1973-74: 2; Boraas and Horn 1975: 106-107).

Since the western edge of the basilica had not yet been reached, and the nature of the newly found structures (including the Early Roman wall in Square C.1, the Iron II wall in Square C.3, and the plastered floor and retaining wall in Area B, Squares 1 and 2) was as yet not ascertained, it was realized that further work was still needed (Boraas and Horn 1975: 115-116). Thus, a fourth season was scheduled for June 26-August 14, 1974. Its announcement appeared in an Andrews University news release in October of 1973 (Heshbon Expedition Archives). The unexpected finding of Iron I material on the tell after the 1971 season (cf. Boraas and Horn 1973: 14-15) also gave rise to the possibility that other gaps in the tell's history might still be found on other sections of the site which were as yet untouched (Boraas and Horn 1975: 116). This observation led to the logical conclusion that earlier (Late Bronze Age) material from the time of Sihon, which could have a bearing on the date of the Exodus, might still be found (Plan Fourth Trip to Jordan 1973; Michigan Scholar Digs in Near East For Exodus Secret 1973). Following the tradition of the previous two seasons, the preliminary report of the third season appeared within two years after the campaign in *Andrews University Seminary Studies*, as well as shorter reports in other journals (Horn 1974: 151-56; 1975: 100-105).

The Beginning of the "New Archaeology"

The "fourth revolution" (Dever 1980a: 46) or the "Explanatory Period" (again borrowing an analogy from Willey and Sabloff 1974; 1980) in Syro-Palestinian archaeology began about 1970. This was a period of expanding horizons. It followed a series of negative reactions to the Albright-Wright school in the late 1950s and 1960s against what was perceived to be their "archaeology proves the Bible" viewpoint. Along with the shift away from various aspects of their philosophical position, there was also a move away from a number of other positions of this paradigm, especially the historicity of the Patriarchs and the Conquest model. De Vaux (1970: 64-80) suggested that written evidence was needed for historical purposes and that the Bible could neither be contradicted nor proved by archaeology, a position that Wright (1971: 70-76) himself adopted within a short period of time. The issue of what archaeology can and cannot be expected to do is also reflected in Geraty's discussion of the problem of Tell Hesban's lack of remains from the time of Sihon (1972: 35; cf. n. 10). About the same time Dever (1974: 27-46) called for a separation between archaeology and biblical studies and suggested that the term "Biblical Archaeology" be dropped in favor of "Syro-Palestinian Archaeology" as the name of the discipline, and further that it should seek to be more professional (cf. King 1983: 269-72).

With the advent of the 1970s, there began to be an emphasis on methodology as theory as opposed to the earlier view of methodology as technique (Dever 1988: 339). American (or New World) Archaeology had gone through a similar series of methodological developments about a decade earlier. In fact, the innovations of what became known as the "new" or processual archaeology were, with one exception, all borrowed from New World Archaeology. The basic tenets of this paradigm were an inter-disciplinary approach (see above); emphasis on ecology; ethnographic parallels; systems theory; the "scientific" method based on formulating and testing hypotheses, constructing models, and using deductive reasoning; research designed to answer specific questions; explicit theory involving explanation instead of mere description; quantitative analysis allowing computerized statistical treatment; a major focus on cultural process and cultural evolution as well as optimism about the possibility of reconstructing social organ-

ization and cognitive systems (Willey and Sabloff 1974: 178-211; 1980; Renfrew and Bahn 1991: 35; Dever 1981: 15-16; 1988: 341; 1992: 355-57). With the earlier focus on stratigraphy and ceramic typology manifesting itself in a long chronological and cultural sequence, there was already a major interest, though rarely articulated, in cultural evolution (Dever 1981: 16). This had not been so in New World Archaeology, where a long series of social anthropological thinkers, culminating in the work of Service (1962), had brought this about.

The Heshbon Expedition in the Geraty Years

With the end of the 1973 season, Horn's funding was exhausted. In addition, he had taken on administrative duties at Andrews University as Dean of the Theological Seminary. These factors led him to give up the directorship of the Heshbon Expedition, which he turned over to Lawrence Geraty, who was now assistant professor of Archaeology and History of Antiquity in the Seminary (Geraty 1994: 42-43). The transition to a new director can be seen in a popular report on the 1973 season authored by both Horn and Geraty (1974: 12-14). In May of 1974, an Andrews University news release announced that not only would the expedition continue to seek evidence for the city of Sihon, but in addition to the coming 1974 season there would be at least one more season of excavation (Heshbon Expedition Archives; cf. Horn 1974: 156; Boraas and Geraty 1976: 6).

There were a number of factors that contributed to the decision to return to the field already in 1974 instead of following the usual alternating year schedule. These included the fact that a trained staff was ready to go back; three of the core staff members were already in Jordan on other assignments and their services could be utilized without additional travel expense; vandalism and illicit digging at Hesban threatened to impede the proper interpretation of the archaeological evidence if too much time elapsed between excavation seasons; the political situation in Jordan was stable; the expedition was encouraged by the government of Jordan to return to the field; and ACOR had promised logistic and financial incentives to do so at a time when funds for excavation were at a premium due to inflation in Jordan, which was causing costs to rise considerably (1974 Heshbon Excavation brochure; Heshbon Expedition Archives).

In order to fund these final seasons, a number of new institutions were added as sponsors. In addition to the three seasons of support by the Archaeological Research Foundation of New York (above), the major sponsor of the dig during the Horn years had been Andrews University. Calvin Theological Seminary and ACOR provided additional support (Boraas and Horn 1973: 1; 1975: 101). Upsala College was also a co-sponsor in the aborted 1970 season (Boraas and Horn 1973: 1, n. 40). However, with the drying up of the original funding after the 1973 season, there was need for expanded institutional support. For the 1974 season, this came, in addition to Calvin Theological Seminary and ACOR, from Covenant Theological Seminary, Grace Theological Seminary, the Graduate School of Loma Linda University, and Hope College through the Kyle-Kelso Archaeological Fund (Boraas and Geraty 1976: 1-2). In addition, sponsorship came from an increased number of individual and private donors (Boraas and Geraty 1976: 2).

Now that Geraty was the director of the expedition, there was an increased commitment to the anthropological concerns and methods of the "new archaeology" (LaBianca 1990: xvii; 1994a: 34). LaBianca submitted another research proposal shortly before the beginning of the season, this time for ethnoarchaeological studies. The content included the purpose; review of the literature; type of research; collection and recording of data; equipment and supplies, as well as suggestions (based on his experience in 1973) and recommendations from anthropological works for the assistants who would be carrying out the work in the coming season (LaBianca 1974: 1-13). Following his visit to the Institute of Archaeology in London a year earlier (above), Boraas was inspired to support the introduction of froth flotation so that carbonized seeds might be collected for research (LaBianca 1994a: 33). He also expanded the locus sheet entries to include data on bone analysis (zoological, ornithological, and human), soil samples, and seed, pollen, micro-faunal, and entomological analyses (Heshbon Expedition Archives).

The 1974 Season

A budget of about $27,500 supported the expanding work at Hesban both in terms of excavation and specialists. The staff (pl. 2.4) consisted of 60 foreign archaeologists and students from the

U.S., Canada, Europe, Australia, New Zealand, and Indonesia as well as 15 Jordanians, including Department of Antiquities representatives and students from the University of Jordan. As usual there were a large number (150) of local laborers as well. Dr. Horn now held the title of senior advisor to the project as well as serving as object registrar for the final three weeks of the season. Geraty, as mentioned above, was the director, and Boraas continued, as in the previous three seasons, as the chief archaeologist. Van Elderen and Sauer continued as the supervisors of Areas A and B respectively, with the latter also serving as the ceramic typologist of the expedition. Area C was now supervised by Harold Mare of Covenant Theological Seminary, and Area D by Larry Herr, a veteran of the 1971 season and at the time a Ph.D. candidate at Harvard. The Area E and F cemeteries were supervised by James Stirling, an anthropologist from Loma Linda University, who was also responsible for the human skeletal remains, and the work in the Area G probes (5-10) was supervised by whomever of the Area C, D, E, and F supervisors, was in closest proximity to these locations. The regional survey and the probes at G.8 (Umm es-Sarab) were supervised by Robert Ibach. The number of specialists this season was increased to three with two anthropologists (LaBianca and Stirling) and a geologist (Harold James). Bert de Vries served as the supervisor of the architectual drafting and surveying team as in the three previous seasons (Boraas and Geraty 1976: 3-5).

The aims of the season revolved around the three unsolved problems that remained at the end of the 1973 season. These were the elusive western edge of the basilica and the unclear nature of both the Roman and Iron Age defense installations in Area C as well as the unclear relationships between portions of the Iron Age reservoir in Area B. The specific aims of the season were: (1) to find the narthex at the western edge of the basilica; (2) to ascertain the dimensions of the Roman period architecture of the acropolis; (3) to fix the northern perimeter of the Area B reservoir; (4) to connect the plastered floor in Square B.1 with the plastered retaining wall/cut bedrock in Squares B.2 and B.4; (5) to improve the stratigraphic link between Areas B and D; (6) to place a sounding (G.5) in another possible reservoir southeast of the tell; (7) to complete the survey of the surrounding region; (8) to make some additional probes on the tell and in the vicinity to see if the archaeological history would

Plate 2.4 Hesban 1974 Staff.

agree with what was found on the upper parts of the mound; (9) to explore other cave-tombs in the cemeteries in order to find burials from the Iron Age; (10) to improve the ecological database and expand the zooarchaeological and ethnoarchaeological components; and (11) to clarify the Roman and Iron Age fortifications in Area C (Boraas and Geraty 1976: 7; Geraty 1975a: 48-49).

It was noted in the preliminary report (Boraas and Geraty 1976: 6, n. 7) that "the excavation and recording methods were extensions of those employed in the previous seasons." These were formulated in a 50-page circular letter (Boraas 1974b), which was a major expansion of the 10-page one which appeared before the first season (Boraas 1968), and as such might be considered the excavation's first "dig manual." It not only included suggested background reading, equipment to bring, and the details of the recording procedure, as in the letter three seasons earlier, but also consisted of detailed explanations of various features and the options for their description; explanations of technical procedures, both archaeological and that of the specialists; definition of terms, and the responsibilities of various supervisory personnel.

The discoveries of the 1974 season included remains from Iron Age I between two vertical bedrock faces in B.2 and B.3, with a sizable wall (B.2:112) on one end; two wall fragments in D.4, and a silt layer at the bottom of a cistern in D.1;

confirmation that the huge feature in Area B (Squares 1, 2, and 4) with its eastern wall (B.2:84) and associated hydraulic system was indeed a reservoir dating to Iron II; the southern extension of the late Iron Age II defensive wall, found the previous season, in Area C; a cave with an associated Rhodian jar handle, used for industrial purposes during the Late Hellenistic period in B.4; additional evidence for a defensive structure consisting of a stone tower and paved flagstone floor from the Early Roman period in Area C; additional portions of Late Roman period walls on the acropolis suggesting that the basilica of the Byzantine period reused features of an earlier Roman Temple and further that this hypothesized structure may be the temple depicted on the two rare Elagabalus "Esbous" coins found in the 1973 and 1974 seasons; an Umayyad period *tabun* cut into the mosaic floor of the basilica; and further features belonging to the Ayyubid/Mamluk period bath house (Boraas and Geraty 1976: 7-15; Geraty 1975a: 51-55).

Other achievements included an additional 22 sites sherded by the survey team. This brought the total to 125 sites within a 10 km radius of the tell and confirmed occupation from Chalcolithic to modern times. The survey team also tested and verified the validity of the survey methodology at the site of Umm es-Sarab (G.8) (Ibach 1976a: 113-17). The cemetery team did not find evidence of any pre-Roman (especially Iron Age) tombs, but did explore and excavate a number of new Roman and Byzantine tombs. A number of new probes were opened around the mound and in its vicinity. These confirmed the occupational history already established on the tell. Probe G.5 confirmed the existence of a Byzantine reservoir to the east of the tell (Boraas and Geraty 1976: 15; Geraty 1975a: 50). That the increased emphasis on the collection of scientific data (anthropological, biological, ecological, and geological) was also a success is indicated by the fact that there were seven specialist studies, besides those on the small finds, in the preliminary report (cf. also LaBianca 1975: 1-6). There was also an attempt to integrate some of this information (bones and seeds) into one of the field reports (Sauer 1976). As was now the custom, the preliminary report as well as shorter reports of the excavation season (Geraty 1974: 1-8; 1975b: 576-86) were published in a timely fashion.

As seen above, the primary objectives of the 1974 excavation season had grown out of the findings of the three previous campaigns. Nevertheless, the emphasis on probes in order to check the occupational history of the tell and the regional survey's search for other sites in the vicinity had implications for the original objective of locating Sihon's Heshbon (Geraty 1994: 43). The probes revealed, as was the case on the tell, that there was no pre-Iron Age I remains in close proximity to the mound. This seemed to rule out Tell Hesban as an option for Heshbon in the time of Moses. Therefore, the most plausible hypothesis, assuming that the name had changed locations as elsewhere, was that one of the other regional sites, where Late Bronze Age remains were found by the Survey, was the capital of Sihon (Geraty 1975d: 11). Though it would appear that the original objective of locating Amorite Heshbon was not totally forgotten, it was the modern methodological innovations that had been embraced by and had come to dominate the Heshbon Expedition that were highlighted even in popular (church-related) reports on the achievements of the excavation (Geraty 1975c: 4-6).

The 1976 Season

The last season of the Heshbon Expedition was carried out between June 15 and August 11, 1976. The much expanded budget of about $35,000 (Heshbon Expedition Archives) was again funded

and sponsored for the most part by the participating institutions including Andrews University, Calvin Theological Seminary, Covenant Theological Seminary, and the Kyle-Kelso Archaeological Fund in cooperation with ACOR. New sponsors included Winebrenner Theological Seminary, Earthwatch, and the Friends of Archaeology (Riverside, California) as well as a number of private donors (Boraas and Geraty 1978: 2-3). The extra-large budget was due to "skyrocketing costs" and logistical difficulties (Geraty 1976: 41). The staff (pl. 2.5) consisted of 83 foreign professors and students from the U.S., Canada, South America, Europe, Australia, and the Far East as well as 13 Jordanians from the Department of Antiquities and the University of Jordan. In addition, there were 11 part-time volunteers. Among this group were eight scientific specialists, the largest contingent to date (Boraas and Geraty 1978: 4, 7-8).

Besides Geraty and Boraas, the field staff included Van Elderen and Herr, supervising Areas A and D (only Squares 2 and 3) respectively. Herr also supervised Area B for Sauer, who as the ceramicist of the expedition was busy with his pottery report. Area C was divided in half (west and east) and supervised by Mare and Thomas Parker respectively. The cemeteries (Areas F and K) were supervised by John Davis and the various Area G probes by Donald Wimmer, Robin Brown, Michael Blaine, and John Lawlor. The regional survey was again supervised by Ibach, and de Vries was in charge of surveying and drafting as in all the previous seasons. Specialists included LaBianca, Little, and Stirling (anthropologists); Boessneck and von den Driesch (zooarchaeologists); Crawford (ethnobotanist); Hare (geologist), and Perkins (computer specialist). Although not specialists themselves, a number of assistants helped to expand the ethnoarchaeological work of the 1973 and 1974 seasons. In addition, Robin Cox conducted a series of meteorological experiments (Boraas and Geraty 1978: 5-8). The field methodology was the same as the much-expanded program of the 1974 season. The locus sheets remained the same and the "manual of instruction" (Boraas and Geraty 1978: 8-9, n. 11) was, with some minor additions and deletions, the same as well (Heshbon Expedition Archives).

Besides reaching bedrock in the squares along the north-south and east-west axes, requiring the opening of four new squares (A.10 and 11; C.9 and 10) for the sake of completeness, the aims of the final season were focused around the remaining

Plate 2.5 Hesban 1976 Staff.

architectural problems. These were: (1) to locate the western edge of the basilica; (2) to clarify the defensive structures in Area C; and (3) to clear up questions surrounding the nature of the Area B reservoir (Boraas and Geraty 1978: 9-10; Geraty 1976: 41-42). Additional aims included the search for the Iron Age cemetery; further work on the regional survey, including an experimental grid-sampling of Jalul (Site 26); the opening of a number of new probes, especially in connection with various cave installations and other surface features, as well as checking the accuracy of the stratigraphy of the tell; a continuation of the froth-flotation sampling in three squares from various portions of the site in order to test the surface-bedrock sequence; an experimental "control" square (C.9) to test data-retrieval; and the expansion of the botanical, environmental, ethnographical, geological, meteorological, and zooarchaeological studies (Boraas and Geraty 1978: 10-11).

Bedrock was reached in every square but one (C.10) along the main north-south and east-west axes by the end of the season with consistent Iron Age I to Mamluk ceramic readings. This temporal sequence was also confirmed in the Area G probes, in that no new periods (earlier or later) were found. Two of these probes (G.14 and 17) revealed two

other Byzantine churches, both of which required further excavation. The location of the western edge of the basilica met with limited success, exposing only the western wall of the nave. In Area C, the Iron Age II defensive structure in Squares 3 and 7 was found to have been repaired, if not originally constructed, in the Hellenistic period with further modifications in Roman and Byzantine times. On the western end of Area C, the Early Roman tower also was shown to have later (Late Roman and Byzantine) modifications. In addition, its defensive nature was called into question by the finding of a doorway and aisle on the west (or outer) side of the building. In Area B, the features in Squares 1, 2, and 4 were indeed found to be connected and the location of both corners of the eastern wall indicated that the shape of the reservoir was probably square (Boraas and Geraty 1978: 11-13; Geraty 1976: 42-45).

The location of the Iron Age cemetery eluded the excavators again, but several new Roman and Byzantine tombs were found. Thirty additional sites were located and sherded by the regional survey, bringing the total number of sites surveyed by the team to 155. The whole 10 km radius surrounding the tell was thus completely surveyed with the exception of three military zones. Among the sites surveyed were Jalul (Site 26) and Tell el-ᶜUmeiri (Site 149), both of which were inhabited during the Bronze Age. The latter was also the object of an intensive grid-survey with implications for survey methodology (Ibach 1978b: 221). The goals of the scientific specialists were also met for the most part with a complete sequence of pollen and seed patterns from surface-bedrock in three squares as a result of the froth-flotation analysis. In terms of ecology, collections of modern flora were made and ornithological observations on current species taken. These analyses were supplemented by ethnographical observations. In addition to the zooarchaeological work of the current season, there was a marathon bone-reading session of the excavated material from all of the previous seasons in a three-week post session. A detailed geological map of the site and its immediate vicinity was also completed (Boraas and Geraty 1978: 13-14; Geraty 1976: 50).

In the process of concluding the excavation of the site, the architects made a general plan of the site for tourist development with suggestions for the preservation of architecture and other features. This was in addition to completing their normal work on the floor-plans, elevations, and architectural sections as well as the contour map extensions. A tentative site-wide stratigraphical history was completed with 24 general strata from Iron Age I through Late Ottoman/Modern periods (Boraas and Geraty 1978: 14-17). Following the tradition which had been established in the previous four seasons, the preliminary report appeared within two years of the last season as well as shorter summary reports (Geraty 1977a: 1-15; 1977b: 404-408; 1980: 251-55).

Though not mentioned in the 1973 report, Tell Jalul (Site 26) had been sherded by the survey team (Ibach 1987: 13). This was done again in 1974 (Ibach 1976b: 123). In the 1973 season no Late Bronze Age sherds had been found on the site (Ibach 1987: 13) and only a few (Ibach 1976b: 123, n. 15), actually two possible LB sherds (Ibach 1987: 13), in 1974. However, Jalul was one of the few sites on which Glueck had found pottery from the Middle and Late Bronze Ages during his earlier survey (1934: 5, 82; 1970: 141). Therefore, the Survey team spent three weeks during the 1976 season conducting an intensive surface survey. This time they found 163 Late Bronze Age sherds (104 on the slopes and 59 on the summit of the tell) out of a total of 26,225 (2,000 diagnostic) pieces (Ibach

1978b: 219, Table 2; 1987: 14). This site along with Tell el-ᶜUmeiri (Site 149), sites 128 and 132, and possibly Iktanu (Site 97) and Umm es-Sarab (Site 54) were the only sites within the 10 km radius of Tell Hesban with Late Bronze Age pottery attested (Ibach 1978a: 209-10; 1987: 157-59).

After the 1974 season it was realized that since the Area G probes had revealed the same site history (Iron I through Mamluk) as on the tell, the only chance of locating Sihon's Heshbon seemed to lay in the possibility that one of the sites in the region with Late Bronze Age evidence might be the site of biblical Heshbon. With the intensive survey of Jalul revealing a relatively heavy Late Bronze concentration, it logically seemed to be the best candidate, assuming that the name had moved from one site to the other. Henceforth, Jalul was to become the focus of any renewed search for Heshbon. However, though this conclusion was the focus in a section of a popular article in a church periodical with the subtitle "still looking for biblical Heshbon," it was nevertheless juxtaposed to a section entitled "new types of scientific data" (Geraty 1977c: 8-9). This would seem to be representative of the fact that while the overall aims and goals of the Heshbon Expedition had grown through the years with the dominating force of the "new archaeology," the original objective of locating the biblical town of Heshbon, though no longer the major focus, was still a consideration to be reckoned with.

Publication Phase

Integration of the various component parts of the Heshbon Expedition including every aspect of the data, whether dug by the archaeologist or gathered by the specialist, could not really begin until the final publication project got started (Geraty 1990: xv). In the 1976-77 academic year, even before the preliminary report of the final excavation season appeared, plans were put into place for the final publication series. Thirty-eight authors accepted writing assignments for this forthcoming series (Final Publication Archives). However, in order to move beyond the mere descriptive accounts of the preliminary reports, the final publication series would need a theoretical framework to integrate the wide range of specialist reports with the stratigraphical analysis (LaBianca 1990: 22). Early attempts to integrate these various lines of research data by LaBianca (1978 and 1986b) were done with Julian Steward's cultural ecology approach (1955) as a framework.

Final publication procedures were adopted for those writing period reports in 1977. These included an outline of agreed-upon definitions, preparative steps, the format of manuscript outlines, periodization and stratification, and a tentative list of the volumes, their contents, and authors (Andrews University Heshbon Expedition 1977: 1-8). At this point four volumes were projected. Volume one was to include periodization studies on the tell, the cemeteries, and the survey as well as chapters on the excavation methodology, the literature on Hesban, the literary and historical information on the site, and appendices including the master locus list and the stratigraphic chart. The other three volumes were to focus on the pottery, the objects, and specialist reports respectively (Andrews University Heshbon Expedition 1977: 6-8). An application was made for a research grant from the National Endowment for the Humanities and funds were received to begin work on the materials for the final publication. In addition, 12 Heshbon authors presented papers at an ASOR symposium on the work in progress. It was the first time a team of excavation authors would use such a format, which has since become a standard (Final Publication Archives; Geraty 1990: xv).

In 1978 there was a short follow-up project of one of the probes (G.14) that were opened up in the 1976 season. There a Byzantine church had been discovered on the northern perimeter of Tell Hesban. This project was directed by John Lawlor with Larry Herr as the chief archaeologist and Larry Geraty as the senior advisor (Lawlor 1980: 65-76). This season contributes little to the overall purpose of this chapter, and therefore is not commented upon here. Its only importance, for our purposes, was that some experimentation, aimed at the improvement of the locus sheets (Herr 1989a: 214), was carried out in preparation for a new project, which was to grow out of the Heshbon Expedition (see below).

Earlier that year (the winter of 1978), the decision had been made to put the Hesban data on computer in order to recall, in an easy way, the vast amount of information as well as to manipulate it (Herr 1989a: 214). This move was essiential in order to facilitate the preparation of the final publication of the excavation results (Brower, LaBianca, and Mitchel 1980: 2). In the spring of that same year a follow-up session was convened for the purpose of arriving at a consensus on format and style.

Larry Mitchel also produced an encoding manual in 1978 and this along with the services of computer expert James Brower, and the systemization of data by a number of others (Final Publication Archives), resulted in what has been lauded as "the most complete computerized data base of field information" to be assembled up to that time (Strange 1988: 311).

The design of the system was guided by three requirements: (1) to accommodate the process of scientific inquiry; (2) to be user-friendly; and (3) to meet the constraints of the work environment. The system met the needs of the first requirement by dealing with multiple variables. With the findspot (or locus number) remaining constant, these were also somewhat relational. Finally, the system was capable of being revised and improved upon. The needs of the second requirement were met by entering the data in terms of abbreviated word form instead of numerical code as was common at the time. This feature made it easy to update the data. The information could thus be edited, sorted, retrieved, and used as raw data, or manipulated extensively if desired. In terms of the third requirement, information could be entered on-line directly into the computer or by punched cards (Brower, LaBianca, and Mitchel 1980: 2-4).

By this time tentative outlines were available for most of the now ten projected final publication volumes. Another application was made to the National Endowment of the Humanities and further funds were received to continue work on the biophysical and ethnological data for the final publication series (Final Publication Archives). A second ASOR symposium was organized for the autumn of the year, with the papers concentrating this time on the scientific and computerization aspects of the excavation (Final Publication Archives).

In 1979 two more projected volumes and a number of additional authors were added to the series. Three of the specialists (Lacelle, Crawford, and James) made a trip to Jordan that summer to do a limited field survey and collect data. In addition, a series of symposia featuring a number of the Heshbon authors were carried out in the autumn in order to share the results that had been achieved so far and so that the research could be critiqued by competent scholars. These were held in conjunction with the annual meetings at the Middle East Studies Association of North America, ASOR, the American Anthropological Association, and the Archaeological Institute of America. Their foci were on the Islamic Era at Hesban, the Iron Age at Tell Hesban, Nomadic-Sedentary relations in Transjordan, and the Hellenistic/Roman and Byzantine/Early Arabic periods respectively. Further, the 24 original strata worked out for the 1976 preliminary report (Boraas and Geraty 1978: 15-16) were recast into 20 strata, with a note on the then current debate over whether this should actually be reduced to 19 (Final Publication Archives).

LaBianca spent the 1980-81 academic year in Jordan doing additional ethnoarchaeological research (LaBianca 1984: 269-82). It was during this time that the food system concept emerged as the means of integrating all the various lines of data that had been generated by the expedition (LaBianca 1990: 27; 109). These consisted of descriptions of archaeological strata, pottery readings, small finds, animal bones, carbonized seeds, the results from the site survey, ecological and ethnoarchaeology data, explorers' accounts, and secondary sources (LaBianca 1990: 24-27, 115-129). Further, the food system concept was designed to answer questions about the environment (climate and topography), settlement, land use, operational facilities (such as tools and equipment), and diet (LaBianca 1984: 272-73; 1990: 114-15). The results were to yield information on three hypothetical food system configurations of low, medium, and high intensity (LaBianca 1984: 277-78; 1990: 131-33).

Also in 1981, a Heshbon author's conference (of 30) was held at Andrews University in conjunction with an exhibit and lectures entitled "Tell Hesban: 3000 Years of Frontier History" (Heshbon Exhibit Featured by Horn Museum 1981; Geraty 1981: 247). The conference/exhibit was supported by funds from the Michigan Council for the Humanities/National Endowment for the Humanities (Final Publication Archives).

By 1982, the Madaba Plains Project had developed out of the Heshbon Expedition with the intention of excavating at Tell Jalul that summer. With the interests of the team members now focusing on this project or others, there was a move away from a preoccupation with Heshbon. Nevertheless, the now 14 projected volumes (LaBianca 1990: 261-63) have continued to appear with seven of them currently available (LaBianca and Lacelle 1986; Ibach 1987; Geraty and Running 1989; LaBianca 1990; Mitchel 1992; LaBianca and von den Driesch 1995; Waterhouse 1998). In addition, a symposium met at Andrews University in March of 1993 to bring the research up to date in a popular manner, 25 years after the beginning of the excavation of Tell Hesban in 1968. This has resulted in a book containing the materials presented at that time (Merling and Geraty 1994).

A large amount of the preparation that has gone into the final publication series (especially what was funded by the National Endowment for the Humanities) and much of the work that has been produced thus far have focused on the rationale of the "food system" perspective (LaBianca 1990), some of the specialists' reports (LaBianca and Lacelle 1986; LaBianca and von den Driesch 1995), and the wider regional approach (Ibach 1987). Nevertheless, material focusing on historical questions, which were part of the original motivation for the excavations, has also appeared. These include a volume on historical and literary backgrounds (Geraty and Running 1989) and one of the periodization volumes (Mitchel 1992). In addition, a bound lecture by Horn has appeared (1982), where the original motivation of finding Sihon's Heshbon and its relationship to the problem of the Exodus were made explicit for the first time in an academic, non-popular medium, as well as an article by Geraty (1983) addressing the problem of bringing the archaeological evidence at Tell Hesban to bear on the Heshbon of the biblical text.

The "State of the Art" in 1976

As mentioned above, the "fourth revolution" or "Explanatory Period" in Syro-Palestinian archaeology began about 1970. This period, as we have seen, was dominated by the "new" or processual archaeology.

Archaeology as practiced in the Middle East has always been very pragmatic, and has rarely even articulated a definition of archaeology much less statements on method (Albright 1969: 1-3; Wright 1969: 149-65). Even the methodological changes brought about by the new archaeology did little to change this pragmatism, as these were made without a "theoretical reformulation of the traditional explanations for cultural change" (Bunimovitz 1995a: 65). Statements of method, with the possible exception of some belated comments on typology (Cross 1973: 2-5; 1982: 121-136), continued to be rare. It was not until the 1970s that the first explicit research designs appeared (Dever 1982: 184; 1985: 49-50). In terms of the Heshbon Expedition, while there was little sophistication in research design for the overall project (Geraty 1994: 44), especially in the early seasons, research designs did appear for various aspects of the anthropological work and other specialist studies (LaBianca 1973b; 1974; 1976b; 1976c; 1978; Crawford 1976a; 1976b).

Acceptance of the "new archaeology" paradigm within Syro-Palestinian archaeology was perhaps facilitated by the emergence of a new generation of archaeologists as a consequence of the deaths, in quick succession, of a number of the pioneering generation including Dajani (1968), Glueck (1971), Albright (1971), de Vaux (1971), and Wright (1974), the latter having already begun to accept some of the major facets of the new archaeology (Wright 1975: 104-15; King 1987: 20-24). Other deaths about this time included Avi-Yonah (1974), Aharoni (1976), and Kenyon (1978).

The interdisciplinary approach, as seen above, had actually begun in the mid-1960s at Gezer. At Hesban, there was at least one specialist each season, with relatively large numbers of them in the final two campaigns. As elsewhere, this took decidedly anthropological and ecological directions, focusing on economic factors and the natural environment. Along with the attention on "ecofacts," there was also an emphasis on the regional approach, a move which expanded archaeological interest from what might be learned from the main tell sites alone to a broader focus on settlement pattern. The regional concept became part of the research strategy of the Heshbon Expedition in the 1973 season and soon became a major component, even though it was at least partially motivated by the desire to find an alternate candidate for biblical Heshbon.

Although there was earlier some speculation and even some study of traditional Arab culture in the Middle East (Dalman 1928-42), the lack of anthropological training left few archaeologists equipped to do ethnological studies. Exceptions were Grant at the villages near Beth Shemesh, Albright at Dura, near Tell Beit Mirism (Grant 1921; Albright 1932b: 68-70; Glock 1985: 469) and the German school under Dalman (Weippert and Weippert 1988: 96-98). In terms of its function within the "new archaeology," there was some initial discussion as to the usefulness of ethnoarchaeological studies of modern traditional societies for archaeological interpretation (Willey and Sabloff 1974: 206-208; 1980; Glock 1983: 172-74). However, by the mid-1970s the general consensus

seemed to be that, used carefully, they could make useful models for understanding ancient ones. This is the case inasmuch as they can be used to develop hypotheses for the interpretation of the archaeological record. This technique was used successfully by the Heshbon Expedition starting in 1973 (LaBianca and LaBianca 1975: 236; LaBianca 1976a; 1976c; 1978: 234-36; 1984; 1986b: 171-73; 1995b: 17-29) and later elsewhere in Jordan as well (Sauer 1982: 79; cf. e.g., Köhler-Rollefson 1987).

The initial thrust towards systems theory by Binford (1962: 218-19) focused on the subsystems of culture (ideological, social, and technological) in relationship to ecosystems. This was a concept borrowed from ecology. Though a major emphasis in the "new archaeology" as practiced in America, it seemed to have trouble being implemented in Syro-Palestinian archaeology (Dever 1981: 17; 1992: 356). Although its possible use for the understanding of technology and agriculture (Rast 1992: 11-13) and its practical and heuristic advantages in terms of organization of research and the collection of data (Dever 1992: 356) have been noted, it was not until the 1980s that it was first applied as a framework for integrating all the diverse lines of evidence generated by the excavation process. Along these lines, the food system theory was developed by LaBianca for the purpose of integrating all the data which resulted from the various components of the Heshbon Expedition (1984, 1986a, 1990; Geraty and LaBianca 1985).

The concept of an explicit scientific format was championed by Binford (1968: 24-26), Flannery (1973: 50-53), and others. Its emphasis on Hempelian positivism, which assumes the testing of general "covering laws," was challenged by Wright (1975). He took these "archaeology as science" enthusiasts to task, noting that whereas science deals with only one or two variables, the social sciences or humanities, where archaeology might be more properly placed, focus on the human being and his brain. Here there are so many variables that it is impossible for there to be any kind of control. Covering laws are possible only when translated into statistics and these ignore human individuality. This includes the artifacts that are made by individuals. These have their own evolutionary process, which is impossible to predict (1975: 110-13).

American archaeology has focused for the most part on prehistory since this is the type of occupational history that presents itself there. Syro-

Palestinian archaeology on the other hand has tended to focus more on the historical periods and the relationship between written evidence and material culture (Rast 1992: 4). Therefore, the latter naturally views archaeology as more of a historical than a scientific discipline. Even with the broad multidiciplinary approach and the use of both equipment and specialists from the natural sciences in the interpretation process, the data must necessarily be related to the historical situation as found in the written records. This was the case as well for the Heshbon Expedition where there was a relatively large amount of written material that relates to the ancient site (Vyhmeister 1989a; 1989b). Thus, despite the move toward more specialists and the broader database available for interpretation, there was always a need on the part of the excavators to relate these data to the historical situation.

With the re-emergence of the evolutionary concept in American archaeology and the new emphasis on cultural evolution (Willey and Sabloff 1974: 178-183; 1980) and cultural process by Flannery (1967) and others in order to explain cultural change, there was a move toward trying to explain behavior in terms of "laws of cultural dynamics" (Binford 1968: 27). Although the cultural evolutionary concept was for the most part an unarticulated "given" in Syro-Palestinian archaeology (Dever 1981: 16), the behaviorist-processualist views were "too esoteric to win many followers" (Dever 1992: 357). In addition to Wright's (1975) arguments (above), there was some question as to whether the archaeological record preserves enough evidence to reveal cultural processes in the past even if they were able to be fully exploited (Dever 1992: 357). While this may be true of Syro-Palestinian archaeology in general, LaBianca (1988: 369, 377; 1990: 33; 110), nevertheless, has used the dynamic processes of sedentarization and nomadization and their corollaries intensification and abatement as the changeable variables (Binford 1962: 217) of his food system concept at Hesban and vicinity without falling into the trap of a self-regulating environmental or economic determinism. In so doing, he did not reject history as a factor in cultural change (Flannery 1967: 122; Dever 1993d: 129) as had been common among some processualists.

Other issues that emerged from the "new archaeology" agenda included salvage archaeology, small exploratory excavations concentrating on specific problems, and site formation and deterioration processes (A. Rosen 1986) or the anatomy of the archaeological sites themselves (geoarchaeology). In addition, several major excavation manuals appeared, among them Dever and Lance (1978), which contributed to the overall literature on methodology.

However, in terms of theory and epistemology, the "new archaeology" proved to be as problematic as what had gone before. Both Wright (1975: 113) and Dever (1981: 21) questioned how far analogy should be taken in archaeological interpretation. Since absolute certainty is an impossibility and the lack of ability to test reconstructions of the past a "given," "confirmation" or rather consensus must be reached by the archaeologists themselves (Wright 1975: 111; Hodder 1992: 123). Leaps of faith are necessary because much of what archaeologists reconstruct is unobservable. Large amounts of literature are thus erected on the basis of unverifiable assumptions. An archaeological hypothesis is not so much tested against archaeological data as it is against an edifice of assumptions and theories of an auxiliary nature which archaeologists have agreed not to question (Hodder 1992: 123-25).

The material culture and systems that archaeologists observe depend on theory and interpretation. For instance, cultural historians, who hold to the "normative model," tend to view artifacts as culture and these are further identified with peoples. Artifacts should instead be understood to reflect culture (Flannery 1967: 119; Bunimovitz 1995a: 63). They must be classified according to a typology which is at least partially (some would say totally) constructed or imposed by the observer on the basis of the attributes which are felt to be relevant (Brandfon 1987: 15; Hodder 1992: 126). Even in so-called middle-range theories such as ethnoarchaeology, archaeologists are still working by consensus. To say something about the past requires moving from data to interpretation and one cannot test interpretation because the data themselves are formulated within the argumentation of theories. Thus, the whole process involves speculation and the subjective (Hodder 1992: 127). This was a major problem for the "new archaeology," which was seeking to be scientific. If, however, archaeology is seen as a cultural (humanities or social science) or even a historical discipline, these problems are lessened or perhaps nonexistent.

The Hesban Legacy

In order to follow up on what had already been learned at Tell Hesban and vicinity between 1968 and 1976, the Madaba Plains Project, a consortium of schools and organizations, was formed. The directors of the project are Geraty, Herr, LaBianca, Randall Younker, and Doug Clark. With the exception of Younker, all were veterans of the Heshbon Expedition. The newly formed project had intended to go into the field in 1982 with excavation to be concentrated at the 18½ acre (7.5 hectare) site of Tell Jalul. A wider regional component in order to test trade and economy within the area was also included. Part of the reason for the interest in Jalul was the fact that on the basis of the 1976 intensive survey, the tell seemed to be occupied throughout the Bronze Ages. This opened up the opportunity to supplement the knowledge already gained in the region at a site that, unlike Tell Hesban and many of the others in the area, was occupied in the Middle and Late Bronze Ages. In addition, this was an opportunity to test the possibility that the site was biblical Heshbon, the capital of Sihon, during the Late Bronze Age.

An illegal search for the ark of the covenant on Mount Nebo in the fall of 1981 and the invasion of Lebanon by the Israelis in early summer of 1982, however, led to the cancellation of the 1982 season (Shanks 1983: 69). The 1983 season was also canceled due to further search for the ark on Mount Nebo in the summer of 1982 (Tompkins 1983: 49, 51-52; Jordan Dig Is Postponed 1983). When the site of Jalul remained off-limits in 1984 as well, it was decided that the majority of the objectives which the project wished to accomplish in the region could be achieved at Tell el-ᶜUmeiri, an 11 acre (4.5 hectare) site to the northeast of Tell Hesban.

Besides the tell, which has now been excavated for seven seasons (1984, 1987, 1989, 1992, 1994, 1996, and 1998), there has been, as with the Heshbon Expedition before it, a large regional component. Both of these operations have been facilitated by the use of a field grid system (cf. Geraty and House 1984). The regional or hinterlands component has used both judgment and random square surveys. As a result, more than 100 new sites have been discovered within a 5 km radius of the tell and several smaller cave (Khirbet Rufeis), farm (Rujm Selim and Site 84), and fortress (el-Dreijat) sites have been excavated as

part of it. Separate studies on the Ammonite towers (Younker 1989b), farmsteads (Younker 1991b), cave villages (LaBianca 1991), and lime kilns (Christopherson 1991) in the region have also resulted from this. In addition, the ᶜUmeiri cemeteries (from the EB IV, MB IIC, and the Roman/Byzantine periods) have been or are presently being excavated (Herr et al. 1996: 76; Younker et al. 1996: 67-68; Krug 1991; Christopherson and Dabrowski 1997). Apart from the survey, the town sites of Tell Jawa (1989-1995), Tell Jalul (1992-present), and Madaba (1996-present), the first and third loosely connected with MPP, are currently adding to the database of tell sites within the region.

Like the Heshbon Expedition, the Madaba Plains Project has had a commitment to scientific specialization and continues to integrate the results gained from these studies. The project maintains anthropologists, palaeobotanists, ethnoarchaeologists, zooarchaeologists, and geologists as well as froth flotation for palynology each season. The interests here have generated data on seismic refraction, ground-penetrating radar, and electromagnetic induction at various sites in the project area (Clark, J. Cole, and Sandness 1997), information on regional plant communities (Younker 1989a), and the geology of the area (Schnurrenberger 1991, 1997a, 1997b, 1997c), an ethnoarchaeological study of potters (G. London and Sinclair 1991), studies on water resources (J. Cole 1989a), bones, carbonized seeds, fauna, and flints (Low and Schnurrenberger 1997), as well as the more traditional interests in architecture, inscriptions, objects, seals and ceramics, the latter broadened somewhat to include ceramic technology (London 1991; London, Plint, and Smith 1991). In addition, there has also been some experimentation with GIS (Levy 1995: 51; Christopherson 1994; 1997c; Christopherson and Guertin 1995; 1996; Christopherson, Guertin, and Borstad 1996; Christopherson and Dabrowski 1997).

The excavation manual has evolved from the one used at Hesban (Herr 1989a: 214). It consists of both excavation and survey versions, which are revised nearly every season (Herr and Younker 1994; Christopherson and Herr 1994; Herr and Christopherson 1998). The locus sheets are computerized so that field data can be entered shortly after it is worked out by the various supervisors. In addition to mechanical and computerized recording, the project has recently (as of the 1996 season) replaced traditional photography with digital photography. This record is supplemented with 35 mm slides and sometimes by video as well. The project has continued its large volunteer base, supplemented by local labor. It has maintained the field school format from its Heshbon days, and there are usually between 100 and 150 foreign participants every season. In terms of publication, the project has continued the admirable record of the Heshbon Expedition, producing four; full-length final reports (Geraty et al. 1989a; Herr et al. 1991a; 1997a; 2000a); full-length preliminary reports of the first three seasons (Geraty et al. 1986; 1990; LaBianca et al. 1995) and shorter preliminary reports of the first seven seasons in various journals (Geraty 1985; Geraty, Herr, and LaBianca 1987; 1988; 1989; Younker et al. 1990; Herr et al. 1991b; Younker et al. 1993; 1996; 1997; Herr et al. 1994; 1996; 1997b; 2000b; Younker and Merling 2000; LaBianca, Ray and Walker 2000).

Unlike the Heshbon Expedition, the Madaba Plains Project does have a sophisticated research design which is submitted before each season to the Department of Antiquities of Jordan, the Committee on Archaeological Policy of the American Schools of Oriental Research, and usually the National Endowment for the Humanities. However, for some reason the latter has been reticent to offer funding to the project for field work, in contrast to the fairly large amounts that were given for the early part of the publication phase of the final publication series of the Hesban volumes.

Perhaps the most important result of the Heshbon Expedition and a major focus by the Madaba Plains Project (MPP) is the interest in the Ammonites and their history (LaBianca and Geraty 1994: 306). Though little has yet been found, there is also the potential to say something about the Moabites (see preliminarily Younker 1997a), as part of the project has moved further south to Jalul and vicinity, in an area which both biblical and extrabiblical sources indicate was under the control of this people at various times during the Iron Age. The interest in food system research, as the integration of all the Hesban material, has continued with the Madaba Plains Project, where new information on the cycles of sedentarization and nomadization continue to come in each season (Geraty et al. 1989b: 5-6), resulting in evidence for long-term patterns of cultural change. Not all of this evidence is represented in terms of settlements, however, as it is now realized that much of the ancient population lived in more makeshift types of dwellings such as habitation caves, rock shelters, and tents (LaBianca 1991; LaBianca and Geraty 1994: 307-309).

Though the research design is now much broader than that of its predecessor, with a major concentration on the regional hinterland component and numerous specialists who have input into the whole excavation process, the Madaba Plains Project nevertheless continues to be interested in history, whether that be Ammonite, Moabite, or Israelite. In fact, though it is seldom articulated and certainly not openly sought after, there is still an interest in finding evidence that can be related to biblical history should it happen to be found. In terms of the original objective of the Heshbon Expedition, there is still a concern for the location of biblical Heshbon. The eight basic options earlier suggested by Geraty (1983: 239-48) for locating Heshbon have recently been rearticulated (Geraty 1994: 47-52), with some of the current MPP staff favoring Heshbon as a region, a combination of Geraty's options 3 and 5 (Merling 1991: 10-12; 48, n. 2), while others suggest an identification with Jalul (Younker 1993: 3-11), Geraty's option 8, originally suggested by Horn (1976: 410).

The Current "State of the Art"

As early as 1984 (39-45), Dever suggested that even with the acceptance of the "new archaeology," the discipline of Syro-Palestinian archaeology still had some maturing to do. He noted that from about 1970 to the mid-1980s it had experienced a true revolution or a "paradigm shift" in the Kuhnian sense (Kuhn 1970) in its acceptance of this new dynamic. However, despite the shift, the new paradigm had not yet become "normal science." He further suggested that archaeologists, who are interested in reconstructing life in ancient times, need to move from an emphasis on political history or the event-oriented upper plane of history (événments) to the middle plane of social or economic history (conjonctures) and the deeper reality (lower plane) of everyday life (the longue durée) as proposed by the Annales school of history (Braudel 1972: 21). He has since expanded on these themes a number of times (1988: 337-40; 1992: 359 364; 1994: 106, 113-24). He felt that there was a need to ask new questions and especially for archaeologists to make explicit what they are trying to learn and how they propose to go about it (1984: 44-45; 1988: 347), in other words the formation of a theoretical hermeneutic for the discipline as well as an archaeological epistemology (Dever 1988: 347, n. 21; 1992: 362-64).

Post-Processual Archaeology

About the same time (especially in Britain), there was a reaction to the "new" or processual archaeology. This was due to the contradiction of retaining a Hempelian positivism, which focuses on objective and independent scientific observation, and at the same time admitting a theory-dependent interpretation of data (Hodder 1992: 150). In addition, the emphasis on science and covering laws or cross-cultural generalization led to the lauding of theory and the devaluation of field archaeology as mere technique (Wright 1975: 113; Hodder 1992: 130).

The main emphasis of post-processual archaeology is context or contextualism. This uses the analogy of the text to move away from a passive identity of the past as a record. The archaeologist is seen as actively reading the material culture. The process that one goes through in order to arrive at meaning is a hermeneutical one or, as it has been described, a double hermeneutic of past and present meanings. The artifact, like the text, had an original meaning, but different people in modern times read the artifact/text differently. Its meaning or significance thus includes what the original maker/author meant and modern interpretations or readings (Hodder 1992: 84, 161, 170). Responses to this double hermeneutic include a post-structuralist position of pluralism and multivocality and a post-modern deconstructionist position[3] which denies the possibility of getting back to any original meaning in the past. Both of these positions have been borrowed from the synchronic approaches in biblical hermeneutics where Ricoeur and Derrida have been their main proponents (Osborne 1991: 374-77; 380-85). Although archaeological data, like texts, must be read differently in different contexts, one interpretation or reading is not as good as another. There must be commitment to understanding the original context as well as modern significance (Hodder 1992: 167).

For coherence, some have advocated a dialectical view, which suggests that interpretation is neither past nor present, but mediates (as an analogy) between both as distant and recent sources of experience and understanding. This process involves both observation and theoretical reconstruction which are in creative tension and thus contribute both to the past and the present. This position is also said to allow for a creative tension between the objective and the subjective and between theory and practice (Hodder 1992: 178-79).

Archaeologists work back and forth between theory and data. Some theories account for more data than others, and when they do not, they need to be adjusted to the data. Both need to be contextualized. Here is where hermeneutics comes in. Meaning is arrived at on the basis of the surrounding data in context. The potential problem here is that the so-called hermeneutical circle, which can be vicious since arguments that may overtly or covertly assume what they are intending to prove, may come into play. We tend to find what we are looking for because it is impossible to come at a problem with blank minds, without presuppositions (Hodder 1992: 213-14). However, it has even been suggested that context itself is illusionary in that the investigator chooses the context out of a number of theoretically possible scenarios (Brandfon 1987: 38-43).

Nevertheless, it is argued that if the hermeneutical process takes the form of a spiral instead of a circle, then it does not become vicious in that the data always force one to adjust one's interpretation because one never returns to the exact same spot in the move between theory and data (Hodder 1992: 214). Osborne (1991: 6) has made basically the same argument from the point of view of biblical hermeneutics. The archaeologist can move from assumptions and knowledge based on previous excavations (and material from other sites in the region) to data analysis of their current excavation, which may cause a shift in interpretation to a more thorough understanding (Hodder 1992: 239).

If processual archaeology concentrated on method, post-processual archaeology seems to be much more concerned with theory. Thus far, Dever, who began to push some of the post-processual agenda in Syro-Palestinian archaeology in the early 1990s, has pointed to its emphasis on cultural context in history (1990: 32; 1992: 357; 1993a: 708; 1994: 112) and the analogy of the artifact with the text (1990: 9-11, 176, n. 9; 1994: 108, 113). This in turn has caused him to partially rethink his position on "biblical archaeology." The previous generation, who embraced the "new archaeology," went too far in severing the archaeology of Palestine from the literary sources and history

(1993a: 707, 710). The move away from history had serious implications on research design, causing archaeologists to retreat even further into the realm of description. Worse yet, archaeology without history, where historical sources are available, is methodologically defective in that it ignores pertinent data (Halpern 1998: 56). In its place, Dever is now willing to make room for a "'new' style of biblical archaeology" or "contextual archaeology" (1993a: 707, 715), with the goal of using both text and artifact within a larger environmental and socio-cultural context as well as a true dialogue between archaeology and biblical studies (1993a: 707). This, it is envisioned, will create the critical balance of the best of the old and new (Dever 1993a: 708; Bunimovitz 1995a: 96).

With the renewed interest in socioeconomic and cultural (as opposed to political) history, studies have slowly begun to appear that focus on Braudel's *longue durée*. This started with Stager's study on the family (1985). Madaba Plains Project studies within this framework include LaBianca (1990; cf. Dever 1993d: 130), dealing with the cycles of sedentarization and nomadization in the Hesban region, and Christopherson (1994; cf. Levy 1995: 51) on aspects of the ᶜUmeiri survey (Madaba Plains Project). Further, Dever has suggested that, because LaBianca has not ignored historical factors and cultural change, his work, written within the framework of the "new archaeology" (1990: xvii-xviii), is transitional and actually anticipates post-processual archaeology (1993d: 129). Though Syro-Palestinian archaeologists have not as yet developed a hermeneutic as Dever would like to see (1994: 116), he himself has made a first attempt at articulating an archaeological epistemology by trying to clarify the nature of facts, data, context, archaeological theory-building, and reasoning (1994: 106-116).

Summary and Conclusions

The Heshbon Expedition, as we have seen, traces its roots to the traditional biblical archaeology of the 1960s at a time when it was considered proper to excavate a site for its potential contribution to biblical history. For Heshbon as a biblical site, the issues centered around the capital of Sihon the Amorite, who endeavored to impede the progress of Israel as they made their way into the land of Canaan from the east and the date of Exodus. The emergence of the expedition into the

"new archaeology" of the 1970s was a natural consequence of a team that was already experimenting in its first season with the interdisiplinary approach, which utilized various specialists to supplement the data gained from the excavation process. This became even more pronounced when evidence for their original objectives seemed not to be forthcoming. With the end of field activity in 1976, the final publication of the material forced the excavators to think about how to integrate the vast amount of data into an interrelated whole. This forced the archaeological team members to computerize the database and to regularly discuss their research. Ultimately, it was the development of the food system concept and the related processes of sedentarization and nomadization which brought about that integration.

As a result of its transformation from biblical archaeology to the "new archaeology," the Heshbon Expedition has been widely acclaimed for its advances in pottery typology of the later periods and, to some extent, Transjordan in general; its regional approach; and actually functioning within the realm of the "new archaeology" (Rast 1974: 434-35; Finkelstein 1993a: 6; Dever 1993d: 127; Joffe 1997: 136). As the Heshbon Expedition has evolved into the Madaba Plains Project, its interests have enlarged and as a project it is now the largest and most well known of all the foreign excavations in the country of Jordan. However, as LaBianca (1994a: 34) has pointed out, the impact of the "new archaeology" on the scope of research of the Heshbon Expedition should not be exaggerated in that it never led to a major change in the goals of the project or in the actual field work despite the awarness of the paradigm by a number of the core staff.

What then should be seen as the most important legacy of the Heshbon Expedition? First, the serendipitous timing of the project when the "new archaeology" was just beginning to take root; second, the openness of Siegfried Horn and Roger Boraas to experimentation, with all its possibilities (LaBianca 1994a: 34); and third, the presence of staff members such as Boraas, Horn, and LaBianca, who became interested in new questions as they became aware of a climate of changing paradigms. Other major contributions include the study of the Ammonites, the emphasis on cultural change, and the discovery that much of the ancient population dwelt outside of towns and villages. Besides these, there are a number of innovations including volunteerism; the consortium; the close relationship with the Department of Antiquities and ASOR; the field school; the emphasis on publication; the Institute of Achaeology and the Horn Archaeological Museum, which empower this; the interdisciplinary approach; and the integration of the results as well as the openness to varied opinion (LaBianca and Geraty 1994: 306-311).

Finally, it must be emphasized that although the research agenda of the Heshbon Expedition did move from one that concentrated on biblical history to the broadened outlook of the "new archaeology," the team never lost its interest in its original objective of locating Sihon's Heshbon and as has been pointed out above, this is still a latent interest of the Madaba Plains Project as well. Thus, while Syro-Palestinian archaeology in general evolved from a strict interest in biblical history to the broad-based paradigm of the "new or processual archaeology," which tended to denigrated history and history writing, the Heshbon Expedition never lost its interest in biblical history even though it also took up this same agenda. With the beginnings of the post-processual paradigm within Syro-Palestinian archaeology, history seems to be on the edge of reemergence. Perhaps this more holistic approach, which has been maintained throughout the years, has helped to give the Heshbon Expedition and its successor, the Madaba Plains Project along with the institutions they represent, an edge with the community that supports archaeology in the Middle East, at a time when other institutions that represent programs in Middle Eastern archaeology but which have rejected biblical history seem to be on the wane (Dever 1995: 53).

Notes

[1]The results of the preliminary reports of the five seasons of the Heshbon Expedition as described here reflect interpretations of the archaeological remains as they were made at the time and do not necessarily reflect current thinking.

[2]This figure found throughout numerous publications (Boraas and Geraty 1976: 5; 1978: 13; Boraas and Horn 1975: 115; Geraty 1975a: 49; 1976: 50; Ibach 1976b: 119; 1978a: 201; LaBianca 1984: 269, 273; 1990: 27) was somewhat idealized in that military zones and other logistical problems kept this from becoming a reality (Ibach 1987: 5). For a map of the actual area covered by the survey, see fig. 1.1 above.

[3]On the effect of this method on the study of biblical history see Dever 1998: 40-46.

Chapter Three

CHRONOLOGY

Chapter Three

Chronology

Introduction

In this chapter, the approximate dates for the Iron Age strata at Tell Hesban are presented, based on the accompanying analysis. These strata are dealt with in detail in chapters 5 and 6. Representative samples of the types of ceramic remains which were found within the architectural and debris layers from each of these six Iron Age strata, are presented both in terms of description and graphics.

Stratum 21

In context ceramic material from the earliest stratum at Tell Hesban (fig. 3.1) was found only in the dump layers on the western side of the mound in Area C. Unfortunately, the amount of material is extremely limited.

The overall ceramic repertoire demonstrates close parallels with the ceramics at Tell el-ᶜUmeiri, Tell Jawa, and Tell Jalul in the same region (Herr 1998: 258; 2000: 177) and possibly Umm ad-Dananir, further north (Herr 1998: 257-58), as well as sites in the central hill country of Cisjordan, north of Jerusalem (Sauer 1994: 237; Finkelstein 1996a: 200, 204; Sauer and Herr 1997: 234; Herr 1998: 256; 2000: 176; in press a; Ji 1997b: 409-11), especially in the Bethel-Shechem region and as far north as the Jezreel Valley. The material from both regions includes collared-rim store jars (fig. 3.1.1-5; Clark 1997: figs. 4.14-20, 21.1; cf. Zertal 1986-87: 129, fig. 12.1, 3-4 6-7, 9; 131, fig. 13.1, 5-6, 8; 133, fig. 14.2; 134; 139, 141, fig. 16.6-11, 13-15; 143, fig. 17.7; 147, fig. 19.7-8), "Manassite" bowls (fig. 3.1.11; Clark 1991: fig. 4.7.24, 27; 1997: fig. 4.25.20; cf. Zertal 1986-87: 125-27, fig. 11: 1-3, 5, 7, 10; 133, fig. 14.5; 139; 141-43 figs. 16.2-3, 17.3-4; 1994: 51-52, fig. 1.a-b) and small carinated bowls similar to their cyma-profiled predecessors (fig. 3.1.14; Clark 1997: fig. 4.25.17-19; cf. Zertal 1986-87: 126-27, fig. 11. 14-15). Zertal (1986-87: 125-26; 140-44) has dated the ceramic material at

the Mount Ebal Site (Strata II-IB) from the Late Bronze Age/Iron Age I transition (late 13th-early 12th centuries B.C.) to the middle of the 12th century B.C. (Iron Age IA). Herr (1998: 253-56) has recognized similarly dated material at Tell el-ᶜUmeiri, where there are also two parallel phases (13 and 12) with basically the same pottery. Since the ceramic material at Tell Hesban Stratum 21 is parallel to that of Tell el-ᶜUmeiri, a similar dating of ca. 1225-1150 B.C. would seem to be indicated. In addition to the Mount Ebal Site (Zertal 1986-87), parallels also include ceramic material from such sites as Giloh (Mazar 1981), Tell en-Nasbeh (Wampler 1947), and Taanach (Rast 1978).

The transition from the Late Bronze Age to the Iron Age has traditionally been dated to ca. 1200 B.C. The rationale for this is the fact that a number of Cisjordanian sites have been found to have destruction layers that date to this approximate time. Most of these layers contained imported Mycenaean IIIB ware along with very late locally made Late Bronze Age ceramic types such as cyma-profiled and hemispherical bowls. These destructions were attributed by Albright (1971: 109) to the Israelite Conquest, an interpretation that has largely been abandoned (Finkelstein 1988), with slightly later destructions to the Sea Peoples.

The following period (Iron Age IA) according to Albright (1932a: 58-61) was dominated by collared-rim store jars. The transition from Mycenaean IIIB to Mycenaean IIIC ware, on the basis of the evidence then available, was thought to have appeared about the same time as the death of Ramses II, and thus was originally dated to ca. 1230 B.C. by Furumark (1941b: 115) using the-then-popular high Egyptian chronology. However, Mycenaean IIIB ware has since been found in a somewhat later context at Deir ᶜAlla in association with a faience drop vase with a cartouche of Tewosret (1193-85 B.C.; Dothan 1982: 294; Franken 1992: 30-31; fig. 3-9.5; 38, 40, 44; fig. 4-3.17-19; 177; 181-82; 187-89; pls. 4b, 5d-e, 6a; Stager 1995: 335-36). This factor, along with the

Figure 3.1   Ceramics from Stratum 21.

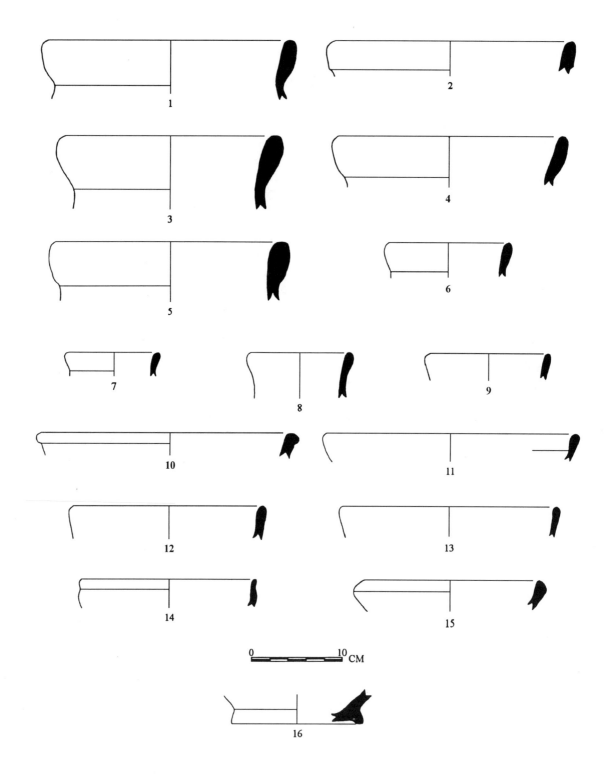

Figure 3.1, *continued.* Ceramics from Stratum 21.

No.	Type	Reg. No.	Locus	Parallel
1	Pithos	979:84071	C.1:142	Zertal 1986-87: 141, fig. 16.13
2	Pithos	979:94936	C.1:142	Zertal 1986-87: 147, fig. 19.8
3	Pithos	978:97965	C.1:142	Zertal 1986-87: 147, fig. 19.7
4	Pithos	982:84736	C.1:143	Wampler 1947: pl. 2.31
5	Pithos	978:83157	C.1:142	Mazar 1981: 26, fig. 9.2
6	Jar/Jug	979:84088	C.1:142	
7	Jar/Jug	979:84086	C.1:142	
8	Jar/Jug	982:8474x	C.1:143	Zertal 1986-87: 143, fig. 17.1
9	Jar/Jug	979:84484	C.1:142	
10	Krater	979:84081	C.1:142	
11	Bowl	982:84731	C.1:143	
12	Bowl	979:84677	C.1:142	
13	Bowl	979:84087	C.1:142	Rast 1978: 79, fig. 8.11
14	Bowl	978:	C.1:142	
15	Chalice	979:32.81/	C.1:142	Rast 1978: 251, fig. 89.5
16	Base	982:84735	C.1:143	Rast 1978: 73, fig. 5.4

now generally accepted low Egyptian chronology at least for the later part of the sequence (Wente and Van Siclen 1976: 217-61), indicates that the ending date of Mycenaean IIIB ware should be lowered to ca. 1175 B.C. The appearance of Mycenaean IIIC:1b (monochrome) ware therefore seems to have begun with the invasion of the Sea Peoples (including the Philistines) in the eighth year (1175 B.C.) of Ramses III (1182-51 B.C.) and lasted through the reign of Ramses VI (1141-33 B.C.), a period coinciding with Iron Age IA (Mazar 1985: 100-101, 107). By the end of this period (ca. 1125 B.C.) the Egyptian empire in Palestine had met its demise (Weinstein 1981: 22-23).

The data presented above would suggest absolute dates of ca. 1225-1150 B.C. for Stratum 21 at Tell Hesban which produced ceramics in the Late Bronze Age/Iron Age I transition through well into the Iron Age IA ceramic tradition. Though the dating here is based on a relative ceramic chronology from Cisjordan, compared with Aegean imports, and further dependent, as it must be, on Egyptian absolute chronology, it is clear that there are a number of solid ceramic parallels between the two sides of the Jordan River at this time. Mycenaean IIIB ware has been found on the east bank of the Jordan. In addition to Deir ᶜAlla (mentioned above), Mycenaean IIIB pottery has been found at such sites as Umm ad-Dananir (McGovern 1980: 55; 1986: 16, 337); the Amman Airport Building (Hennessy 1966: 155; Hankey 1974: 133-43), Sahab (Dajani 1970: pl. 5. SA72, 82, 204;

Furumark 1941a: 31; fig. 6.179-180; 33; 44; fig. 12.183; Leonard 1987: 262) and Madaba (Harding and Isserlin 1953b: 39.69; fig. 15.69; Furumark 1941a: 116; Leonard 1987: 262). However, with the possible exception of Umm ad-Dananir (cf. Herr 1998: 257-58), Mycenaean IIIB ware has not been found at the same sites with the locally made wares mentioned above. Hence this reasoning seems justified.

Stratum 20

The ceramics from Stratum 20 (figs. 3.2 and 3.3) were found in the bedrock trench in Areas B and D on the southern shelf of the mound. Although these debris still included a relatively large quantity of Iron Age IA ceramic material, they also included pottery which was typologically later than that of the previous stratum. Hence, the ceramic repertoire from this stratum is mixed and includes both Iron Age IA and IB material. This material was found among the destruction debris of the Stratum 20 settlement. It includes collared-rim store jars (fig. 3.2.1-8), incurved bowls (fig. 3.3.2) and strainer-spouted jugs (fig. 3.3.16) as well as Manassite (fig. 3.3.3; 5-6) and carinated (fig. 3.3.7-9) bowls as in the previous stratum. Though the surface treatment is generally light, dark cores were common (Sauer 1986: 10-11, fig. 11; 1994: 235, 236 plate). The Iron Age IB material includes collared-rim store jars (fig. 3.2.7) which were thinner than their precedents and cooking pots with elon-

Figure 3.2   Ceramics from Stratum 20.

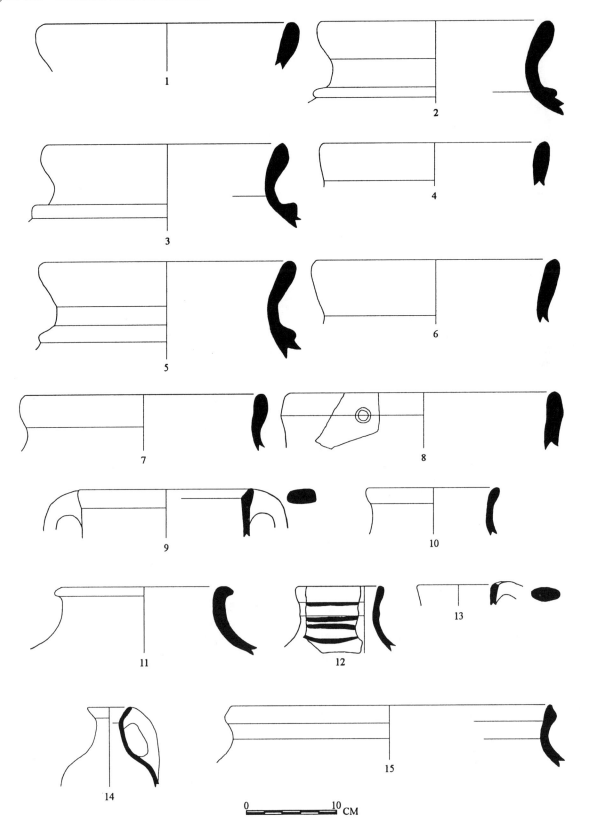

Figure 3.3   Ceramics from Stratum 20.

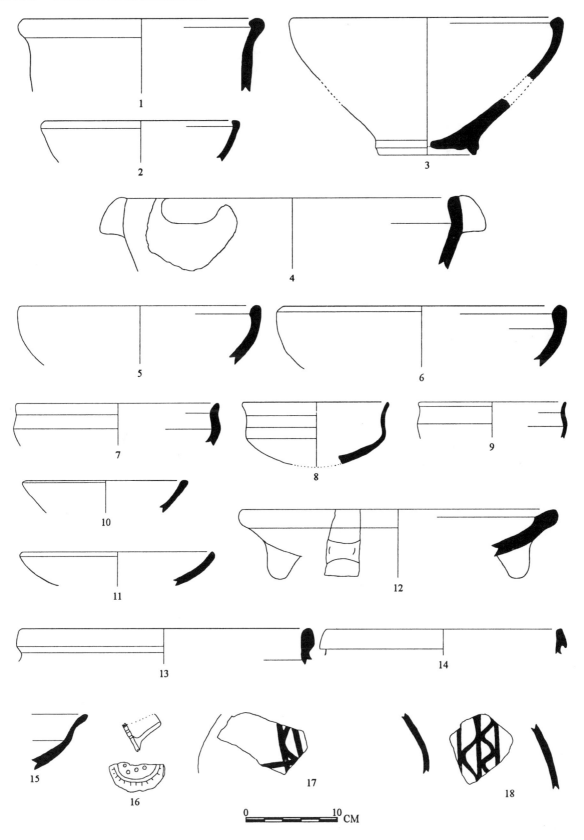

Figure 3.2, *continued.*   Ceramics from Stratum 20.

No.	Type	Reg. No.	Locus	Parallel
1	Pithos	286:31626	D.4:135	Wampler 1947: pl. 2.18
2	Pithos	141:14805	B.3:82	Buhl and Holm-Nielsen 1969: pl. 16.192
3	Pithos	135:14193	B.3:77	N. Lapp 1981: 205, pl. 47.5
4	Pithos	294.31748	D.4:138	Marquet-Krause 1949: pl. 69.439
5	Pithos	299:31818	D.4:141	
6	Pithos	299:31819	D.4:141	Wampler 1947: pl. 2.31
7	Pithos	307A:31975	D.4:142	Finkelstein 1993b: 166, fig. 6.48.4
8	Pithos	307A:31971	D.4:142	Finkelstein 1993b: 166, fig. 6.53.5
9	Jar	305:31922	D.4:142	
10	Jar	286:31622	D.4:135	Albright and Kelso 1968: pl. 59.6
11	Jar	133:14194	B.3:77	Albright and Kelso 1968: pl. 61.5
12	Jug/Jar	300:31835	D.4:141	Finkelstein 1993b: 166, fig. 6.47.7
13	Jug	276:31540	D.4:125	Loud 1948: pl. 81.13 ?
14	Jug	152:10397	B.3:92	Albright and Kelso 1968: pl. 61.15
15	Krater	286:31625	D.4:135	Dever 1986: pl. 44.4

Figure 3.3, *continued.*   Ceramics from Stratum 20.

No.	Type	Reg. No.	Locus	Parallel
1	Krater	284:31678	D.4:133	N. Lapp 1981: 205, pl. 47.13
2	Bowl	295:31755	D.4:139	Boraas 1986: 257, fig. 1.8
3	Bowl	H97.D7.19.1-2	D.7.19	Zertal 1986-87: 127, fig. 11.10
4	Bowl	297:31783	D.4:140	Dever 1986: pl. 44.7
5	Bowl	148:10178	B.3:83	Gitin 1990: pl. 6.6
6	Bowl	288:31662	D.4:135	Gitin 1990: pl. 6.10
7	Bowl	152:10398	B.3:92	Zertal 1986-87: 127, fig. 11.14
8	Bowl	H97.D7.24.1	D.7:24	Gitin 1990: pl. 3.9
9	Bowl	289:31670	D.4:137	Boraas 1986: 262, fig. 5.12
10	Chalice	155:10512	B.3:94	Loud 1948: pl. 87.8
11	Chalice	307A:31974	D.4:142	
12	Plate?	307A:31978	D.4:142	
13	Cooking pot	313:32037	D.4:144	
14	Cooking pot	289:31677	D.4:137	Dever 1986: pl. 40.12
15	Lamp	159:10678	B.3:97	
16	Sherd	128:13961	B.3:75	Buhl and Holm-Nielsen 1969: pl 5.51
17	Sherd	286:31633	D.4:135	
18	Sherd	155:10518	B.3:94	

Figure 3.4 Ceramics from Stratum 19.

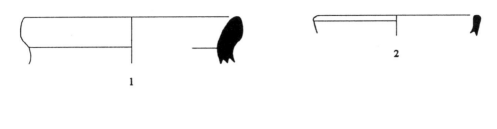

No.   Type   Reg. No.   Locus   Parallel

No.	Type	Reg. No.	Locus	Parallel
1	Pithos	279:11824	B.2:112	Albright and Kelso 1968: pl. 56.5
2	Bowl	278:11774	B.2:112	

gated rims (fig. 3.3.14). Dark monochrome surface treatment appears at this time (Sauer 1994: 238-39, plate), as well as evidence of early burnishing as at Bethel (cf. Sauer 1994: 237). Parallels are found at Tell el-Ful (N. Lapp 1981), Tell en-Nasbeh (Wampler 1947), et-Tell (Marquet-Krause 1949), Bethel (Albright and Kelso 1968), the Mount Ebal Site (Zertal 1986-87), Shechem (Boraas 1986), Shiloh (Buhl and Holm-Nielsen 1969; Finkelstein 1993b), Megiddo (Loud 1948) and Gezer (Dever 1986; Gitin 1990).

Following Albright's sequence (1932a: 61-67) at Tell Beit Mirism, Iron Age IB has traditionally been defined by the presence of locally made wares, including collared-rim store jars with Philistine Bichrome ware. However, with the exception of Deir ᶜAlla (Franken 1969: figs. 47.4; 51.52-64; 52.3-5; 57.51) and possibly Pella (Sauer 1994: 237), Philistine bichrome ware has not shown up in Transjordan, and there is little if any evidence of the Philistines or other Sea Peoples in the Jordan Valley in the Early Iron Age (Negbi 1991: 219). Nevertheless, as in Iron Age IA, the presence of comparable Iron Age IB locally made wares on both sides of the Jordan River again suggests a chronological equivalence. It appears that the best parallels to the Iron Age IB ceramic material at Hesban are found at Bethel (Albright and Kelso 1968: pls. 56-60) and hill country sites within its proximity (Sauer 1994: 237, 239). It would seem that the Stratum 20 settlement at Tell Hesban was built in late Iron Age IA and flourished during

Iron Age IB. A date of 1150-1100 B.C. would seem to be reasonable.

Stratum 19

The remains of this stratum are extremely limited and are again found on the southern shelf of the mound in Area B. The ceramic material (fig. 3.4) is likewise comparatively limited and consists only of sherds that were excavated from Wall B.2:112, which is the only extant locus from this stratum. Like the Iron Age IB ceramic material from the previous stratum, it consists of collared-rim store jars (fig. 3.4.1) and incurved bowls (fig. 3.4.2). Parallel ceramic material is found at Bethel (Albright and Kelso 1968). This material would seem to indicate a date of ca. 1100-1050 B.C. for this stratum.

Stratum 18

Much of the ceramic material from Stratum 18 (figs. 3.5 and 3.6) was again found in the dump layers on the western side of the mound in Area C. While still containing some Iron IA and IB ceramics, much of this material was Iron IIA. Reflecting repeated scraping activities on the summit, it seems to have been dumped in an orderly manner but in reverse chronological order, with layers of stratigraphically later material found below layers with earlier ceramics (Mare 1978: 70; Herr 1979a: 16-17). Iron Age IIA sherds were also found in Area D in the uppermost layer of the bedrock trench as

Figure 3.5   Ceramics from Stratum 18.

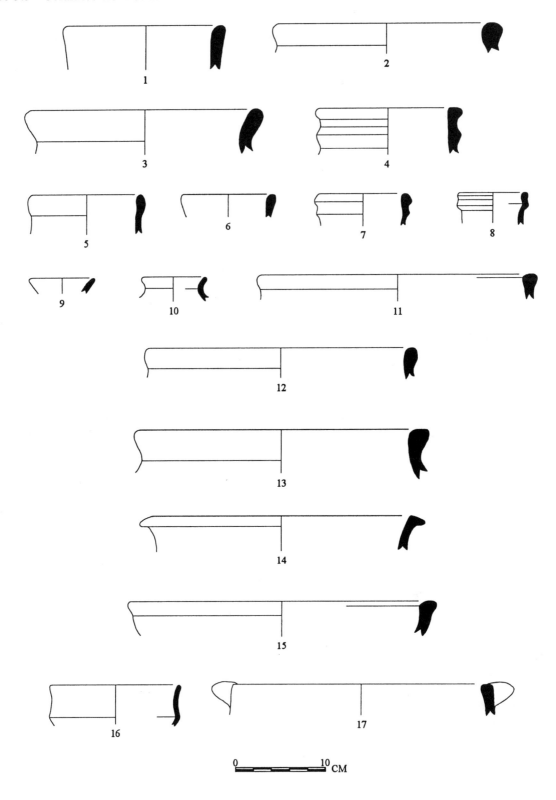

Figure 3.6   Ceramics from Stratum 18.

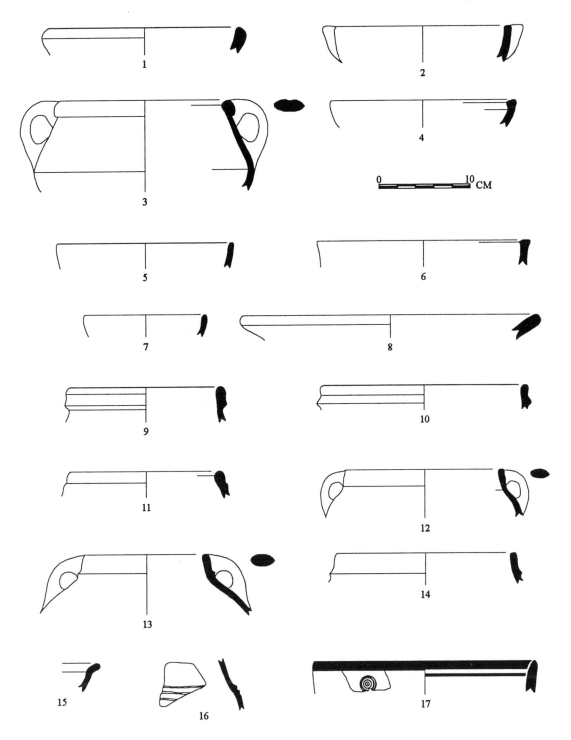

Figure 3.5, *continued.* Ceramics from Stratum 18.

No.	Type	Reg. No.	Locus	Parallel
1	Pithos	899:23667	C.1:124	
2	Pithos	905:24453	C.1:126	
3	Pithos	918:25810	C.1:126	
4	Jar	889:23109	C.1:124	N. Lapp 1981: 207, pl. 48.12
5	Jar	174:34677	D.4:63	Rast 1978: 133, fig. 34.5
6	Jug/Jar	204:35815	D.4:82	Finkelstein 1990: 189, fig. 18.5
7	Jug/Jar	897:23657	C.1:126	Rast 1978: 103, fig. 19.6
8	Jug	918:25811	C.1:126	Finkelstein 1990: 183, fig. 15.5
9	Juglet	918:25814	C.1:126	
10	Juglet	918:25813	C.1:126	Low 1991: 174, fig. 8.6.21
11	Krater	897:23656	C.1:126	Finkelstein 1990: 181, fig. 14.6
12	Krater	202:35805	D.4:74	
13	Krater	903:24157	C.1:127	
14	Krater	899:23672	C.1:124	Wampler 1947: pl. 64.1464
15	Bowl	202:35804	D.4:74	Finkelstein 1990: 187, fig. 17.4
16	Bowl	174:34676	D.4:63	
17	Bowl	903:24159	C.1:127	

Figure 3.6, *continued.* Ceramics from Stratum 18 (no. 17 unstratified).

No.	Type	Reg. No.	Locus	Parallel
1	Bowl	287:31845	D.4:136	Yadin et al. 1961, pl. 171.8
2	Bowl	902:24147	C.1:126	
3	Bowl	889:23116	C.1:124	
4	Bowl	905:24443	C.1:126	Rast 1978: 121, fig. 28.5
5	Bowl	885:21296	C.1:124	Finkelstein 1990: 181, fig. 14.2 ?
6	Bowl	891:22398	C.1:126	Rast 1978: 259, fig. 93.1
7	Bowl	905:24446	C.1:126	Rast 1978: 101, fig. 18.5
8	Chalice	905:24450	C.1:126	Loud 1948: pl. 90.8
9	Cooking pot	918:25803	C.1:126	
10	Cooking pot	905:24447	C.1:126	Rast 1978: 123, fig. 29.1
11	Cooking pot	887:21790	C.1:124	Wampler 1947: pl. 47.993
12	Cooking pot	889:23115	C.1:124	
13	Cooking pot	909:24818	C.1:124	Rast 1978: 111, fig. 23.10
14	Cooking pot	913:25247	C.1:126	
15	Lamp	908:24794	C.1:126	Rast 1978: 173, fig. 51.1
16	Sherd	899:23673	C.1:124	
17	Cypro-Phoenician ware	78:10735X	B.7:19	Hamilton 1935: 6, fig. 8

well as in connection with a structure that was built into it at this time. The Iron Age IIA ceramic remains from this stratum include collared-rim store jars that have become more bulbous (fig. 3.5.2) and cooking pot rims, which, though continuing to be elongated, also have rounded profiles (fig. 3.6.11). Hand-burnishing had come into vogue, and this is found over red, tan, and to a lesser extent dark brown and black slip (Sauer 1994: 239-40, plate). Ceramic parallels occur at Tell el-Ful (N. Lapp 1981), Tell en-Nasbeh (Wampler 1947), Khirbet ed-Dawwara (Finkelstein 1990), Taanach (Rast 1978), Megiddo (Loud 1948), Hazor (Yadin et al. 1961), and Tell Abu Hawam (Hamilton 1935).

The hallmark of Iron Age IC (now = IIA), again according to Albright's sequence (1932a: 61-67) at Tell Beit Mirism, was the advent of hand-burnishing on red slip with wheel-burnished red slips beginning in Iron Age IIA (now = IIB) (cf. Sauer 1994: 236-37).

Holladay (1990: 25-63) has attempted to date the appearance and development of red slip pottery more precisely using the preliminary evidence from what he describes as the finely detailed and closely dated context from the gateway in Field III at Gezer. He compares the evidence there with a number of other sites and suggests the provisional introduction of red slip during the reign of David (1010-970 B.C.), with incipient red-burnish from about the beginning of the reign of Solomon (970-30 B.C.), and the introduction of hand-burnishing on red slip at ca. 950 B.C. (Holladay 1990: 49-54; Table 2, 62, fig. 18, 63). It is after the destruction of Stratum VIII (UG 2 = Phase II, PG 2-UG 2) at Gezer by Sheshonq I (biblical Shishak) in 925 B.C., that the first significant introduction of wheel-burnished red slip occurs (Holladay 1990: 53; Table 4), with mixed burnish included as it should be, with hand-burnish (i.e., before true wheel-burnish).

Mazar (1998: 369-71) has pointed out considerable flaws in Holladay's methodology. His reevaluation of the red slipped ceramics at Gezer with reference to his work at Tell Qasile, where there was total retrieval of all diagnostic shapes, suggests a sequence closer in line with Albright's original proposals (1932a, 1943). He argues that red slip makes its first appearance on the northern plain of Philistia at Tell Qasile (Stratum X) in the 11th century B.C. with incipient hand-burnishing toward the end of the same century, at a time before it was common elsewhere. It is during the tenth century

B.C. (Tell Qasile Strata IX-VIII) that hand-burnish on dark red slip becomes the common technique (Mazar 1998: 373-77). This evidence would suggest that red slip on late Iron Age I wares had a longer, more gradual development (Mazar 1998: 377) than advocated by Holladay.

The ceramic material at Taanach Periods IIA (ca. 1020-960 B.C.) (Rast 1978: 6, 17-2; 100-123, figs. 18-29) and IIB (960-918 B.C.) (Rast 1978: 6, 23-39; 124-211, figs. 30-69) appears to be parallel with Stratum 18 at Hesban (Sauer 1994: 241). Taanach Period IIB ends with the destruction by Shishak (row II, no. 14 on the Karnak reliefs) (Rast 1978: 26-27; Sauer 1994: 241). However, with the exception of a few sites north of the Wadi Zerqa, there is no literary or archaeological evidence for Shishak's raid of 925 B.C. in Transjordan. Nevertheless, the fact remains that there are destruction layers at relatively large numbers of sites in the region at approximately the same time as the end of the United Monarchy in Jerusalem. These events, no doubt, brought about momentous changes in the sociopolitical and economic conditions throughout the whole region which significantly affected the material culture as well (Herr 1997d: 134). On the basis of the above discussion, I suggest a date of ca. 1050-925 B.C. for Stratum 18 at Tell Hesban. The Cypro-Phoenician piece (fig. 3.6.17), though stratigraphically the earliest sherd from a much later locus, fits well within this time frame.

Stratum 17

As we have seen above, the transitional Iron Age I/II ceramic material from Stratum 18 dates from the last half of the 11th century B.C. to the last quarter of the tenth century B.C., with the Iron Age II pottery typologically early in the sequence (cf. Herr 1979a: 19). Further, this was at a time when there was still interregional similarity between Transjordan and Cisjordan (cf. Herr 1997d: 117). The ceramic remains from Stratum 17 (figs. 3.7 and 3.8) are somewhat different. They were rather sparse and found exclusively in Area C on the western side of the mound. The Tell Hesban repertoire of this period includes cooking pots with double-grooved rims (fig. 3.8.13), pierced tripod cups, angle-rimmed kraters (fig. 3.7.10-11), and angular bowls (fig. 3.8.1, 7). Thin, non-brittle wares occur in predominately brown and tan colors, although red and black also exist. Other surface treatments

Figure 3.7 Ceramics from Stratum 17.

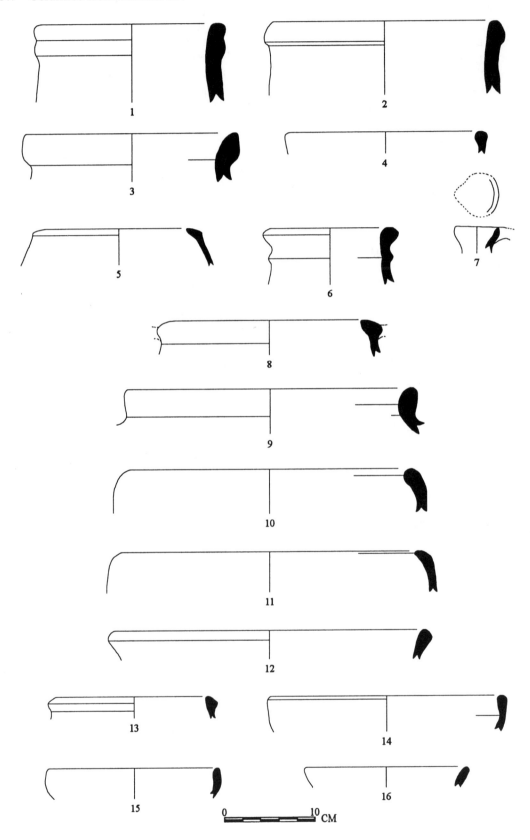

Figure 3.8 Ceramics from Stratum 17.

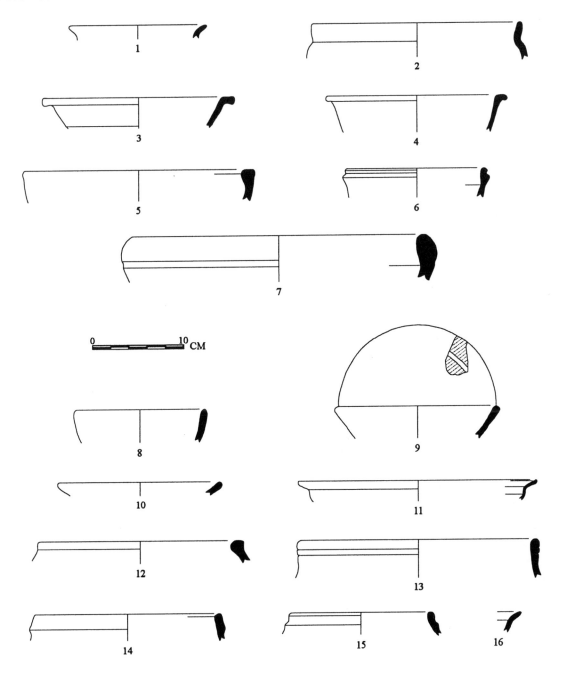

Figure 3.7, *continued.*   Ceramics from Stratum 17.

No.	Type	Reg. No.	Locus	Parallel
1	Pithos	872:26697	C.1:118	
2	Pithos	883:20859	C.1:123B	
3	Pithos	890:22381	C.1:123B	
4	Jar	576:22913	C.2:95	
5	Jar	419:28065	C.5:163	Tushingham 1972: fig. 14.3 (?)
6	Jug/Jar	883:20856	C.1:123B	Tubb 1988:36, fig. 11.2
7	Juglet	419:23066	C.5:163	Tushingham 1972: fig. 24.6
8	Krater	553:21443	C.2:73	Winnett and Reed 1964: pl. 76.1
9	Krater	883:20857	C.1:123B	
10	Krater	865:26246	C.1:118	Tubb 1988: 36, fig. 11.21
11	Krater	871:26462	C.1:118	
12	Krater	862:25988	C.1:118	
13	Bowl	510:83207	C.5:187	Tushingham 1972: fig. 1.63
14	Bowl	861:25710	C.1:118	Tushingham 1972: fig. 1.76
15	Bowl	579:23145	C.2:97	Tushingham 1972: fig. 2.1
16	Bowl	412:27740	C.5:155	Tushingham 1972: fig. 1.70

Figure 3.8, *continued.*   Ceramics from Stratum 17.

No.	Type	Reg. No.	Locus	Parallel
1	Bowl	570:22608	C.2:89	Tushingham 1972: fig. 18.5
2	Bowl	553:21442	C.2:73	Tushingham 1972: fig. 1.67
3	Bowl	553:21437	C.2:73	Tushingham 1972: fig. 2.17
4	Bowl	570:22609	C.2:89	Saller 1966: 215, fig. 18:19 (?)
5	Bowl	886:21760	C.1:123B	Olavarri 1965: 85, fig. 1.7
6	Bowl	883:20863	C.1:123B	
7	Bowl	893:23073	C.1:123B	
8	Bowl	886:21758	C.1:123B	Saller 1966: 215, fig. 18.2
9	Bowl	388:26410	C.5:147	Tushingham 1972: fig. 2.34
10	Bowl	576:22914	C.2:95	Tushingham 1972: fig. 2.32
11	Bowl (Chalice)	900:24113	C.1:123B	Olavarri 1965: 87, fig. 2.9
12	Cooking pot	890:22382	C.1:123B	Tushingham 1972: fig. 1.36
13	Cooking pot	893:23079	C.1:123B	
14	Cooking pot	886:21767	C.1:123B	McNicoll, Smith, & Hennessy 1982: 129, pl.124.6
15	Cooking pot	862:26005	C.1:118	Tubb 1988: 36, fig. 11.24
16	Lamp	570:22606	C.2:89	Tushingham 1972: fig. 2.42

include wheel-burnishing and paint (Sauer 1994: 244, 245 plate). Besides comparable material nearby, at Nebo (Saller 1966), and sites within the wider region such as Pella (McNicoll, Smith, and Hennessy 1982) and Tell es-Saᶜidiyeh (Tubb 1988), there are close parallels with the ceramic remains from Aroer (Olavarri 1965) and especially Dibon (Winnett and Reed 1964; Tushingham 1972). This most likely indicates a Moabite element in the ceramic repertoire at Hesban (Sauer 1994: 244-45) and thus also a trend toward regional assemblages (Herr 1997d: 117).

Sauer (1975b: 105) has suggested that all of the ceramic material from Dibon can best be dated from 850-701 B.C. The ceramic material from Hesban, being parallel, therefore, would also seem to date to the last half of Iron Age IIB. However, more recent analysis (Sauer and Herr forthcoming) would seem to indicate that the Hesban material covers the entire period, not just the later part as was formerly thought (Herr 1979a: 19, 24). Nevertheless, the end of the stratum, on the basis of Sauer's dating of the parallel material at Dibon, would still seem to fall at the end of the eighth century B.C. Hence a date of ca. 925-700 B.C. for this stratum seems to be justified.

Stratum 16

The Iron Age IIC/Persian ceramic material (figs. 3.10 and 3.11) was found in Areas B and C (cf. fig. 6.13) as well as in an occasional bedrock pocket on the summit in Area A. It is much different than the ceramics of the previous stratum and consists of a large variety of bowls (fig. 3.11.1-13), of which the offset-rimmed (fig. 3.11.1-2) appears to be the most popular. Other ceramic forms include short-necked cooking pots (fig. 3.11.16), tripod bowls (cups) (fig. 6.13.8), holemouth kraters (fig. 3.10.11-14), and mortaria (fig. 3.10.15-16) (Lugenbeal and Sauer 1972: 33-61; Sauer 1994: 247). Collared-rim store jars (fig. 3.10.1, 3) continue to be attested (Lugenbeal and Sauer 1972: 52-53, pl. 7.376-87; Herr in press b), unlike in Cisjordan where they seem to have disappeared at the end of Iron Age I. Surface treatment especially on bowls consists of red and black burnish as well as painting in a variety of banded decorations (Lugenbeal and Sauer 1972: 61-62). The overall corpus suggests that Stratum 16 was occupied at least until the end of the sixth century B.C. (Lugenbeal and Sauer 1972: 63-64; Herr 1979a: 33,

Figure 3.9   Hesban Ostracon A6.

37), although the presence of a few Attic ware sherds (Stern 1982: 138-39; cf. Waldbaum 1991: 243) would seem to indicate a slightly later date within the fifth century B.C. The Attic ware (fig. 3.11.22) sherds, while being the earliest sherds in loci from later time periods, contribute to the overall understanding of this stratum. Besides forms already attested at Tell Hesban itself (Lugenbeal and Sauer 1972), parallels occur at such nearby sites as Tell el-ᶜUmeiri (Herr 1989c; Clark 1991; Lawlor 1991; 1997; Low 1991; 1997); Amman (Dornemann 1983); and Jawa (Daviau 1994), as well as farther north at Tell es-Saᶜidiyeh (Pritchard 1985).

Stratum 16 appears to have begun with the arrival of the Assyrians in the late eighth century B.C. They were no doubt an instrument for change in the material culture (Herr 1997d: 134-35) at a time of growing nationalism (Herr 1997d: 118) which saw the Ammonites become the dominant indigenous group in this region. The stratum continued throughout the Neo-Babylonian and Persian periods as is also attested by the latest ostraca (A5; A6, fig. 3.9) found in the reservoir (Cross: 1969:

Figure 3.10   Ceramics from Stratum 16.

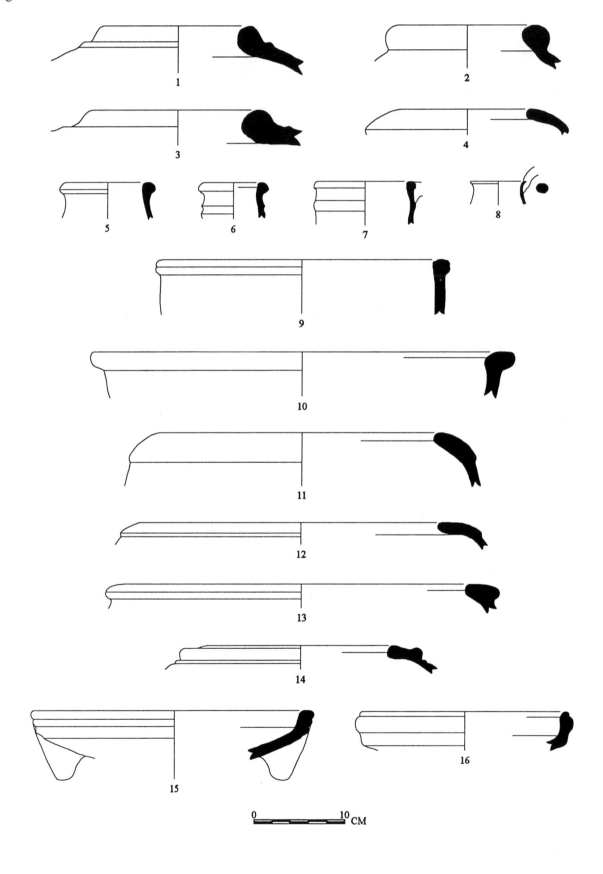

Figure 3.11   Ceramics from Stratum 16.

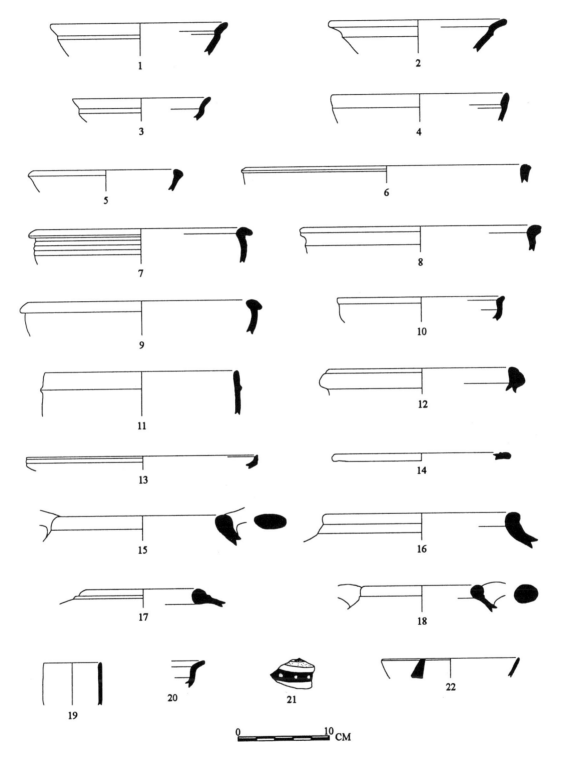

0 _____ 10 CM

Figure 3.10, *continued.*   Ceramics from Stratum 16.

No.	Type	Reg. No.	Locus	Parallel
1	Pithos	396:13336	B.1:143	Low 1991: 191, fig. 8.13.4
2	Pithos	394:13296	B.1:143	Pritchard 1985, fig. 17.22
3	Pithos	397:13359	B.1:143	Lawlor 1997: 34, fig. 3.15.2
4	Jar	394:13299	B.1:143	Lawlor 1997: 47, fig. 3.22.2
5	Jar	327:10741	B.1:119	Lawlor 1997: 47, fig. 3.22.9
6	Jug	397:13378	B.1:143	Low 1991: 191, fig. 8.13.33
7	Jug	374:13060	B.1:143	
8	Juglet	329:10790	B.1:119	
9	Basin	397:13362	B.1:143	
10	Basin	394:13298	B.1:143	Herr 1989c: 337, fig. 19.13.1
11	Krater	396:13340	B.1:143	Lawlor 1997: 47, fig. 3.22.14
12	Krater	396:13342	B.1:143	Lawlor 1997: 34, fig. 3.15.27
13	Krater	330:10808	B.1:119	Low 1991: 195, fig. 8.14.17
14	Krater	393:13274	B.1:143	
15	Mortar	326:10716	B.1:119	Daviau 1994: 186, fig. 11.7
16	Mortar	372:12956	B.1:143	Low 1997: 220, fig. 7.22.4

Figure 3.11, *continued.*   Ceramics from Stratum 16 (no. 22 unstratified).

No.	Type	Reg. No.	Locus	Parallel
1	Bowl	372:1296X	B.1:143	Lawlor 1997: 37, fig. 3.16.5
2	Bowl	394:13301	B.1:143	Low 1991: 180, fig. 8.8.23
3	Bowl	326:10724	B.1:119	Dornemann 1983: 249, fig. 56.583
4	Bowl	321:10383	B.1:119	Herr 1989c: 325, fig. 19.7.19
5	Bowl	372:12946	B.1:143	Pritchard 1985, fig. 15.1
6	Bowl	330:10807	B.1:119	
7	Bowl	372:12966	B.1:143	Low 1991: 201, fig. 8.16.11
8	Bowl	324:10464	B.1:119	Dornemann 1983: 249, fig. 56.595
9	Bowl	325:10689	B.1:119	Clark 1991: 64, fig. 4.9.10
10	Bowl	321:10378	B.1:119	
11	Bowl	325:10684	B.1:119	Lawlor 1991: 42, fig. 3.25.22
12	Bowl	396:13341	B.1:143	Low 1997: 212, fig. 7.16.13
13	Bowl	326:10709	B.1:119	Lugenbeal and Sauer 1972, pl. 10.523
14	Plate (Saucer)	325:10687	B.1:119	Daviau 1994: 186, fig. 11.2
15	Cooking pot	330:10826	B.1:119	Pritchard 1985, fig. 15.30
16	Cooking pot	326:10708	B.1:119	Lawlor 1997: 47, fig. 3.22.26
17	Cooking pot	374:13071	B.1:143	Clark 1991: 64, fig. 4.9.13
18	Cooking pot	393:13278	B.1:143	Lugenbeal and Sauer 1972, pl. 5.306
19	Cup ?	327:10755	B.1:119	
20	Lamp	396:13347	B.1:143	Low 1991: 219, fig. 8.22.15
21	Sherd	372:12949	B.1:143	
22	Attic ware	55:1077	A.2:11	

228; Cross and Geraty 1994: 170 Table, 173), and should thus be dated from ca. 700-500/450 B.C. The ceramics as well as the language and the script on ostraca from this stratum indicate that the tell was occupied by Ammonites during Stratum 16.

Summary

As is well known, it was W. F. Albright who established the overall Iron Age pottery sequence at the Cisjordanian sites of Tell Beit Mirsim (Albright 1932a: 53-89) and Bethel (Albright and Kelso 1968: 63-67). Recently, Finkelstein (1995b; 1996b; 1998b; 1998c) has suggested a lower chronology (1998d; 1999a; 1999b). His conclusions are based on: (1) the lack of Philistine wares (monochrome and bichrome) at Lachish, whereby he suggests that these were introduced somewhat later, and (2) the mid-ninth century B.C. ceramic assemblage at Tell Jezreel, to which he compares other sites (especially Megiddo) in an attempt to pull the tenth century B.C. wares down into the following century. However, both Mazar (1997; cf. Mazar and Camp 2000: 47-48; 50-51) and Ben-Tor and Ben-Ami (1998; cf. Ben-Tor 2000a) have persuasively argued that: (1) two clearly defined cultures living in close proximity to each other can and do coexist during the same period (cf. also Stager 1995: 341-44), and (2) that pottery types have a long range and develop slowly. Since these arguments seem to be more cogent, it would appear that the traditional pottery chronology is closer to reality (cf. Master 2001: 117-22) despite Finkelstein's (1998b) polemics to the contrary.

While this standard pottery terminology (Iron Age IA, B and C = IIA, B and C), which is based on a sequence that was originally developed for sites west of the Jordan River and corresponding in Iron Age II to the united monarchy at Jerusalem, does not seem to be appropriate for southern Jordan below the Wadi Hesa (Bienkowski 1992: 7), it still seems to be adequate for northern and central Jordan where it corresponds in a number of ways. In addition, both archaeological and ethnographical evidence would seem to indicate that itinerant potters diffused domestic wares relatively rapidly throughout Palestine. Since the production process was generally consistent across the country resulting in a basic uniformity of style, temporal changes were much the same through the various parts of Palestine (Wood 1990: 92-93) and, as we have seen, also in Transjordan, at least in Iron Age I. This might even be said to extend to such things as decorative motifs on rims and handles, as the same incised circular motif on a Stratum 20 pithos rim (fig. 3.2.8) can be seen on pithoi from Shiloh (cf. Finkelstein 1993b: 172, fig. 6.53.4, and 180, fig. 6.60.5). As is now known, the Ammonites and probably the other Transjordan cultures of Moab and Edom did not disappear with the arrival of the Babylonians, but continued to flourish throughout the Persian period (Herr 1993a: 29, 35; 1995b: 617-19; Sauer 1986: 18; 1994: 248; Younker 1994a: 314-15; Stern 2001: 257; 329; 457) and, perhaps, later. The lack of a cultural break and the clear continuity of the Iron Age through the end of the sixth century B.C., at least, is now beginning to be recognized in Cisjordan as well (Barkay 1992: 373; 1993: 106-109; Zorn 1997a: 36-38; 1997b: 61-63).

Table 3.1 summarizes the stratigraphic and ceramic correspondences as arrived at above.

Table 3.1. Iron Age Strata at Tell Hesban.

Stratum	Period	Dates
21	LB/Iron I Transition-Iron IA	1225-1150 B.C.
20	Iron IA-IB	1150-1100 B.C.
19	Iron IB	1100-1050 B.C.
18	Iron IB-IIA	1050-925 B.C
17	Iron IIB	925-700 B.C.
16	Iron IIC/Persian	700-500/450 B.C

Chapter Four

HESBAN AND VICINITY
IN THE LATE BRONZE AGE

Chapter Four

Hesban and Vicinity in the Late Bronze Age

Introduction

In order to put Iron Age Tell Hesban and its environs into context it is necessary to look at what was happening at the tell and the wider region during the Late Bronze Age.

Tell Hesban in the Late Bronze Age

Several Late Bronze Age and possible Late Bronze Age sherds were said to have been found in the deepest levels reached in the sounding in Area B (= Square B.1) during the 1968 season (Horn 1968-69: 2.4; Hesban 1968 Area B locus sheets). Unfortunately, most of these can no longer be located. James Sauer (1994: 233-34, plate) also suggested the possibility of a few Late Bronze Age sherds from mixed loci found during the 1974 season in Square D.2, and Larry Herr (personal communication) has since informed the author that there is a Cypriot base-ring II ware sherd among the material that he is analyzing for the forthcoming volume on Hesban pottery. In addition, Bjornar Storfjell (personal communication) claims to have found a Late Bronze Age sherd on the surface of Tell Hesban some years ago, which has since been lost. Most, if not all, of these sherds probably fit within the Late Bronze II/Iron Age IA transitional phase of Stratum 21 (cf. chapters 3 and 5).

Irrespective of the above-mentioned sherd evidence, no Late Bronze Age occupational layers were found during the five seasons of excavation on the tell. This is not to say that there never was any evidence to be found or that no one lived on the tell at this time because no remains were located by the excavators. It just means that so far there is no evidence for sedentary occupation on the site at this time. No evidence is not the same as negative evidence. It is just nonevidence (Fischer 1970: 47-48; Kitchen 1993: 48; Merling 1996: 238-62; 2001: 61-72). As we have seen above (chapter 2), suggestions have been made that evidence could potentially have been found on parts of the mound so far

unexcavated, especially in light of the possible sherd evidence mentioned above, or that the site of biblical Heshbon, if Tell Hesban is to be so equated, might be located elsewhere (Geraty 1983: 243-47; 1994: 47-52; J. M. Miller 1997: 199-200, 202, n. 8).

It could also be argued that the tell was used by pastoral nomads, living in tents and caves (LaBianca 1991: 355; 1997: 254; van der Steen 1995: 146, 151) on the site at this time. Indeed, to some degree, the Late Bronze Age has been considered as a nomadic interlude throughout much of the Middle East (Adams 1974: 9; Rowton 1977: 182, 195; Finkelstein 1988: 341-45; 1992: 138-39) especially in Transjordan (Glueck 1934: 82; 1935: 138; 1939: 268-69; 1940: 114, 125-47; 1951: 423; 1970: 140-41; McGovern 1986: 343; Boling 1988: 13; Hopkins 1993: 208-210), where literary evidence indicates that groups of *Šзśw*, who are usually considered to have been bedouin tribes, existed at the time (Papyri Anastasi VI and Harris I; cf. *ANET* 259, 262; Giveon 1971: 235; Ward 1972: 35-60; Weippert 1974: 265-80; McGovern 1987: 268; Redford 1992: 271-75; Worschech 1997: 229-30).

However, the above view is gradually being modified to one where the period is characterized by urbanism on a reduced scale, with a diminished rural sector and a large nomadic population on the frontier zones (McGovern 1987: 267-71; Bienkowski 1989: 59; Bunimovitz 1995b: 324-28; Younker 1997b: 87-92; 99-105). It would seem that this came about, at least in part, as a reaction to the heavy taxation, labor (the corvée), and military conscription demands (Bunimovitz 1995b: 327) as well as the deportation policies (Younker 1997b: 98-99) of the Egyptians. Earlier models tended to view villagers and pastoral nomads as a dichotomy (Eickelman 1981: 56; Eph[c]al 1982: 5, 13), often in opposition to each other (e.g., Noth 1958: 69) or in terms of a cultural-evolutionary process where nomads became sedentarized (e.g., Finkelstein 1984: 201). Newer models, however, have been inclined to see a symbiotic relationship between nomadic and sedentary elements of society (Rowton 1974; 1976; Marx 1977: 345; Eickelman 1981: 56, 73-74; McGovern 1987: 268-69; Köhler-Rollefson 1992: 11), which tend be fluid and part of a continuum, with some combination of pastoral and agricultural pursuits being carried out by the same group of people (Swidler 1973: 23-42; LaBianca 1990: 38; Marx 1992: 259). Thus, at any one time a certain amount of sedentarization and nomadization occurs within the same segment of society even within the same household (LaBianca and Younker 1995: 404; LaBianca 1997: 253). Ethnological (Barth 1961) and ethnoarchaeological studies (Köhler-Rollefson 1987) have brought out various aspects of pastoralism that have a bearing on ancient practices and some studies have been successful in finding recently abandoned pastoral encampments (Cribb 1991: 113-211). More importantly, some nomadic sites, which were occupied at various points in history from the Early Bronze Age through the Islamic periods, have indeed been found (S. Rosen: 1988: 49-52; S. Rosen and Avni 1993: 193-96), though for some reason similar sites from the Late Bronze Age have been particularly difficult to locate (S. Rosen 1988: 53; 1992: 81-82). The excavators of Tell Hesban, likewise, have found no evidence for pastoral encampments on the site during the Late Bronze Age.

The Regional Context

We will next look at sites located between the Wadi Zerqa and the Wadi Mujib, which were occupied during the Late Bronze Age. Unfortunately, archaeological reports (mainly surveys) make no inner-period distinctions. However, it is likely that many of these sites date to the Late Bronze/Iron Age I transition period.

Barakat's 1973 study listed six Late Bronze Age sites within this region (Amman, no number; Hesban, Site 166; Jalul, Site 183; Madaba, Site 227; Safut, Site 324; and Sahab, Site 325) though no criterion are provided for his assignments (Barakat 1973: 72, Map 6). It may be surmised that Hesban was included on the basis of the sherds mentioned in the 1968 preliminary report. In 1976, a survey was conducted in the southern half of the East Jordan Valley between Wadi Rajib and the Dead Sea. Three Late Bronze Age sites (189, 193 and 200) were found between the Wadi Nimrin/Shuᶜeib and the Wadi Kefrein (Yassine, Ibrahim, and Sauer 1988: 192, 197, 203). Tell

Nimrin also now appears to have very early Late Bronze ceramics (Dornemann 1990: 160, 164, 180, pl. 9.1). In the region around Telul edh-Dhahab, two sites (Khirbet Umm el-ᶜIdham, Site 17, and Tell Ghreimun, Site 24), just south of Wadi Zerqa, were found to have possible Late Bronze Age sherds (Gordon and Villiers 1983: 276, fig. 1, 286-87, Table 1). The er-Rumman Survey also found six sites (2/4, 4, 6/1, 27, 41, and 42) with Late Bronze Age sherds (Gordon and Knauf 1987: 290, fig. 1; 294-97) with the possibility of four others (7/1, 23, 26, and 35; cf. p. 292).

In the Umm ad-Dananir region, the Baqᶜah Valley Project surveyed seven sites, three (Rujm al-Henu East, Site 1; Rujm al-Henu West, Site 2; and Khirbet Umm ad-Dananir, Site 3) contained some evidence from the Late Bronze Age (McGovern 1980: 62, 64; 1986: 8). In addition, they found two groups of burial caves, a number of which were used at this time. The Jebel al-Hawayah (Group A) tombs consisted of three burial caves. Tomb A1 was used in Late Bronze Age I A, A2 primarily in Late Bronze Age I A, with some further use in Late Bronze Age II, and A3 in Late Bronze/Iron Age I transition. The Jebel al-Qesir (Group B) tombs consisted of 30 burial caves, of which 16 (B3, B5-14, 26-30) were used some time within the Late Bronze Age (B7, 11, 12, and 13 in Middle Bronze/Late Bronze Age; B5, 6, and 9 in Late Bronze Age I A; B3, 8, 28, 29, and 30 in Late Bronze Age II; and B10, 14, 26 and 27 some time within Late Bronze Age). Besides local wares from this period, there were some fragments of Mycenaean III B sherds (McGovern 1980: 55-60; 1986: 13-16).

A survey of the Wadi Nimrin/Shuᶜeib described three Late Bronze Age sites (1, 16, and 19) in the area near the city of Salt (Wright, Schick, and Brown 1989: 347-348). In a survey of the Greater Amman area, four other of Late Bronze Age sites (56-29.4, 56-29.7, 56-38.1, and 56-41.1, cf. *JADIS* Site 2415.061) were located (Abu Dayyah et al. 1991: 390-92). Glueck Sites 250 and 293, *JADIS* Sites 2016.002 and 2113.022, and al-Hadid = Parker Site 7 (Parker 1976: 23, 29) also had Late Bronze Age sherds. The Hesban Regional Survey (Ibach 1976b: 124-25; 1978a: 213; 1987: 157-58, 159, fig. 3.3) yielded six sites (26, 54, 97, 128, 132, and 149) with Late Bronze Age sherds, two (Jalul, 26, and Tell el-ᶜUmeiri West, 149) of which have since been partially excavated (see below) and one site (Umm es-Sarab, 54) where a two-square sounding found no additional Late Bronze Age materials (Ibach 1976a: 113-117). Khirbet el ꞋAl (*JADIS* Site 2213.009) is also known to have been occupied during the Late Bronze Age, though the Hesban Survey did not find any sherds from this time. The Hesban Survey was followed up by the Madaba Plains Project Survey which found three sites (34, 36, and 37) with possible Late Bronze Age sherds in the 1984 season (Cole 1989b: 54-55; Boling 1989: 99, 188). No Late Bronze Age sites were found in the 1987 or 1989 seasons (Younker 1991a: 269-334; Christopherson 1997b: 291-302). Further south the sites of Umm el-Walid = Glueck Site 65 and Parker Site 9, and Khirbet el-Jumaiyil also had Late Bronze Age sherd evidence.

Late Bronze Age tombs have been found in central Jordan in the Baqᶜah Valley, at Amman, Sahab, Madaba, and possibly at Nebo. At Amman, the Jabal Nuzha tomb was dated to 1300-1150 B.C. (Late Bronze/Iron Age I), with the majority of the pottery belonging to the Late Bronze Age (Dajani 1966b: 48-49). At the Citadel, a Middle Bronze II/Late Bronze Age I tomb was found at Jebel Jofeh el-Gharbi. While there was a lack of base-ring and white slip (milk bowls) wares, other ceramic evidence leaned toward a Late Bronze Age I date for at least some of the tomb deposits (Harding and Isserlin 1953a: 14-15, 19-20). In addition, Ward (1966: 15-16) has confirmed a Late Bronze Age date for Cave 2 Tomb at Jebel el-Qalaᶜ on the basis of the cylinder seals found there.

At Sahab, three tombs have been found. Tombs A and B were both dated to Iron Age II, but Tomb C had remains from the 14th century to the end of the ninth century B.C. (Late Bronze Age II-Iron Age II). It had previously been used as a dwelling, and the ceramic evidence, including imported Mycenaean wares as well as local imitations of the same ware, indicated that it was used as a tomb throughout Late Bronze Age II (Dajani 1970: 29-31). A seal with a corrupt form of the prenomen of Thutmose III was also found within this tomb (Horn 1971: 103). A tomb at Madaba yielded evidence from the Late Bronze/Iron Age I transition. It contained Mycenaean imports but no base-ring or white slip (milk bowl) wares, so its beginning phase was dated to the Late Bronze Age II B (Harding and Isserlin 1953b: 27-28, 34-36). It also had parallels to Tomb C at Sahab (Dajani 1970: 31). Finally, a cave tomb in Wadi Abu en-Naml near Mount Nebo produced sherd evidence and other objects from Middle Bronze Age II, but a few

pieces that could be dated to Late Bronze Age I (Saller and Bagatti 1949: 24-29).

Considering sites in the Baqᶜah Valley (mentioned above), Rujm al-Henu East (Site 1) is about 650 m southeast of the Jebel al-Hawayah (group A) burial caves. Its structure is laid out in a square with a central courtyard and is surrounded by outer rooms. This type of architecture is known as a *Quadratbau* structure. It is similar in nature to the Amman Airport Building (see below) as well as other sites of this type in Cisjordan, e.g., at Tananir on the lower slope of Mt. Gerizim (Boling 1969: 84). The pre-excavation survey had found several Middle Bronze/Late Bronze Age and Late Bronze/Iron Age I sherds. Test soundings in 1980 consisted of five squares (III.0, III.1, III.11, III.23, and III.32). The walls of the structure were founded on bedrock and revealed additional Late Bronze Age and Late Bronze/Iron Age I sherds in mixed loci (McGovern 1983: 105-108, 116, 122-127; 1986: 12-13).

Rujm al-Henu West (Site 2) had revealed only one pre-excavation Late Bronze Age II sherd. Excavation (Field IV, areas 1-3) revealed a circular (Rujum Malfuf type) tower which dated exclusively to Iron Age IIC/Persian, but no further Late Bronze Age evidence was found (McGovern 1983: 110-112, 127-37). Khirbet Umm ad-Dananir (Site 3) was the major settlement in the region in the Late Bronze and Iron Age. The site was associated with both the cemeteries of Jebel al-Hawayah and Jebel al-Qesir. A building similar to Rujim al-Henu East and the Amman Airport Building was found in squares V2, V5, and V7 with a 60 cm thick "dedicatory fill" including both burnt and unburnt animal remains including sheep/goat, equid, and cattle. In the foundation trenches of the building walls, there were whole pottery vessels including miniatures and a Cypriot-type shaved juglet as well as Egyptian blue frit beads. Against the central pillar was a fireplace. This building was destroyed sometime during Late Bronze Age IIB. A refuse pit dug into the destruction debris contained half of a bull rhyton and animal bones of the same species as those found in the "dedicatory fill." A cultic function for the refuse pit has been suggested. Large amounts of Late Bronze Age sherds were found on the uppermost terrace of the site (McGovern 1986: 9-11, 61-63; 1989: 128-134).

Tell Safut overlooks the Baqᶜah Valley. The earliest occupation on the site is Late Bronze Age, though there were mixed Middle Bronze/Late

Bronze Age ceramic finds. This is connected in Area B.2 with the inside of an outer perimeter wall (B.2:2) of 0.75 m long stones, which evidently encircled the acropolis. It was traced through a narrow foundation trench to bedrock. This wall ran the length of Area B enclosing what may have been a holy place in which a chalice, a large quantity of charred two-row barley beneath a large mudbrick tumble, and a bronze Ba^{C}al statue were found (Wimmer 1987a: 162, 164, fig. 4, 165-66; 1987b: 279-80).

At the Amman Citadel (Jebel el Qala^C), the British excavations found a few Late Bronze Age sherds (Bennett 1979a: 159), as well as a Middle Bronze/Late Bronze Age jug in area C.XXX in 1976, but no other Late Bronze Age materials (Bennett 1979b: 166). A small collection of Late Bronze Age sherds found from unstratified contexts at the citadel (Dornemann 1983: 22, figs. 49.76-77, 92, 94-95; 50) also attests Late Bronze Age presence here. In 1969, a Middle Bronze Age II glacis was located north of the Roman Wall and came up against Walls E and F. The sherd material in the glacis dated to the Middle Bronze Age II with a few possible Late Bronze Age sherds as well (Dornemann 1983: 19, 89, 90, n.1, 198, fig. 5). Recently, after the clearing of modern constructions in the area, two parallel walls were found. The lower (2015) was ca. 1.60 m wide and the upper (2005) was massive, averaging 2 m wide. There was a sloping glacis in between the two walls. The sherd evidence is Middle Bronze Age II (Zayadine, Humbert, and Najjar 1989: 357, 359-61, figs. 3 and 4, 363). Inside these walls was the entrance to a water system which was used in the Iron Age, though possibly earlier (Zayadine, Humbert, and Najjar 1989: 357). Water systems are notoriously difficult to date, but it has been noted that the arched ceiling is similar to Late Bronze Age tombs at Ugarit, which had corbeled roofs (Dornemann 1983: 90, n. 1).

The site of Sahab was also inhabited during Late Bronze Age. A 75 m stretch of the town wall was excavated in Areas G II, G III, and G IV and soundings which traced it on the south and southeast (H III and H IV), east (H II), and north (H II and B 019). The associated pottery yielded both local (including a storage jar handle with the seal of Thutmose III) and imported (Mycenaean) wares. The town was inhabited from the 15th through the 13th centuries B.C. and enclosed over 20 dunums. Sahab seems to have had an unbroken history of

occupation from the beginning of the Middle Bronze Age to late Iron Age II (Ibrahim 1987: 76-77). Additional evidence for Late Bronze Age occupation comes from a public building in Area E consisting of a massive wall over 17 m long and a tower-like room which projects from it. It has also yielded Mycenaean sherds (Ibrahim 1974: 60-61, 196-98, pls. 31.2, 32-33; 1975: 78, fig. 5, 80, 178, pl. 34.3).

In a pre-excavation random survey of Tell el-^{C}Umeiri before its initial season in 1984, 64 randomly selected squares were dug into the upper .10 m of topsoil for surface pottery. It was found that the eastern shelf had the greatest concentration of Late Bronze Age sherds, with a relatively strong concentration on the northern shelf as well. Concentrations on the acropolis were rather weak, but the heavy Iron Age II deposits there may have allowed few Late Bronze Age remains to erode onto the upper slopes (Herr 1989b: 216, 219-220, figs. 14.2, 14.3, 222). Field Phase 5 in Area C on the northern slope yielded some Late Bronze Age sherds in the 1984 and 1987 seasons (Battenfield and Herr 1989: 267; Battenfield 1991: 81, 82, fig. 5.12:25-29, 31-34, 85; Herr 1991: 241). In the 1989 season, Field F (Field Phase 10), on the eastern shelf, produced a layer of Late Bronze Age pottery including a Cypriot base-ring sherd (Younker et al. 1990: 21; LaBianca et al. 1995: 101; Low 1997: 191-95, figs. 7.6:3-33; 7.7; Herr 1997c: 233-37). Late Bronze remains were found in Field A in the 1992 season below three large boulders (Younker et al. 1993: 219). In addition, the Middle Bronze Age II earthen rampart (Area B) appears to have been reused in the Late Bronze Age (Field Phase 14; cf. Herr 1998: 253) much as the defensive systems in Cisjordan were reused at this time (Gonen 1984: 62, 70). However, the settlement seems to have been reduced to about half of its Middle Bronze Age II size (Herr 1992: 176; Herr 2000: 170). Either extra-urban activities such as terracing occurred on the northern and eastern slopes or the materials represent material eroded from the acropolis (Herr 1992: 176; 1997c: 233).

Tell Jawa produced a fill behind two Iron Age II walls containing sherds from the Middle Bronze Age, Late Bronze Age, and Iron Age I periods (Younker et al. 1990: 15). Fills below Iron Age II pavements and walls in Areas A and B on the acropolis at Jalul contained some Late Bronze Age pottery including biconical vessels in the initial (1992) season (Younker et al. 1993: 216). Late

Bronze Age pottery (a chalice base and two lamps) were also found in fills (?) in Area C during the 1994 season (Younker et al. 1996: 70).

Glueck found Late Bronze Age II/Iron Age I pottery at Khirbet el-Mekhayyet (Site 239; Glueck 1935: 110-11). Saller and Bagatti later found Late Bronze Age materials in Wadi el-Mekhayyat and Wadi Abu en-Naml that would seem to confirm this (Glueck 1970: 141; Saller and Bagatti 1949: 29, 210). Glueck (1970: 141-42) also claimed to have found Middle Bronze Age and/or Late Bronze Age sherds at Khirbet el-Medeineh on the Wadi eth-Themed (Site 68), though the new excavations at the site have not yet reached levels earlier than Iron Age II (Daviau 1997: 223; 1998: 2). Dibon yielded a few Late Bronze Age sherds in Areas B and C in the 1950-52 campaigns (Winnett and Reed 1964: 52), but no architecture or occupational levels were located. Nevertheless, the place name *Tpn* or *Tpwn* (Ti-pu-n or Tibunu = Dibon) appears on some war-scenes from the forecourt of Ramses II (1279-1213 B.C.) at the temple of Luxor in Thebes (Kitchen 1964: 53, 63; 1992: 28-29) and as number 98 in a list of toponyms (Nos. 89-101) of Thutmose III (1504-1450 B.C.), which seem to follow an itinerary through Transjordan from Syria to Kerak via Dibon (Redford 1982a: 119; 1982b: 62). Therefore, the lack of Late Bronze material at the site (based on the limited amount of excavation done there to date) does not necessarily rule out its occupation during the Late Bronze Age (Kitchen 1992: 28-29).

Aroer, on the north slope of the Wadi Mujib, was excavated between 1964 and 1966. It seems to have been inhabited during the Late Bronze/Iron Age I transition (level 5) as houses from this time were found (Olavarri 1965: 82-83, 91; 1993: 1:93). Late Bronze houses were also found at Lehun, just east of Aroer on the Wadi Mujib (Homès-Fredericq 1989: 354-355; 1992: 188-191). The houses contained Late Bronze Age ceramics (local and imported) and grinding stones.

An isolated building at the Amman Airport was found in 1955. It was re-excavated in 1966 by Hennessy (1966: 155-62) to clarify the initial salvage excavations of 1955, which found a *Quadratbau* or middle courtyard building with large numbers of Late Bronze Age ceramics both local and imported (Mycenaean II and III A -B as well as Late Helladic II Palace Ware, Cypriot base-ring I, and red lustrous ware). Egyptian stone vessels, scarabs (ranging from Hyksos to Thutmose

III), and cylinder seals were also found. While it has been variously interpreted (temples of various types, tribal league shrine, watchtower, cultic center for human sacrifice, and mortuary using cremation), it is agreed that its period of use was during Late Bronze Age IIB (13th century B.C.) if not earlier (Hennessy 1966: 162; Herr 1983a: 21; 1983b: 227). About 4 km southeast of the Amman Airport Building, another structure of this type was found at el-Mabrak. A number of non-descript body sherds, which were dated to Late Bronze/Iron Age, were associated with it (Yassine 1988: 61-64). While this dating is uncertain, similar structures at the Amman Airport, Rujm al-Henu East, and Khirbet Umm ad-Dananir might suggest a Late Bronze Age date for this structure as well, though arguments from architecture alone are not sufficient.

Interpretation

To a certain extent the northern part of central Transjordan might be seen as an extension of the Late Bronze Age city-state system of Cisjordan (McGovern 1986: 336; 1987: 267; Boling 1988: 17), possibly centering around Umm ad-Dananir (cf. McGovern 1986: 336), Safut, Sahab, and Amman, which seem to have been the only walled towns at the time. In terms of Amman, this is only an assumption. In addition to sites in the north of the country (Irbid, Pella, Tell es-Saᶜidiyeh, and Deir ᶜAlla) four others between the Wadis Zerqa and Mujib (Umm ad-Dananir, Amman, Sahab, and Madaba) have revealed Mycenaean pottery, leading Leonard (1987: 261-66) to suggest an extended trade network which brought Mycenaean and Cypriot imports from the Mediterranean to these sites. From the coast at Tell Abu Hawam these wares would have been brought through the Jezreel Valley as far as Beth-shean, then across the Jordan River to Pella. At this point one route would have gone south through the Jordan Valley and then to Amman, while the other route went first north through the Wadi Ziqlab and/or the Wadi Taiyiba to Irbid and then south through Umm ad-Dananir to Amman, Sahab, and Madaba (Leonard 1987: 264, 265, fig. 3). The central portion of the itinerary of Thutmose III (Redford 1982a: 115-119; 1982b: 55-74), passing through the Baqᶜah Valley and south through the Amman region and then past Dibon and over the Wadi Mujib, appears to have followed a route later known as the King's Highway and would appear to substantiate at least one of the routes suggested by Leonard. In addition, items of trade appear to have been brought from both Egypt (evidenced at Sahab and the Amman Airport Building) and the north (cylinder seals at Amman and the Baqᶜah Valley tombs), with Egypt evidently interested in exploitation of the local economy (Redford, 1982b: 73; Franken 1992: 175, 178-79).

To a certain extent the sites in the southern part of central Transjordan seem to have been distributed along the main north-south highway. There appear to have been only a few sites in the southern Jordan Valley, but a number of others were located along the east-west wadi systems, especially Wadi Nimrin/Shuᶜeib. Toward the desert there were also a few sites (Sahab, the Amman Airport Building and el-Mabrak).

The few sites in the southern Jordan Valley, by extrapolations from similar activities during the nineteenth century A.D., may represent pastoral-transhumance activities (see Borowski 1998: 42-43). Here, as well as in the Wadi Zerqa valley, semi-nomads would have had permanent settlements of huts and caves, grazing their herds in the winter and spring as well as planting and harvesting grain in the fertile valleys. During the summer months they would have moved their flocks up onto the plateau at which time they also lived in tents (LaBianca 1990: 80-81; Prag 1991: 49, 59; 1992: 156-157; van der Steen 1995: 144-52). On the plateau there may have been a few market towns playing the kind of role that Salt and Madaba did during the 19th and the early 20th centuries A.D. (Prag 1992: 157-59). Another mark of pas-

toral-nomadism during the Late Bronze Age was the phenomenon of isolated cemeteries and shrines unattached to permanent settlements (Finkelstein 1988: 343-34; 1992: 139; Hopkins 1993: 210) for which there is evidence of the former at Madaba and perhaps Nebo and the latter at the Amman Airport structure and el-Mabrak. The lack of evidence at Tell Hesban makes it impossible to suggest any kind of function for the site during this time.

Summary

Other than transitional ceramic forms, which probably place the earliest stratum of Tell Hesban (like that of Tell el-ᶜUmeiri) in the Late Bronze/Iron Age I transitional period (cf. Chapter 3), there is no evidence that the mound was occupied during the Late Bronze Age proper. In the region, the Late Bronze Age evidence consists of relatively few town sites with a number of smaller sites, tombs (a few in isolated areas), and an occasional cultic site, the latter also for the most part unconnected with permanent settlements (cf. Younker 1997b: 87-91, 101). As in all periods, there is a mixture of nomadic and sedentary activities reflected in the archaeological record, though it would seem that a large part of the Late Bronze Age society in central Transjordan was more on the pastoral end of the nomadic-sedentary continuum. Although it is possible that Tell Hesban was also used for pastoral-nomadic activities at this time, there is no evidence to suggest that this was the case.

Chapter Five

HESBAN AND VICINITY
IN IRON AGE I

Chapter Five

Hesban and Vicinity in Iron Age I

Introduction

Although a few earlier sherds may have been found at Tell Hesban (Sauer 1994: 230-235), it is with the Iron Age that the first clear evidence of sedentary occupation appears. Even these remains are very limited in that the acropolis and upper slopes were almost completely denuded by those who inhabited the mound in the centuries that followed. It was on the acropolis that the occupants of the site settled during most of the Iron Age, with the exception of Stratum 16 when the settlement was large enough to spread out on the lower slopes. Unfortunately, the remnant of the Iron Age materials is almost completely confined to bedrock and sub-bedrock installations as well as dump layers on the lower slopes below the acropolis. Due to these limitations, the interpretations found below necessarily need to remain more tentative than if we were dealing with layers where more definite stratigraphic connections could be made.

The tentative periodization of the tell at the conclusion of the 1976 season included 24 strata, with three (XXII-XXIV) belonging to the Iron Age-Persian Periods (Boraas and Geraty 1978: 15-16). This was modified in 1979 (cf. chapter 2) to twenty strata, with five strata (16-20) reflecting the Iron Age-Persian Period remains (Final Publication Archives). Larry Herr, who has done the most complete study of the Iron Age remains before this one, also identified five Iron Age strata (1-5 = Hesban Strata 16-20), but left open the possibility that Strata 5 and 4 were local phases within a larger Iron Age stratum (1979a: 12, 15). Hence, the more recent view on the Hesban stratigraphy has been that there are actually four Iron Age strata (16-19) (Storfjell 1983: 9; Mitchel 1992: 7; Table 1.1). Fisher has correlated these as follows: Herr's Strata 5-4 = Hesban Stratum 19 and his Strata 3-1 = Hesban Strata 18-16 respectively (1994: 94, n. 1). Recent reexamination of some of the original ceramic readings from the earliest strata (Sauer and

Herr forthcoming), however, now warrant a modification of this view. Due to the clear separation of pottery which has now been recognized, a six-strata scheme (16-21) seems to be justified (cf. Table 3.1).

Stratum 21

Stratigraphy

The remains of the earliest stratum at Tell Hesban are extremely limited and would seem to consist only of a number of dump layers located on the lower slope of the western side of the mound (in Squares C.1 and C.2; cf. fig. 1.2), well below the acropolis (cf. C.1 east and west balks and C.2 west balk; figs. 5.1-3).

Stage C

No evidence for the preparatory stage of this stratum was found among the fragmentary remains.

Stage B

Several soil layers in Squares C.1 and C.2 on the western slope of the tell would seem to represent the remnant of the use layers of the occupational phase of this stratum. The settlement at this time was probably localized on the acropolis and possibly the upper slopes of the mound. These dump layers, which were deposited here by later inhabitants of the tell, consist of loci C.1:95, 96B, 97, 98, 99, 142, 143, 144; C.2:54, 55, 92, 93, 94, 96, 98, and 99 (Thompson 1975: 181; Mare 1976: 68, 77). Loci C.2:54 and 55 were originally dug as cleanup debris and exhibit a wide range of ceramics. They were uncovered in the west balk of C.2, seemingly parallel with and equal to Stratum 21 layers (C.1:95 and 97) on the other side of the balk in Square C.1. Four spindle whorls and a slingstone (pl. 5.1) were found within these dump layers.

Figure 5.1   Area C, Square 1, East Balk.

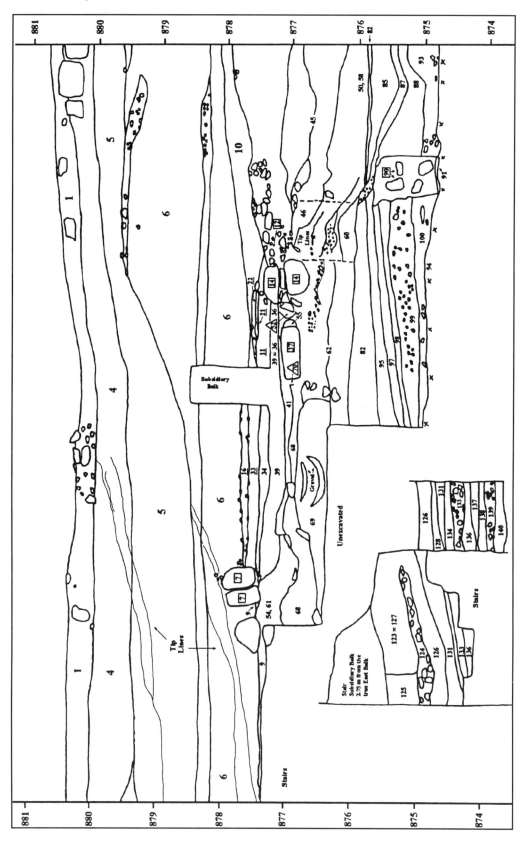

Figure 5.2   Area C, Square 1, West Balk (North Side).

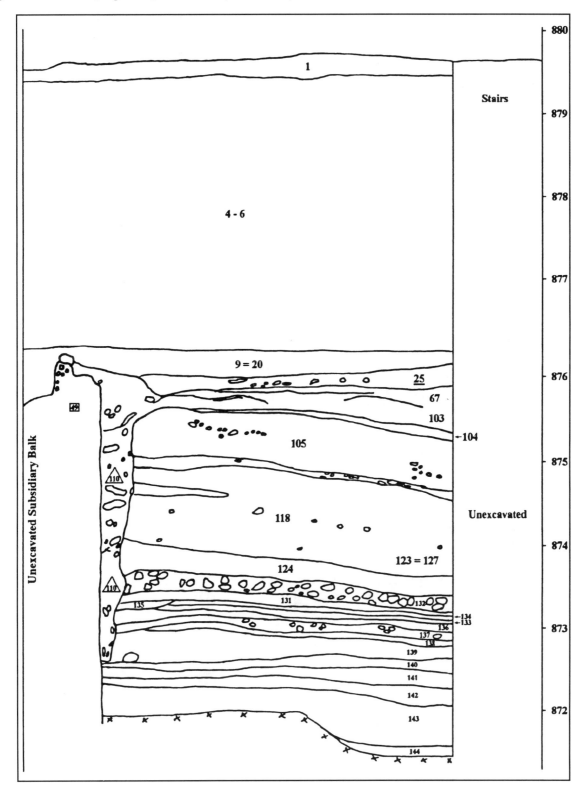

Figure 5.3   Area C, Square 2, West Balk (South Side).

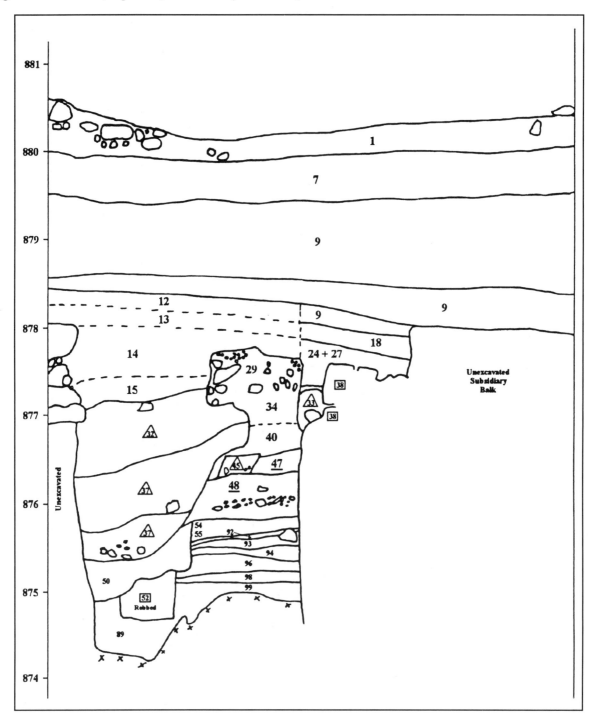

Plate 5.1 Slingstone (Object 1817).

Stage A

As was the case with Stage C, there is no evidence for a destruction/abandonment stage for this stratum.

Interpretation

The built-up remains of this earliest stratum at Tell Hesban are extremely poor and consist entirely of soil layers containing debris that was most likely dumped from the acropolis when the occupants of the following stratum began to build within that same area. This makes the interpretation of this stratum difficult. Nevertheless, there is still enough material remains (ceramic, faunal, and artifactual) to make some inferences about the original occupants and the character of the settlement.

The question of the identity of the occupants of the tell during Stratum 21 is a difficult one. Though it is impossible to know for sure, two lines of evidence (ceramic and textual) seem to suggest that they might have been a tribe or an alliance of tribes related to other tribal entities in Cisjordan. The ceramic repertoire of early Iron Age I Hesban, as well as those of Tell el-ᶜUmeiri, Tell Jawa, and Tell Jalul from the same period (Herr 1998: 258; 2000: 177), closely parallels those of towns and villages in the central hill country, north of Jerusalem (Sauer 1994: 237; Finkelstein 1996a: 200; 204; Sauer and Herr 1997: 234; Herr 1998: 256; 2000: 176; in press a), in the Bethel-Shechem region.

This repertoire includes collared-rim store jars (Zertal 1986-87: 129, fig. 12:1; 131, fig. 13.1, 134; cf. chapter 3, fig. 3.1.1-5 above), "Manassite" bowls (Zertal 1986-87: 125-26, 127, fig. 11.1-3, 5, 7, 10; 1994: 51-52, fig. 1.a-b; cf. chapter 3, fig. 3.1.11), and small carinated bowls similar to their cyma-profiled predecessors (Zertal 1986-87: 126, 127, fig. 11.14-15; cf. chapter 3, fig. 3.1.14). Finally, unless one dismisses the biblical narratives as late and irrelevant (e.g., Finkelstein 1996a: 200), there is abundant testimony to early Israelite settlement in Transjordan (Num 21:25-35; 32:1-42; Deut 29:7-8; Josh 12:1-6; 13:8-32; Judg 11:19-26). The combination of these factors would suggest that Hesban was inhabited by a people belonging to one of the Israelite tribes (possibly Reuben) (Herr 1998: 260; 1999a: 72*; 2000: 178; Herr and Clark 2001: 64; cf. Ji 1995: 137; 1997b: 410-112) at this time.

On the other hand, the rather large (3.25) percentage of pig bones at Hesban[1] might suggest occupation by groups (Sauer 1994: 237; Finkelstein 1996a: 206) other than the Israelite tribes. However, a number of other factors need to be considered. First, the tribal populations (Ammonite, Reubenite, Gadite, Moabite, and possibly even Amorite) living within, and claiming the same general area, were fluid (LaBianca and Younker 1995: 403-5; Herr 1998: 258-59). Thus, it is probable that not everyone within a given area and possibly even the same site was of the same ethnic origin. Second, pig distribution is influenced by factors other than consumption such as scavenging (waste consumption) and turning over harvested gardens (Hesse 1986: 25; Zeder 1996: 301-302). Third, the presence of the dog, which in the Middle East was never a pet and had to fend for itself in obtaining food, has been found in a recent ethnoarchaeological study of modern Hesban to have been responsible for the large numbers of bones of "unclean animals" being transported from outlying areas into the village (LaBianca 1990: 196; 1995b: 22, 27-29). Fourth, while prohibition against pig keeping and consumption is also proscribed among Moslems, pigs were nevertheless found to consist of from 1.0-12.2% of the faunal remains in the Islamic strata at Tell Hesban (LaBianca 1990: 220, Table 7.1). Finally, Finkelstein assumes Iron Age I Hesban was a "proto-Ammonite site" due to the high percentage of pig bones (1996a: 206). However, Stratum 16, which, as we will see, has the best evidence for Ammonite settlement, had very few pig bones. The sample, unfortunately, is statistically invalid (cf. Appendix C, introduction), but on the basis of the available data would be less than 1%. Even if the Iron II/Persian remains in the Stratum 15 reservoir fill are taken into consideration, the result would be the same.

It would seem that the above caveats would mitigate against leaning too heavily on the prohibition against swine as the determining factor of ethnicity, which in any case cannot be determined by their mere presence or absence (Hesse and Wapnish 1994 in Borowski 1998: 142). The above discussion and probably other factors need to be figured into strategies based on food as an indicator of ethnicity.

It is impossible to know how or why this stratum came to an end. Nevertheless, it might be inferred from historical considerations. The stabilizing influence of Egypt was gone from the region by the end of the reign of Ramses VI (1141-33 B.C.) (Weinstein 1981: 22-23; 1998: 191). Areas farther removed from Egypt itself, such as Transjordan, no doubt became vulnerable even earlier. The garrison at Beth-shean, for example, does not seem to have outlasted Ramses III (1182-1151 B.C.), the last great pharaoh of the Twentieth Dynasty (Weinstein 1981: 23). This destabilizing situation no doubt opened the door to those with an eye to take advantage of the resulting power vacuum. If this was the case, it may have prompted the inhabitants of the village to embark on a new building plan which included defensive measures to protect the settlement.

The faunal remains from this stratum include cattle, sheep, goats, and pig as well as gazelle among the wild species. These data along with the relatively high percentage of cattle, which appear to have been used as draft animals for cereal cultivation (B. Rosen 1994: 343), would seem to indicate a mixed agro-pastoral subsistence economy based on the production of grain and the products of sheep and goats (wool/hair, milk, and meat; cf. Borowski 1998: 52-58, 63-65, 70-71), which made up 81% of the faunal assemblage (cf. Table 5.1). This appears to have been supplemented on occasion by the hunting of wild animals (gazelle). The four spindle whorls found within the debris of this stratum would suggest some kind of cottage industry (Herr 1979a: 11). These rather thick and crudely built whorls made from reused potsherds were probably used for spinning a rather thick thread such as goat's hair, which can be used for making tents (D. Irvin personal communication; Herr

Table 5.1 Stratum 21 Bone Data.		
Bone Type	#	%
Cattle	11	12.0
Sheep/Goat	76	81.0
Pig	3	3.25
Wild Species	4	3.75
Total	94	100.00

1997d: 120; London and Clark 1997: 38, fig. 48; Friend 1998: 68, n. 19). The cottage industry would seem to have been associated closely with those clan or family members who were on the more pastoral end of the nomadic-sedentary continuum.

Of the four determining considerations usually associated with tell habitation (Wright 1974: 127), it would seem that communications, food supply, and defense were the principle motivations for its original occupation. Water supply would seem to have played a lesser role in the choice of the tell in that it is located about 3 km southeast from the closest perennial spring at ᶜAin Hesban (Geraty 1993: 626). Though cisterns probably played a major role in water harvesting, the presence of relatively large numbers of collared-rim store jars (pithoi) from this stratum would suggest that water was transported by donkey and stored in these vessels (B. Rosen 1994: 340; Finkelstein 1996a: 201-2). Bones of donkeys have not been found in this stratum. The reason for this might be that as "unclean animals" their remains were deposited away from the settlement and that the few bones which were found in later strata owe their existence to dogs and other scavenging animals who brought them back on to the tell (LaBianca 1990: 196).

On the basis of the meager finds described above, one would not like to go much beyond Herr's assessment that Hesban was a small, unfortified village settlement (1979a: 11), perhaps with some sort of shrine (cf. the chalice, fig. 3.1.15) at this time.

Stratum 20

Stratigraphy

The meager remains of this stratum are confined to a bedrock trench on the southern shelf (in Squares B.2, B.3, and D.4; figs. 5.4-9) and a cistern

Figure 5.4   East Balks of Squares B.2 and B.4.

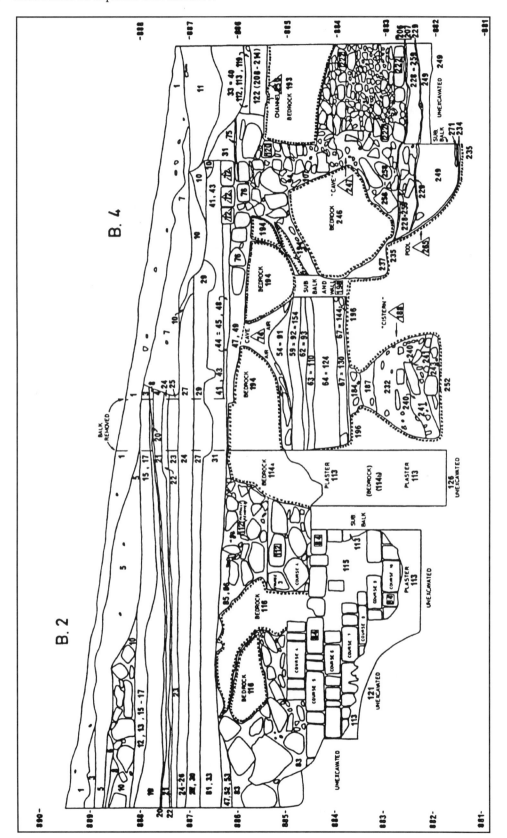

Figure 5.5   Area B, Square 3, East Balk.

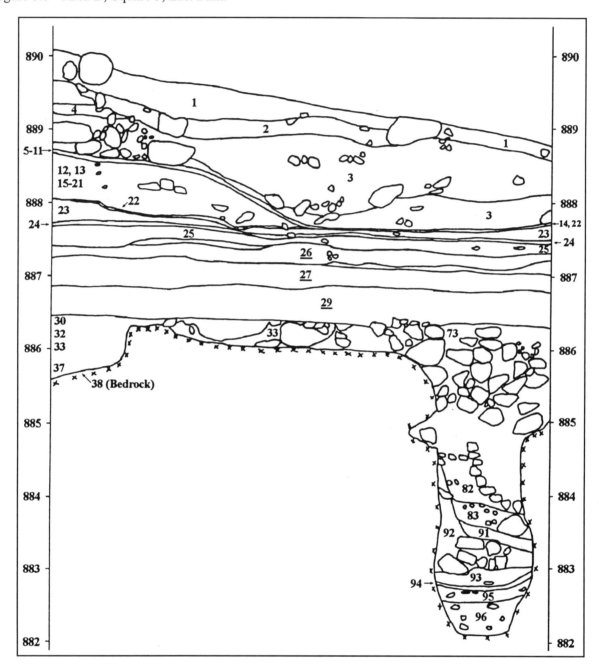

Figure 5.6   Area B, Square 3, West Balk.

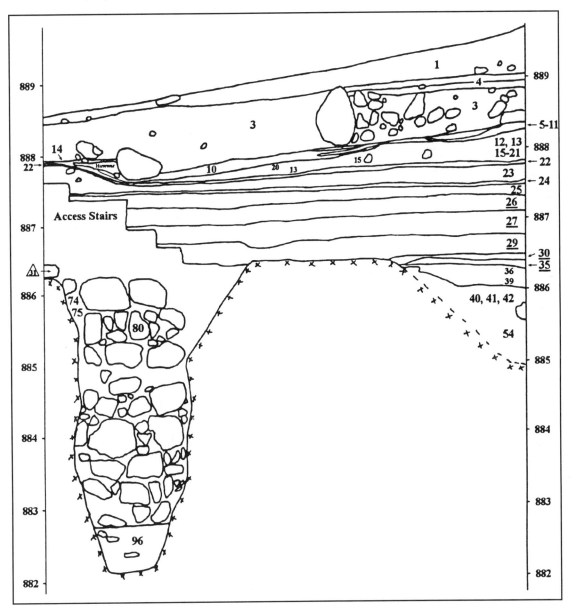

Figure 5.7   Area B, Square 3, South Balk.

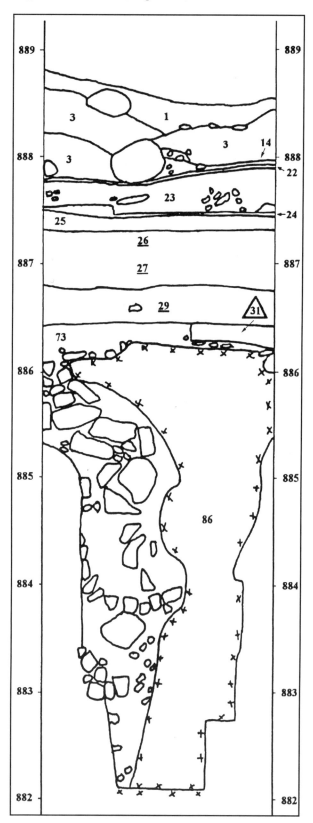

along with its bottommost soil layer on the Acropolis in Square D.1.

Stage C

A bedrock trench (see fig. 5.10) measuring between 2-2.50 m in width at the top and about .75 m at the bottom, with an average depth of around 4.00 m, represents the construction stage of this stratum. The excavated portion of the trench, until recently,[2] was ca. 11.85 m in length. The 13 m figure mentioned by Sauer (1976: 62; 1978: 49) does not include the part that extends into the east balk of D.4. This length was evidently calculated on the basis of the uppermost portion of the north face of the trench (D.4:25) that was exposed. The additional 2.00 m to the east were not actually excavated until 1996, when parts of the site were cleaned for restoration purposes. In 1997 an additional 3.00 m were partially excavated further to the east in Square D.7. The exposed section, now ca. 17 m, begins in Square D.7 and enters the east balk of Square D.4 just below a cave complex. From here it runs to the west throughout the length of Squares D.4 and B.3 and ends abruptly about a meter into Square B.2, where a reservoir, built later in the Iron Age, was cut. The north face consists of loci B.2:116; B.3:84, 85, 90; and D.4:25 and the south face, loci B.2:114A; B.3:86; D.4:67; and possibly 154, the latter being partly outside of the excavation area within the south balk of Square D.4. The bottom or "floor" (Sauer 1976: 61) of the trench, where isolated, consists of locus D.3:98. Herr (1979a: 6) also suggested a 3.00 m subsidiary cut to the north in Square B.2, hence his total excavated length of 16.85 m. However, this cut, whether or not it was a continuation of the trench or some other feature, was probably made at a later time (in Stratum 19), a possibility also allowed by Herr (1979a: 7, 13-14). In addition, but stratigraphically unconnected, is a 3.50 m by 2.25 m by 1.75 m cistern (D.1:63) with a plaster lining of .05 m (D1:63H=102) near the edge of the acropolis (D.1 plan; see fig. 5.11) on the south side of the tell. It is dated generally to Iron Age I, but was possibly dug at this time.

Stage B

The only remains from the use stage of this stratum consist of a thin layer of water-laid silt with a few pieces of Iron Age IA pottery (Herr 1976: 99;

Figure 5.8   Area D, Square 4, West Balk.

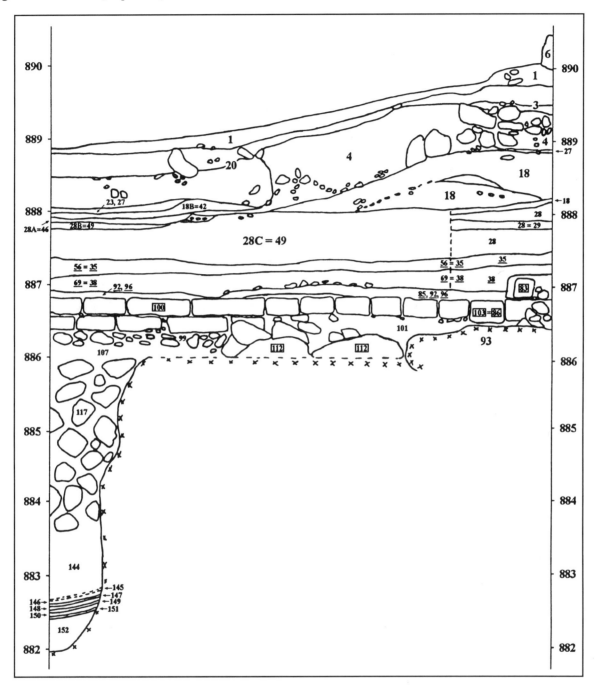

Figure 5.9   Area D, Square 4, South Balk.

Figure 5.10 Stratum 20 Bedrock Trench (with Stratum 19 Wall and Stratum 18 House).

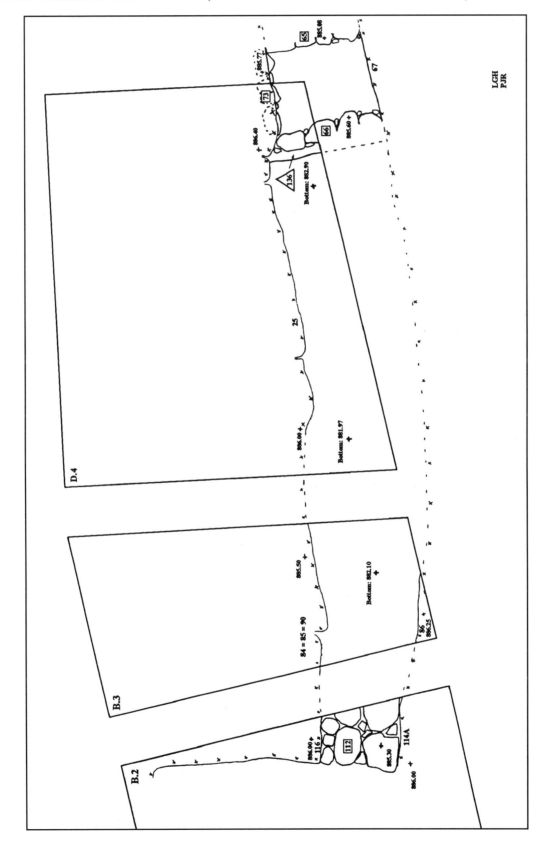

Figure 5.11   D.1 Cistern 63.

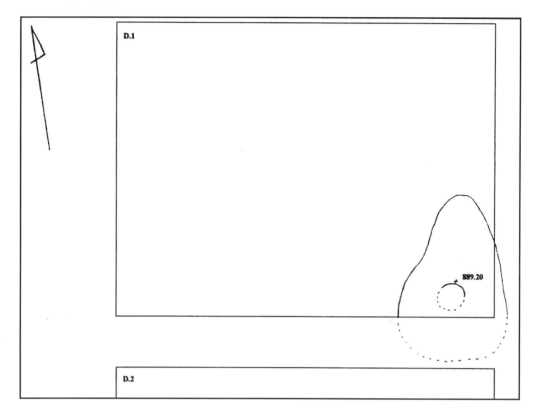

1978a: 110) in the bottom of the D.1 cistern (D.1:63G=101).

Stage A

The bedrock trench in Squares B.3 and D.4 was filled to the top with debris. This material contained a mixture of Iron Age IA and IB pottery along with the destruction debris of Stratum 20 which were found in loci B.3:74, 75, 76, 77, 78, 80, 81, 82, 83, 89, 91, 92, 93, 94, 95, 96, 97, 99; D.4:111?, 124, 125, 126, 128, 129, 130, 131, 132, 133, 134, 135, 137, 138, 139, 140, 141, 142, 143, 144, 145, 146, 147, 148, 149, 150, 151, and 152. These layers consist of superimposed, and sometimes alternating, layers of soil, ash (B.3:74, 77, 94; D.4:126, 128, 129, 131, 132, 137, 145, 147, 149, and 151), and rock tumble (B.3:78, 80, 83, 92; D.4:144) (Sauer 1976: 60-61; 1978: 48; Herr 1979a: 9). A mortar, a door socket, four spindle whorls, and five pottery discs (pl. 5.2) which could have been blanks for other spindle whorls or alternatively may have served as jar stoppers or lids (Kotter 1979: 8; London 1991: 414, 417), spindle rests (Platt 1983:

3), game pieces, "bats" for the production of pottery or counters for accounting and business exchange (London 1991: 414, 417) were found within these layers.

Interpretation

Because of its depth and relative narrowness, the bedrock trench, which is the most notable feature of this stratum, is somewhat enigmatic, and exact parallels seem to be lacking. Therefore, a number of suggestions have been made regarding its function (Sauer 1976: 49; Geraty 1993: 628), most of which (dry storage and subterranean habitation) have been dismissed (Herr 1979a: 7-8). Although the so-called "Israelite shrine (?)" at Samaria (Crowfoot, Kenyon and Sukenik 1942: 23-24, fig. 11; pl. 1, feature 27, see also Steiner 1997: 19-21) remotely resembles the trench, this trapezoid-shaped feature is too dissimilar both in terms of its dimensions (4.00-6.00 m in width) and date (Iron Age II) to be a feasible parallel (Herr 1979b: 4). Other suggestions include water channel and dry moat (defensive cut) options (Fisher 1994: 86-

Plate 5.2 Pottery Disc (Object 2846).

87; Sauer and Herr 1997: 233).

Herr (1979a: 8) has suggested that this feature is a water channel. In favor of this proposal is the .80 cm decline of the trench from east (882.90 m) to west (882.10 m), suggesting that water flowed in this direction to a possible reservoir farther west (Herr 1979a: 5, 8). Herr did, however, note a number of problems with his own suggestion, the most significant being the irregularity of the bottom of the trench (e.g., it slopes to 881.97 m in one spot on the western end of Square D.4). He has also noted the lack of water-laid silt that would be expected to have been deposited in a facility bearing water. Although, on the basis of a suggestion from John Holladay (Herr 1979a: 8, n. 4), he attempted to explain the depth of the channel as being necessary because of the height of the bedrock at this spot, he pointed out that it would have been easier to cut the channel around the bedrock spur to the south (1979a: 8). Further, it should be noted that two of the feeder channels (B.4:242 and 244) for the large (ca. 17.5 m x 17.5 m, with a depth of 7.00 m) reservoir, which was built later on in the Iron Age and which is estimated to have had a capacity of 2,200,000 ℓ (Sauer 1978: 48; Merling 1994: 215), were only ca. 0.25 m and 0.20 m wide and 0.25 m and 0.15 m deep, respectively. The former was plastered while the latter was not (Sauer 1976: 57). Though some of this bedrock area has collapsed since the Iron Age, it has been estimated that channel B.4:275C would have been ca. 0.65 m wide and ca. 0.55 m in depth (Sauer 1976: 58). Two factors mitigate against the suggestion that the bedrock

trench was designed as a water channel. First, there was an easier route for channeling of water available only a short distance away. Second, the trench's width and depth would suggest that another solution needs to be reached.

Another early suggestion for the function of the bedrock trench was that it was a defensive cut (Sauer 1978: 49) or dry moat. This was rejected by Herr (1979a: 7) partially because the trench was deeper than other Iron Age dry moats in the region. Iron Age sites with dry moats in the immediate region include Khirbet ᶜAyun Musa (el-Meshhed; Site 108 of the Hesban Survey) (Glueck 1935: 110; 184, pl. 22, Site 238; Ibach 1987: 25), Khirbet Mekhayyat (Glueck 1935: 110-11, Site 239; Saller and Bagatti 1949: 2, fig. 2) and Khirbet ᶜAtarus (Musil 1907: 395; 396, fig. 189).³ Outside of this region, sites with dry moats include Khirbet el-Medeinet South (ᶜAliya) (Glueck 1934: 52; 98, pl. 12; Routledge 1995: 236 plan; 2000: 41, fig. 4; 48-49; Mattingly 1996: 355-57, fig. 3), Khirbet el-Medeinet North (Muᶜarradjeh) (Olavarri 1983: 166, fig. 1; J. M. Miller 1991: 71) and Khirbet el-ᶜAkkuzeh (Glueck 1939: 61-62, 84, 90; J. M. Miller 1991: 158-60; Mattingly 1996: 363-64, fig. 9). However, since as yet none of these moats have been thoroughly investigated, their exact depth is unknown. Therefore, their potential relationship to the bedrock trench at Hesban can only be inferred in a general way. Since Herr made his original proposal (1979a), he himself has found a dry moat that is quite similar, in terms of its depth, to the bedrock trench at Tell Hesban at Tell el-ᶜUmeiri, on its western side in Field B. Here the Iron Age inhabitants of the site reused the top 4.00 m of an almost 5.00 m deep and ca. 6.00 m wide dry moat which was originally dug in the Middle Bronze Age (Herr et al. 1991b: 159; Clark 1994: 142; 1997: 54, 63, fig. 4.9, 85, 87; Herr et al. 1994: 153; Herr 1998: 251-52, 254; 2000: 171; LaBianca et al. 1995: 102).

In another draft of his paper, Herr (1979b: 4) noted a further reason for rejecting the dry moat interpretation of the bedrock trench in that no trace of the trench was found on the western side of the mound, which means that it did not completely encircle the site. Shea (1979: 20-21), however, postulated that it did just that. Picking up on Herr's suggestion that there was a subsidiary cut in the trench to the north, he extended this cut along an imaginary line on the western side of the tell just below the acropolis, and suggested that it might have been missed archaeologically in an unexca-

Figure 5.12 Model for Tell Slope Erosion (from A. Rosen 1986: 35).

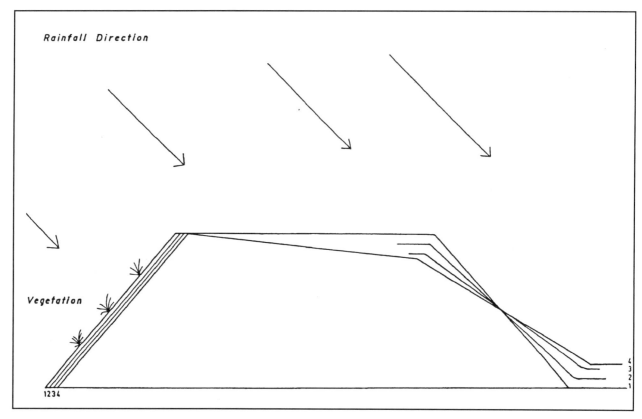

vated portion of Square C.10. While I agree that the dry moat interpretation has merit as the possible function of the bedrock trench, I believe that it is unlikely, indeed even unnecessary, for the trench to extend to the north on the western side or for that matter any where else on the mound.

Like most natural hills, the shape of tells appear to be the result of a combination of slope decline and parallel retreat (A. Rosen 1986: 27). According to slope evolution studies, at least one steep slope, often the one facing northwest, will usually develop (fig. 5.12). This occurs because it is exposed to the direct erosional agents of wind and rainfall. If it is flanked by a wadi, its steepness will be further accentuated by the removal of erosional debris at its base. The result is a phenomenon known as parallel retreat, where there is equal weathering along the entire face of the slope. A low, more gentle slope will develop on the other side of the mound where the rain strikes the surface obliquely and thus produces less vegetation. In other words, this side of the mound will erode through the process of slope decline caused by soil

creep from its upper to lower portions (i.e., declining in height and lengthening out; A. Rosen 1986: 29, 31-33).

Irrespective of the accumulated sediments of cultural material which developed later, the first inhabitants of Tell Hesban evidently settled on a mound which had the same basic shape as is found at present. This is because Hesban is not a true tell (Geraty 1983: 247), but rather a natural hill formed on the basis of geological activities. Conforming to the model described above, geomorphologically speaking, a crosssection of Tell Hesban would look asymmetrical, with relatively steep slopes on three sides and a gentle slope on the other (fig. 5.13). The large gradually sloping shelf, upon which the acropolis sits in its center, drops rapidly on all sides of the mound except the southwest, which consists of a long sloping ridge. Contributing to the steepness of the other slopes of the mound (pl. 5.3) are the Wadis el-Marbat and Majar flanking its east and west sides respectively (Boraas and Horn 1969a: 97-98; Younker 1994b: 55). Thus, the mound, even to its earliest inhabitants, would seem to have been

Figure 5.13   Topographical Map of Tell Hesban.

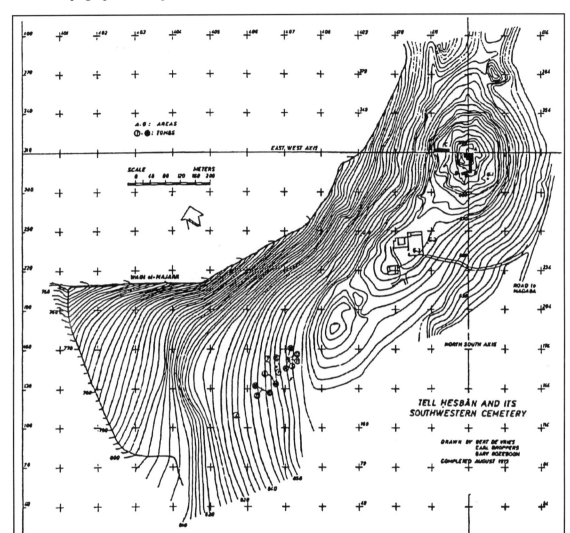

defensible on all sides except the south. To the extent that it has been excavated, it is on this southern vulnerable side of the mound where the bedrock trench was found.   The later Hellenistic (Sauer 1975a: 148, fig. 4; 156, 160; 1976: 54; 1978: 46; 1994: 250) or Early Roman (Mitchel 1992: 51-55) defense wall (B.1:17=B.2:62), which ran roughly parallel but slightly south of the bedrock trench (fig. 5.17), is evidence that even later inhabitants saw a need for additional defense at this side of the tell.

Both Clark (1994: 141) and Herr (1997b: 15) have noted that it is likely that the moat at Tell el-ʿUmeiri probably existed only on its vulnerable western side of the tell. This seems to have been the case with all of the other contemporaneous dry moats mentioned above as well. Although they occur at different directions of their respective tells, each of these moats has been found only on its one gently sloping side.[4] It would seem then that these tells also exhibit the same asymmetrical geomorphology, described above. The difference in the direction of their gently sloping side, which necessitated the contruction of a dry moat on that same slope in each case, is due to the complex topography of the region, which is impacted by locally altered wind patterns among the hills and valleys as well as the direction of flow of the deeply incised

Plate 5.3   Tell Hesban (Western Side) on the Wadi Majar.

wadis (A. Rosen 1986: 31).

It would seem that a moat would be a necessity at Tell Hesban. At this site the gently sloping side of the tell is on the south-southwest. The bedrock trench was found in that area of the tell and thus conforms to the pattern of dry moat placement which we have seen at other sites. The one weakness of this argument is that the moat at Tell Hesban is rather high up on the tell instead of at its base.

It should also be noted that the moats at the sites previously referenced appear to have been much wider (6.00 m +) than the bedrock trench at Hesban and to have had walls in connection with them. Although the 2.00-2.50 m width of this feature is certainly not as impressive as the dry moats found at these other sites, it nevertheless could possibly have served a defensive function as a deterrent against military attack, especially in combination with its 4.00 m depth. Its narrow width might reflect the limited manpower of Iron Age I Tell

Hesban. Another possibility is that what has been found represents a moat that was never finished (Herr 1979a: 9; Shea 1979: 21).

It is also true that no walls have been found in connection with this trench. While there was a large amount of rock tumble in the western part of the trench (in Square B.3), which perhaps might have once been part of a defense wall or some other structure near it, there is no way of knowing for sure if that was the case. Since very little remains of this stratum, one could easily over-or underestimate the value of that which was not found. Nevertheless, unlike these other sites with dry moats, which were shorter lived, Hesban was occupied almost continuously up to modern times, with ongoing removal and robbing of earlier occupational features. Thus, the possibility exists that there originally was a wall or that one was intended, but never built before the trench went out of use. Further, it should also be pointed out that if such a wall did exist, the evidence indicates that it was not placed around the periphery of the mound, as the site was settled only on the Acropolis and its upper slopes at this time. Hesban is larger than the above-mentioned sites, and its Iron Age I inhabitants were unable to occupy all of its available space, a situation roughly analogous to Iron Age I and early Iron Age II Hazor (Yadin et al. 1989: 165-66; Ben-Tor 1995: 65-66), which also had a dry moat (Yadin et al. 1989: 53).

These same factors (the large size of the mound and the restricted area of settlement) may also account for the placement of the moat in a location higher up, on one of the shelves of the mound, rather than at its base as is typical of the other dry moats in the region. Though designed to deal with sherd distribution, the tell formation model of Portugali (1982: 171-72, fig. 1; cf. A. Rosen 1986: 47, fig. 14) may help to illustrate the point (fig. 5.14). Most of the above-mentioned sites with dry moats appear to be sealed structures (fig. 5.14.B) and would seem to lend themselves to dry moat placement at the base of the tell. Both ᶜUmeiri and Hesban are shelved structures (fig. 5.14.A) although the location of the dry moat at ᶜUmeiri is also at the base of the tell. This was necessary because the vulnerable side of the tell leading up to the acropolis, where the Iron Age settlement was located, is joined to a saddle connecting to a nearby ridge (Clark 1994: 140). The shelves, however, are located on the steep sides of the tell. At Hesban, on the other hand, the acropolis is located in the center of the mound with one of the shelves on its weak side (fig. 5.14.C). It is on that shelf that the bedrock trench is located.[5] The settlement, restricted basically to the acropolis, was thus a considerable distance from the base of the mound, making the location of a dry moat in that position an impractical solution. Regardless of its placement on the shelf, the bedrock trench or moat appears to have cut off the settlement from its approach on the southwest and thus functioned in the same manner as if it had been located at its base.

With the exception of an intrusive Early Roman pit (D.4:117) which contained loose rock, the bedrock trench was completely filled with debris from this stratum. The ceramic material was mixed Iron Age IA and IB and includes collared-rim store jars, incurved bowls, and strainer-spouted jugs (Sauer 1986: 10-11, fig. 11; 1994: 235, 236 pl.; cf. chapter 3, figs. 3.2.1-8; 3.3.2, 16 above). As in the previous stratum, there are also "Manassite" bowls (fig. 3.3.3, 5-6, cf. fig. 3.1.11) and small carinated

bowls (fig. 3.3.7-9; cf. fig. 3.1.14). Both the debris and the ceramic remains were homogeneous, containing no surfaces, wind, and water-sorted soil layers or flat-lying pottery, which indicates a rather quick filling process (Herr 1979a: 10). This, along with numerous ash layers (see above and Sauer 1976: 62 on B.3:94) and one human bone (D.4:142 cf. Sauer 1978: 48, n. 18), would suggest the destruction of the site (Herr 1979a: 10-11, contra Sauer 1994: 237). Thus, irrespective of whether the trench was finished or not and whether or not there were accompanying walls, the site would seem to have been attacked and destroyed rather early in its existence.

It is impossible to know for sure the identity of those who attacked and destroyed Hesban. A very tentative suggestion based, as all proposed perpetrators of ancient destructions are, on textual evidence is that of the desert peoples. The Midianites, Amalekites, and other tribes from the desert to the east plundered both eastern (Judg 8:4-11) and western Palestine, sometimes on an annual basis (Judg 6:1-3) during Iron Age I and there is ample analogy throughout the history of the Middle East of this kind of activity. It is possible, therefore, that Hesban was destroyed by some group of nomadic raiders as they moved about from place to place plundering the settled population. Another possibility is that it was the Ammonites (or other nearby neighbors) who began a short period of military expansion about this time (Judg 10:7-12:7).

As we have seen, the tell was naturally defensible and if the bedrock trench was indeed a dry moat (whether just underway or completed), fortification seems to have been at least attempted. Further, the coordination of the labor involved in digging the bedrock trench would seem to have necessitated a socioeconomic sophistication beyond the means of the small village of the previous stratum. Tell Hesban is located at the crossroads of the main north-south (or King's highway) and the so-called way of Beth-Jeshimoth (Josh 12:3), the precursors to the *Via Nova Traiana* and the *Esbus-Livias Road* (Waterhouse and Ibach 1975: 217; Ibach 1994: 65). Assuming that this advantage was exploited, something on the scale of a large village could easily be posited. While London (1992: 72*) is surely correct that a full-blown central place theory is not applicable for ancient Palestine (eastern as well as western), Dever's suggestion (within a tentative typology of tells) that Tell Hesban was a small (border) town (1996: 39, table 1; cf. Younker 1994b:

Figure 5.14   Tell Structures (Modified from Portugali 1982: 172, 182).

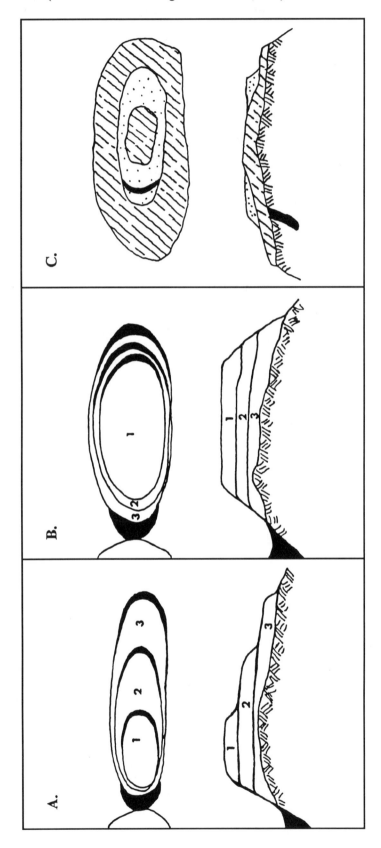

Figure 5.15 Stone Bass, *Polyprion americanus* (from Tortonese 1975: 61).

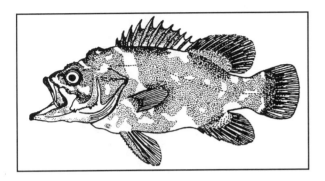

59) might be a little premature for this early in the history of the settlement. We therefore suggest that the site was a large village of Reubenites (cf. above p. 125 and Num 32:37; Josh 13:15, 17), which contained some sort of shrine (cf. the chalices, fig. 3.3.10-11), and perhaps with smaller satellite settlements (Josh 13:17) at this time.

The steepness of most of the slopes of Tell Hesban, as already mentioned, gives it a natural defensive position. Recent studies on visibility and settlement strategy indicate that the viewshed of Tell Hesban contained 27% of its 10 km surrounding region (Christopherson and Guertin 1996: 9). It is possible that a number of smaller sites served as watchtowers in its immediate vicinity and would have acted as an early warning system.

Though one cannot say much from the few remains that have been located from this stratum, it would nevertheless appear that there was perhaps a bit of growth in prosperity from the previous stratum. This supposition is supported by a limestone (possibly *mizzi yahudi*) door socket that was found in locus D.4:142, which may suggest the presence of a public building (Reich 1992: 2, 13). Further, the two fish bones (one stone bass, *Polyprion americanus* [fig. 5.15] and one sea bream, *Sparus auratus*) that were found in the soil layers (D.4:135 and 138) of this stratum would seem to have been "imported" from the Mediterranean Sea (von den Driesch and Boessneck 1995: 100; Lepiksaar 1995: 182-88, pls. 9.19, 9:37 and Table 9.29), which confirms trade connections with entities in Cisjordan.

Hesban's location at the junction of three topographical zones (the highlands, the Madaba Plains [the Mishor], and the mountains of Abarim) (Younker 1994b: 56) provided it with an ample food supply. Carbonized seeds of cultivated plants from the debris layers of this stratum (Heshbon Expedition Archives; Gilliland 1986: 126-27, fig. 7.1) included wheat (*Triticum aestivum*; fig. 5.16a) (D.4:129, 139, 141, 143; D.7:15, 16); barley (*Hordeum vulgare*; fig. 5.16b) (D.4:128, 129, 139, 141; D.7:15, 16); lentils (*Lens sp.*; fig. 5.16c)

Figure 5.16 Seeds: (a) Wheat, *Triticum aestivum*; (b) Barley, *Hordeum vulgare*; and (c) Lentils, *Lens sp.* (Modified from *FFB* 133, 194, 196).

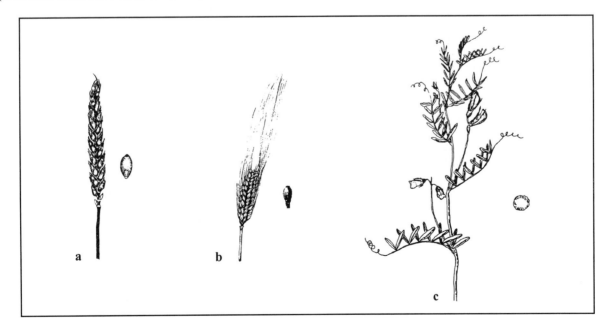

Table 5.2 Stratum 20 Bone Data.		
Bone Type	#	%
Cattle	140	22.33
Sheep/Goat	440	70.33
Pig	27	4.34
Camel	3	0.5
Equids	7	1.15
Chicken	2	.33
Fish	2	.33
Wild Species	4	.69
Total	625	100.00

Plate 5.4 Spindle Whorl (Object 2845).

(D.4:129; D.7:15, 16); grapes (*Vitis vinifera*) (D.4:129, 139; D.7:15, 16); figs(?) (*ficus sp.*) (D.7:15) and pea (*pisum sp.*) (D.7:16). Seeds from uncultivated plants included rye grass or tares (*Lolium temulentum*) (D.4:128, 129; 141) and an unidentified species of wild grass (*Gramineae*) (D.4:129), both of which were probably used as fodder or forage for animals (Crawford 1986: 80-82; 89-90). Bones of domesticated animals used by the residents of the tell during this stratum included the better represented cattle, sheep, goats, and pig, with smaller numbers of camel, horse, donkey, and chicken, with only the last of this latter group normally used as food. Represented wild species include fish, which were occasional imports from the Mediterranean coast, and gazelle.

It would appear from the above that the subsistence economy of Tell Hesban during Stratum 20 was a mixed agro-pastoral one, heavily dependent on grain production (cf. also the mortar for grain preparation found in Locus B.3:93) and the products from sheep and goats. The central role of cereals in the diet also seems to throw light on the high proportion of cattle (22.33%) reflected in the faunal assemblage (cf. Table 5.2). They were evidently used as draft animals for cereal cultivation (B. Rosen 1994: 343), though possibly also for food production (LaBianca 1990: 146). These subsistence strategies were occasionally supplemented with wild fish and game. A number of spindle whorls (pl. 5.4) (not loom weights as formerly thought) and pottery discs, which may have been blanks for other spindle whorls, are evidence for the continuation of the cottage industry begun already in the previous stratum. Two other seed species found at the tell suggest the possible

sophistication of its occupants. Though the presence of these seeds does not necessarily mean that they were used in this way, knotweed (*Polygonum sp.*) (D.4:129) can be used medicinally to make poultices (Crawford 1986: 80) and heliotrope (*Heliotropium sp.*) (D.4:128, 129) and can be cultivated in gardens for ornamental purposes (Gilliland: 1986: 131).

Stratum 19

Stratigraphy

One cannot totally rule out the possibility that the bedrock trench was simply abandoned as an impractical installation that got out of hand and was filled in preparation for the building of new features, an indication of sub-phasing (Herr 1979a: 11, 12, 15). However, we have suggested that the evidence favors the destruction of the bedrock trench. The remains of Stratum 19 are practically non-existent. What has been found to date has been located on the southern shelf of the mound. It consists of only one wall behind which are the soil and ash layers of Stage A of Stratum 20 that filled the bedrock trench (cf. B.2 plan; fig. 5.17).

Stage C

The construction stage of this stratum consists of a substantial 2.5 m wall (B.2:112) made of large semi-hewn boulders blocking the western end of the bedrock trench of Stratum 20 (cf. Square B.2 plan; fig. 5.17), behind which is the destruction debris of Stratum 20, Stage A.

Figure 5.17   Area B, Squares 1-3.

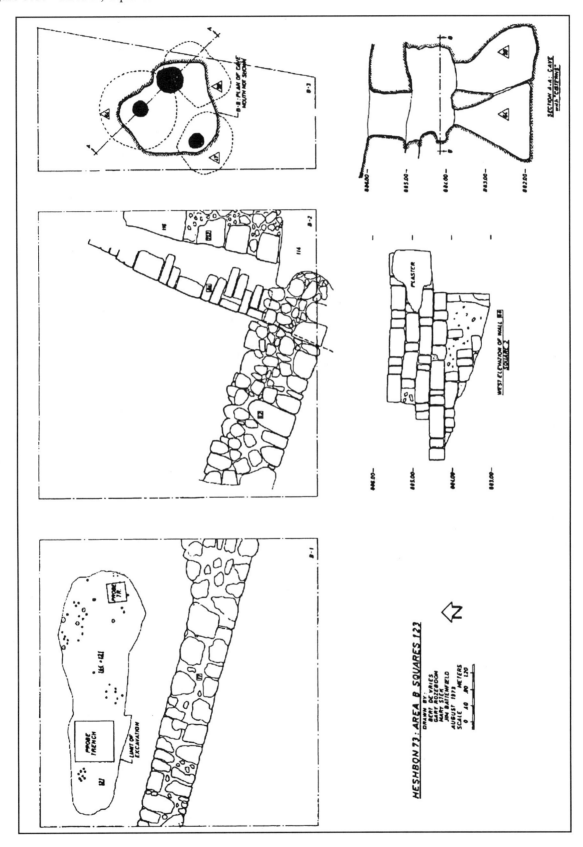

Figure 5.18   Area B Hypothetical Reservoir of Stratum 19.

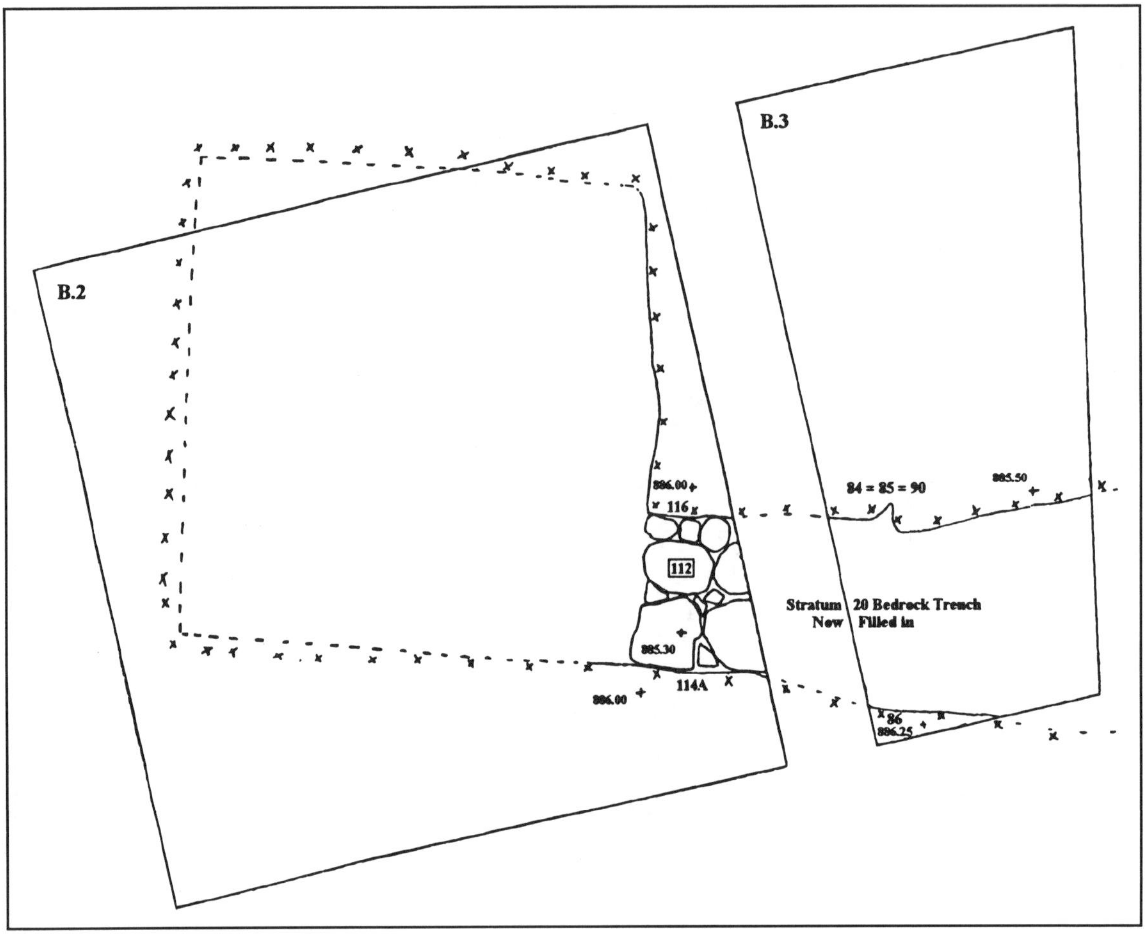

Stage B

No remains of the use stage of this stratum have been found. Either they were totally removed by the later inhabitants of the tell or they exist in some unexcavated area.

Stage A

Likewise, no trace has been found of the destruction/abandonment debris of this stratum. As with the Stage B remains, they were either totally removed by later earth-moving operations or they exist where the excavator's spade has not yet touched.

Interpretation

Whether parts of the bedrock trench were destroyed beyond use or it simply was not finished

at the time, it was quickly filled with debris and went out of use. Wall B.2:112 spanned the entire 2.50 m width of the current western end of the bedrock trench and its western face was aligned with a 3.00 m cut in bedrock running to the north that was probably made at this time. We agree with the suggestion made by Herr (1979a: 6-7, 14) that this wall and the northern bedrock cut in Square B.2 may have functioned as the eastern side of a reservoir, which would have been the precursor of the larger one built later in the next stratum. Since the wall was otherwise not needed to merely fill up the trench, the suggestion seems to make good sense. The depth of Wall B.2:112 is unknown, but, according to this scenario, would have to have been at least the depth of the bedrock trench. If that was the case, the proposed reservoir would have been at least 5.50 m square (extrapolating from its eastern side) and ca. 4.00 m deep (fig. 5.18).

It has been suggested that cistern D.1:63, just

below the acropolis, was built during the previous stratum. It no doubt continued to function, along with others that were not found. It is also possible that cistern A.2:11 on the acropolis could have been brought into operation at this time. Mitchel calls this feature a silo and dates its construction to the Iron Age (1992: 21, Table 2.1, 23, 25-26; cf. 1994: 101-2), but Merling (1994: 220, 223 n. 7) has noted its bell shape and settling basin, even though he believes it was much later in date. The cisterns, along with the proposed reservoir above, denote an increased attention to water. On the basis of lake-level changes in the terminal lake of the Dead Sea, Bruins (1994: 303, fig. 2, 305) has noted that there was a gradual drying of the climate throughout Iron Age I when Dead Sea levels declined to between -383 m to -397 m down from Late Bronze Age levels, which remained around -375 m. The dry climatic conditions at this time have also been noted elsewhere in the Middle East (Neumann and Parpola 1987: 163-65; 166, Table 1; 168-82).

The ceramics from this stratum are Iron Age IB in date and are a continuation from earlier (Iron Age IA) forms including collared-rim pithoi (cf. fig. 3.4.1). Dark monochrome surface treatment appears on bowls (cf. fig. 3.4.2), but there is as yet no burnishing (Sauer 1994: 238-39, pl.).

Unless Wall B.2:112 served some kind of defensive function (Sauer 1975a: 166; 1994: 243), which appears unlikely, the settlement would seem to have been unwalled at this time. In fact, the filling of the bedrock trench of Stratum 20, if it actually functioned as a dry moat as maintained above, would also suggest that the settlement was without defenses. The fact that the trench was filled in, and with destruction debris at that, would seem to indicate that after the destruction of the site at the end of the previous stratum there was an outside force which kept Tell Hesban unfortified.

The nature of Stratum 19 would seem to be fairly similar to that of its predecessors (Strata 21 and 20), except for the lack of defenses and the increased emphasis on its water supply. It appears to have been a small village of the tribe of Reuben (see above) as the paucity of finds would seem to indicate its somewhat diminished character. Due to the lack of flora and faunal material, it is impossible to say anything about the food system during this stratum. However, it is unlikely that it differed much from that of Stratum 21. Since there is no evidence of a Stage A, it is also impossible to say anything about how the stratum came to an end.

Stratum 18

Stratigraphy

In Herr's original analysis of this stratum (1979a: 16-19) he came to the conclusion that there were no *in situ* (Stage C) remains. Since Hesban's large reservoir was dated by Sauer to the ninth-seventh centuries B.C. (1975a: 165; 1976: 60) and attributed to Stratum 17 (Herr's Stratum 2), there was nothing between it and the previous stratum (19, his Stratum 4) except debris layers on the western side of the mound. However, one would think that such a large facility would have been constructed in a time of prosperity possibly under some kind of royal auspices. It is interesting that 71 artifacts were found in Stratum 18 while there were only 12 found in connection with the Stratum 17 remains. While the majority of these objects are still textile related, as we shall see there are also a number of other objects which can be connected with commercial or mercantile, trade, administrative, domestic, ornamental, and religious activities. One might therefore expect something significant to have happened architecturally during Stratum 18. Recently, Sauer (1994: 241-44) has reevaluated his dating of the reservoir and has suggested that it was originally built in the tenth century B.C., which would place it according to this scenario in Stratum 18, and this dating now seems to have been accepted as a possibility by Herr (1997d: 150; 1999b: 227) as well. On the basis of these considerations, the following analysis is considerably different from previous appraisals of this stratum.

Stage C

The construction/preparation stage of this stratum consists of a reservoir which was cut deep into bedrock. It appears to have measured 17.50 m x 17.50 m (fig. 5.19) based on its east bedrock face (B.2:114B=B.4:191=192=193=194=195 and 246, the latter now collapsed, but once a part of locus B.4:194). A section of this eastern face was a 5.75 m long and ca. 1.20 m thick wall (B.2:84=115) of ashlar masonry (pl. 5.5) laid in an alternating double-header, single-stretcher fashion (cf. B.2 and B.4 east balks; fig. 5.4 and plan; figs. 5.17 and 20). Its finely squared stones measured ca. .80 x .22 x .35 m (Sauer 1975a: 162). Some of the southern face of the reservoir (B.4:277) was also found. The overall feature was 7.00 m deep and, where exposed, its

Figure 5.19   Area B Reservoir of Stratum 18.

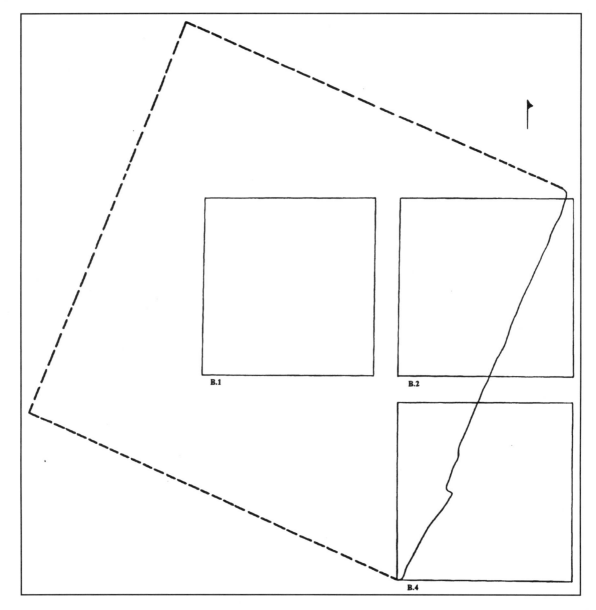

floor consisted of horizontal bedrock loci B.1:148=152 (cf. B.1 north balk; fig. 5.21). The original layer of three layers of plaster (the middle and outer layers, presumably being applied in Strata 17 and 16 respectively) was found on the floor (Locus B.1:147=151 from a probe in Square B.1) and on its east face (B.2:92, 113C=B.4:190C). Tripartite Channel B.4:168=250 fed the reservoir (cf. fig. 5.20). It was carved out of the bedrock shelf above and to its east. Each of its sections was ca. .12 m wide (Sauer 1975a: 162).

A subterranean room was built into the eastern-most excavated portion of the bedrock trench. This room (cf. D.4 south balk; fig. 5.9 and plan, fig. 5.10) was dug ca. 1.75 m into the trench fill and was about 2.10 m north-south between the edges of the trench (D.4:25 and 67, the latter outside the square) and about 1.60 m east-west. It was bounded by two single-row walls (D.4:65, 66) running north-south. These were constructed of small to medium-sized (ca. 0.25-0.40 m) unhewn boulders and chinkstones, two to three courses high (1.05-1.39 m). The foundation trench (D.4:136) for Wall D.4:66 was also found. Sealing against these walls

Plate 5.5   Ashlar Wall B.2:84.

on the north was a crude single-row wall (D.4:73), four courses high (1.22 m), underneath and indented ca. .37 m under the lip of the northern bedrock face (D.4:25). A flat, tightly fitted cobbled surface (D.4:75) was found between these three walls (Sauer 1976: 35; Herr 1979a: 12-13). It should be noted that Sauer (1978: 45) attributed this room to the Hellenistic period on the basis of one "probable Hellenistic" sherd found in the foundation trench (D.4:136) of wall D.4:66. Herr (1979a: 40 n. 8a), however, has pointed out that the Iron Age I layers sealed against this wall on its east side and also noted that the probable origin of this sherd was from the Hellenistic period pit in the south balk where much of this room was found.

Unrelated stratigraphically, a cone-shaped cistern (C.5:228) located on the lower western slope, outside the settlement, could possibly have been dug at this time (cf. locus summaries). It is also possible that cistern G.1:47, on the eastern shelf of

the mound, was brought into operation at this time (Beegle 1975: 213; Mitchel 1992: 21).

Stage B

As in Stratum 21, the loci making up the use stage of this stratum were located mainly on the western slope of the tell and consisted of dump layers (C.1 east and west balks; figs. 5.1 and 2; and C.5 east and west balks; figs. 5.22-23). While containing Iron Age IA and IB ceramics as well, much of this material was Iron Age IIA. It was dumped in an orderly manner but in reverse chronological order, with layers of stratigraphically later material found below layers with earlier ceramics (Mare 1978: 70; Herr 1979a: 16-17). To a certain extent, the earlier soil layers were found farther up the slope (Square C.1) than the later ones (in Square C.5), indicating that they cascaded or spilled over and passed each other as they accumulated (Herr

Figure 5.20   Squares B.2 and B.4.

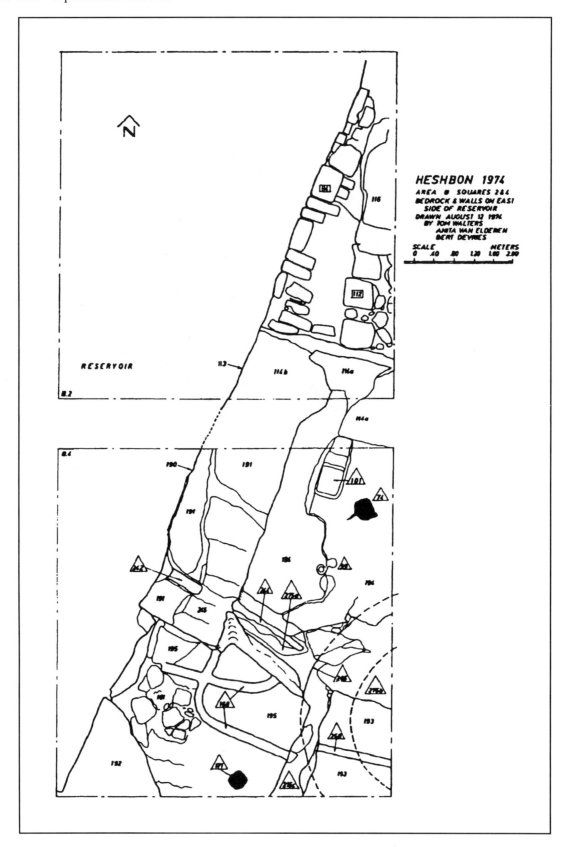

Figure 5.21   Area B, Square 1, North Balk.

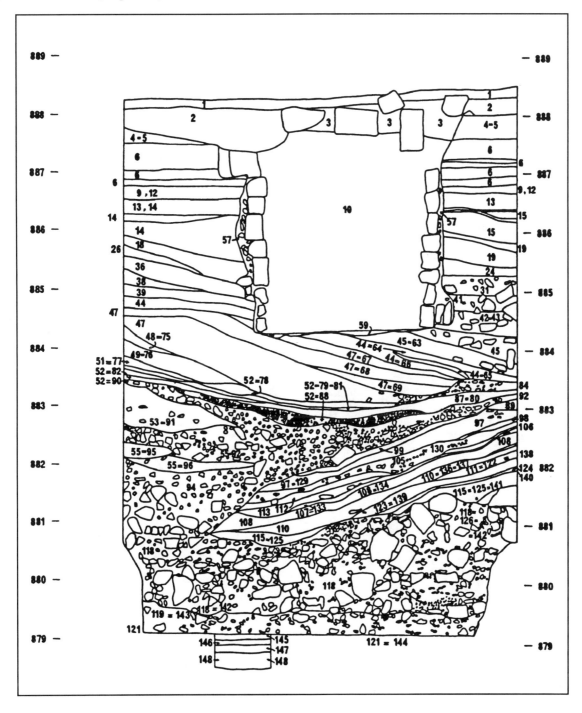

Figure 5.22   Area C, Square 5, East Balk (North Side).

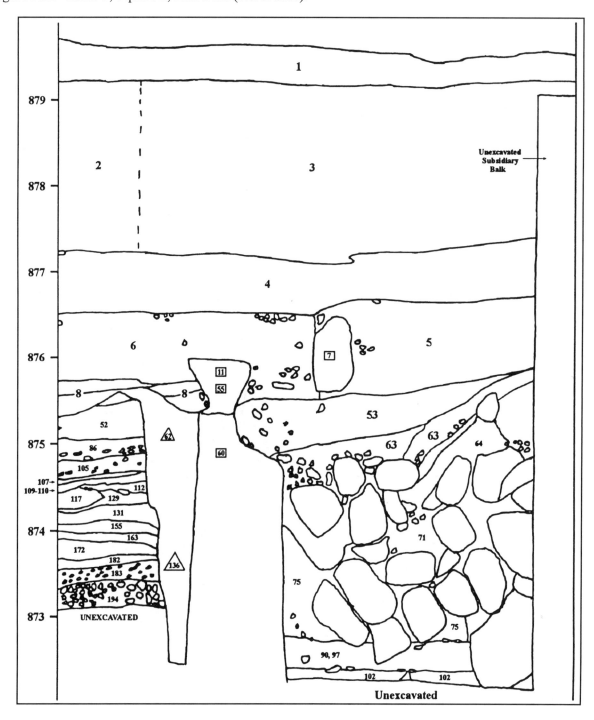

Figure 5.23   Area C, Square 5, West Balk (North Side).

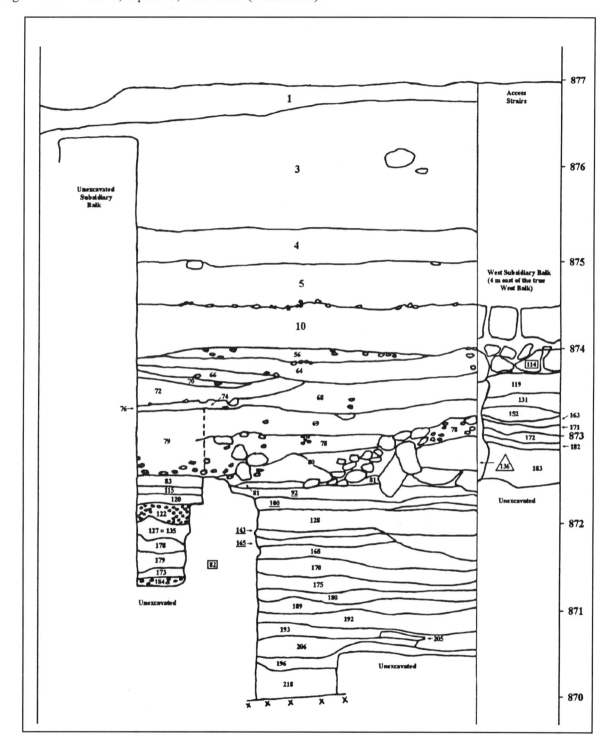

Plate 5.6   Weight (Object 2306).

1979a: 17). As Herr has pointed out (1979a: 17-18), it would seem that this type of sorting, with ceramic horizons of typologically different material but little mixture within individual layers, suggests the excavation of debris from the foundation trenches (construction stage) and pits (use stage) of this stratum which were dumped down the hill from the expanding settlement. In this way earlier material found its way on top of later.

These dump layers included loci C.1:124, 126, 127, 128, 129, 130, 131, 132, 133, 134, 135, 136, 137, 138, 139, 140, and 141; C.5:171, 172, 182, 183, 193, 194, 196, 205, 206, and 218. In addition, C.5:227B[6] should also be considered a part of this stage (cf. locus summaries). They consisted of an assortment of stony rubble material, clay, loess, white chalky and ash layers, with and without inclusions, reflecting various construction (thick, rubbly layers) and use (thin loess layers with few inclusions) activities over a long period of time. It is possible that there were one or more breaks in occupation although the mixed nature of the material does not allow that kind of differentiation (Herr 1979a: 16, 18). Herr (1979a: 18) has suggested a possible destruction in the late 11th century B.C., which is reflected in this material, but the limited quantity of the evidence makes it impossible to be certain. Seventy-one objects were found within these layers. They include fifty-five spindle whorls and fragments of whorls, four pottery discs, three stone weights (pl. 5.6), one muller, one stone

Plate 5.7   Ring Inset (Object 2806).

bowl, one door socket, one slingstone, one bead, one inset of a ring (pl. 5.7), two seals (pl. 5.8), and one figurine (pl. 5.9) (cf. Appendix B).

Plate 5.8   Seal (Object 2452).

There were also some use phase loci on the southern slope of the tell (D.4 South; fig. 5.9). These consist of two soil layers (D.4:63, 74) in the subterranean room of the house structure, which was dug into the upper layers of the Stratum 20 fill, within the bedrock trench. They were located above the floor (D.4:75) of Stage C. Two other soil layers (D.4:81 and 82) were also located in a probe below this same floor. All of these soil layers sealed against the walls of the subterranean room. The layers (D.4:63 and 74) above floor D.4:75 sealed against Walls D.4:65, 66, and 73 and the lay-

Plate 5.9   Figurine Fragment (Object 2826).

ers (D.4:81 and 82) below the floor against walls D.4:66 and 73. All four soil layers contained pottery which was typologically later (i.e., Iron Age IC now = IIA) than the latest material (Iron Age IB) that was found in the Stratum 20 fill below it.

Stage A

Locus D.4:115 represents the uppermost soil layer within the bedrock trench fill. It also contained Iron Age IIA ceramic material indicating that it was deposited later than the fill layers below it, where the latest pottery dated to Iron Age IB. It appears that this locus belongs to the destruction/abandonment stage of this stratum.

Interpretation

James Sauer originally dated the reservoir to Iron Age IIB (1975a: 162, 165; 1976: 56-57, 60) on the basis of four body sherds (Sauer 1994: 242 pl.) taken from the removal of several stones from the ashlar Wall B.2:84 on its east face. This wall was then compared to ninth-eighth century B.C. header-stretcher masonry at Samaria (Sauer 1975a: 165; Herr 1979a: 24). Of these sherds, one was smoothly burnished, but not done on a wheel, with a dark color on its interior. This, along with the lack of pre-Iron IIC/Persian sherds in the reservoir layers, especially near its bottom, caused him to suggest the above dating for the facility (Sauer 1994: 241-42).

However, as mentioned above, he has recently reevaluated this dating and come to the conclusion that an Iron Age IC (= IIA) date is just as, if not more, feasible. The factors in this reevaluation included: (1) the possibility that the reservoir was completely cleaned out periodically; (2) the absence of wheel-burnishing on the above-mentioned sherd could indicate that it was earlier typologically (i.e., hand-burnished); (3) the absence of Iron Age IIB sherds anywhere in Area B; (4) the presence of a few Iron Age IC (=IIA) sherds at the uppermost levels of the bedrock trench, and (5) that the ashlar wall was so well constructed that its probable date of construction fits best in Iron Age IC (= IIA), in the time of Solomon, when Phoenician craftsmen were used in public works programs (Sauer 1994: 242-44). He (1994: 242) correctly notes that the four body sherds sample is too small to be conclusive. I cautiously accept his line of reasoning as supported by the reasons that

he suggests and because the paucity of finds from Stratum 17 (above and chapter 6) seems to mitigate against the earlier suggested alternative.

If Wall B.2:84 is dated to Iron Age IIA, it finds an interesting parallel in the walls of gallery 629 at Megiddo (VA-IVB) (Lamon 1935: 10-12, fig. 8; cf. Yadin 1975: 227-31), which was also connected with a water facility. Like the walls of the gallery, which was probably a roofed-over tunnel (Lamon 1935: 10), this impressive wall was hidden under a plaster face and consequently not seen (for remnants of this plaster still adhering to the wall see fig. 20). Another reservoir built at this same time (tenth century B.C.) has recently been discovered at Beth-Shemesh (Bunimovitz and Lederman 1997: 44, plan, 46, plan 76-77), though it is cruciform rather than square in shape.

Sauer (1994: 243-44) suggests that the purpose of Hesban reservoir, which was akin to the imposing gates at Gezer, Megiddo, and Hazor along the main commercial highways, was to control international trade, especially the lucrative camel caravans, along the King's Highway. Thus, if this is correct, it would seem that this incentive was beyond the interest of a single town or village (Herr 1979a: 24) and was evidently done under royal auspices.

Instead of reusing the northern cut and Wall B.2:112 of Stratum 19 as the eastern face of this new, greatly enlarged reservoir, the builders chose to build a fresh line slightly to the west, necessitating the cutting of more bedrock and the insertion of a new well-built ashlar wall (B.2:84) into the earlier Strata 20 and 19 bedrock activities (Sauer 1976: 49, fig. 9). Further, as Herr (1979a: 21; 1997d: 150; 1999b: 227) has pointed out, with only about 4,500 m² of area equivalent to or above it, the reservoir had the capacity (2,200,000) to hold perhaps five times the amount of water that could have run into it in a normal rainy season and was well beyond the needs of the inhabitants of the site. Water would have had to have been imported, perhaps by donkey, in order to have kept it filled.

The subterranean room which was dug into the easternmost excavated portion of the bedrock trench was evidently a basement or cellar connected to a house above it (Herr 1979a: 13) that was later removed. This type of facility, which is usually used for containerized dry storage, is rare in this part of the world (Borowski 1987: 72, 75-76). There were two soil layers above its cobbled floor (D.4:75). Locus D.4:74 is described in the locus

Plate 5.10 Door Socket Fragment (Object 2445).

summary as a "hard ash layer with some charcoal fragments." This material was unfortunately not floated, so any remaining organic matter was not analyzed (Herr 1979a: 13). Locus D.4:63 immediately above it did include one bone of either sheep or goat.

While the majority of the objects that were found in loci from Stratum 18 are still textile related (probably a continuation of the cottage industry of the previous strata), a number of them seem to support the assumption that the reservoir was built during a time of prosperity. Although not giving a clear picture of a fixed standard or able to be correlated with other known standards from the ancient world (Kotter 1979: 8; 25), the three limestone weights (pl. 5.6) found in Square C.1 would still seem to reflect commercial or mercantile activities. The four pottery discs found among the objects in this stratum, if they functioned as counters for accounting and business exchange (G. London 1991: 417), would also reflect mercantile activities. While the exact function of the female plaque figurine (object 2826, pl. 5.9) from Locus C.5:194 is unknown (Dabrowski 1993: 22-24), it was evidently associated with religious activities. The disc-shaped object held in its hands was probably some kind of percussion instrument (Dabrowski 1993: 4-5), and would indicate an interest in music and ritual. The appearance of seals (one unfinished), the symbol of aristocratic office (Platt 1992: 829), alludes to administrative activities, and the limestone (possibly *mizzi yahudi*) door socket (pl. 5.10) suggests the possible presence of some kind of public building (Reich 1992: 2, 13).

Several objects indicate long-distance trade at this time. A Cypro-Phoenician sherd was found in Locus B.7:19 (cf. Amiran 1969: 288-89, pl. 97.6, 11, cf. chapter 3, fig. 3.6.17 above) as the earliest sherd in a locus from a later period. The basalt stone bowl (Object 2823) was probably produced and imported from either southern or eastern Transjordan or as far away as Galilee or the Negev (Herr 1997d: 119). The bead (Object 2428) was made from carnelian. Although this semiprecious stone can be found in the desert regions in Transjordan (Bender 1974: 167), it and other stones were also imported into Jordan from India, Iran, Afghanistan, Mesopotamia, and Egypt and made into beads, pendants, and seals by itinerant lapidaries within the region (Homes-Fredericq 1995: 472-73). The unfinished seal (Object 2459) might also reflect trade in semiprecious stones, with production of such artifacts possibly carried out at the site itself. The six fish bones (sea bream, *Sparus auratus*; fig. 5.24) in Loci B.2:84; C.1:124; 136 and 137 would seem to have been imported from the Mediterranean Sea (von den Driesch and Boessneck 1995: 98 Table 5.22, 100; Lepiksaar 1995: 186-87, pls. 9.38, 9.39 and Table 9.29), suggesting a continued trade connection with Cisjordan (cf. Stratum 20).

The faunal remains from this stratum further round out the above picture. Sheep and goats continue to dominate the faunal assemblage (78.30%) with cattle (14.0%) and pigs (5.70%) also appearing in relatively high proportions (cf. Table 5.3). The smaller percentage of cattle (14.0%) during this stratum as opposed to Stratum 20 (22.33%) might possibly indicate a transition from a complete dominance of cereals (objects associated with domestic activities include a muller and a stone bowl from C.1:132 and 139 respectively) to an

Figure 5.24 Sea Bream, *Sparus auratus* (from U.N. Food and Agriculture Organization 1973).

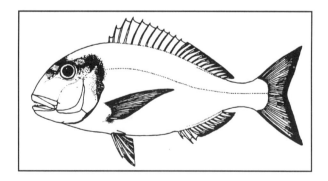

Table 5.3   Stratum 18 Bone Data.

Bone Type	#	%
Cattle	234	14.00
Sheep/Goat	1311	78.30
Pig	95	5.70
Camel	4	0.25
Equids	8	0.48
Fish	6	.36
Wild Species	16	.95
Total	1674	100.00

expansion into other types of subsistence strategies such as fruit trees, which seem to have been of marginal importance earlier in the period (B. Rosen 1994: 342), though there is admittedly no data from carbonized seeds to quantify this. On the presence of pigs, see above (Stratum 21). Smaller numbers of camel, horse, and donkey are also present. In addition to fish (above), there is also a relatively high incidence of wild mammal species including gazelle (*Gazella dorcas*, fig. 5.25; and *Gazella gazella*, fig. 5.26), fallow deer, wild sheep (fig. 5.27), goat, and pig (cf. Appendix C), indicating the importation of exotic foods into the diet. With this stratum, there is thus a transition to high intensity food production (LaBianca 1984: 278-79; 1989a: 172; 1990: 131-32; fig. 4.4).

Figure 5.25   Gazelle, *Gazella dorcas* (from Sclater and Thomas 1897/98: pl. 57).

The latest ceramics from this stratum are Iron II A in date and include pithoi. These become more bulbous, however, and the cooking pot rims, though continuing to elongate, also have rounded profiles (cf. chapter 3, fig. 3.5.2 and 3.6.11). Hand-burnishing came into vogue at this time as it did in Cisjordan (Holladay 1990: 49-54; Table 2, 62, fig. 18), and this is found over red, tan, and to a lesser extent dark brown and black slip (Sauer 1994: 239-40, pl.).

We have suggested above that the Stratum 20 bedrock trench could have functioned as a dry moat. If that were the case, it would also suggest that it was perceived as roughly the southern

Figure 5.26   Gazelle, *Gazella gazella* (from Sclater and Thomas 1897/98: pl. 59).

perimeter of the settlement. In Stratum 20, the trench was filled and in Stratum 18 at least one house was built into parts of it. The presence of a house at the edge of the settlement further suggests the possibility of a peripheral belt of houses used for defense, a common feature in 11th century B.C. provincial towns in Cisjordan with their prototypes seemingly appearing at Megiddo (Strata VII B and VII A) as early as the LB/Iron I transition (Herzog 1992: 233-34, fig. 3; 245-46, fig. 11). Also known as enclosed settlements, the back walls of these houses functioned as a defense wall, with the roofs for observation and a place to fire down on attackers (Herzog 1992: 269). Since the meager remains of every feature in these early strata leave their

Figure 5.27 Wild Sheep, *Ovis orientalis* (from Vinogradov et al. 1953: 265).

function unclear, this suggestion is very tentative. If this were the case, however, the inhabitants of Tell Hesban would have merely exchanged one type of defense (a dry moat and possible wall) in Stratum 20 for another (enclosed settlement) in Stratum 18.

While no trace of a wall has been found which could be connected with Stratum 18, if an enclosed settlement did exist on the site at this time, its most likely location would have been in the unexcavated area immediately to the south of Area B. A peripheral belt of houses situated here would have incorporated the new reservoir which extended 10.50 m to the southwest from the southern edge of the bedrock trench in which the basement structure was found. This would be consistent with the tenth century B.C. reservoir at Beth-Shemesh which was located not far from its contemporary defense system (Bunimovitz and Lederman 1997: 44, fig.; 75-77). Other Iron Age I water systems such as Megiddo (Lamon 1935: 10-12, fig. 8); Jerusalem (Gill 1994: 30; Reich and Shukron 1999: 31), and Gibeon (Pritchard 1962: 71-72) were also located just within or near the walls of their respective settlements.

On the basis of the above data, it would appear that there was an expansion of the settlement at this time. Besides the enlargement of the reservoir and its accompanying movement to the south, there was the use of the western slope, possibly extra-murally, where the cistern in Square C.5 was located, perhaps for collection of irrigation water for tree crops

(horticulture) in the Wadi Majar below. The same might be said for the cistern in probe G.1 on the southeastern slope on the Wadi el-Marbat. It would seem then that Hesban must have finally reached the status of a small provincial town at least by the tenth century B.C. (cf. Dever 1996: 39, Table 1; Younker 1994b: 59) in Iron Age IIA. As in Strata 21 and 20, there is also evidence of a possible shrine (cf. the chalice, fig. 3.6.8). The earlier village begun by members of the tribe of Reuben (see above) apparently blossomed into a town as a result of the prosperity which resulted from its location at the crossroads of two major highways. Under the auspices of the "tribal kingdom" of Israel (on this concept, which suggests the complexity of a state, but unlike a state is still organized along kinship lines, see LaBianca and Younker 1995: 399; 408-10; Younker 1997a: 238-45; Ray 1995: 25-31; cf. Renfrew and Bahn 1991: 154-57 and Kamp and Yoffee 1980: 87) under King Solomon, a public works project was initiated evidently in order to control traffic on the major north-south (or King's) highway, resulting in a huge reservoir. If Tell Hesban is to be equated with Iron Age Heshbon, this facility might be considered one of the "pools" mentioned in Song of Solomon 7:4 (7:5 Heb).

Iron Age I: Tell Hesban and Vicinity

Although it is usually assumed that the seasonal nomadic-pastoral subsistence patterns of the Late Bronze Age accompanied a drier climate (van der Steen 1996: 65; Sauer and Herr 1997: 233), as mentioned above, Dead Sea lake levels seem to indicate that this was actually a rather moist period which was followed by a gradual drying of the climate in the Iron Age (Bruins 1994: 305). Though there is as yet no consensus on climatic change in the historical periods (Finkelstein 1995a: 32-35), the work mentioned above takes into account a number of studies on various aspects of environmental change within the Dead Sea catchment, and therefore should probably be considered as representative. Though the historical reality was probably far more complex than a simplistic model of climatic determinism, nevertheless, if the above scenario is correct, the freedom of the more loose and flexible networks of cooperation of kin-based alignments, which maintained control over widespread pasture land and water resources during a period of relative moisture, would have eventually given way to a more ridged system where parts of these same kin-based groups began to invest in crops and expend labor on ploughing and planting (LaBianca and Younker 1995: 404) as the climate grew dryer. Younker (1997b: 118-20) has suggested that it was at this time that there was a resurgence of sedentary activities in the highlands on both sides of the Jordan River by such groups as the *Ḫab/piru* and *Š3św*, following a period of more markedly nomadic subsistence activities during the Late Bronze Age. By the end of Iron I, as this drying trend developed further, these activities no doubt would have extended to terracing, watering (irrigation), and protection (watch towers) of their investment in the land, with a heightened sense of cooperation with and obligation to one another.

While throughout the period there was a continuation of nomadic activity on the rocky slopes of the steppe zone in the Jordan Valley and on the desert fringe to the east, there was also an emphasis on land-tied cereal production (and pulses) on the shallow soils of the highland plateau and sometimes on the deep soils of the wadis along with fruit and olive trees (Lacelle 1986: 110-19, figs. 6.4, 6.5; Danin 1995: 30). Since the climax vegetation included oak trees (*Quercus calliprinos*, fig. 5.28) (al-Eisawi 1985: 50, 53; Lacelle 1986: 105; Younker 1989a: 33-37; Danin 1995: 27, fig. 1, 30) and "cupholes" were present at a number of sites, especially in the ᶜUmeiri region (4, 10, 19, 23, 28, 43 and 129), it would seem that the Iron Age I population also exploited acorns (Younker 1995: 687-89). Nuts such as almond (*Amygdalus communis*) and pistachio (*Pistacia*) were also used (Crawford 1986: 79).

Iron

While there are exceptions (McGovern 1986: 59; 338), large numbers of iron artifacts have not been attested at Iron Age I sites in Palestine (Waldbaum 1978: 17-36). Though the early development of metallurgical processes eventually led to a preference for iron over bronze (Muhly 1980; 1982; Waldbaum 1980), it was not until the early tenth century B.C. that iron objects appear in significant numbers (Waldbaum 1978: 26; Frick 1985: 187). The artifactual assemblage at Hesban, however, does not contribute anything to the above synthesis in that no iron objects were found in any of the Iron Age I strata. Interestingly, no bronze objects were found either. This situation probably does not indicate that there was a lack of bronze

Figure 5.28   Oak, *Quercus sp.* (from *FFB* 155).

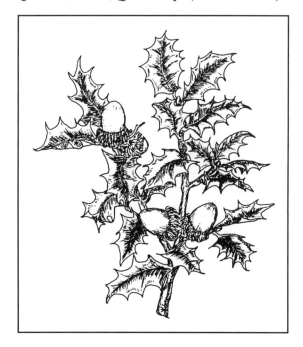

artifacts, but only reflects the accidental nature of object finds.

Settlement Pattern

The Hesban Regional Survey located 30 Iron Age I sites (1, 6, 7, 26, 29, 39, 40, 44, 45, 47, 49, 54, 72, 91, 95, 97, 101, 102, 103, 105, 108, 114, 129, 135, 137, 141, 146, 147, 149, 150) within a 10 km radius of Tell Hesban between 1973 and 1976. Of these there were five major sites, three large sites, six medium sites, nine small sites, and seven very small sites (Ibach 1987: 160-64, Tables 3.8 and 3.10; fig. 3.5).[7] In addition, Madaba is now known to have been inhabited in Iron Age I (Harrison 1996: 7; cf. tomb evidence in Harding and Isserlin 1953b: 28, 34-36; Thompson 1986: 345). The ᶜUmeiri Survey located another 15 Iron Age I sites (4, 10, 19, 22, 23, 25, 28, 29, 30, 37, 43, 55, 88, 129 and 130) in the 1984, 1987, and 1992 seasons (Boling 1989: 99, fig. 8.1; 188; fig. 8.117; Younker 1991a: 270, fig 12.2; 296, figs. 12.62 and 63; Christopherson et al. 1997: 37-38) within a 5 km radius of Tell el-ᶜUmeiri. An additional nine random squares produced Iron Age I pottery (J. Cole 1989b: 54-55, figs. 7.3 and 4). Other sites in the immediate area which have yielded Iron Age I sherds include Naur, the Abu Jaber village site (Kan Zaman = *JADIS* Site 2313.044), and *JADIS*

Site 2314.123. The East Jordan Valley Survey also found nine Iron Age I sites (137 = Glueck Site 194 [Glueck 1951], 151, 173, 182, 183, 190, 191 = Tell Iktanu, Hesban Survey Site 97, 195 = Tell er-Rameh, Hesban Survey Site 95 and Glueck Site 214, and 196 = Glueck Site 216) south of the Wadi Zerqa (Yassine, Ibrahim and Sauer 1988: 191-92, 197-98). Tell ᶜIraq el-Emir (though this is disputed by Ji, personal communication) and Glueck Site 221 (Glueck 1951: 385, 387) also seem to have been occupied during Iron Age I.

The largest sites within the area immediately surrounding Tell Hesban (fig. 5.29) at this time would have been Madaba, Jalul, and Umm el-ᶜAmad (possibly biblical Bezer, cf. Dearman 1989: 186) on the northern end of the Madaba Plains (the Mishor). These sites were medium to large towns[8] located within the bread basket of the region. In addition, both Madaba and Umm el-ᶜAmad were located along major north-south roads, the former on the "King's Highway" and the latter on a secondary north-south road on the eastern border of the plateau (Dearman 1989: 182, 192, 302, Map 4). Other major town sites included Tell el-ᶜUmeiri, Khirbet el ᵓAl, and possibly Tell Iktanu (Yassine, Ibrahim and Sauer 1988: 192, 198; Dearman 1992: 69), also on major road systems. Khirbet el ᵓAl and Tell el-ᶜUmeiri were located on the main north-south highway and one of its branches within the highlands, the latter also having its own spring. Tell Ikhtanu, if occupied at this time, was located on the main east-west trunk road in the Jordan Valley (Ghor). Smaller town sites included probably Tell Jawa (Daviau 1992: 147; 1995: 607, n. 3) and Tell er-Rameh, again along the road systems, the former on the secondary north-south road (mentioned above) and the latter on the main east-west trunk road. Tell Hesban, itself probably a small town by Iron Age IIA, was located, as mentioned above, at the crossroads of the main north-south (King's Highway) and the main east-west trunk road. Other small town sites included Umm el-Hanafish on the plateau and Umm el-Qanafid guarding the spring of ᶜAin Rawda on the Wadi Hesban. The latter is surrounded by four small village sites (40, 44, 45, 47). Another site protecting water sources was the small fortress site of Khirbet ᶜAyun Musa which guards the spring of the same name. Just to its south was the small town of Nebo (Khirbet Mekhayyat, Glueck Site 239), which also seems to have been occupied at this time.

The remainder of the sites in the Hesban region were probably small villages, farmsteads, and watchtowers. The majority of these sites were located within the highland plateau region (1, 6, 54, 72, 101, 114, 129, 135, 137, 141, 146, 147, 150) with a smaller number in the wadis (39, 49, 91, 105 = Glueck Site 194). The large number of sites on the highland plateau reflect the emphais on land-tied cereal production of the Iron Age I economy. This was for the most part dependent on the ridge soils (silty loam) (Christopherson and Guertin 1995: 16; Christopherson, Guertin and Borstad 1996: 11, 16). The few sites located in the wadis either protected water sources or had begun (probably late in Iron I) to expand the subsistence base into horticulture (fruit and olive trees). It would seem that the use of agricultural terraces probably began at this time (Christopherson and Guertin 1995: 17; Christopherson, Guertin and Borstad 1996: 19), in late Iron I (= IIA). The very specific environmental signature, described above, with sites located for the most part on the plateau had the added feature of maintaining good visual contact with the main sites in the region (Christopherson 1994: 9). In fact, a number of the sites from the ᶜUmeiri survey which were designated as farmsteads could have also functioned as watchtowers (Christopherson and Guertin 1996: 9) for Tell el-ᶜUmeiri or Hesban or both. This was certainly the case later on in Iron Age II (Kletter 1991: 39-41), but may have begun already at this time (Younker 1989b: 196).

By the latter part of Iron Age IB, the kingdom of Ammon (on its approximate boundaries cf. Younker 1994b: 60-63, Map) existed to the northeast of the area described above and there was probably occasional warfare between the two regions (1 Sam 11:1-11; 2 Sam 10:1-12:31). The capital of Rabbath-Ammon, at the headwaters of the Wadi Zerqa (biblical Jabbok), has not been completely excavated, but the water system has recently been re-explored and if it is to be connected with the "city of waters" (2 Sam 12:27) could possibly date to Iron I (Zayadine, Humbert and Najjar 1989: 357-59, figs. 1 and 2). However, Iron Age I wall sections and ceramics have been found at the Citadel (Dornemann 1983: 90; Zayadine 1973: 30) and Iron Age I ceramics at the Forum (Hadidi 1974: 82-85). Otherwise, evidence for this time frame comes from tombs (Dajani 1966b: 48-49). To its north, other sites connected with this kingdom during Iron I were Safut (Wimmer 1989: 513-14), Khirbet Umm ad-Dananir (Site 3), Rujm

Figure 5.29   Hesban Region in Iron Age I.

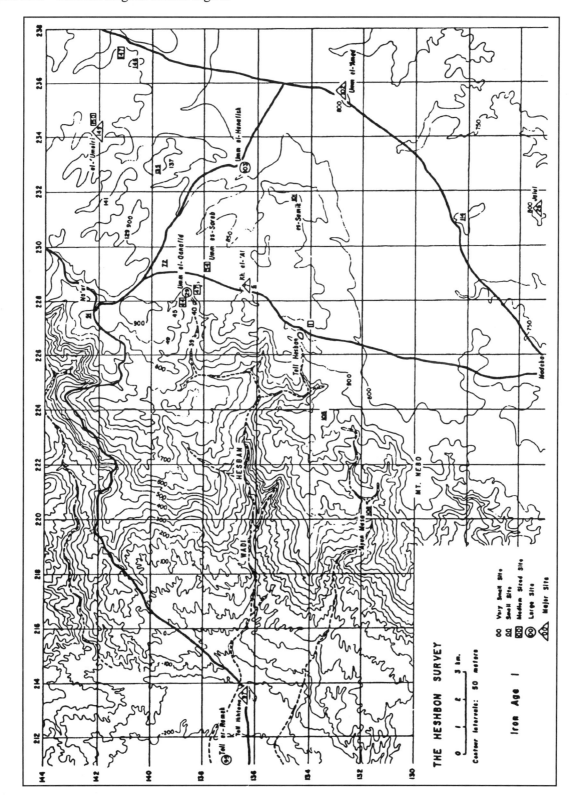

al-Hawayah (Site 4) with its nearby Jabal al-Hawayah-Group A Cave-tombs (McGovern 1986: 8, Table 1, 9; 13-16, Tables 2 and 3; 53-61), and Penuel (Telul edh-Dhahab el-Sharqiyeh, Site 22; Gordon and Villiers 1983: 276, fig. 1; 279, fig. 1A). A survey in the vicinity of Penuel has located six other Iron Age I sites (7, 17, 23, 24, 25 = Glueck Site 303, and 26) on the south side of the Wadi Zerqa (Gordon and Villiers: 1983: 276, fig. 1; 286-87; Tables 1-2). Further east, three more early Iron Age sites (1, 23 = Glueck Site 300, and 41) have been found in the vicinity of er-Rumman (Gordon and Knauf 1987: 290, fig. 1; 294-97). Other sites to the north of Amman include Glueck (1939) sites 208, 220, 221, 245, 250, 251, 270, 272, 293, 306, 315, 316, 327, and 333.

To the south of the capital was the site of Sahab (Ibrahim 1972: 24-27, 30; 1974: 55-58; 1987: 77-78). A number of smaller Iron Age I sites (2, 4, 22, 29, 30, 37, 38, 39, 56, 61, 80, 85, 94, 96, 103, 104, 105, 106, 124, 125, 126, 128, and Sahab SW) have recently been surveyed within its hinterland (*JADIS* 2.158-161; 2.171). Eleven other Iron Age I sites (*JADIS* Sites 2413.027, 2414.011, 2414.028, 2414.037, 2414.041, 2414.049, 2514.004, 2514.008, 2514.014, 2514.017, and 2514.020) have also been found within the vicinity.

Other Iron Age I sites in immediate proximity to Amman include Muqablein, Khirbet el-Hajjar, el-Mabrak, and the Amman Airport site. There was only one site (Khirbet Jeranin South, Site 54-38.3 = Glueck Site 242) within the Greater Amman survey, besides Tell el-ʿUmeiri (Site 42-34.1), that was occupied at this time (Glueck 1939: 177; Abu Dayyah et al. 1991: 391, Table 2), though the latter would appear to have been at least lightly occupied at the Iron I/II transition (Herr in press b).

Farther to the south there were a number of sites between Madaba and the Wadi Mujib (biblical Arnon). Included here are Qasr ez-Zaʿferan, Libb, Glueck Site 182, and *Limes Arabicus* Site 10 (Parker 1976: 23) = Glueck Site 72 (?). These sites would seem to represent settlements belonging to the tribe of Gad (Num 32:34-36; cf. Mesha Inscription line 10).[9] Sites south of the eth-Themed/Wala/el-Heidan wadi system may also have been occupied by the Gadites (Num 32:34; Josh 13:25) or possibly already represent settlements of the kingdom of Moab by this time. These sites include Khirbet Medeiniyeh on the Wadi eth-Themed, possibly = biblical Jahaz (Dearman 1989: 182), Dibon (Morton 1989: 240, 245; fig. 14),

Lehun (Homès-Fredericq 1989: 354-55; 1992: 188-198), Saliyeh = Glueck Site 92 = Parker Site 15 = Dhiban Plateau Site 3 and possibly biblical Kedemoth (Ray 2000a), er-Rumeil = Glueck Site 176 = Parker Site 12 = Dhiban Plateau Site 11 and Glueck sites 87 = Parker Site 14, 94 = Dhiban Plateau Site 4, 157 = Dhiban Plateau Site 1, 162 = Dhiban Plateau Site 6 and 174.

The exact time of occupation within Iron Age I of most of the sites in the region is unknown.[10] Preliminary evidence within the vicinity of Amman would seem to indicate, however, that the settlement pattern consisted of many small and dispersed sites (Herr 1992: 176; McGovern 1992: 181), but with diminished occupation toward the latter part of Iron I. This is generally consistent with the situation throughout the region as a whole during late Iron Age I (Dornemann 1983: 25; Ji 1995: 131-34; 1997a: 23-26; 29-34; Sauer and Herr 1997: 233), though several sites (Jalul, Umm el-Qanafid, and Khirbet ʿAyun Musa) in the Hesban region would seem to have been occupied throughout the whole period (Ibach 1987: 162, Table 3.8).

Summary

On the basis of the above analysis of the archaeological remains, it would appear that Tell Hesban developed from a series of oscillating small to large villages (Strata 21 through 19) which centered in the tribal activities of the biblical Reubenites (Num 32:37; Josh 13:15-17) to a small town in Stratum 18 under the auspices of the kingdom of Solomon. The earliest villages exhibited medium intensity food production regimes, consisting of mixed agro-pastoralism heavily dependent on cereal cultivation, which utilized large amounts of cattle as draft animals, and the products from sheep and goats. The later town had a high intensity food production regime, which, while still producing significant amounts of grain and keeping herd animals, also hunted wild species, imported fish from distant salt water ports, and was in the process of extending its repertoire to include horticulture (olive and fruit orchards) and the beginnings of wine production. This occurred at a time when the settlement was part of the administrative district of "Gilead" (1 Kgs 4:19) and like the other 11 districts had to provide agricultural products as well as domestic and wild animals (1 Kgs 4:22-23) for the royal table one month of each year (1 Kgs 4:7). While the overall Iron Age I population appears to have been generally low, the Stratum 18 settlement evidently had grown to relatively significant numbers. At all stages of the early Iron Age, the settlement must have consisted of extended family household units (Stager 1985: 18-23) based on the principle of unilineal descent, with various parts representing different proportions along the sedentarization-nomadization continuum (LaBianca and Younker 1995: 404).

Economically, the village, at the beginning of the Iron Age, attests a cottage industry and some minor trade with Cisjordan neighboring tribes by Iron Age 1B (Stratum 20), reflecting the transitional nature of their partially subsistence-oriented, partially market-oriented economy. It was evidently sophisticated enough to mount such labor-intensive projects as the Stratum 20 bedrock trench and possibly a reservoir in Stratum 19. In terms of social organization, the above level of complexity would suggest that the tribally oriented kin-based society of which Tell Hesban was a part during early Iron

Age I should probably be classed as a chiefdom (a kin-based society ranked under a hereditary leader or chief of the senior linage, cf. Renfrew and Bahn 1991: 156). By the tenth century B.C., however, the settlement had expanded somewhat, with evidence of mercantile activities and a wider trade network, indicating the beginning of a market-oriented economy (LaBianca 1984: 278). Under royal auspices a large public works project (probably by use of forced labor, cf. 1 Kgs 9:15) gave Hesban a huge reservoir. This would seem to have helped the town to dominate the caravan traffic (cf. 1 Kgs 10:2) on the main north-south highway (Rasmussen 1986: 156-62; Sauer 1994: 243-44) as well as, no doubt, the east-west trunk road from Cisjordan. It would appear that Stratum 18 Hesban belonged to a society that had reached the level of a tribal kingdom (i.e., a complex social organization with more simple kin-based structures embedded within it; Younker 1997a: 242).

Notes

[1]Strata 20 through 18 are also connected with the Reubenites/Israelites (above). The percentages of pig bones for these strata are 4.33 (Stratum 20) and 5.70 (Stratum 18) respectively. In addition, a pig bone was found in the eastern extension of the bedrock trench (D.7:15:22) in the 1997 season. This merely supplements the information on Stratum 20.

[2]In 1997 another 3.00 m was partially exposed farther to the east in Square D.7 when Øystein LaBianca and the author returned to Tell Hesban to begin phase 2 operations. Preliminary goals include the restoration of the site for tourist purposes, to deal with specific problem areas, and to gain additional exposure for the purpose of broadening knowledge of the site. LaBianca served as the director, and the author as the chief archaeologist (cf. LaBianca and Ray 1998 and LaBianca and Ray 1999). Lael Caesar was the supervisor for Square D.7. Among the specific objectives for the 1997 season were to gain additional lateral exposure of the bedrock trench and to expand the database on carbonized seeds (see below). The data presented here from the 1997 season (see also chapter 6) will figure into the analysis only as they supplement our understanding of the features originally excavated during phase 1. Since the results are preliminary and still under study, a complete analysis will not be undertaken here. Thus, specific loci, objects, and seed data from the 1997 season do not appear in the summaries within Appendices A-C.

[3]Ataroth (Khirbet ⊂Atarus), if indeed an Iron Age I site (cf. n. 9 below), had two dry moats, one on the north side of the mound and the other on the south (Musil 1907: 395; 396, fig. 189). The entire site is situated on an extensive ridge. The moats cut the settlement off from the remainder of the ridge at its weak points. Steep wadis border the site on its east and west sides.

[4]Ataroth, with dry moats on two sides of the mound, might seem to be an exception (cf. nn. 3 and 9 below). Nevertheless, these moats were found on the vulnerable sides of the tell and, thus, still conform in a general way to this pattern.

[5]Though the tell formation model makes a reasonably good analogy it should be emphasized that the moat was dug into the bedrock core (hence the descriptive term "bedrock trench") of the natural shelf of the hill rather than into the tell materials as at Hazor (Yadin et al. 1989: 50, plan XVI, 53; Ben-Tor 2000b: 247-48), which in any case at Hesban would not have been built up to any significant depth at this early point in time. The new moat typology of Oredsson (2000) is a bit too imprecise to be of help. He correctly points out the Early Bronze Age and Iron Age tendency for hilltop sites which have one or two strategically weak sides to cut themselves off from neighboring hills with a dry moat, and further notes the defensive purpose for this strategy (2000: 40, 47; 91; 176-77). However, in terms of Hesban (2000: 135-36), while suggesting the likelihood that the bedrock trench also functioned as a quarry, he returns to the water channel hypothesis because it is trapezoidal (V-shaped); rectangular (U-shaped) moats (2000: 19, 181) being the preferred form for Iron Age defensive moats. He points to Tell es-Sawwan on the Tigris River as a parallel. While sites on flood plains such as Tell es-Sawwan did use moats to protect their walls against erosion, Hesban is a hilltop site, where a defensive intention seems more logical, especially on the gentle slope which probably also served as the entrance to the site. In addition, Iron Age sites typically used trench-cut, stone-lined and stone-covered channels to divert water from heavy rainstorms. The drains at Gezer, Lachish, and Beer Sheba are rectangular (U-shaped) structures between .5 and 1 m in width (Holladay 1990: 25, fig.1, 29, 31, cf. Dever 1993e: 503, pl; 1997: 400, fig. 3; Tufnell 1953: 95-96, fig. 8,

pls. 14.1-2; 15.2-3, 111, 114; Aharoni 1973b: 14, pl. 9.2, cf. Herzog 1984: 2, 5, 29, figs. 2-3, 13) and about 1 m in depth (Tufnell 1953: 95, pl. 113).

[6]This subdivision was made by the author on the basis of the fact that there was a successive layering of debris here. Though this anomaly was noted by the original excavators, no attempt was made to divide the locus at that time.

[7]A main shortcoming of the Hesban survey (as with many others) is the lack of site size criteria beyond general indications (Finkelstein 1998a: 122-23). Ibach (1987: 9) defines a very small site as one which comprises a single feature, a cluster of tombs or a sherd scatter; a small site as one with a combination of the above, including clusters of industrial installations as well as settlements; a medium site as one which covers several acres with considerable architecture and was occupied during several periods; a large site as one which has a substantial depth of debris and is placed on the 1:25,000 map; and a major site as one which covers 10 to 20 acres in size including town and city sites. In comparison, it must be noted that in terms of Gonen's (1984: 63) site size hierarchy for Cisjordan, all of the above site categories would have to be classified within the range of "tiny" to "medium-sized" settlements in that even Ibach's "major sites" covering 10 to 20 acres fall only within her "small" (11-50 dunams = 2.5-12.5 acres) to "medium-sized" settlement (51-100 dunams = 12.75 to 25 acres) criteria.

[8]Due to the various problems in defining site size (G. London 1992; Dever 1996; Finkelstein 1998a) not to mention the lack of precise definitions for such concepts as "hamlet," "village," "town," and "city," sites here have been ranked intuitively. This site hierarchy is based loosely on Ibach's (1987: 9) site categories (cf. n. 7) with very small sites being referred to as watchtowers or installations, small sites as farmsteads, fortresses, and outposts, medium sites as villages, large sites as small towns, and major sites as medium to large towns. In my opinion no site in Palestine should be designated a "city" before the classical periods (Falconer 1987).

[9]While the Mesha Inscription specifically mentions that the land of Ataroth (cf. Dearman 1989: 195; 303 Map 5) had always belonged to the Gadites, the site of Ataroth (khirbet ᶜAtarus) may or may not have been occupied during Iron Age I. Biblical references (cf. Num 32:3; 34) would suggest that it was occupied at this time, if not even earlier. Although this site appears to have been occupied in Iron Age II, when it was mentioned by Mesha, the survey pottery found there (Glueck 1939: 135-36 = Site 180 cf. JADIS 2.58, Site 2110.002) was undifferentiated between Iron I and II and so it is not referenced here as an Iron Age I site.

[10]Younker (1997b: 116-20; 1999: 203-5) suggests that the initial settlement of the highland villages near Amman occurred during the period of Egyptian weakness and decline between the reigns of Pharaohs Merenptah and Ramses III (ca. 1203-1182 B.C.).

Chapter Six

HESBAN AND VICINITY
IN IRON AGE II

Chapter Six

Hesban and Vicinity in Iron Age II

Introduction

By the fourth quarter of the tenth century B.C., the Stratum 18 town at Tell Hesban seems to have come to an end. No signs of destruction have been found and, thus, the reason(s) for its termination are not apparent in the archaeological record. It is possible that this resulted from the breakup of the united monarchy after the death of Solomon in 931/30 B.C. (1 Kgs 12:1-20). Another possibility is that it was due to repercussions from the raid on (or destruction of) several sites (Adamah, Succoth, Penuel, and Mahanaim) to the north along the Wadi Zerqa (biblical Jabbok) by Pharaoh Sheshonq I (945-924 B.C.) in 925 B.C., as depicted in rows II (no. 22) and V (nos. 53, 55-56) of his reliefs on the southern wall of the Temple of Amun at Karnak (Hughes and Nims 1954, pls. 2-9; Kitchen 1973: 297-98, fig. 2; 434, fig. 9, 438; 1992: 29) and mentioned in passing in the Old Testament (1 Kgs 14:25; 2 Chr 12:2-4). Yet another possibility is that Moabites moved into the region, filling the power vacuum left by the passing of the kingdom of Solomon (Van Zyl 1960: 137; Dearman 1989: 156). A combination of these or other unknown factors seems probable.

It was formerly thought that there was a gap of at least a century, as the next ceramic horizon, as it appeared then, did not begin until the late ninth or early eighth centuries B.C. (Herr 1979a: 19, 24). Lack of settlement at this time would not be unique to Tell Hesban, as there is little evidence of early Iron Age II occupation at central Transjordan sites before the eighth century B.C., though this may actually be more of a reflection on the small number of sites excavated so far (McGovern 1992: 181; Sauer and Herr 1997: 234). However, it now appears that the pottery of Stratum 17, though not abundant, covers the entire period (Sauer and Herr forthcoming). This is consistent with a number of sites in Cisjordan where there is evidence for a slow continuous development of Iron Age II pottery

from the tenth to the eighth centuries B.C. (Mazar 997: 160-63).

Stratum 17

Stratigraphy

As was the case with Iron Age I strata 20-18, the meager remains of this stratum were found on the southern shelf and the western slope of the mound. The remains from Area B are associated with the plastered reservoir (cf. B.1 north balk, fig. 5.21; B.2 east balk and B.4 plan; figs. 5.4, 5.20), while those from Area C consist of dump layers (cf. C.1 west, C.2 west and south balks, figs. 5.2-3 and 6.1 and C.5 east and west balks, figs. 5.22-23).

Stage C

The loci which make up the preparation stage of this stratum include plaster layers on the bottom (B.1:146=150) and the east side (B.2:113B= B.4:190B) of the reservoir. The layer of "cement" at the bottom, like the ones below (Stratum 18) and above (Stratum 16) it, was gray and yellow in color and ca. .08-.10 m in thickness (Sauer 1975a: 161-62), while the plaster surface on its east face was ca. .01-.03 m thick (Herr 1979a: 23). On the bedrock shelf above and to the east of the reservoir, two channels (B.4:275B and 275C) converged into one (B.4:275A) at its entrance. Their function was to channel water for catchment in the reservoir. Channel B.4:275C apparently put Stratum 18 Channel B.4:168=250 out of use as it cut completely through the earlier system (Sauer 1976: 49, fig. 9; 58; Herr 1979a: 23; cf. fig. 5.20 above). Some of this bedrock shelf is now collapsed due to post-Iron Age seismic activities, and therefore, the measurements of these channels can only be estimated. The size of channel B.4:275C, accordingly, seems to have been ca. 0.65 m wide and ca. 0.55 m in depth (Sauer 1976: 58).

Figure 6.1   Area C, Square 2, South Balk.

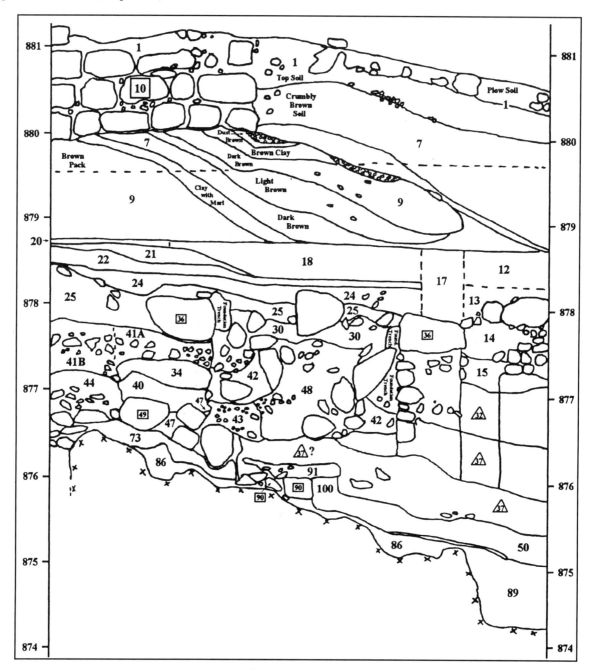

Plate 6.1   Spindle Rest (Object 2399).

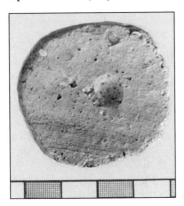

Stage B

The loci which make up the use stage of this stratum were found in three isolated locations (their farthest points some 10.00 m apart) on the western slope of the mound. Like the dump layers of the previous strata on this part of the tell, they seem to consist of materials from pitting and construction activity. These debris were either thrown or washed down in a "cascading" fashion on top of and farther down hill than their predecessors (Herr 1979a: 19-20). They include C.1:118, 123B, C.2:73, 86, 89, 95, 97; C.5:130, 147, 152, 155, 159, 163, 173, 175, 180, 184, 185, 187, 189, and 192. Since these soil layers included a sizable amount of Iron Age I ceramic material, but were deposited over layers of Iron Age II material, they evidently reflect fill material used in building and construction activities (Herr 1979a: 20). Only 12 artifacts were found within these layers (cf. Appendix B).

Stage A

Plate 6.2   Weight (Object 2439).

No Stratum 17 destruction or abandonment loci have been discovered. Unless they are located in areas as yet untouched by excavation, it would seem that there was a smooth transition to the next stratum (Herr 1979a: 20-21, 25).

Interpretation

As mentioned in the previous chapter, James

Sauer originally dated the Area B reservoir to Iron Age II (1975a: 162, 165; 1976: 56-57, 60) and thus to Stratum 17, an interpretation also followed by Herr (1979a: 21-26). However, as we have seen, Sauer has recently reevaluated his earlier conclusions and now dates this feature to Iron Age IC = IIA (Stratum 18) instead (1994: 241-44). This dating seems to have been accepted as a possibility by Herr (1997d: 150; 1999b: 227) as well and we have elaborated on it somewhat above (chapter 5).

Plate 6.3   Bronze Ring (Object 2385).

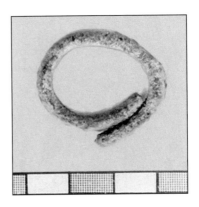

With the redating of the reservoir to Stratum 18, Stratum 17 is left with only a few extant remains, which include, in addition to the above-mentioned loci, only a few (12) objects, besides ceramic and faunal evidence, as no architecture was found. The objects were still mostly textile related (eight spindle whorls and a spindle rest [pl. 6.1]). The others, however, are more far reaching. The limestone weight (pl. 6.2), like those found in Stratum 18, suggests mercantile activities (Kotter 1979). The bronze ring (pl. 6.3), if originally connected with a precious or semi-precious stone, would indicate long-distance trade as does the obsidian bead (pl. 6.4), of which the nearest source is Anatolia. There is also the remote possibility that an animal figurine

Plate 6.4   Bead (Object 2440).

fragment (Object 817; fig. 6.2) found in a locus belonging to a much later period could have originally come from this stratum on the basis of typological comparison with an analogous object from Megiddo during this

Figure 6.2 Figurine Fragment (Object 817).

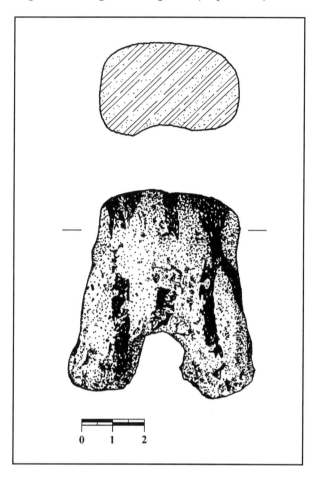

period (Dabrowski 1993: 19).

The ceramic remains from this stratum (cf. chapter 3, figs. 3.7 and 3.8) include thin, non-brittle wares in predominately brown and tan colors, though red and black also exist. Other surface treatments include wheel-burnishing and paint. Cooking pots with double-grooved rims (fig. 3.8.13), pierced tripod cups, angle-rimmed kraters (fig. 3.7.10-11) and angular bowls (fig. 3.8.1, 7) are among the common forms (Dornemann 1983: 49-58; Sauer 1994: 244, 245 pl.). The closest parallels to the material here are the ceramic remains from such sites as Aroer and especially Dibon, indicating a definite Moabite element in the ceramic repertoire at Hesban at this time (Sauer 1994: 244-45). Since the Mesha stela reflects Israel as existing in this general area of Transjordan at the time of his conquest in the mid-ninth century B.C., it is possible that the Moabite element within the ceramic repertoire of the stratum began at this time.

However, the extant remains of this stratum are very scant and there does not seem to be any evidence for separate phases. Therefore, it seems that the site was inhabited by Moabites throughout the entire stratum.

In terms of the faunal assemblage (Table 6.1), the little material that was found seems to reflect a basically pastoral economy dominated by the raising of sheep and goats (78.25%), though the relatively high percentage (18.25%) of cattle (cf. Appendix C), which were evidently used as plough animals, would also suggest at least some emphasis on cereal production (LaBianca 1984: 277; B. Rosen 1994: 343). One fish bone, that of a parrot fish (*Pseudoscarus sp.*; fig. 6.3), found in Locus C.5:184, seems to have come from the Red Sea (Gulf of Aqaba) (von den Driesch and Boessneck 1995: 98, Table 5.22, 102; Lepiksaar 1995: 193, Table 9.40), indicating that it was imported from the south (through Edom and Moab), but the two sea bream (*Sparus auratus*) bones from Locus C.1:123B could have been imported from either the Red Sea or the Mediterranean Sea (Lepiksaar 1995: 186-87, Table 9.29). If it was the latter, it would suggest a continued trade connection with Cisjordan as in some of the previous strata. Outside of the above-mentioned fish bones and the wild goat (fig. 6.4) (cf. Appendix C), indicating the importation of exotic foods into the diet, the overall picture, from a food systems perspective, would seem to be one of a low to medium intensity food regime (LaBianca 1984: 277-78; 1990: 131-32, fig. 4.4).

Judging from the data presented above, it would seem that the site was inhabited rather lightly during Iron Age II. Though it is possible that there are other remains in as yet unexcavated portions of the mound, based on the accumulated evidence, one could not postulate much more than some kind of

Table 6.1   Stratum 17 Bone Data.

Bone Type	#	%
Cattle	61	18.25
Sheep/Goat	261	78.25
Pig	7	2.20
Fish	3	1.0
Wild Species	1	0.30
Total	333	100.00

Figure 6.3   Parrot Fish, *Pseudoscarus sp.* (from Carcasson 1977: pl. 33.1358).

squatter settlement, on the basis of the ceramic remains, it would seem, by Moabites. While Herr (1979a: 24-25) also attributed this stratum to the Moabites, he postulated that the site was a village developing into a town. This was of course espoused on the basis of the then-current view that the reservoir was built at this time, a reconstruction which now seems to be untenable. A Moabite occupation of Hesban would nullify the suggestion that the site was still Israelite at this time (Kallai 1986: 85). Similarly, Na²aman's (1997: 90-91) supposition that Hesban was fortified by the Omrides and became a central town in the ninth century would also be out of the question.

Figure 6.4   Wild Goat, *Capra aegagrus* (from Vinogradov et al. 1953: 250).

That the Moabites inhabited Hesban at this time agrees with the literary evidence from the Mesha Stela (*ANET* 320) and the Old Testament (2 Kgs 1:1; 3:4-5) (Vyhmeister 1989a: 8-9). Mesha was a pastoralist (2 Kgs 3:4) and is also known for his water conservation projects (reservoirs) at Baalmeon (line 9) and Qarḥoh (line 23), the latter probably the royal acropolis of Dibon rather than a separate site (van Zyl 1960: 78-80; Dearman 1989: 171-74; Morton 1989: 239; Tushingham 1990: 186-87; J. M. Miller 1992: 886). It is possible that the Moabites worked the same way at Hesban. If they "(re)built" the reservoir at Hesban, which is what Mesha claimed to have done elsewhere, this would have consisted of merely cleaning out and replastering the structure. Though Heshbon is not mentioned in the extant text of the Mesha Stela, Moabite presence at such nearby sites as Nebo (line 14), probably Khirbet Mukhayyat (Ray 2000b), Madaba (lines 7-8; 30), and Bezer (Umm el-ᶜAmad) (line 27), forming a rough west-to-east line just to the south and east of it, suggest that the Moabites had moved that far north at this time or slightly later (2 Kgs 13:20, cf. also Na²aman 1997: 91-92). These towns are just south of a natural border of high hills running south-west to north-east which separate the hill country of the Ammonites from the Madaba Plains (at this time northern Moab). Since Hesban is located on the edge of this natural border, it would not have been too difficult for the Moabites to have extended their territory further north from points in its immediate vicinity (Younker and Daviau 1993: 27-28, n. 25).

Although it is debatable as to whether Mesha undertook one or two campaigns (Dearman 1989: 204-5), 2 Kgs 1:1; 3:5 places Mesha's rebellion after the death of Ahab (853 B.C.). Since all of the activities mentioned on the Mesha Stela (Moabite Stone) must have occurred over an extended period of time, it is likely that the inscription itself dates to a decade or so after the last of the events described on it, or approximately 830 B.C. (Dearman 1989: 208; Mattingly 1994: 327; 1992: 707). It is possible that Mesha extended his domain further north to Hesban shortly after the inscription was written and hence its lack of mention. On the other hand, it is possible that it was later Moabites who attempted to push the border further to the north after the death of Elisha (2 Kgs 13:20) around the beginning of the eighth century B.C. (Vyhmeister 1989a: 8). It must be remembered that a major goal of Mesha's rebellion was to gain control of the main north-south highway (Dearman 1989: 156-57). As mentioned above (chapter 5), Hesban is located at the crossroads of both this highway and the main east-west trunk road.

It is possible then that either Mesha or later Moabites around the beginning of the eighth century B.C., following his policy, merely extended their territory north to Hesban, which, as surmised above, was possibly already nominally Moabite since the end of the tenth century B.C., and made use of its dominating position at the crossroads of these major highways. It would appear that they renovated the reservoir, completely cleaning out the debris which had accumulated for the previous century (or slightly more) as no ceramic material from this period was found within it. They evidently also added another layer of plaster to its bottom and sides as the long period of casual use and lack of upkeep would have quickly contributed to its decay. The occupants seem to have been basically pastoralists (cf. faunal remains), and the site appears to have been used mainly to gather tolls and for its water resources; hence, the rather sparse remains that have been unearthed from this stratum.

The Moabites would seem to have remained in possession of Hesban throughout the remainder of Iron Age IIB (late ninth-eighth centuries B.C.) until the Assyrians became the dominant force in the region. The Moabite king Salamanu, along with the kings of Ammon and Edom, agreed to pay tribute to Tiglath-pileser III in 733-32 B.C. in order to preserve their independence (*ANET* 282, van Zyl 1960: 149; MacDonald 1994: 18). Heshbon was evidently still Moabite at the time (Isa 15:4; 16:8-9). They may have lost it in 712-11 B.C. after their rebellion, along with the Philistines, Judah, and Edom, against Sargon II (*ANET* 286-87, cf. Isa 20:1).

Stratum 16

Stratigraphy

The fill layers of Stratum 17 reveal no evidence for a destruction/abandonment phase (Stage A) at its end, so we can say nothing about the transition to the next period of occupation. The nature of the Stratum 16 settlement is considerably different from that of Stratum 17. Since the Stratum 15 (Stage C) reservoir fill, which is included in the following analysis, contained essentially pure Iron Age IIC/Persian period pottery (Sauer 1975a: 159;

1976: 55) and practically no earlier ceramic material, it is likely that the builders of the Stratum 16 settlement completely scraped off and removed whatever remained of the previous strata (Sauer 1978: 46; Herr 1979a: 26) in preparation for the new settlement. This would seem to imply the occupation of the site by a different people from that of the previous stratum. Though the remains of this stratum are still rather limited, the settlement at this time had begun to expand beyond the acropolis and upper slopes, where all of the previous occupants of the site had confined themselves, to include part of the lower slopes, at least on the western side of the mound. The Stratum 16 remains are better preserved than those of the earlier strata, and the artifact assemblage, which is rounded out by the large number of objects from the Stratum 15 reservoir fill, is much more varied, including inscriptional material.

Stage C

On the western side of the mound on the lower slope in Area C, a wall (C.3:26A=34=C.7:44A) was found running along a bedrock shelf (C.3 south balk, fig. 6.5; C.7 north balk and plans, figs. 6.6-6.8). Phase A of Wall C.3:26 (erroneously equated with C.3:60 = a soil layer west of Wall C.3:26A, in the 1974 season cf. Mare 1976: 69, fig. 12; 70-71, 77) consisted of smooth, partly dressed field stones. Small (.25-.50 m) slabs of stone were founded in a small bedrock trough with larger (.85-.95 m) ones on top of them. The wall, according to the date of the ceramics found in the soil layers at its northern base (locus summary sheets; Thompson 1975: 179), was Iron IIC/Persian. A later (Hellenistic/Early Roman) wall (C.3:26B=C.2:26; cf. stones within C.7:60, 69 and 76, C.7 north balk, figs. 6.5-6), consisting of at least three courses of small to medium rough field stones, extended to the northwest abutting Wall C.3:26A on its western face by means of a .35 m fill of small stones (C.3:26C). Wall C.3:26A continues to the south, being interrupted by the balk between Squares C.3 and C.7, with Wall C.7:44A. It is abutted on the east by Wall C.3:34, which extends to the northeast. Together, this whole system forms one large zigzag or offset-inset wall along the bedrock shelf. Wall C.3:34 was made of massive (.50-.90 m) unhewn boulders surviving 1.00 m high in some places. A probe within it recovered Iron Age sherds (Thompson 1975: 180). Wall C.7:44A was built of large (.70-.90 m)

Figure 6.5   Area C, Square 3, South Balk.

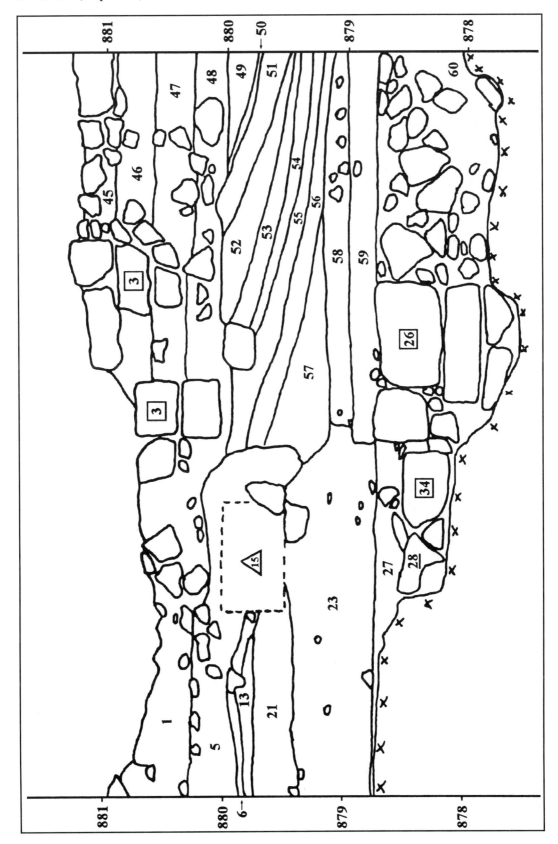

Figure 6.6 Area C, Square 7, North Balk.

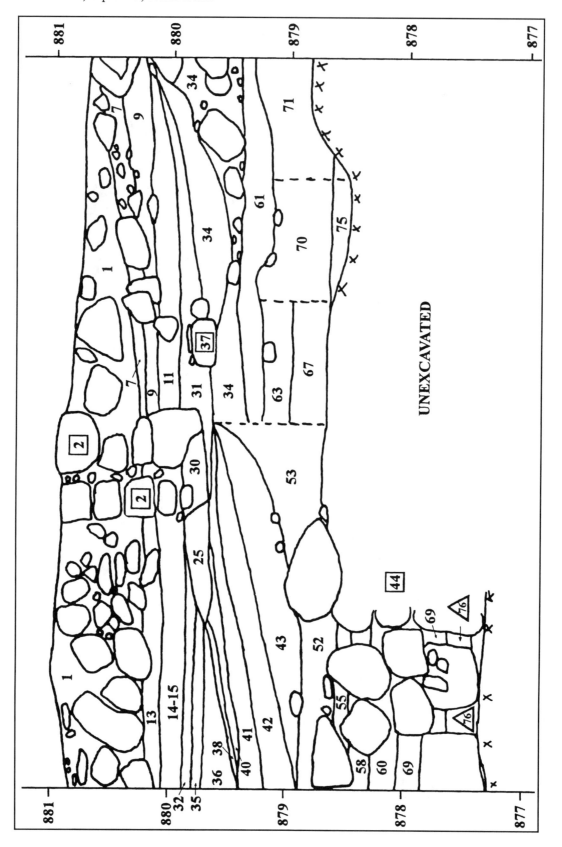

Figure 6.7   Area C, Square 3 Features.

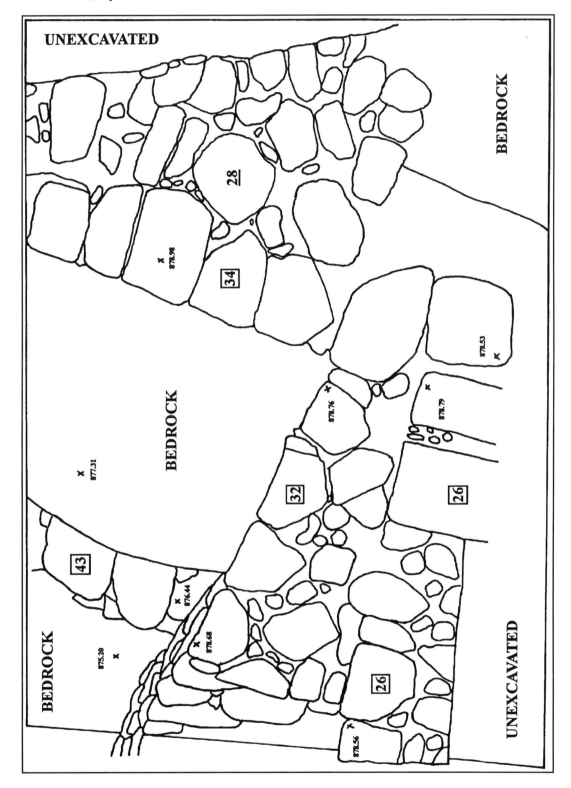

Figure 6.8   Walls C.3:26, 34, and C.7:44.

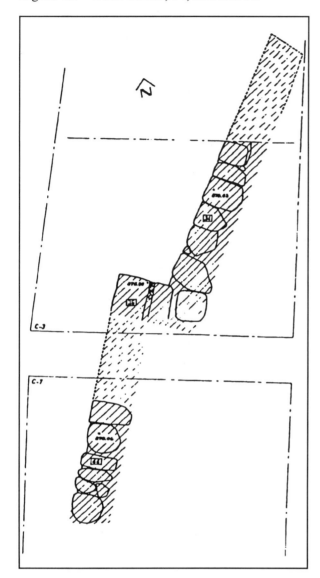

was founded within a small crevice, which was cut into the bedrock. Consisting of 10-11 courses of undressed (.40-.70 m) field stones, it was stepped up slightly for 3.50 m. The eastern, upper two courses (phase B) were laid above phase A and made of unhewn boulders and cobble chink stones (Thompson 1975: 179; Herr 1979a: 27). The overall structure (cf. plan, fig. 6.7; pl. 6.5) appears to have been a buttress or revetment wall anchored in bedrock with the intention of holding up Wall C.3:26A=34 (Mare 1978: 68). Running parallel and underneath this wall was a line of large unhewn boulders (.75-1.00 m), two courses high and one row wide set against the east side of the bedrock part way down in the crevice or trench (locus summary sheets; Herr 1979a: 27). This wall (C.3:43 cf. figs. 6.7 and 6.9) appears to have been a retaining wall for Wall C.3:32.

To the west, and outside of the above complex of walls, was a single coursed (.40 m) crudely built wall (C.2:49) not founded on bedrock (C.2 plan, fig. 6.10). It was made of a single row of rough, undressed (.55 m) stones at least 3.00 m in length (Thompson 1975: 178). It was partially robbed by Hellenistic pitting. Farther to the west, another wall (C.2:52=90=C.1:90) was found (Thompson 1975: 180-81; C.2 west and south balks, cf. figs. 5.3 and 6.1; C.1 east balk and plan, figs. 5.1 and 6.10). It emerged out of the south balk as C.2:90 for length of 1.35 m. The extant remains here consist of only the remnant of a one-course wall with a large (.40 x .50 m) stone at its corner. The wall then turns west as Wall C.2:52 for 3.75 m, where it enters the west balk, further reemerging on the other side of the balk as Wall C.1:90 for a distance of 2.10 m in its bottom course (.90 m in its top two courses). Wall C.2:52 consists of one to two courses depending on the slope of the bedrock, which is steep in places, and is one row wide. It is made up of .45-.60 m wide undressed stones. Wall C.1:90 consists of three rows of partially dressed and undressed stones. It, too, was partially destroyed by Hellenistic pitting activities. Soil layer C.2:88, between two stones of Wall C.2:52, confirmed a Iron IIC/Persian dating from the sherds found within it. The wall's (unnumbered) foundation trench (Mare 1976: 68; Herr 1979a: 28) indicates that it cut through soil layers of all the previous strata and was founded on virgin soil (C.1:91; cf. fig. 5.1).

On the southern shelf, there was more activity in the area of the reservoir (B.1 north balk, fig. 5.21; B.2 east balk and B.4 east balk, fig. 5.4). A thick

stones, with a surviving length of 3.10 m (Mare 1976: 71). Soil layer loci (C.7:74 and 97) contained Iron IIC/Persian sherds on bedrock immediately below the first course and on either side of the wall (locus summary sheets; Herr 1979a: 29), though Hellenistic sherds were found under the second and third (or top extant) courses of the wall, indicating a later rebuild (C.7:44B).

Wall C.3:32 (figs. 6.7 and 6.9) abutted Walls C.3:26A and 34 (Thompson 1975: 179) and possibly ran underneath Wall C.3:26B as well (Herr 1979a: 27). It seems to have been built in two construction stages. The western, lower part (phase A)

Figure 6.9   Area C, Square 3, Wall 32.

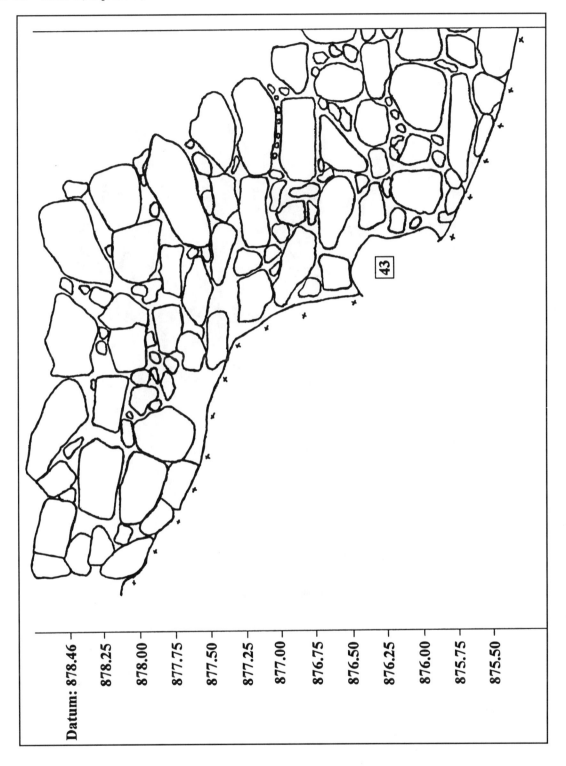

Datum: 878.46

878.25

878.00

877.75

877.50

877.25

877.00

876.75

876.50

876.25

876.00

875.75

875.50

43

Plate 6.5   Walls C.3:32 and 34.

layer of plaster was found at the bottom of the reservoir. It consisted of a very thin (.02 m in thickness) layer (B.1:121=128=144), which contained layer B.1:145=149 (Sauer 1975a: 164), which in turn is equal to B.2:138. Plaster layer B.1:145=149, like the two below it (in Strata 17 and 18), was gray and yellow in color and measured ca. .08-.10 m in thickness (Sauer 1975a: 161-62). In addition, part of the upper lining (B.1:144A) had a series of cupmarks. As in the two strata that preceded it, the sides of the reservoir also received new coats of plaster as represented on the eastern side by Loci B.2:113A=B.4:190A=282. On the bedrock shelf above and to the east of the reservoir, a series of new channels were apparently added at this time as Channel B.4:242=244 was cut into and along the same line as the earlier Channel B.4:275A of Stratum 17 (Sauer 1976: 49, fig. 9; 58; Herr 1979a: 24; cf. fig. 5.20). Plastered Channel B.4:242 was ca. .25 m wide, .25 m deep, and .70 m long, while

Figure 6.10   Area C, Square 1 and 2 Walls.

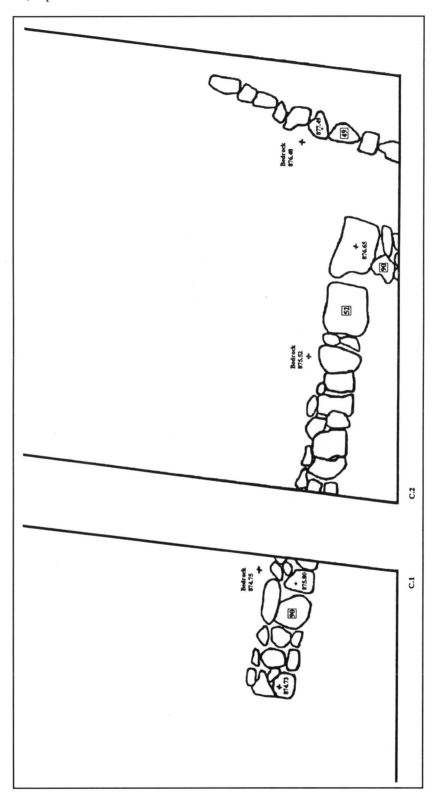

Plate 6.6 Weaving Pattern Spatula (Object 1669).

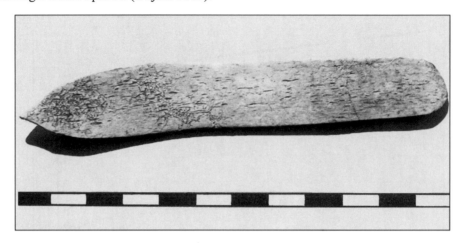

unplastered Channel B.4:244 was ca. .20 m wide, .15 m deep, and 1.70 m long. Both of these ran in an east-west direction (Sauer 1976: 49, fig. 9; 57) to the lip of the reservoir. Running north-south and intersecting both of these features was Channel B.4:245, which evidently led water into Channel B.4:242. In addition to the above features, a pool (B.4:265) was cut into the bedrock shelf to the east of the reservoir. It was ca. 1.50 m deep and 4.00-5.00 m in diameter and was plastered with three layers (B.4:234A, B, C) of plaster (Sauer 1976: 54; Merling 1994: 215). Though it seems to have been used throughout the Late Hellenistic Period as some kind of industrial installation (Sauer 1976: 55), it was evidently founded in the Iron IIC/Persian period (Sauer 1976: 59; cf. Stage B for the sherds within its earliest soil layer).

Stage B

A number of soil layers were connected with the Stage C features above and make up the use stage of this stratum (C.2 south and east balks, figs. 6.1 and 6.11). Unfortunately, only one of these soil layers (C.2:44) can possibly be considered a living surface, though not a "floor" (Herr 1979a: 29). This locus sealed against Terrace Wall C.2:49 on its eastern side. Three objects (an incised ceramic fragment, an ostracon, and a horse head figurine) were found on this surface. Locus C.2:51, slightly farther to the north, was also retained by this wall. This locus also contained objects (two slingstones, a rubbing stone, and a weaving pattern spatula [pl.

6.6]). Soil layers C.2:56, 57, 58, 59, 60, 61, 62, 63, 64, 65, 66, 67, 68, 72, 82, 83, and 101 were located on the west side of Wall C.2:49 and to the north of Wall C.2:52=90. All of these layers were rather thin and were separated from each other by thin layers of water-sorted sand grains (cf. locus summary sheets and Herr 1979a: 29). A slingstone was found in Locus C.2:58. Soil layers C.3:39, 40, and 41, the latter containing a slingstone, were found in the bedrock basin, all sealing against Wall C.3:32 on the northwest (C.3 west balk; fig. 6.12). There is also one isolated Iron IIC/Persian deposit (A.3:56) up in the settlement (Harvey 1973: 34).

As was the case with all of the previous strata, there are also a number of soil layers that were merely dumped or thrown down from the settlement above. These were found very far down on the western slope in Square C.5 and consist of Loci C.5:86, 105, 107, 109, 110, 112, 117, 119, 129, 131, 168, 170, 178, and 179 (C.5 east and west balks, figs. 5.22-23). Locus C.5:114 is a row of stones amidst these dump layers. In Area B, on the south side of the mound, soil layers B.4:159 and 164 were found in bedrock pockets above and to the east of the reservoir. In addition, soil layer B.4:271 (B.4 east balk; fig. 5.4) was the earliest layer within the plastered pool (B.4:265), found immediately above the plaster lining. It contained only Iron IIC/Persian ceramics along with Iron Age body sherds (cf. locus summary sheets contra Sauer 1976: 59), which would seem to date the original founding of the pool at this time.

Figure 6.11   Area C, Square 2 East Balk (South Side).

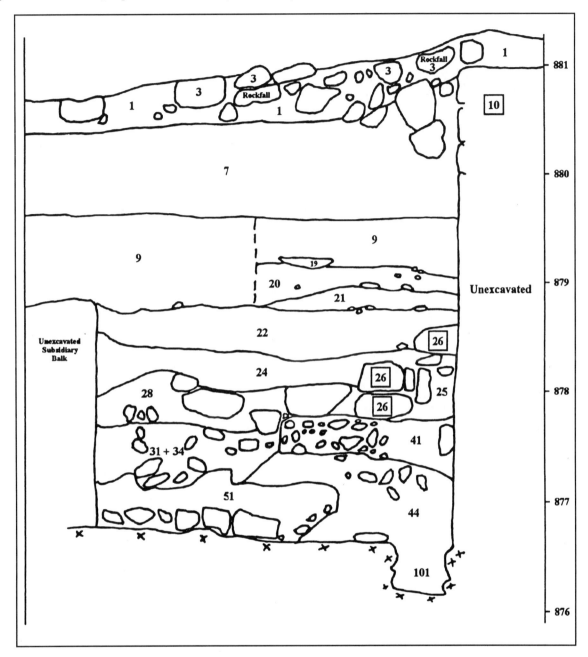

Figure 6.12   Area C, Square 3 West Balk (South Side).

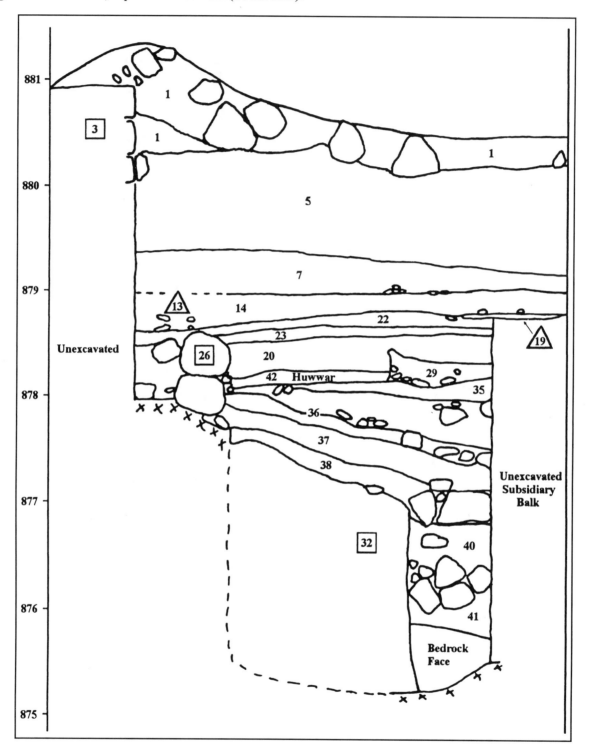

Stage A

Several soil and fill layers make up the destruction/abandonment debris of this stratum. On the lower western slope Locus C.3:38 sealed against the destroyed or abandoned Wall C.3:32, the lack of rock tumble on either side of the wall suggesting that there had been enough time for robbing of stones to have taken place before it was deposited (Herr 1979a: 30). This soil layer equals C.2:41 which ran to the west and probably over Wall C.2:49. Similarly, Locus C.2:50=100 sealed against the destroyed or abandoned Wall C.2:52 further down slope (Thompson 1975: 178). On the southern shelf a moist gray compact clay soil layer (B.1:119=143=B.2:137) .30-.40 m in depth, with over 1000 Iron IIC/Persian sherds within it (Sauer 1975a: 161), was found at the bottom of the reservoir. It represents either the silt which collected on the bottom of the reservoir during its last period of use (Stage B) (Sauer 1975a: 164; 1978: 47) or the debris which washed into it during the gap in occupation of the tell between Stratum 16 and its filling during the late Hellenistic Period. Since this material was deposited on the clean plaster bottom (B.1:121=128=144), it seems best to interpret it as representing the post-occupational buildup on the bottom of a frequently cleaned reservoir (Herr 1979a: 31). A number of objects were found within this layer including two figurines (pl. 6.7), an ostracon (pl. 6.8), another possible ostracon, an iron arrowhead (pl. 6.9), an iron blade point, and some lamp fragments.

Plate 6.7 Horse Figurine (Object 1576).

Plate 6.8 Ostracon A1 (Object 1657).

Unassigned Loci

A number of Huwwar layers in the southeast corner of Square C.2 (Loci C.2:75, 76, 77, 78, 79, 80, 81, and 91) could not be assigned with any degree of assurance to a particular stage. Since Iron IIC/Persian ceramics were the latest found in some of these successive layers, they appear to belong to this stratum. They likely belong either to the use (Stage B) or abandonment (Stage C) phases of this stratum. A spindle rest was found within Locus C.2:76. In addition, a number of structures, which likely functioned as silos (A.5:61, 62, 79, 90; B.3:47, 59, 64; B.4:188; D.2:77, 80, 95; D.3:57; D.6:47, 48), probably belong to this stratum. Although all of these silos were originally assigned to the Hellenistic period on the basis of loci from that period found in "Storage Silo" D.2:77 (Mitchel 1992: 23), it has rightly been noted that their probable original cutting was in the Iron Age, with most of the parallels (see below) coming from Iron II (Mitchel 1992: 23-27; 1994: 100-102).

Plate 6.9 Arrowhead (Object 1547).

Stratum 15 (Stratum 16 Fill)

This material technically belongs to a discussion on Hellenistic period stratigraphy inasmuch as one *in situ* Hellenistic fishplate sherd was found in the rock tumble of Locus B.1:118=126=142 in 1973 (Sauer 1975a: 159, fig. 5A, 160-61, n. 22; 1976: 55). A few additional Hellenistic sherds in other reservoir loci were also found in 1976 (Sauer 1978: 45). Nevertheless, the reservoir produced essentially pure Iron IIC/Persian pottery (Sauer 1978: 45), and although this material has been treated as belonging to the Hellenistic Period (Mitchel 1992: 18-19; 144-45; 161) most of the artifacts and bones probably date to the Iron IIC/Persian period (Sauer 1975a: 161). Due to the above circumstances, the fill, which contains the remains of Stratum 16, has rightly been discussed under the Iron Age rubric throughout the preliminary reports (Sauer 1975a: 161; 976: 55, 58-59; 1978: 45, 46-47) as well as in Herr's analysis (1979a: 33-35).

Stage C

A series of debris layers deposited as a fill, 7.00 m in depth, was found on top of Stratum 16 soil layer B.1:119=143=B.2:137 in the Area B reservoir (Sauer 1975a: 158). This fill includes Loci B.1:14C, 15B, 18, 19, 23B, 24, 26, 30, 31, 32, 33, 34, 36, 37, 38, 39, 41, 42, 43, 44, 45A, 45B, 47, 48, 49, 50, 51, 52, 53, 54, 55, 56, 63, 64, 65, 66, 67, 68, 69, 75, 76, 77, 78, 79, 80, 81, 82, 83, 84, 85, 86, 87, 88, 89, 90, 91, 92, 93, 94, 95, 96, 97, 98, 99, 100, 101, 102, 104, 105, 106, 107, 108, 109, 110, 111, 112, 113, 114, 115, 116, 118, 122, 123, 124, 125, 126, 129, 130, 131, 132, 133, 134, 135, 136, 137, 138, 139, 140, 141, 142; B.2:35B, 36, 37, 38, 39, 40, 41, 42, 56, 57, 58, 59, 60, 61, 65, 66, 67, 68, 70, 72, 73, 74, 79, 80, 81, 83, 91, 94, 100, 107, 111,

118, 119, 120, 121, 122, 124, 125, 126, 128, 129, 130, 131, 132, 133, 134, 135, 136; B.4:202, 203, 205, 207, 215, 216, 218, 219, 220, 224, 272, 273, 274; and B.7:39.

The soil layers making up this material contained a fair amount of rocky inclusions, especially near the bottom of the reservoir, on top of the Iron IIC/Persian clay Soil Layer B.1:119=143 (Sauer 1975a: 159). This material represents a 1.00-2.00 m deep rock tumble locus (B.1:118=126=142) containing (hewn and unhewn) stones (possibly from walls), which were evidently the first items to be thrown in the reservoir. As pointed out by Herr (1979a: 33-34), the tip lines of the fill sloped sharply near the plastered face of the reservoir (cf. B.1 north balk, fig. 5.21), but leveled out in the approximate center of the facility, assuming that the debris was thrown in from various points along its edge. The tan and brown soil layers making up the fill alternated with gray and black ashy layers (B.1:14C, 15B, 19, 24 [in part], 44=64, 47=67, 51, 79, 81, 85, 106=131, 109=136, 124=140; B.2:37, 39, 67, 107, 120, 126, 129, 132, 133, 134 and 135) (cf. Sauer 1975a: 159), the latter (ashy) material possibly representing the remains of a destruction. Since there were no flat-lying sherds or evidence of wind- or water-sorted soil layers, it would seem that these layers were deposited rather rapidly. This material was evidently not washed down into the reservoir over a long period of time, but represents destroyed remains from some time earlier (Herr 1979a: 35).

The varied artifactual material within this fill includes an Egyptian-style frit of "Bes" (pl. 6.10), a loom weight (pl. 6.11), a piece of scale armor (pl. 6.12), seven slingstones, a pottery disc, six stone vessel fragments, a pin or hook, three stone weights, three weaving pattern spatulas, two spindle whorls, a mortar (pl. 6.13), one fibula, two fibu-

Plate 6.10 Bes Figurine (Object 152).

la springs, worked flints, a bead, two whetstones (pl. 6.14), a bronze spatula, an awl (pl. 6.15), three rubbing stones, two shell ornaments, a pendant, a brace, a copper bar, a button, two ivory inlays, three figurines, and six ostraca (cf. Appendix B). The second-fourth centuries A.D. Roman coin in Locus B.2:80 is obviously out of place here and most likely arrived in that location as the result of rodent activity. The above objects as well as the bones and carbonized seed remains (see below) help to round out the picture of everyday life for the inhabitants of Stratum 16. Thus, they will be used, along with those of Stratum 16 proper, in the interpretation of this stratum.

Interpretation

The C.3:26A=34=C.7:44A (pl. 6.16) wall system running along the bedrock shelf on the western slope was attributed to the Iron IIC/Persian period in the preliminary reports (Thompson 1975: 178-79; Mare 1976: 69, fig. 12; 77; 1978: 68-69). It was originally suggested that Wall C.3:34 was part of the Iron II city wall and that Wall C.3:32/26 was

Plate 6.11 Loom Weight (Object 184).

a bastion or tower (Thompson 1975: 179, n. 4). The whole system was also described as a "major defense perimeter wall" (Mare 1976: 69, fig. 12; 1978: 68). This was later rejected by Herr (1979a: 27). Because parts of this wall system yielded

Plate 6.12 Scale Armor (Object 186).

nothing later than Iron IIC/Persian ceramics, while other parts contained Hellenistic sherds on a consistent basis, he felt that positing a Hellenistic rebuild of the wall on the basis of ceramics alone was going beyond the evidence (1979a: 42, n. 35).

As pointed out above, Wall C.3:34 produced Iron Age sherds in a probe within the wall itself (Thompson 1975: 180). Wall C.3:26A produced Iron IIC/Persian ceramics in the soil layers at its

Plate 6.13 Mortar (Object 310).

northern base (locus summary sheets; Thompson 1975: 179), and Wall C.3:32, which abutted Walls C.3:26A and 34, and probably functioned as a revetment wall for the latter, contained nothing later than Iron IIC/Persian ceramics in 18 baskets

Plate 6.14   Whetstone Fragment (Object 566).

Plate 6.15   Awl (Object 768).

(cf. locus summary sheets). Wall C.3:43, while having no associated pottery, ran underneath Wall C.3:32 (pl. 6.17) and must therefore have been contemporary or earlier than it. Although a probe under the third (top extant) and second courses of Wall C.7:44 produced Hellenistic sherds in Loci C.7:100 and 106 (locus summary sheets, Mitchel 1992: 20), Soil Layers C.7:74 and 97, immediately below the first course and on either side of the wall, produced Iron IIC/Persian sherds on bedrock (locus summary sheets; Herr 1979a: 29). This would seem to indicate an original Iron IIC/Persian period wall (C.7:44A), which went with other parts of the system (C.3:26A=34, 32, 43), and a later Hellenistic rebuild of at least part of it (Wall C.7:44B). It is likely that Wall C.3:26B=26C=C.2:26 (cf. stones

Plate 6.16   Offset-Inset Wall on the Western Shelf, Area C (Looking South).

Plate 6.17   Walls C.3:43 (Foreground), and C.3:32 (Right) (Left Wall Retains a Modern Viewing Platform).

within C.7:60, 69 and 76, C.7 north balk; figs. 6.5-6) was built in the Hellenistic period and used as late as the Early Roman period. This wall was not part of the original system, but was added on to Wall C.3:26A at a later time.

A parallel for this type of phenomenon has been found at Gezer, where the so-called "Outer Wall," built originally in Late Bronze Age II, was rebuilt in Iron I (tenth century B.C.), again in Iron II (ninth-eighth centuries B.C.) with the addition of offsets constructed at various points during the period (ninth and eighth centuries B.C.) and then rebuilt yet again (the upper two or three courses) in the Hellenistic Period by the Maccabees/Hasmoneans (Dever, Lance and Wright 1970: 6, 67), reusing ashlars from the earlier Iron Age phases of the wall (Younker 1991c: 26-33, figs. 4, 14-15, 17-19; Dever and Younker 1991: 284-86, figs. 1-3; Dever 1993c: 40-50, figs. 10-11, 13, 15-16, 18; Ray 1993: 48-49). In addition, at Jerusalem, the Iron II city wall and tower on the western hill were reutilized in the Hellenistic period by the Hasmoneans with the addition of a new tower integrated into the earlier wall after a gap in occupation on this part of the site of some 400 years (Avigad 1980: 39, fig. 14; 49, 50, fig. 30; 59, 68-71). It would seem that basically the same thing happened at Hesban where the Iron IIC/Persian wall was par-

tially reused and partially rebuilt in the Hellenistic period by the Hasmoneans (Mitchel 1992: 33-35) after a gap in occupation of several hundred years.

In order to test the above interpretation of this wall system, I reexcavated some parts of Tell Hesban in 1997.[1] Along the edge of a sub-balk left by the original excavators in the north central part of Square C.3, a 7.00 x 2.00 m trench was laid perpendicular to Wall C.3:34. After the removal of 23 years of inter-seasonal debris, a 1.00 x 2.00 m probe (pl. 6.18) along the western (or outer) face of the wall was excavated. Because of the rocky nature of the sediment, no stratigraphy was encountered there. Pottery pails were therefore arbitrarily changed every 30 cm in order to gain control of datable pottery. Iron Age II through the Umayyad (or Early Islamic) period sherds were located in the uppermost 30 cm, but the remaining 60+ cm yielded pure Iron IIC/Persian pottery (cf. fig. 6.13) including burnished black ware sherds. A clearly datable seventh century B.C. wheel-burnished rim sherd (cf. fig. 6.13.6) was found almost on bedrock.

Though an attempt to find a foundation trench on the eastern (or inner) side of the wall (pl. 6.19) was made, this yielded mostly large stones with a small amount of soil. This fill was laid between the wall and another, vertical section of bedrock. Only a very few (mostly body) sherds were located here,

Plate 6.18   Newly Excavated Section of Wall C.3:34 in 1997 (Looking East).

and the last several centimeters over bedrock yielded no pottery whatsoever. At the level of the greatest extant in height of the wall, flagstones (C.3:28) were laid between the wall and the vertical section of bedrock, above the fill. These seem to have been laid in the Late Roman or Early Byzantine period, accounting for the few sherds from that time frame found immediately beneath them.

Wall C.3:26A=34=C.7:44A would thus seem to have been the western wall of the site during Stratum 16. Wall C.3:32 evidently functioned as a buttress or revetment wall. Anchored in bedrock, this wall would have helped to maintain the overall structure (or at least part of it, i.e., Wall C.3:26A=34) on the bedrock shelf above. Wall C.3:43 would seem to have been a retaining wall for Wall C.3:32. At the point where the extant part of Wall C.3:32 abuts Wall C.3:34, the system (to the extent that it has been excavated) is slightly over 4.00 m thick. Though there is no evidence for one, the southern wall of the site, assuming an extension of its western counterpart, would have had to have been south of the reservoir, perhaps along the same lines as the peripheral belt of houses hypothetically placed there in Stratum 18 (cf. chapter 5). Walls C.2:52=90=C.1:90 appear to have been the northern and part of the eastern walls of some kind of extra-mural domestic structure (a house). Other Iron II sites with buildings just outside of their perimeter walls include Jerusalem (Shiloh 1984: 28-29), Ḥorvat ᶜUza, in the Negev

(Beit-Arieh and Cresson 1991: 132), and Dibon in Area C (Winnett and Reed 1964: 43, pls. 49.2, 50.1, 88, 93; Tushingham 1972: 16, 23, sheet 3, plan 2). Wall C.2:49 would seem to have been a terrace wall. The Stratum 16 occupants of Hesban added an additional layer of plaster on the bottom (B.1:145=149=B.2:138) and sides (B.2:113A= B.4:190A=282) of the reservoir as well as three new channels (B.4:242, B.4:244, and B.4:245) for bringing water into the facility. Pool B.4:265 also appears to have been cut into the bedrock shelf to the east of the reservoir at this time.

Although still in use in the Hellenistic period, silos A.5:61, 62, 79, 90; B.3:47, 59, 64; B.4:188; D.2:77, 80, 95; D.3:57; and D.6:47, 48 were probably originally cut during the Iron Age and most likely within the period under discussion. Their shape and size (cf. fig. 5.17; Van Elderen 1976: 26, fig. 3, 27-28; Sauer 1975a: 148, fig. 4; 1976: fig. 10; Herr 1976: 88, fig. 16; Geraty 1973: 102, fig. 6) are similar to installations found at Gibeon. Based on the 26 adjacent, interconnected, and mostly unplastered Iron II silos there (106, 113, 135, 136, 137, 139, 140, 142, 145, 149, 150, 153, 155, 208, 108S, 209, 209W, 211, 213, 215, 216, 218, 219, 223, 224, and 229), as well as a large number of storage jar handles and stoppers found in the nearby pool (Pritchard 1962: 89-99, figs. 7-8, pls. 42-53; 1964: 1-17, 14-15, Table, figs. 6-11), the silos at Hesban, like those at Gibeon, appear to have been used for wine storage (Mitchel 1992: 23-27;

Figure 6.13 Stratum 16: Area C, Square 3 Ceramics from 1997.

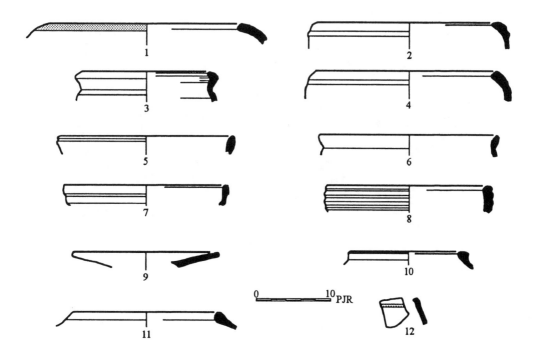

No.	Type	Reg. No.	Locus	Parallel
1	Krater	H97C3.8.2	C.3:65	Low 1991: 195, fig. 8.14.8
2	Krater	H97C3.9.1	C.3:65	Low 1991: 195, fig. 8.14.15
3	Jar	H97C3.8.4	C.3:65	
4	Krater	H97C3.9.3	C.3:65	Lawlor 1997: 47, fig. 3.22.15
5	Bowl	H97C3.12.1	C.3:65	Lugenbeal and Sauer 1972: pl. 5.266
6	Bowl	H97C3.12.2	C.3:65	Lugenbeal and Sauer 1972: pl. 4.257
7	Bowl	H97C3.8.1	C.3:65	
8	Bowl	H97C3.9.2	C.3:65	Pritchard 1985, fig. 17.33
9	Plate	H97C3.9.4	C.3:65	Lugenbeal and Sauer 1972: pl. 9A.504
10	Cooking pot	H97C3.10.2	C.3:65	Lawlor 1997: 43, fig. 3.18.3
11	Cooking pot	H97C3.10.3-4	C.3:65	Lawlor 1997: 40, fig. 3.17.26
12	Sherd	H97C3.7.1	C.3:65	

Plate 6.19   Inner/Eastern Side of Wall C.3:34 (Looking South).

1994: 100-102; Borowski 1987: 112). Other parallels exist at Tel el-Ful, dated to various points in the Iron Age, and at Tell Zakariya, though undated (Mitchel 1992: 24-25; 1994: 102). The fact that lines seven and eight of Hesban Ostracon A1 (pl.6.8), which appears to be a record by a royal steward containing the assignment or distribution from the royal storehouses (Cross 1975: 2, 7; 1993; Cross and Geraty 1994: 170), mention fairly large quantities of wine, would seem to support wine production at or near the site. Sibmah (ᶜAin Sumia; Hesban Survey Site 59), a site nearby Heshbon, was well known for its vineyards (Isa 16:8; Jer 48:32). The numerous wine presses in the Nebo (Saller and Bagatti 1949: 14-15), Hesban (Ibach 1987: 199), and ᶜUmeiri (Younker 1991b: 337; Herr 1995a: 121-25; 1997d: 170; 1999b: 231-32) hinterland regions attest to fairly extensive wine-production activities in this area in the Iron IIC/Persian period.

The Iron IIC/Persian ceramic material (cf. chapter 3, figs. 3.10 and 3.11) comprises numerous bowls (fig. 3.11.1-13), the offset-rimmed (fig. 3.11.1-2), red-burnished, and black ware varieties being among the most popular. Other forms include short-necked cooking pots (fig. 3.11.16), tripod bowls (cups) (cf. fig. 6.13.8), holemouth kraters (fig. 3.10.11-14), and mortaria (fig. 3.10.15-16) (Lugenbeal and Sauer 1972: 33-61; Sauer 1994: 247). In addition, collared-rim pithoi (fig. 3.10.1, 3) continue to be attested this late

(Lugenbeal and Sauer 1972: 52-53, pl. 7; Herr in press b) unlike in Cisjordan where they disappeared at the end of Iron Age I. Surface treatment especially on bowls consists of painting in a variety of banded decorations (Lugenbeal and Sauer 1972: 61-62). This material, as well as the latest ostraca (A5, A6) found in the reservoir (Cross: 1969: 228; Cross and Geraty 1994: 170 Table, 173), suggests that Stratum 16 was occupied at least until the end of the sixth century B.C. (Lugenbeal and Sauer 1972: 63-64; Herr 1979a: 33, 37), although the presence of a few Attic ware sherds (Stern 1982: 138-39; cf. Waldbaum 1991: 243) as well as other late locally made forms (Herr 1995b: 617) might indicate a slightly later date, within the fifth century B.C. This same ceramic evidence, along with the ten ostraca, all but one found in the reservoir (Cross and Geraty 1994: 170 Table; Geraty 1997: 2) and written in the Ammonite language either in Ammonite script, or, toward the end of the sixth century B.C., in Aramaic script (Cross and Geraty 1994: 172, 174), makes it clear that Stratum 16 was Ammonite in character (Herr 1997d: 169), contra Hübner (1992) who suggests that Heshbon was still Moabite at this time. Parallels with ceramic, seal, and ostraca evidence (Herr 1978b: 55-78, figs. 34-45; 1980: 21-26, figs. 1, 1a, 1b; Aufrecht 1989) from other sites within the vicinity of Amman also bear this out (Herr 1993a: 35).

The occupants of the Stratum 16 built the most prosperous settlement on the tell thus far. Dever's

Plate 6.20   Cup Fragment (Object 806).

suggestion that Tell Hesban was a small (border) town (1996: 39, Table 1) fits very well for this stratum (Herr 1979a: 31-32, 37). This prosperity was due in part to trade, evidence for which exists in the form of Attic ware sherds (from Loci A.2:11, cf. chapter 3, fig. 3.11.22; A.4:8 and B.1:40), though these were all found as the earliest sherds in loci from later time periods. A number of basalt artifacts including rubbing stones (Objects 1317, 1319 and 1674), stone bowls (Objects 300, 1313 and 2309), a weight (Object 1396), and one whose identification is uncertain (Object 769) were probably produced and imported from either southern or eastern Transjordan or as far away as Galilee or the Negev (Herr 1997d: 119). A cup made of alabaster (Object 806, pl. 6.20), which was quarried mainly in the eastern desert of Egypt and transported in blocks throughout the Levant for artisans to shape into vessels (Mattingly 1997: 217), is good evi-

Plate 6.21   Weight (Object 245).

dence of long-distance trade. Hematite and lead weights (Objects 245 [pl. 6.21], and 805) are made of materials that are not native to the region. Two ivory inlays (Objects 1827 and 2275 [pl. 6.22]), probably used for wooden furniture or small boxes, also indicate trade (Kotter 1979: 11) as do the shell artifacts (Objects 820 and 1728), which were brought from either the Mediterranean Sea or the Gulf of Aqaba (Crawford 1976c: 171, 173) and the fish bone (stone bass, *Polyprion americanus*) from Locus B.1:142. This bone probably came from the Mediterranean Sea (von den Driesch and Boessneck 1995:100; Lepiksaar 1995: 184-85), suggesting that the trading partner was either Phoenicia (cf. Neh 13:16) or Judah. Since Ammon and Judah were normally at odds with one another, if the partner was Judah, this relationship probably occurred in the early sixth century when they, along with several other kingdoms, including Moab and Edom, participated in a short-lived rebellion (or at least an attempt at forming a coalition) against Babylon in 593 B.C. (Jer 27:3, cf. 28:1). The relatively high number (36) of camel bones (as compared to only three and four in Strata 19 and 18 respectively, cf. Appendix C) would also seem to indicate an emphasis on long-distance trade (Sauer 1994: 235) at this time. Ostracon A5 (Object 309; fig. 6.14), dating to ca. 500 B.C. would seem to bear this out as it represents a list of names of Aramaized Arab traders who moved along the caravan routes (the King's Highway and the east-west road to Jericho and Jerusalem) which crossed at Hesban (Cross 1969: 228; Cross and Geraty 1994: 173). Two other ostraca (A1 and A2; Objects 1657 [pl. 6.8] and 2092), dating to ca. 600 and 575 B.C. respectively, appear to represent tax, if not trade-related, receipts (Cross and Geraty 1994: 170-71; Herr 1997d: 171; 1999b: 224-25).

The prosperity of this period is further evidenced by two stone weights (Objects 245 and 1396). As was the case for similar objects found in earlier strata, these do not give a clear picture of a fixed standard nor are they able to be correlated with other known standards from the ancient world

Plate 6.22   Ivory Inlay (Object 2275).

Figure 6.14   Ostracon A5 (Object 309).

(Kotter 1979: 8, cf. Bienkowski 1995: 88-89). Nevertheless, they still seem to reflect commercial or mercantile activities (Kotter 1979: 11, 25). The same could be said for the pottery disc, if it functioned as a counter for accounting or business exchange (London 1991: 417). The jewelry objects (button, fibulae [fig. 6.15],[2] pendant [fig. 6.16] and pins) and cosmetic tools also attest to interests

Figure 6.15   Fibula (Object 1343).

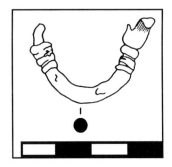

beyond mere subsistence. The ostraca (pl. 6.23) and a scarab seal (Object 1625 [pl. 6.24], cf. Horn and Platt 1990) further indicate administrative activities. The remaining artifacts are illustrative of various aspects of daily life such as domestic activities (ceramic and stone vessels), cottage industries (textile tools), building (construction and other tool kit objects), and cultic (figurines) activities. The latter, mostly fragments of horse and rider or zoomorphic (bovine and ram) figurines, could also have functioned as recreational (toys) objects (Dabrowski 1993: 22-24; Herr 1997d: 172; 1999b: 226). A number of artifacts associated with warfare (arrowheads, blade points, scale armor, and slingstones[3]) were also found.

Figure 6.16   Pendant (Object 1228).

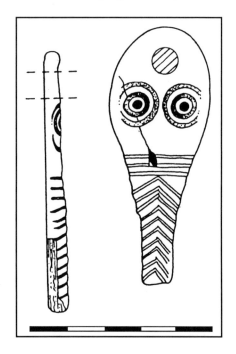

The transition from Moabite to Ammonite Hesban may have occurred in 712-11 B.C. after Moab rebelled (along with the Philistines, Judah, and Edom), against Sargon II (*ANET* 286-87, cf. Isa 20:1). Ammon appears not to have taken part in this rebellion and may have received Hesban (possibly along with other sites in the immediate area) for her loyalty. There is no evidence for a destruction or a gap in occupation, so the transition must have been fairly smooth. By the end of the seventh century B.C. there is also textual evidence that Ammon was in control of Hesban (Jer 49:3).

Plate 6.23   Ostracon (Object 1656).

Whatever, the exact meaning of Jer 48:2, 45, Hesban seems to be no longer Moabite. Verse 34 appears to reflect Isa 15 and within the context of the chapter would appear to be non-Moabite. This interpretation would also seem to be in line with Sauer's lastest observations about the ceramics from this stratum, which he now feels do not really reflect the Assyrian period, but are rather mostly Neo-Babylonian and Persian in date (Sauer 1994: 247).

In terms of the end of the stratum, one possibility is that the site was destroyed in 582 B.C. when, according to Josephus (Ant 10.9.3-4 @163-73), Nebuchadnezzar conducted a punitive campaign against the Ammonites for the murder of Gedaliah, the Babylonian appointed leader of the remnant of the Jewish population in Judah (Jer 40:11-41:18) (Herr 1979a: 32; Younker 1994a: 313-14). If so, the destruction would be reflected in the numerous ash layers found within the reservoir fill (Herr 1979a: 32, 35; Geraty 1997: 21). On the basis of this scenario, Hesban would have continued to have been occupied within the remains of the ruined town, its inhabitants (the Ammonites) utilizing the reservoir until it fell into disrepair, at which time the site was abandoned. The time frame here, based upon the remains discussed above, would have been throughout the remainder of the Neo-Babylonian period and into

Plate 6.24   Scarab (Object 1625).

the Persian period at least until ca. 500 B.C., if not some years into the fifth century B.C.

The possibility also exists that the site was not destroyed until the early to mid-fifth century B.C. as the result of either desert tribes (Herr 1979a: 33, 37), local problems, or revolts, the latter probably due to overtaxation. Although not specifically mentioned as rebelling, Ammon was part of the satrapy of "Across the River" (*Abar Nahara; Ebir-Nari*) which revolted under Megabyzus in 448 B.C. Imperial armies were sent to the satrapy on two occasions before the conflict was over (Olmstead 1948: 312; Yamauchi 1996: 250). Egypt had revolted earlier between 486-84 B.C. (Herodotus *Hist.* 7.1.7). If *Abar Nahara* was even mildly sympathetic, a possibility since an accusation was made against the Jews at this time (Ezra 4:6), there could have been reprisals when Xerxes was in Palestine on his way to Egypt to settle the rebellion (Olmstead 1948: 234-35; Yamauchi 1996: 193).

Carbonized seeds from the debris layers of Stratum 16 and the Stratum 15, Stage C reservoir fill from both the 1974 and 1976 seasons (Sauer 1976: 58; Herr 1979a: 30; Heshbon Expedition Archives; Gilliland 1986: 126-27, fig. 7.1) include wheat, both bread wheat (*Triticum aestivum*, pl. 6.25a) (B.2:128; B.4:207) and *Triticum sp.* (B.2:128), and barley, both six-row (*Hordeum vulgare*) (B.2:128, 132; B.4:207) and *Hordeum sp.* (B.2:128). These grains were commonly used for bread and porridge. Pulses included lentils (*Lens sp.*) (B.2:128); bitter vetch (*Vicia ervilia*) (B.2:128,

Plate 6.25   Seeds: (a) Wheat, *Triticum aestivum*; and (b) Rye Grass, *Lolium temulentum* (from Dimbleby 1967: pl. 18.a, m).

Figure 6.17   Seeds: (a) Grapes, *Vitis vinifera*; and (b) Olives, *Olea sp.* (Modified from *FFB* 157, 189).

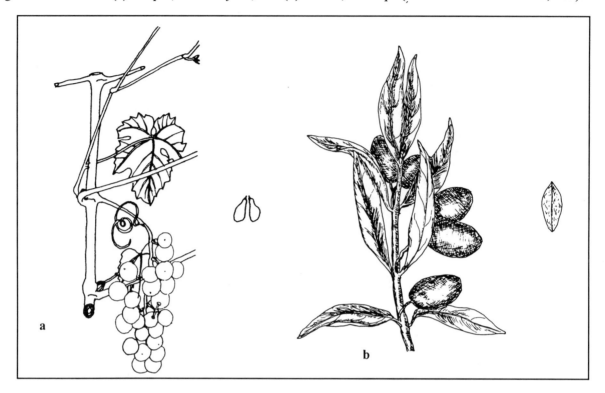

132; B.4:207), and sweat pea or broad bean (*Lathyrus sativus*) (B.2:128). Seeds from fruit crops consisted of grapes (*Vitis vinifera*, fig. 6.17a) (B.2:132; C.3:65),[4] olives (*Olea sp.*, fig. 6.17b) (B.2:118, 128; B.4:203, 205, 207; C.3:65), and dates (*Phoenix dactylifera*) (according to Herr 1979a: 30). Vegetables included pigweed (*Amaranthaceae/Chenopodiaceae*) (B.2:128) and mallow (*Malvaceae*) (B.2:128). Seeds from uncultivated plants included rye grass or tares (*Lolium temulentum*, pl. 6.25b) (B.2:128), burclover (*Medicago sp.*) (B.2:128), clover (*Trifolium sp.*) (B.2:128, 132), and an unidentified species of wild grass (*Gramineae*) (B.2:128), all of which were probably used as fodder or forage for animals (Crawford 1986: 80-82; Gilliland 1986: 131, 133). While the presence of the following seeds does not necessarily mean that they were used in this way, Knotweed (*Polygonum sp.*) (B.2:128) can be used medicinally to make poultices (Crawford 1986: 80) and fumitory (*fumaria sp.*, pl. 6.26) (B.2:128) can be cultivated in gardens for ornamental use (Gilliland 1986: 133). Gromwell (*Lithospermum arvense*) (B.2:128, 132; C.7:74) is merely a troublesome weed found among wheat crops (Gilliland 1986: 133).

Bones of domesticated animals used by the residents of the tell during Stratum 16 as well as those from the reservoir fill (Stratum 15), which also represent a large part of the faunal remains of this stratum, include cattle, sheep, goat, pig, camel, horse, donkey, and chicken. Represented wild species include fish, which were an occasional import from the Mediterranean coast, gazelle, fallow deer (fig. 6.18), and wild sheep or goat (Appendix C).

It would appear from the above that the subsistence economy of Tell Hesban in Stratum 16 was a mixed agro-pastoral one, as it had been in Iron Age I. However, it seems to have been less dependent on grain production as the proportion of cattle reflected in the faunal assemblage (Table 6.2) had dropped from Stratum 18 levels (14.0%) to just below eight percent. They no doubt continued to be used as draft animals in cereal cultivation (LaBianca 1990: 146), which throughout the Iron Age played a major role (cf. the relatively large number and variety [mortars, rubbing stones, whetstones, and stone vessels] of food preparation objects from this stratum, see Appendix B). Nevertheless, there was a definite move away from a complete dominance of cereals to an expansion into other types of subsistence strategies such as

Plate 6.26 Pollen: Fumitory, *fumaria sp.* (from Dimbleby 1967: pl. 12.m).

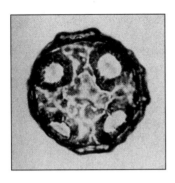

Table 6.2 Strata 16 and 15C Bone Data.

Bone Type	#	%
Cattle	295	7.51
Sheep/Goat	3471	88.43
Pig	13	.33
Camel	36	.92
Equids	44	1.13
Chicken	29	.75
Fish	1	.03
Wild Species	36	0.92
Total	3925	100.00

fruit trees (including grapevines), which seem only to have been of marginal importance earlier in the Iron Age (B. Rosen 1994: 342). The relatively high number (43) of donkey bones reflects their use as draft animals on terraces. In addition, pulses and vegetables (cf. the data on the carbonized seeds above) were grown and eaten. Sheep and goats continued to dominate the faunal assemblage, their products (wool/hair, milk, and meat) assuming an important role. Pigs also appear, but in very small (less than 1%) quantities (on their presence and significance in the faunal assemblage, see chapter 5, Stratum 21). Smaller numbers of camel, horse, donkey, and chicken were also present. These subsistence strategies were occasionally supplemented with wild fish and game, the relatively high inci-

dence of wild species including gazelle, fallow deer, wild sheep, or goat (cf. Appendix C) indicating, as it did in Stratum 18, the use of exotic foods in the diet. These observations would seem to indicate that occupants of the tell at this time were involved in a high intensity food production regime (LaBianca 1984: 278-79; 1989a: 172; 1990: 131-32; fig. 4.4). This conclusion is further supported by the rise in number of donkeys (as draft animals for terrace horticulture) and chickens (29 bones) as barnyard animals (LaBianca 1984: 279).

Iron Age II: Tell Hesban and Vicinity

As pointed out above (chapter 5), Dead Sea lake levels would seem to indicate that there was a grad-

Figure 6.18 European, *Dama dama* (Left) and Persian Fallow Dear, *Dama mesopotamica* (Right), (from Haltenorth 1959: fig. 46).

ual drying of the climate throughout the Iron Age, with Iron Age II levels averaging ca. -400 m (Bruins 1994: 305). Initially, however, instead of a further intensification in crop investment as was the trend in Iron Age IC/IIA, the complex political situation (the changing fortunes of the kingdoms of Israel and Moab) in Iron Age IIB seems to have dictated at least a partial return to range-tied pastoralism and with it the more loose and flexible networks of cooperation between kin-based alignments, which maintained control over widespread pasture land and water resources (LaBianca and Younker 1995: 404). It is only in Iron IIC/Persian, as the climate grew even drier, that the region, now dominated by the Ammonites, once again began to invest in crops and expend labor on ploughing and planting with the return of a stable political system under foreign vassalage to Assyria, Babylonia, and Persia. With the emphasis on and expansion of land-tied agriculture there was a return to a more rigid system, which maintained a heightened sense of cooperation with and obligation to one another, among these same kin-based groups (LaBianca and Younker 1995: 404). These activities included terracing, irrigation, and protection (watch towers) (Christopherson and Guertin 1996: 8-9, 15-16) of their investment in the land.

In Iron Age IIB it would seem that much of the land was used for pastoral-nomadic activities, but with the return to the more sedentary end of the continuum in Iron IIC/Persian these activities were no doubt once again confined to the rocky slopes of the steppe zone in the Jordan Valley and on the desert fringe to the east. On the Plateau the emphasis would have been on land-tied cereal production (and pulses) with fruit, olive trees, and especially vineyards in the deep soils of the wadis (Lacelle 1986: 110-19, figs. 6.4, 6.5; Danin 1995: 30). The presence of fallow deer (cf. Appendix C) would seem to indicate a relatively lush habitat and a fairly balanced approach to the removal of the forests for agricultural purposes (Younker 1989a: 36-37; for a different view see LaBianca 1998: 7). The climax vegetation included oak trees (*Quercus calliprinos*) (al-Eisawi 1985: 50, 53; Lacelle 1986: 105; Younker 1989a: 33-37; and Danin 1995: 27, fig. 1, 30) and since "cupholes" were present at numerous sites, especially in the ᶜUmeiri region (4, 10, 17, 19, 23, 28, 33, 36, 43, 46, 52, 69, 74, 83, 84, 101, 128, 129, and 133), it would seem that the late Iron Age II population continued to exploit acorns as an alternate subsistence strategy, probably also

Figure 6.19 Almond, *Amygdalus communis* (from *FFB* 89).

using them for animal fodder and tanning of hides (Younker 1995: 686-89). Nuts such as almond (*Amygdalus communis*, fig. 6.19) and pistachio (*Pistacia*, fig. 6.20) (Crawford 1986: 79) no doubt continued to be part of the diet as well.

Iron

As pointed out above (chapter 5), it was not until the early tenth century B.C. that iron objects appear in significant numbers in the Levant (Waldbaum 1978: 26; Frick 1985: 187). The artifactual assemblage from Hesban, however, does not contribute anything to this repertoire until Stratum 16 and then only in very small numbers. The two objects, a knife blade point and an arrowhead (Objects 1329 and 1547), represented here, do show evidence of carburization or steeling, however (B. London 1981: 8, 11, Table 1).

Settlement Pattern

The sparsely settled conditions during Iron Age IIB, mentioned above, are reflected throughout the region (McGovern 1992: 181; Sauer and Herr 1997: 234; Herr 1997d: 146 [box], 148; 1999b:

Figure 6.20 Pistachio, *Pistacia* (from *FFB* 164).

222). Only 16 sites (1, 26, 29, 39, 95, 96, 97, 102, 108, 110, 135, 143, 146, 149, 151, and 153) out of the 63 Iron Age II sites from the Hesban Survey were settled at this time. Of these, ten (1, 26, 102, 110, 135, 143, 146, 149, 151, and 153) were located on the plateau; three (29, 39, 108) in the wadis and three (95, 96, and 97) in the Jordan Valley. All but four (96, 110, 151, and 153) of these sites were occupied in Iron Age I, with three of the new ones (110, 151, and 153) only inhabited during this subdivision of the Iron Age.

In Iron IIC/Persian the number of sites in the Hesban region increased to 58 (1, 2, 3, 4, 5, 6, 7, 8, 9, 10, 21, 26, 29, 36, 40, 41, 42, 44, 47, 59, 72, 74, 80, 82, 91, 92, 94, 95, 96, 97, 98, 99, 100, 101, 102, 103, 104, 105, 108, 127, 128, 129, 131, 132, 133, 136, 138, 139, 140, 141, 143, 144, 145, 146, 147, 148, 149, and 150). For 33 of these sites (2, 3, 4, 5, 8, 9, 10, 21, 36, 41, 42, 59, 74, 80, 82, 92, 94, 98, 99, 100, 104, 127, 128, 131, 132, 133, 136, 138, 139, 140, 144, 145, and 148), this was the first time during the Iron Age that they were settled. Of these there were five major sites, six large sites, eleven medium sites, twenty-one small sites, and fifteen very small sites (fig. 6.21; Ibach 1987: 164-68, Table 3.11).[5] In addition, Madaba also seems to have been inhabited at this time (Harrison 1996: 7;

Herr 1997d: 170) with tomb evidence (Thompson 1986: 334-45) even earlier (Iron Age IIA-B). The ᶜUmeiri Survey located another 52 Iron Age IIC/Persian sites (4, 6, 8, 9, 10, 13, 14, 17, 18, 19, 21, 22, 23, 25, 26, 27, 28, 29, 30, 31, 33, 34, 35, 36, 37, 38, 43, 45, 46, 49, 51, 52, 54, 55, 64, 68, 69, 74, 83, 84, 85, 100, 101, 116B, 116D, 118, 122, 125, 126, 128, 129, and 133) during the 1984, 1987, 1989, and 1992 seasons (Boling 1989: 99, fig. 8.1; 188; fig. 8.117; Younker 1991a: 270, fig. 12.2; Christopherson 1997b: 291-302; Christopherson et al. 1997: 36-42). These were found within a 5 km radius of Tell el-ᶜUmeiri. Twenty-three of the random squares visited in the 1984 season produced Iron II/Persian pottery (J. Cole 1989b: 54-55, figs. 7.3 and 4) as well. Other sites within the immediate vicinity which have yielded Iron Age II sherds include Naur, the Abu Jaber village site (Kan Zaman = *JADIS* Site 2313.044), and *JADIS* Site 2314.123. In addition, the East Jordan Valley Survey located 20 sites (137 = Glueck Site 194 [Glueck 1951], 145, 148, 149, 151, 159, 182, 183, 185 = Tell el-Kafrein, Hesban Survey Site 96; 186, 189, 190, 191 = Tell Iktanu, 195 = Tell er-Rameh, Hesban Survey Site 95 and Glueck Site 214, 196 = Glueck Site 216; 199, 211, 217, 219, and 221) south of the Wadi Zerqa (Yassine, Ibrahim and Sauer 1988: 191-93, 198-99). Glueck Site 221 (Glueck 1951: 385, 387) and *JADIS* Site 2212.006 also seem to have been occupied at this time.

The largest sites within the 10 km radius immediately surrounding Tell Hesban during the Iron IIC/Persian period were the same as those in Iron Age I. These were Madaba, Jalul, and Umm el-ᶜAmad on the northern end of the Madaba Plains (the Mishor). These sites, located within the bread basket of the region, were probably now large towns.[6] In addition, both Madaba and Umm el-ᶜAmad were located along major and secondary north-south roads respectively. The other major town sites likewise continued from Iron Age I. These included Tell el-ᶜUmeiri, Khirbet el ᵓAl, and Tell Ikhtanu, also on major road systems. Tell Jawa, now (as already in Iron Age IIB) with a casemate wall (Daviau 1992: 145, 152-53; 1994: 174-78; 1996: 83-94), and Tell er-Rameh were both located along the road systems. Tell Jawa, as well as the large site of el-Yaduda (Site 143), was located on a secondary north-south road, while Tell er-Rameh was located on the east-west trunk road. Both of these sites were no doubt important towns.

Figure 6.21   Hesban Region in Iron Age II.

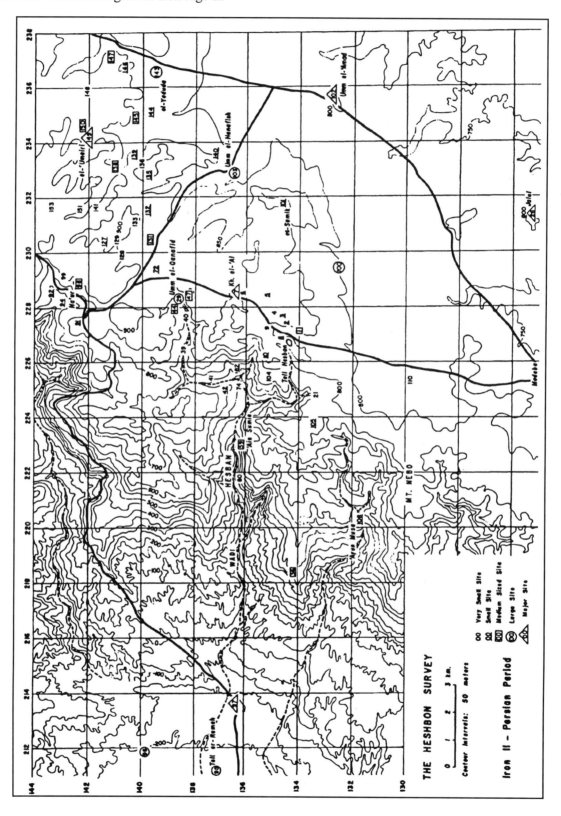

Tell Hesban, strategically located at the crossroads of the main north-south and the east-west trunk road, reached new heights in prosperity and was now somewhat larger than its Stratum 18 (Iron Age IC/IIA) predecessor. Other town sites included Umm el-Hanafish (Site 103) on the plateau and Umm el-Qanafid (Site 29) guarding the spring of ᶜAin Rawda on the Wadi Hesban. ᶜAyun Musa (Site 108), though still a relatively small fortress, continued to guard the spring of the same name. In addition, there was now Masuh (Site 100) on the plateau and Tell el-Kafrein (Site 96) in the Jordan Valley. Though both are prominent sites, neither seem to have been connected with a road system. The latter may have functioned as yet another barrier to would-be attackers from the west.

The rest of the sites in the Hesban region were probably small villages, farmsteads, and watchtowers. The majority of these were located within the highland plateau region (1, 2, 3, 4, 5, 6, 8, 9, 10, 72, 98, 99, 101, 127, 128, 129, 131, 132, 133, 136, 138, 139, 140, 141, 144, 145, 146, 147, 148, and 150) with a smaller, but significant number in the wadis (21, 36, 40, 41, 42, 44, 47, 59, 74, 80, 82, 91, 92, 94, 104, and 105). The large number of sites on the highland plateau would seem to reflect the continued emphasis on land-tied cereal production in the Iron Age II economy. This remained for the most part dependent on ridge soils (silty loam) (Christopherson and Guertin 1995: 18-19; Christopherson, Guertin and Borstad 1996: 11, 17, 19, 24). Though there was still the need to protect water sources (Sites 29 and 108), most of the sites located in the wadis (as with those in the ᶜUmeiri region) reflect the utilization of less desirable areas for food production. In addition to the drying of the climate (mentioned above), this probably came about as a result of population pressures as well as being a response to a wider diversity of subsistence strategies (Christopherson, Guertin and Borstad 1996: 24). The system of agricultural terraces, already in use in Iron Age I, was evidently expanded considerably at this time (Christopherson and Guertin 1995: 17, 19; Christopherson, Guertin and Borstad 1996: 17, 19).

Both the Hesban and ᶜUmeiri regions were no doubt part of the kingdom of Ammon at this time. Very little of the Iron Age II capital of Rabbath-Ammon, at the headwaters of the Wadi Zerqa (biblical Jabbok), has been excavated. However, walls of a residential (or palace ?) area on the lower terrace (Zayadine 1973: 28-29; 31-35; Bennett 1975:

141; Zayadine, Humbert and Najjar 1989: 360, fig. 3, 362) and part of the (casemate) fortification system (Dornemann 1983: 90-93) have been found on the citadel. Iron Age II sherds have also been found at the Amman Forum (Hadidi 1974: 82-85). Otherwise evidence comes from tombs (Harding 1945; 1951; Harding and Tufnell 1953; Dajani 1966a: 41-47; Yassine 1975: 57-68, and *JADIS* 2.143, Site 2315.144).

Other Iron Age II sites in the Ammon region include Safut (Wimmer 1987a: 166-72; 1987b: 281; 1989: 513-14), ᶜAin el-Basha (*JADIS* Site 2216.002), Rujm al-Henu West (Site 2), Khirbet Umm ad-Dananir (Site 3/Field V), Rujm al-Hawayah (Site 4), Rujm al-Hawi (Site 5), and Rujm ᶜAin Umm-ad Dananir (Site 6) (McGovern 1986: 8, Table 1, 9) in the Baqᶜah Valley. The er-Rumman Survey, farther to the north, found 14 (2/3, 2/4, 3/3, 4, 6/1, 6/2, 15/3, 21, 23 = Glueck Site 300; 26, 27, 28, 34 and 40) Iron Age II sites (Gordon and Knauf 1987: 290, fig. 1; 294-97). Other sites to the north of Amman include Tell Siran (Thompson 1973a: 7), Salt (*JADIS* Site 2116.003), *JADIS* Sites 2315.008, 2316.001, 2416.001, 2516.016, 2516.017, 2517.051, and Glueck (1939) Sites 208, 220, 221, 224, 239, 245, 250, 251, 267, 270, 272, 293, 315, 316, 320, 327, and 333.

In addition, the Survey of Greater Amman (Abu Dayyah et al. 1991) located 70 (53-39.1, 53-39.3, 53-39.5, 53-39.8, 54-36.3, 54-36.7, 54-36.8, 54-36.9, 54-38.7, 54-38.10, 54-39.6, 54-40.7, 54-41.3, 55-36.10, 55-36.11, 55-36.12, 55-37.2, 55-37.6, 55-37.8, 55-38.1, 55-38.2, 55-39.4 & 5, 55-39.6, 56-38.1, 56.41.1, 42.34.1 [= Tell el-ᶜUmeiri], 48-37.1, 48-37.3, 48-37.4, 48-37.5, 48-37.6, 54-33.1, 54-33.2, 54-33.3, 54-46.1, 55-29.1, 55-30.1, 55-30.2, 55-32.1, 55-35.1, 55-35.2, 55-35.4, 56-29.3, 56-29.5, 56-29.9, 56-29.11, 56-30.1, 56-30.3, 56-30.4, 56-30.5, 56-30.6, 56-30.8, 56-30.10, 56-30.11, 56-32.1, 56-34.1, 56-34.2, 57-30.1, 57-30.2, 57-31.1, 57-32.1 [cf. Bikai 1993: 521], 58-31.2, 58-33?.1, 58-34.1, 58-34.2, 58-35.1, 59-33.1, 59-33.1, 59-33.3, and 60-33.1) Iron Age II (many probably Iron IIC/Persian period) sites.

Thirty-eight (53-39.1, 53-39.3, 53-39.8, 54-36.7, 54-36.9, 54-39.6, 54-41.3, 55-38.2, 56-41.1, 48-37.1, 48-37.3, 48-37.4, 48-37.5, 48-37.6, 54-33.1, 54-33.3, 54-46.1, 55-29.1, 55-30.1, 55-30.2, 55-32.1, 55-35.1, 55-35.4, 56-29.5, 56-29.11, 56-30.1, 56-30.3, 56-30.4, 56-30.5, 56-30.6, 56-30.8, 56-30.10, 56-30.11, 56-34.1, 56-34.2, 57-30.1, 57-

30.2, and 58-35.1) of the above sites were either towers or had towers on them. As these sites were for the most part on the plateau, they probably served agricultural functions as well as maintaining good visual contact with the main sites in the area. Since Christopherson and Guertin (1996: 9) have suggested that a number of sites designated as farmsteads from the ᶜUmeiri Survey could also have functioned as watchtowers, one could make a similar case for related sites in the Amman and Hesban regions (Younker 1989b: 196-97). Kletter (1991: 39-41) has also suggested that the towers or Rujm el-Malfuf buildings throughout the region served more than one function. That most of the towers in the Ammonite region that have been excavated so far (Rujm el-Malfuf South, Khirbet el-Hajjar, Rujm el-Mekheizin, and Rujm al-Henu West) have dated to the Iron IIC/Persian period (Thompson 1972: 63; 1973b: 49; 1984: 31, 38; and McGovern 1983: 112, 127, 134-36) would seem only to strengthen the case. Indeed, several of the towers, formerly interpreted as "forts," were found in the Hesban (Site 73 = Fohrer Site N; 132 = Fohrer Site C; 137 = Fohrer Site F; and ᶜUmeiri Site 12) and ᶜUmeiri (Site 46 = Fohrer Site E) regions (Kletter 1991: 39-42, fig. 10, Table 1).

To the south of the capital was the site of Sahab (Ibrahim 1975: 70-74; 1987: 78-79). A number of smaller Iron Age II sites (2, 4, 30, 38, 39, 45, 46, 56, 61, 78, 80, 90, 94, 96, 105, 106, 110, 114, and Sahab SW) have recently been surveyed within its hinterland (*JADIS* 2.158-161; 2.171). Other Iron Age II sites in immediate proximity to Amman include Muqablein, el-Mabrak, and *JADIS* Sites 2413.027, 2413.028, 2414.011, 2414.026, 2414.028, 2414.037, 2414.042, 2514.004, 2514.008, 2514.014, and 2514.020.

Notwithstanding the occasional downward trend or mini-cycle (late Iron I and early Iron Age II), the number and size of the Iron Age I and early Iron Age II sites remained fairly stable in this part of Jordan. However, during the Iron IIC/Persian period there seems to have been a mushrooming of sites (Herr 1992: 176; McGovern 1992: 181), the intensification process finally reaching its climax (LaBianca 1990: 156; LaBianca and Younker 1995: 409-10). Though most of these sites were rather small (cf. above), with some of the larger ones such as Tell el-ᶜUmeiri even apparently becoming smaller (Herr 1992: 176), the region still appears to have been fairly prosperous, much of it connected with wine production (Herr 1995a: 121-25). As is

now known, the Ammonites did not disappear with the arrival of the Babylonians, but continued to flourish well into, if not throughout, the Persian period (Herr 1993a: 29, 35; Sauer 1986: 18; 1994: 248; Younker 1994a: 314-15).

During Iron Age II B, sites from Hesban, south to as far as the Wadi Mujib (biblical Arnon), would seem to have fallen into Moabite hands under Mesha and his successors (see above). These sites earlier belonging to the tribe of Gad (Num 32:34-36; Josh 13:25, cf. Mesha Inscription line 10) included Madaba, Jalul, Umm el-ᶜAmad (possibly Bezer), Khirbet Mukhayyat (Nebo), Libb (possibly Beth Bamoth, cf. Dearman 1989: 185-86), Khirbet el-Heri (Herr 1997d: 169-70; Daviau 1997: 226-27), Glueck Site 182, and Qasr ez-Zaᶜfaran = *Limes Arabicus* Site 10 (Parker 1976: 23) = Glueck Site 72 (?). Sites with undifferentiated Iron Age ceramics, but probably also inhabited in Iron Age II B as indicated by their inclusion on the Mesha Inscription, include khirbet ᶜAtarus (biblical Ataroth) and Khirbet et-Teim (Kiriathaim ?). To the south of the eth-Themed/Wala/el-Heidan wadi system there is Khirbet Medeiniyeh on the Wadi eth-Themed, with a recently discovered six-chambered gate (Daviau 1997: 223-24; 1998: 2, 4). This site possibly = biblical Jahaz (Dearman 1989: 182). Other sites include Dibon (Morton 1989: 241-246; figs. 4-5, 7-13, 15-18; Tushingham 1972: 5-23; 1990: 183-92, and Ray 1997), Lehun (Homès-Fredericq 1989: 354-55; 1992: 191-98), Aroer (Olavarri 1965: 77-94, 1983: 165-78; 1993: 92-93), Saliyeh = Glueck Site 92 = Parker Site 15 = Dhiban Plateau Site 3 and possibly biblical Kedemoth (Ray 2000a), Khirbet el-Jemeil = Glueck Site 94 = Dhiban Plateau Site 4, ᶜAleiyan = Glueck Site 162 = Dhiban Plateau Site 6 and possibly Kerioth from the Mesha Inscription (Dearman 1989: 179), er-Rumeil = Glueck Site 176 = Parker Site 12 = Dhiban Plateau Site 11, and Glueck Sites 87 = Parker Site 14, 157 = Dhiban Plateau Site 1 (possibly occupied at this time) and 174. Still others include *Limes Arabicus* Sites 18 (Parker 1976: 23) and 814 and probably Umm er-Rasas = Mephaath (Younker and Daviau 1993: 23-25; Dearman 1997: 210) with undifferentiated Iron Age remains.

Recent ceramic and inscriptional evidence indicates that in Iron Age II C the eth-Themed/Wala/el-Heidan wadi system represented the border between Ammon and Moab (Herr 1997d: 169-70; Dearman 1997: 209; Daviau 1997: 226-27). Notwithstanding some fluidity, settlements north of this wadi system would have been under the control of the Ammonites while sites south of it belonged to the kingdom of Moab.

Summary

The above analysis of the Iron Age I/II (chapter 5) remains at Tell Hesban indicates that the small town that existed there in Stratum 18, under the auspices of the tribal kingdom of Israel in the time of Solomon, was abandoned in the fourth quarter of the tenth century B.C. Stratum 17, which followed, seems to have been inhabited rather lightly and appears to have been a Moabite squatter settlement. The high intensity food production regime of Stratum 18, which produced significant amounts of grain and animal products, while in the process of intensifying its agricultural repertoire to include horticulture and vineyards, was followed for a short time by a partial abatement, returning to range-tied pastoralism and a low to medium intensity food regime. While the Iron Age population in the region through Iron Age IIB appears to have been generally low, with the number and size of sites remaining fairly stable and the occasional abatement cycle representing but a different proportion along the sedentarization-nomadization continuum (LaBianca and Younker 1995: 404), in the Iron IIC/Persian period the number of sites mushroomed as the gradual intensification process that had continued throughout the Iron Age reached its climax. At this time, Stratum 16 Hesban, once again a thriving town, returned to a high intensity food produc-

tion regime.

Economically, the Stratum 17 Moabite squatter settlement at Hesban was no doubt merely subsistence-oriented, with a major focus on range-tied pastoralism, supplemented by dry farming of cereals and possibly some limited control of the trade routes. This tribally oriented kin-based society making minimal use of Tell Hesban at this time should probably be classed as a chiefdom. With the return to town life in the Iron IIC/Persian period, the Ammonites under the dominance of the Assyrians, Babylonians, and Persians moved to a market-oriented economy (LaBianca 1984: 278), probably heavily involved, like a number of other sites in the region, in wine production (cf. the silos). The town was extended to the west and with it the building of an offset-inset wall on this side of the settlement to protect its growing population. In addition, the Stratum 18 reservoir was repaired (i.e., replastered) and several feeder channels were added. There is evidence of mercantile activities and a fairly wide trade network. The location of the site on the crossroads of the main north-south highway and the east-west trunk road from Cisjordan would seem to have helped it to continue to dominate the caravan traffic which traveled through the region. These characteristics helped to make Stratum 16 the most prosperous Iron Age settlement on the tell. In terms of social organization, it would appear that Ammonite Stratum 16 Hesban belonged to a society that had once again reached the level of a tribal kingdom.

Notes

[1]Although the primary reasons for returning to Tell Hesban in 1997 were its restoration and development as a tourist site and to expand our knowledge of its cultural history (see chapter 5, n. 1), the author also used it as an opportunity to deal with two interpretational issues involving Iron Age features (cf. LaBianca and Ray 1999). The supervisor for Square C.3 was Phil Drey.

[2]This type of utilitarian jewelry increased in popularity during the eighth century B.C. to the point that by the next century it had replaced the toggle pin as a fastener for clothing (Stronach 1959: 204; Platt 1989: 356).

[3]Bienkowski (1995: 88) suggests that the primary function of slingstones was as grinding stones, pestles, and pounders.

Homès-Fredericq (1992: 198) suggests that they have different war-time and peace-time functions. This last suggestion is more likely.

[4]Loci C.3:63-70 were excavated in 1997.

[5]For Ibach's definition of the various sized sites, cf. chapter 5, n. 7.

[6]On the site hierarchy used here, cf. chapter 5, n. 8. Numerous other sites were no doubt located on the plain in antiquity, but have been removed by modern farm machinery (Christopherson 1997b: 4-5).

Chapter Seven

HESBAN AND VICINITY
IN THE HELLENISTIC PERIOD

Chapter Seven

Hesban and Vicinity in the Hellenistic Period

Introduction

Earlier in this study (chapter 4), we looked at the tell and the region during the Late Bronze Age in order to put Iron Age Tell Hesban and its environs into context. To round things out, we will also take a brief look at what was happening at the tell and the wider region during the period immediately following the Iron Age.

Tell Hesban in the Hellenistic Period

Since the Hellenistic period at Tell Hesban has been published in depth (Mitchel 1992: 17-39; 1994: 90-103), for the most part we shall merely summarize the details as outlined elsewhere.

There appears to have been a gap in occupation at Tell Hesban of ca. 350-400 years from the end of the sixth or possibly as late as the mid-fifth century B.C. (cf. chapter 6) until the beginning of the second century B.C. The tell does not seem to have been settled in the Early Hellenistic (or Ptolemaic) period (Mitchel 1992: 31) though it is possible that there could be more than a few ceramic findings from this time (Mitchel 1992: 17; Sauer 1994: 248, 250).

The construction stage of the Hellenistic period (Stratum 15) involved the complete denuding of the entire summit of the mound to bedrock. As we have seen (chapter 6; cf. Mitchel 1992: 18), much of the Iron IIC/Persian period debris and its cultural contents ended up being scraped into the reservoir which had been in use between the Iron IC/IIA (Stratum 18) and the Iron IIC/Persian periods (Stratum 16). As with the Iron Age strata before it, the architectural remains from the Hellenistic stratum are rather sparse due to their later removal by the successive occupants of the tell. What remains of the architecture of Stratum 15 consists of two ca. 2.00 m thick walls (A.11:49 and D.1:4D) of a perimeter wall (Mitchel 1992: 19-20; fig. 2.3), which can be traced along the periphery of the summit. The overall feature was interpreted as a

fortress (Mitchel 1992: 38), which may certainly have been the case, although the majority of the artifacts (mostly slingstones),[1] which Mitchel (cautiously) used to infer a military function (Mitchel 1992: 38, Table 2.4; cf. 161, Appendix B; 1994: 102-103) for the structure, were found in the reservoir and thus would have been used during the Iron Age rather than the Hellenistic period, at which time they were included as fill material beneath the settlement.

Mitchel (1992: 20; 39; cf. locus summary sheets) assigned Wall C.3:26=C.7:44 to the Hellenistic period on the basis of the fact that a probe under the third (top extant) and second courses of Wall C.7:44 produced Hellenistic sherds in Loci C.7:100 and 106. However, as we have seen (cf. chapter 6), this overall wall system, which also includes Wall C.3:34 moving further to the north and Walls C.3:32 and 43 as revetment and retaining walls, actually originated in the Iron IIC/Persian period though parts (at least the above-ground structures) of the system were reused during the Hellenistic period and later. This was hypothesized in early versions of this study, and then confirmed by excavation in the 1997 season, when excavations were renewed at the site. Therefore, it would seem that this wall system on the western side of the mound, rather than having a mere soil-retaining function (Mitchel 1992: 20), was part of a second line of defense at the site at this time.

It is possible that this wall met up with and continued along the southern part of the tell as Wall B.1:17=B.2:62. This wall (cf. fig. 5.17) appears to have been built for defensive purposes (Beegle 1969: 124; Sauer 1973: 67; 1975a: 160; 1994: 250) and was dug into the massive fill that was dumped into the Iron Age reservoir in the Late Hellenistic period (Sauer 1975a: 156; 1976: 53-54). Mitchel (1992: 51-55) on the other hand assigned this wall to the Early Roman period on the basis of the few sherds from this period that were found among the primarily Hellenistic period ceramics within the foundation trench (B.1:40=103=B.2:69=105) and the fact that several partially excavated smaller walls (B.1:23, 27, and 28) abutted Wall B.1:17 on its southern face. He further implies (1992: 51) that it could not have been the Greeks who built the wall because, while they were the ones who filled the reservoir with the earlier debris,[2] those who built the wall seemed to have been unaware of the depth of this fill in that its foundation trench was filled with ca. 1.25 m of stone before the courses were begun.

While I have nothing to urge in either direction, if the wall was built in the Late Hellenistic period, it could have been constructed during a second phase of activity when the site was taken from the Seleucids by the Hasmonaeans (Mitchel 1992: 31-35). This would be analogous to Gezer, which was also captured from the Seleucids by the Hasmonaeans after which the "Outer Wall" was hastily repaired (Dever, Lance and Wright 1970: 6; Dever et al. 1974: 41-43). Both sites (Gezer and Tell Hesban) are located at the crossroads of major north-south highways and east-west trunk roads leading to Jerusalem. Securing these sites with garrisons would have been important to the Hasmonaeans in their struggle to hold on to their recent gains on both sides of the Jordan, for protecting the flanks of the capital at Jerusalem, and as potential bases of operation for further acquisitions. If the wall was built at this time, the few Roman period sherds could possibly be accounted for by a rechecking of the foundation trench when it was repaired or rebuilt in the early stages of the Early Roman period. The remnants of the walls on its southern face could have simply belonged to extramural structures. In this way it is possible that the Hasmonaeans could have rebuilt parts of the Iron Age town wall at Hesban and built a new section on the south, assuming that the earlier southern wall was either destroyed or in too poor shape to reuse. However, if Wall B.1:17=B.2:62 was indeed built in the Early Roman period as Mitchel maintains, it would merely mean that the southern extension of the western wall of the Late Hellenistic period has not been found.

Other than the silos (Mitchel 1992: 21, Table 2.1), which were reused at this time, but were probably originally dug and used for the first time during the Iron Age (chapter 6; Mitchel 1992: 23-27; 1994: 102), no other construction (Stage C) remains from Stratum 15 were found. Loci from the use Stage (B) of Stratum 15 were few and other

than one crude wall (G.1:36), a floor (A.11:47), several occupational surfaces (B.3:66, 68; B.4:229; D.2:77B, 80E), two soil surfaces (A.9:113; C.2:48), and two fire pits (C.2:46; C.7:99), it consisted of mostly soil layers (A.5:56, 90E; A.11:51; B.3:62, 67, 71; B.4:182, 249, 271; G.1:39; G.12:29, 31, 33, 34B, 35B), fill layers (A.11:46, 52, 53; B.2:110), ash layers (C.3:29; G.1:40), huwwar layers (B.4:180; C.2:47), and zirs (B.2:75, 82; B.4:174). Destruction/abandonment Stage (A) loci consisted of a capstone (B.3:70), a number of soil layers (B.3:51, 63; B.4:175, 178, 183; D.2:77A; G.1:35), two fill layers (B.3:50, 52), a huwwar layer (B.2:77), and an ash layer (B.4:176).

The Regional Context

We will next look at sites that were occupied between the Wadi Zerqa and the Wadi Mujib during the Hellenistic period. Most of the surveys, from which this information is drawn, make no inner-period distinctions. However, it is likely that many of these sites fall within the Late Hellenistic period[3] as Ptolemaic Transjordan, like most of Cisjordan, other than the Mediterranean coast, the Shephelah, and the Negev (by the Nabateans), was sparsely populated, with the few sedentary villages engaged basically in subsistence agriculture (Berlin 1997: 4-14). In terms of Transjordan cities, Amman alone was refounded (as Philadelphia) by the Ptolemies (Mitchel 1992: 31; Berlin 1997: 11).

In addition to Tell Hesban itself (see above), the Hesban regional survey found 21 (7, 26, 29, 31, 36, 54, 59, 95 = Glueck Site 214; 96, 97, 99, 104, 109, 123, 129, 130, 132, 139, 141, 142, and 149) Hellenistic period sites. Of these, four (7, 26, 97, and 149) were major sites, three (29, 95, and 96) were large sites, six (36, 54, 59, 109, 130, and 142) were medium sites, four (31, 123, 132, and 139) were small sites, and four (99, 104, 129, and 141) were very small sites (Ibach 1987: 170, Table 3.14).[4] Glueck earlier (1935: 110-11) found Hellenistic pottery at Khirbet Meshhed, Site 238, though the Hesban Survey (Site 108) found none on the site. Besides Tell el-ᶜUmeiri itself, the ᶜUmeiri survey found five (116D, 116H, 122, 124, 126 = el-Dreijat) Hellenistic sites within its 5 km radius (Christopherson 1997b: 291-302; Christopherson et al. 1997) as well as one (number 4) random square of those visited in the 1984 season (J. Cole 1989b: 54-55, figs. 7.3 and 4) and eight (63, 66, 76, 79, 82,

83, 86, and 95) random squares of those visited during the 1989 season (Christopherson 1997a: 252; fig. 10.3; 250-90). Excavation of Rujim Selim (ᶜUmeiri Survey Site 34 = Fohrer Site D) produced Late Hellenistic sherds and a Ptolemaic coin during the 1987 season (Younker 1991b: 338; J. E. Miller 1991: 381-82; Christopherson et al. 1997). While no pottery was found there, it is possible that ᶜUmeiri Survey Site 39 (Boling 1989: 156-57, figs. 8.74-76), which was a columbarium (or dovecote), had its beginnings in the Hellenistic period in that the practice of dove breeding, common in Egypt since Dynastic times, was spread into other areas of Greek dominance beginning in Ptolemaic times (Berlin 1997: 8). Not far away, ᶜIraq el-Emir (Qaṣr el-ᶜAbd; Stratum III) and Tell ᶜIraq el-Emir (Stratum IV) were both inhabited at this time (N. Lapp 1983: 8-11; Lapp and Lapp 1993: 647-49).

The East Jordan Valley Survey located seven (185 = Tell el-Kafrein, Hesban Survey Site 96, and Glueck Site 210; 187, 191 = Tell Iktanu, Hesban Survey Site 97; 199 = Glueck Site 203; 203 = Glueck Site 218; 204 and 223) sites. Tell Nimrin, which is also in this area, is now known to have both Early and Late Hellenistic ceramics (Dornemann 1990: 155-160, figs. 2-3; 174-76, pls. 3.2, 4.1-2, 5.1).

As mentioned above, Amman (Philadelphia) was the only city to be refounded by the Ptolemies (Mitchel 1992: 31; Berlin 1997: 11). Hellenistic remains have been found at the Citadel (Zayadine 1973: 25-28; Bennett 1979b: 166, 168; Dornemann 1983: 19, 89, 90, 198, fig. 5; Zayadine, Najjar and Greene 1987: 309) and the Forum (Hadidi 1974: 80-85) as well as at Murabbaᵓat Musa (Zayadine 1981: 344) and Tell Siran (Thompson 1973a: 7). The Greater Amman Survey located 13 (54-36.3, 55-30.1, 55-35.4, 55-36.8, 55-36.10, 55-41.5, 56-30.5, 56-32.1, 57-31.1, 57-32.1 [cf. Bikai 1993: 521-22], 58-31.3, 58-34.1, and 59-33.1) Hellenistic period sites (Abu Dayyah et al. 1991: 387-93, Table 2). Other Hellenistic period sites in the Amman region include ᶜAin el-Basha (JADIS Site 2216.002), and Khirbet Umm ad-Dananir (Site 3), in the Baqᶜah Valley. Further north near the Wadi Zerqa, 11 Hellenistic period sites (12, 13, 14, 17, 19, 20, 23, 24, 25 = Glueck Site 303; 28 and 30) were located (Gordon and Villiers: 1983: 276, fig. 1; 286-87; Tables 1-2). Farther to the east, 13 (2/4, 4, 7/1, 10, 11, 14, 16, 25/1, 28, 34, 37/3, 39, and 40) more Hellenistic period sites have been found in the vicinity of er-Rumman (Gordon and Knauf 1987:

290, fig. 1; 294-97). Other sites to the north of Amman include Glueck (1939) sites 206, 223, 225, 267, 277, and 328.

To the south of Amman there were Sahab Sites 18, 37, 38, and 103 (JADIS 2.158-161; 2.171) as well as JADIS Sites 2514.007 and 2514.008, which were also inhabited at this time. Near Madaba, the site of Zabayir el-Qastal (Glueck 1934: 7; Site 55) had Hellenistic period sherds as did Khirbet ᶜAtarus (Glueck Site 180), Machaerus (Loffreda 1980: 381, 391, pl. 92.1-5; 1992: 458; Corbo and Loffreda 1981: 268, 278, figs. 35.14-18, 21, 36.1-9), the Ez-Zara Oasis (JADIS Site 2011.001) and Aroer (Olavarri 1965: 92-94; 1993: 93) farther to the south on the Wadi Mujib.

Interpretation

Since so little is known about the Hellenistic period in Transjordan it is difficult to suggest what the settlement pattern might have been like at this time. Ibach (1987: 170, Table 3.14) placed the Hesban Survey sites within various size categories (cf. n. 4). However, he qualified this by noting that the actual quantity of sherds from the Hellenistic period found on the majority of sites was rather small (1987: 168). This would suggest that even though the physical size of a site could be quite large, perhaps only a fraction of it was actually being used during this period.

Amman was probably the only site of any size at the time and would either have been a large town or small city after its refounding as Philadelphia by the Ptolemies in the Early Hellenistic period. The site of Tell Hesban seems to have been a fortress (Mitchel 1992: 38) as was Machaerus (Loffreda 1992: 458) during the Late Hellenistic period. Khirbet Umm ad-Dananir, Tell er-Rameh, Iktanu, Khirbet el ᵓAl, Tell el-ᶜUmeiri, Jalul, Khirbet ᶜAtarus, and Aroer, all sites along the various road systems, may also have functioned as fortresses at this time. Although El-Dreijat (ᶜUmeiri Survey Site 126) appears to have been a fortress during Iron II (Younker 1991b: 341), the clearing of the site to bedrock and its modification with the use of caves below it (Younker et al. 1990: 13) suggest a domestic structure of some kind during the Hellenistic period. Domestic structures with steps leading to subterranean cave complexes seem to have been fairly common at sites in both eastern and western Palestine at this time (Mitchel 1994: 99; Kloner 1997: 29). Qaṣr el-ᶜAbd at ᶜIraq el-

Emir would seem to have been a water (or pleasure) palace with a reflecting pool for the entertainment of guests (Netzer 1999: 52, 55). This, together with the structures surrounding it, appears to have been part of a large palatial estate or villa (Lapp and Lapp 1993: 649; Netzer 1999: 54-55). Beyond its defensive function, Machaerus may have also been a villa (Berlin 1997: 42). It is likely that the majority of the other sites mentioned above were small agricultural complexes like Rujim Selim (ᶜUmeiri Survey Site 34; cf. Younker 1991b: 338-39) at this time.

Summary

Tell Hesban appears to have served as a fortress during the Late Hellenistic period, first under the Seleucids and then the Hasmonaeans. In the region, the Hellenistic period evidence suggests only one major town site (Philadelphia-Amman), an occasional villa, a number of possible fortresses, and numerous agricultural complexes. As in all periods, there was no doubt a mixture of nomadic and sedentary activities. The Hellenistic evidence, however, especially toward the end of the period, appears to reflect the transition to a more settled economy. The local population was no doubt mixed, consisting of Tobiad-Ammonites, and Nabataeans, and by the tail end of the period with many Jews. It is possible that the slight increase in sedentary activity in the region was a result of the relative stability under Hasmonaean rule.

Notes

[1]As noted above (chapter 6), Bienkowski (1995: 88) has recently suggested that the primary function of slingstones was as grinding stones, pestles, and pounders. Homès-Fredericq (1992: 198) sees them as having different war-time and peace-time functions. Though this is probably closer to reality, one should be cautious about assigning a military function to these objects when they are not included within an obvious destruction layer with other military-related objects.

[2]Actually they most likely completed a process begun naturally by weathering during the gap in occupation of the tell between Strata 16 and 15, at which time a significant amount of debris would have already washed into it (cf. the discussion on Locus B.1:119=143=B.2:137 in chapter 6).

[3]Sauer (1994: 250) suggests that the so-called Early Hellenistic period gap may actually be a lack of ceramic knowledge.

[4]For Ibach's definition of the various sized sites, cf. chapter 5, n. 7. On the site hierarchy used here, cf. chapter 5, n. 8.

Chapter Eight

CONCLUSIONS

Conclusions

Summary of the Research

Certain limiting factors have made the analysis of the Iron Age stratigraphy at Tell Hesban a challenge. First, the lateral exposure of the archaeological remains at the site has been primarily confined to the summit and the southern and western shelves. More than this, later scraping and occupational activities have limited the remnants of the earliest occupational layers to bedrock features and dump and fill layers for the most part. Nevertheless, it has still been possible to isolate six distinct strata.

The exact temporal parameters of these strata have been arrived at by a comparison of representative samples of the ceramic remains, which were gathered as the tell was excavated, with those of the wider region, and where available, with historical sources and placed within an absolute chronological framework. Wherever possible, evidence such as distinctive ceramics, ostraca, and seals were also taken into account in order to isolate specific ethnic material cultures.

Stratum 21

Very little exists from the first recognizable settlement that was built on Tell Hesban. The extant remains consist of ceramic material found within dump layers on the western side of the mound. Nevertheless, this evidence, when compared with that of some other tells in the immediate region as well as sites in the Central Hill Country of Cisjordan, suggests that a small village of Reubenites existed on the tell during the Late Bronze Age/Iron Age I transition.

Stratum 20

Tell Hesban appears to have been a large fortified village during this stratum. Though the tell was naturally defensible on three sides because of its steep sides and deep wadis, the occupants of this early settlement dug a trench in bedrock on the weak southern side of the mound. This feature appears to have functioned as a dry moat. Large amounts of stone within the destruction debris found in the trench suggest the possibility that a fortification wall may also have originally stood above it. The ceramic evidence would again suggest that the village was inhabited by Reubenites.

Stratum 19

Stratum 20 seems to have been destroyed. The moat went out of use, apparently leaving the now smaller village without fortifications. A wall was built across the trench possibly as part of a new reservoir. The little that is available of the remains of Stratum 19 would suggest that its character and ethnic makeup remained pretty much the same as the previous settlement.

The villages of Strata 21 through 19 appear to have relied upon a medium intensity food production regime, which consisted of a mixed agro-pastoralism, heavily dependent on cereal cultivation and the products from sheep and goats. Cottage industries seemed to have played a major role among the economic activities.

Stratum 18

The Reubenite village of Stratum 19 appears to have grown into a small town during Stratum 18 under the auspices of the kingdom of Solomon. A large reservoir was built at this time. The sophistication of the ashlar masonry of the extant wall of this feature suggests that it was built under royal patronage. There is also evidence for a basement structure of a house dug into the upper layers of the bedrock trench. It is possible that the town had a peripheral belt of houses surrounding it that functioned as a kind of a fortification during this stratum.

The settlement at this time appears to have had a high intensity food production regime. Though still producing large amounts of grain and keeping herd animals, it was also in the process of extending its repertoire into olive, fruit, and wine production. Though still basically a subsistence-oriented economy, evidence of mercantile activities and a fairly wide trade network indicate the beginnings of a market-oriented economy. Its position at the crossroads of the main north-south highway and the east-west trunk road from Cisjordan allowed it to dominate the caravan traffic along these roads.

Stratum 17

Iron Age IIB Hesban appears to have been rather sparsely inhabited and would seem to have been a Moabite squatter settlement as indicated by its ceramic makeup. I have suggested that an early Moabite occupation toward the end of the tenth century B.C. was expanded (slightly) by either Mesha or still later Moabites. They appear to have extended their territory north to Hesban and made use of its dominating position at the crossroads of the major highways to gather tolls. I have further suggested that they cleaned out and replastered the reservoir and used it for its capacity to hold large amounts of water. On the basis of the faunal remains, the occupants of the tell at this time seem to have been mainly pastoralists. Thus, this period appears to have been one of abatement, when the inhabitants of the site returned to range-tied pastoralism and a low to medium intensity food regime.

Stratum 16

Probably in the beginning of the seventh century B.C., in the Iron IIC/Persian period, Tell Hesban became Ammonite, under the dominance of the Assyrians and then later the Babylonians and Persians. The site once again grew to the size of a small town extending even beyond the size of the Stratum 18 settlement, as an offset-inset wall was built on the western shelf. Water needs were taken care of by the addition of several new feeder channels to the reservoir. Stratum 16 was the most prosperous of the Iron Age settlements on the tell. It moved to a market-oriented economy heavily involved in wine production. The latter is indicated, besides evidence from the seeds, by a number of silos, which appear to have been used for wine storage. Evidence, including weights, jewelry, ostraca, and seals, indicates mercantile activities and a fair-

ly wide trade network. The location of the site on the crossroads of the main north-south highway and the east-west trunk road from Cisjordan would seem to have helped the site, as at earlier times, to continue to dominate the caravan traffic which traveled through the region. Seed and faunal evidence indicate a return to a high intensity food production regime.

Regional Context

In terms of settlement pattern in the region, in Iron Age I it appears that there were a few small-medium towns, located either on the Madaba Plains, within the bread basket of the region, or along the road systems, as well as a few fortresses guarding the main water sources and numerous small villages, farmsteads, and watchtowers. The majority of the sites were located on the highland plateau and involved in land-tied cereal production, while a smaller number were located in the wadis, and gradually, toward the end of the period, began planting fruit and olive trees.

As at Tell Hesban itself, the region in Iron Age IIB seems to have gone through a period of abatement with a partial return to range-tied pastoralism. It is only during the Iron IIC/Persian period, as it came under the domination of the Ammonites with the return of a stable political system under foreign vassalage to Assyria and later to Babylonia and Persia, that it once again began to invest in crops and to expend labor on ploughing and planting. Most of the Iron Age I towns, located within the bread basket area and along the road systems, grew to be large towns at this time. There was a major increase in settlements of all sizes, but especially numerous were small villages and farmsteads as well as a large number of towers, which evidently served agricultural as well as watchtower functions. Again, the majority of the sites were located on the highland plateau, but there was also a considerable growth in the number of sites located in the wadis, as population pressures necessitated a wider diversity of subsistence strategies. There was thus an increase in the use of agricultural terraces, which had already begun toward the end of Iron Age I.

Peripheral Strata

To round out the picture of the Iron Age, we also looked at the tell and the surrounding region in the preceding (Late Bronze Age) and following

(Hellenistic) periods. While there is evidence during the former of a few towns and a number of smaller sites, tombs, and occasional cultic places, there is no evidence that Tell Hesban was occupied during this time other than a few Late Bronze II/Iron Age IA transitional ceramic forms. While there was a mixture of nomadic and sedentary activity, the Late Bronze Age population of this part of Transjordan was more on the pastoral end of the nomadic-sedentary continuum.

Tell Hesban appears to have been first a Seleucid and then later a Hasmonaean fortress during the Late Hellenistic period. As in the Late Bronze Age, the regional picture suggests that it was sparsely populated, at least in terms of sedentary sites. At this time there is evidence in the region for only the town of Philadelphia-Amman, a palatial estate at ᶜIraq el-Emir, an occasional villa, a few fortresses, and numerous agricultural complexes.

Excavation Methodology

In terms of methodology (chapter 2), it was found that the Heshbon Expedition began with a traditional biblical archaeology approach, which at the time (the late 1960s) was considered appropriate for the potential contribution that a site could make to biblical history. Nevertheless, the Expedition began experimenting already in the first season with an interdisciplinary approach, which utilized various specialists to supplement the data gained from the excavation process. Its emergence into the "new" or processual archaeology of the 1970s was therefore a natural consequence. Later, with the final publication in view, the excavators were forced to think about how to integrate the vast amount of data into an interrelated whole. This led to the computerization of the Hesban database and the eventual development of the food systems concept and the related processes of sedentarization and nomadization, which have continued to guide the research design of the succeeding Madaba Plains Project.

Further Study

One unresolved problem is that of whether or not Tell Hesban is to be equated with biblical Heshbon. For the sake of dealing with historical questions related to the occupation of the site during the Iron Age, that equation was assumed. Nevertheless, there is no definitive evidence that that is the case. Sauer's (1994: 241-44) redating of the reservoir to the end of Stratum 18 in Iron Age IC (=IIA), during the time of Solomon, makes it possible that it could be one of the pools, located by the gate of Bath-rabbim, referred to in Song of Solomon 7:4 (7:5 Heb). Although no gate has been found at Tell Hesban, the logical place for one would be near the reservoir on the gentle southern slope. However, there remains the question of whether the excavated structure fits the definition of what the author of the passage had in mind. For one thing, the reference is in the plural (cf. Eccl 2:6) and only one reservoir was found. This of course does not negate the possibility that there could be another as yet unlocated reservoir on the mound. Be that as it may, as Herr (1979a: 21; 1997d: 150; 1999b: 227) has noted, the reservoir was capable of holding perhaps five times the amount of water that could have potentially run into it during a normal rainy season and that this was well beyond the needs of the inhabitants of the site. If this observation, which assumes the reservoir did not serve caravan traffic as well, is accurate the likelihood of the existence of a second such structure is minimal. There is also the possibility that the pools were not on the tell proper, but rather were located along the Wadi Hesban (Conder 1882: 8; 1892: 142, cf. Geraty 1972: 34; Vyhmeister 1989b: 69-70).

In addition, the lack of evidence for settlement on the mound during the Late Bronze Age, during the time of Sihon the Amorite, though potentially explainable by a different understanding of the occupation (chapter 4) or its location on a different site at the time (chapter 2), still makes the Tell Hesban/Heshbon equation a problematic one. An in-depth discussion of this problem is beyond the scope of research that was intended in the present study. However, the implications of the present research open up some potentially fruitful possibilities for future discussions of this problem.

Appendix A

ABBREVIATED LOCUS LIST
FOR STRATA 21-16

Appendix A

Abbreviated Locus List for Strata 21-16

This appendix presents the Iron Age loci in an abbreviated and modified format from the comprehensive master locus list found in the archives of the Heshbon Expedition. The majority of these loci were originally assigned to their present position (Stratum and Stage) by Larry G. Herr (LGH), with a small number being assigned by Larry A. Mitchel (LAM). Their arrangement is followed here except where otherwise indicated. Those loci that differ from their original assignment are explained more fully in chapters 5 and 6.

Most of the loci of Stratum 21 were originally assigned by LGH to Stratum 20 = Herr's Stratum 5 (1979a: 9) except loci C.1:142, 143, and 144 which were earlier assigned by him to Stratum 19 = Herr's Stratum 4 (1979a: 15). In addition, there are loci C.2:54, and 55, which were unassigned earlier as well as C.2:92, 93, 94, and 96, which were originally assigned to Stratum 17. However, these were later reassigned to Stratum 5 (Herr 1979a: 9). All the loci of Stratum 21 are assigned to their current positions by the present author on the basis of the implications of Sauer and Herr forthcoming.

All of the loci of Stratum 20 were originally assigned by LGH and LAM (D.4:154) to Stratum 20 = Herr's Stratum 5 (1979a: 5-7, 9) except loci D.1:63, 63G, 63H, 101, and 102 which were earlier assigned by LGH to Stratum 19 = Herr's Stratum 4 (1979a: 14). The current configuration of this Stratum is due however to the implications of Sauer and Herr forthcoming.

Locus B.2:112, which is the only one assigned to Stratum 19, was originally assigned by LGH to Stratum 19 = Herr's Stratum 4 (1979a: 13), but is in its current position because of the implications of Sauer and Herr forthcoming.

Most of the loci that are currently found in Stratum 18, Stage C were originally assigned to Stratum 17 and in one case (C.5:228) Stratum 11 by LGH and LAM respectively. These loci have been reassigned by the present author on the basis of the implications of Sauer (1994: 241-44) and remarks from the original locus sheets (C.5:228). In addition, loci D.4:65, 66, 73, 75, and 136 were originally assigned by LGH to Stratum 19 = Herr's Stratum 4 (1979a: 12-13), but have been assigned to their current positions due to the implications of Sauer and Herr forthcoming.

All the loci of Stratum 18, Stage B remain as originally assigned by LGH except Loci D.4:63, 74, 81, and 82 which have been reassigned to their current positions due to the implications of Sauer and Herr forthcoming. In addition, Locus C.5:227B was assigned by LAM to Stratum 14, but has been reassigned to its current position on the basis of the present authors' understanding of its function. Locus D.4:115 of Stratum 18, Stage A was originally assigned by LGH to Stratum 20 = Herr's Stratum 5 (1979a: 9), but has been reassigned to its current position on the basis of the implications of Sauer and Herr forthcoming.

All of the loci of Stratum 17 were originally assigned by LGH to their present positions except C.2:95, 97, and C.5:130, which were unassigned at the time and C.5:173, which was originally thought to belong to Stratum 18. These were later reassigned by him to their current positions (Herr 1979a: 19). Loci C.1:118, and 123B, originally thought to belong to Strata 16, and 18 respectively, have been reassigned to their current positions by the author on the basis of the implications of Sauer and Herr forthcoming.

The loci of Stratum 16 were assigned by LGH and LAM (B2:245) except B.1:144A; B.4:234, 265, 271; C.3:26A; 34; C.5:86, 105, 107, 109, 110, 112, 114, 117, 119, 129, 131, 168, 170, 178, 179, and C.7:44A, which have been reassigned by the present author on the basis of his present understanding of the stratigraphy. Loci C.7:74, and 97 have been repositioned within this stratum for the same reason.

Stratum 15, Stage C (Stratum 16 fill) loci were originally assigned by LGH except B.1:127, which he added later (Herr 1979a: Table 3).

Abbreviations

The following abbreviations have been used in this appendix:

Conf	Confidence	ER	Early Roman
Asn	Assignment	LR	Late Roman
Lat	Latest	Byz	Byzantine
Earl	Earliest	Abbd	Abbasid
Cert	Certain	AM	Ayyubid/Mamluk
Unct	Uncertain		
Prob	Probable	Bedrtrn	Bedrock Trench
Poss	Possible	Cissilt	Cistern Silt
		Cobsurf	Cobble Surface
I1	Iron I	Founda	Foundation
I2	Iron II	Ftrench	Foundation Trench
I2/P	Iron II/Persian	Huwlay	Huwwar Layer
Hel	Hellenistic	Plaslay	Plaster Layer
		Plaslin	Plaster Lining
		Reservr	Reservoir
		Retwall	Retaining Wall
		Soillay	Soil Layer
		Soilsur	Soil Surface

Locus	Conf	Asn	Lat.	Earl.	Stratification	Function	Description
Stratum 21 **Stage B**							
C.1:95	Prob	I1	I2/P	I1	Equals: 144?, C.2:54; Under: 82; Over: 97; Cut by: 90	Dump	Soil layer on slopes below Settlement
C.1:96B	Prob	I1	I1	I1	Equals: 143?: Under: 83. 95; Over 94; Cut by 51	Dump	Soil layer on slopes below Settlement
C.1:97	Cert.	I1	I1	I1	Equals: 142?, C.2:55, 99; Under: 95; Over: 98; Cut by: 90	Dump	Soil layer on slopes below Settlement
C.1:98	Cert.	I1	I1	I1	Equals: 141?, C.2:92, 93; Under: 97; Over: 99; Cut by: 90	Dump	Soil layer on slopes below Settlement
C.1:99	Cert.	I1	I1	I1	Equals: 126? C.2:94, 96, 98, 99; Under: 90; Over: 100; Cut by: 90	Dump	Soil layer on slopes below Settlement
C.1:142	Cert.	I1	I1A	I1A	Under: 141; Over: 143	Dump	Soil layer on slope below Settlement
C.1:143	Cert.	I1	I1A	I1A	Under: 142; Over: 144	Dump	Soil layer on slope below Settlement
C.1:144	Cert.	I1	Iron	Iron	Under: 143; Over: Bedrock	Dump	Soil layer on slope below Settlement
C.2:54	Unct	I1	A/M	I1	Equals: C.1:95	Cleanup	Cleanup Locus
C.2:55	Unct	I1	A/M	I1	Equals: C.1:97	Cleanup	Cleanup Locus
C.2:92	Poss	I1	I1	I1	Equals: 73?, 86?, C.1:98; Under: 55; Over: 93; Cut by: 52	Dump	Soil layer on slope below Settlement
C.2:93	Poss	I1	Hel?	I1	Equals: 73?, 86?, C.1:98; Under: 92; Over: 94; Cut by: 52	Dump	Soil layer on slope below Settlement
C.2:94	Poss.	I1	I2	I1	Equals: 73?, 86?, C.1: 99; Under: 93; Over: 96; Cut by: 52	Dump	Soil layer on slope below Settlement
C.2:96	Poss	I1	I2	I1	Equals: C.1:99; Under: 94; Over: 98; Cut by: 52	Dump	Soil layer on slope below Settlement
C.2:98	Prob	I1	I1	I1	Equals: C.1:99; Under: 96; Over: 99; Cut by: 52	Dump	Soil layer on slope below Settlement
C.2:99	Prob	I1	Hel?	I1	Equals: C.1:99; Under: 98; Over: Bedrock; Cut by: 52	Dump	Soil layer on slope below Settlement
Stratum 20 **Stage C**							
B.2:114A	Cert	I1	-	-	Equals: B.3:86, D.4:67; Under 31; Cut by: 114E	Bedrock	S face of Bedrock Trench
B.2:116	Cert	I1	-	-	Equals: B.3:84=85=90, D.4:25; Under 31=33	Bedrock	N face of Bedrock Trench

Locus	Reliability				Relationships	Type	Description
B.3:84	Cert	II	--		Equals: B.3:85; B.2:116, D.4:25; Over 90	Bedrock	N face of Bedrock Trench
B.3:85	Cert	II	--		Equals: B.3:84; B.2:116, D.4:25; Over 90	Bedrock	N face of Bedrock Trench
B.3:86	Cert	II	--		Equals: B.2:114A, D.4:67	Bedrock	S face of Bedrock Trench
B.3:90	Cert	II	--		Under: 84=85	Bedrock	N face of Bedrock Trench
B.3:98	Cert	II	--		Equals: D.4:154; Under: 97; Seals Against: 86, 90	Bedrm	Bottom of Bedrock Trench
D.1:63	Prob	II	--		Under: 66; Sealed by: 66	Cistern	Plastered Cistern
D.1:63H	Prob	II	--		Equals: 102; Under: 63G, 101	Plaslin	Plaster lining of Cistern
D.1:102	Prob	II	--		Equals: 63H	Plaslin	--
D.4:25	Cert	II	--		Equals: B.3:84=85, 90, B.2:116; Under: 19=21	Bedrock	N face of Bedrock Trench
D.4:67	Cert	II	--		Equals: B.3:86. B.2:114A; Cut by 68	Bedrock	S face of Bedrock Trench
D.4:154	Prob	II	--		Equals: B.3:98	Bedrock	Bedrock Trench along S Balk

Stage B

Locus	Reliability				Relationships	Type	Description
D.1:63G	Prob	II	Hel?		Equals: 101; Under: 63F; Over: 63H	Cissilt	Water laid Soil Layer on bottom of Cistern 63
D.1:101	Prob	II	II		Equals: 63G	Cissilt	--

Stage A

Locus	Reliability				Relationships	Type	Description
B.3:74	Cert	II	IIB	IIA	Under: 73; Over:75; Seals Against: 84=85, 86	Fill	Soil layer in Bedrock Trench Fill
B.3:75	Cert.	II	Hel	IIA	Under: 74; Over: 77; Seals Against: 84=85, 86	Fill	Soil layer in Bedrock Trench Fill
B.3:76	Cert.	II	--	--	Under: 74; Over: 77; Seals Against: 84=85, 86	Fill	Soil layer in Bedrock Trench Fill
B.3:77	Cert.	II	Hel	II	Under: 75, 76; Over: 81, 82; Seals Against: 84=85, 86	Fill	Soil layer in Bedrock Trench Fill
B.3:78	Cert.	II	IIB	IIA	Under: 48; Over: 81?; Seals Against: 84=85, 86	Fill	Rock Tumble in Bedrock Trench Fill
B.3:80	Cert.	II	IIB	IIA	Equals: B.2:112?-unlikely; Under: 77; Over: 77?; Seals Against: 84=85, 86	Fill	Rock Tumble in Bedrock Trench Fill
B.3:81	Cert.	II	IIB	IIA	Under: 77; Over: 82; Seals Against: 84=85, 86	Fill	Soil layer in Bedrock Trench Fill
B.3:82	Cert.	II	IIB	IIA	Under: 81; Over: 83; Seals Against: 84=85, 86	Fill	Soil layer in Bedrock Trench Fill

Locus							
B.3:83	Cert.	II	IIB	IIA	Under: 81, 82; Over: 91; Seals Against: 84=85, 86	Fill	Soil layer in Bedrock Trench Fill
B.3:89	Cert.	II	IIB	IIA	Seals Against: 84	Fill	Soil layer in Bedrock Trench Fill
B.3:91	Cert.	II	IIB	IIA	Under: 83; Over: 92; Seals Against: 86, 90	Fill	Soil layer in Bedrock Trench Fill
B.3:92	Cert.	II	IIB	IIA	Equals: D.4:144?; Under: 91; Over: 93; Seals Against: 86, 90	Fill	Soil layer in Bedrock Trench Fill
B.3:93	Cert.	II	IIB	IIA	Equals: D.4:144?; Under: 92; Over: 94; Seals Against: 86, 90	Fill	Soil layer in Bedrock Trench Fill
B.3:94	Cert.	II	IIB	IIA	Equals: D.4:145-151; Under: 93; Over: 95; Seals Against: 86, 90	Fill	Soil layer in Bedrock Trench Fill
B.3:95	Cert.	II	IIB	IIA	Equals: D.4:145-151; Under: 94; Over: 96; Seals Against: 86, 90	Fill	Soil layer in Bedrock Trench Fill
B.3:96	Cert.	II	IIB	IIA	Equals: D.4:152?; Under: 95; Over: 97; Seals Against: 86, 90	Fill	Soil layer in Bedrock Trench Fill
B.3:97	Cert.	II	IIB	IIA	Under: 96; Over: 98; Seals Against: 86, 90	Fill	Soil layer in Bedrock Trench Fill
B.3:99	Cert.	II	IIB	IIA	Seals against :90	Fill	Soil or plaster layer in Trench fill; possibly water laid
D.4:111	Prob.	II	II	II	Under: 99; Over: Bedrock	Soillay	Soil layer on Bedrock
D.4:124	Cert.	II	IIB	IIA	Under: 115; Over: 125; Seals Against: 25; Cut by: 117, 122	Fill	Soil layer in Bedrock Trench Fill
D.4:125	Cert.	II	IIB	IIA	Under: 124; Over: 126; Seals Against: 25; Cut by: 117, 122	Fill	Soil layer in Bedrock Trench Fill
D.4:126	Cert.	II	ER	IIA	Under: 125; Over: 128; Seals Against: 25; Cut by: 117, 122	Fill	Soil layer in Bedrock Trench Fill
D.4:128	Cert.	II	IIB	IIA	Under: 126; Over: 129; Seals Against: 25; Cut by: 117	Fill	Soil layer in Bedrock Trench Fill
D.4:129	Cert.	II	IIB	IIA	Under: 126, 128; Over: 130; Seals Against: 25; Cut by: 117, 122	Fill	Soil layer in Bedrock Trench Fill
D.4:130	Cert.	II	IIB	IIA	Under: 129; Over: 131; Seals Against: 25; Cut by: 117, 122	Fill	Soil layer in Bedrock Trench Fill
D.4:131	Cert.	II	IIB	IIA	Under: 122, 130; Over: 133; Seals Against: 25; Cut by: 117	Fill	Soil layer in Bedrock Trench Fill
D.4:132	Cert.	II	IIB	IIA	Equals: 126? 129-131?; Under: 120, 121; Over: 134; Seals Against: 25; Cut by: 122, 136	Fill	Soil layer in Bedrock Trench Fill
D.4:133	Cert.	II	IIB	IIA	Equals: 133, 134; Under: 131; Over: 137; Seals Against: 25; Cut by: 117	Fill	Soil layer in Bedrock Trench Fill
D.4:134	Cert.	II	IIB	IIA	Equals: 133, 135; Under: 132; Over: 138; Seals Against: 25; Cut by: 136	Fill	Soil layer in Bedrock Trench Fill
D.4:135	Cert.	II	LR	IIA	Equals: 133, 134; Under: 131; Over: 137; Seals Against: 25; Cut by: 117	Fill	Soil layer in Bedrock Trench Fill
D.4:137	Cert.	II	IIB	IIA	Under: 133=134=135; Over: 138; Seals Against: 25; Cut by: 117	Fill	Soil layer in Bedrock Trench Fill
D.4:138	Cert.	II	Hel	IIA	Under: 134, 137; Over: 139; Seals Against: 25; Cut by: 117	Fill	Soil layer in Bedrock Trench Fill
D.4:139	Cert.	II	Hel?	IIA	Under: 138; Over: 140; Seals Against: 25; Cut by: 117	Fill	Soil layer in Bedrock Trench Fill
D.4:140	Cert.	II	IIB	IIA	Under: 139; Over: 141; Seals Against: 25; Cut by: 117	Fill	Soil layer in Bedrock Trench Fill

Locus							
D.4:141	Cert.	11	11B	11A	Under: 140; Over: 142; Seals Against: 25; Cut by: 117	Fill	Soil layer in Bedrock Trench Fill
D.4:142	Cert.	11	11B	11A	Under: 141; Over: 143; Seals Against: 25; Cut by: 117	Fill	Soil layer in Bedrock Trench Fill
D.4:143	Cert.	11	11A	11A	Under: 142; Over: 144; Seals Against: 25; Cut by: 117	Fill	Soil layer in Bedrock Trench Fill
D.4:144	Cert.	11	11B	11A	Equals: B.3:92; Under: 143; Over: 145; Seals Against: 25	Fill	Soil layer in Bedrock Trench Fill
D.4:145	Cert.	11	11B	11A	Under: 144; Over: 146; Seals Against 25	Fill	Soil layer in Bedrock Trench Fill
D.4:146	Cert.	11	11A	11A	Under: 145; Over: 147; Seals Against 25	Fill	Soil layer in Bedrock Trench Fill
D.4:147	Cert.	11	11A	11A	Under: 146; Over: 148; Seals Against 25	Fill	Soil layer in Bedrock Trench Fill
D.4:148	Cert.	11	11A	11A	Under: 147; Over: 149; Seals Against 25	Fill	Soil layer in Bedrock Trench Fill
D.4:149	Cert	11	11A	11A	Under: 148; Over: 150; Seals Against 25	Fill	Soil layer in Bedrock Trench Fill
D.4:150	Cert.	11	11A	11A	Under: 149; Over: 151; Seals Against 25	Fill	Soil layer in Bedrock Trench Fill
D.4:151	Cert.	11	ER	11A	Under: 150; Over: 152; Seals Against 25	Fill	Soil layer in Bedrock Trench Fill
D.4:152	Cert.	11	11A	11A	Equals: B.3:96; Under: 151; Over Bedrock; Seals Against 25	Fill	Soil layer in Bedrock Trench Fill

Stratum 19
Stage C

Locus							
B.2:112	Prob	11	11		Under: 31, Seals Against: 114A, Sealed By: 31; Cut by 84?	Founda	Foundation Wall in Iron 1 Trench

Stratum 18
Stage C

Locus							
B.1:147	Poss	11	i	-	Equals: 151; Under: 146=150; Over 148=152	Plaslin	Plaster Lining of Reservoir
B.1:148	Poss	11	i	-	Equals: 152; Under 147=151	Bedrock	Bedrock floor of Reservoir
B.1:151	Poss	11	ii	-	Equals: 147; Under 146=150; Over 148=152	Plaslin	Plaster Lining of Reservoir
B.1:152	Poss	11	-	-	Equals: 148; Under 147=151	Bedrock	Bedrock floor of Reservoir
B.2:84	Poss	11	Hel	11	Equals: 115; Under: 83; Seals Against: 112, 114A; Sealed by: 113; Cuts: 112?	Retwall	Side Wall of Reservoir

Locus	Cert				Relationships	Type	Description
B.2:92	Poss	I1	I2/P	I2/P	Seals Against: 84=115; Sealed by: Reservoir Fill	Plaslin	Plaster Lining of Reservoir
B.2:113C	Poss	I1	--	--	Equals: B.4:190C; Under: 113B; Over: 84; 114	Plaslin	Plaster Lining of Reservoir
B.2:114B	Poss	I1	--	--	Equals: B.1:148, 152; Under: 113C; Cuts: Iron I Bedrock Trench	Bedrock	Bedrock E face of Reservoir
B.2:115	Poss	I1	--	--	Equals: 84	Retwall	Side Wall of Reservoir
B.4:168	Poss	I1	--	--	Under: 167	Channel	3-pronged Bedrock channel feeding Reservoir
B.4:190C	Poss	I1	--	--	Equals: B.2:113C; Under: 190B; Over: Bedrock	Plaslin	Plaster Lining on Reservoir E face
B.4:191	Poss	I1	--	--	Equals: 192, B.2:114B; Cut by: 115? 120? 127?	Bedrock	Bedrock E face of Reservoir
B.4:192	Poss	I1	--	--	Equals: 191, 195, B.2:114B; Under: 161; Cut by: 120?	Bedrock	Bedrock E face of Reservoir
B.4:193	Unct	I1	--	--	Equals: 192, 195, before earthquake; Cut by: 168	Bedrock	Bedrock Slab in SE Corner
B.4:194	Poss	I1	--	--	Equals: part of B.2:114B; Cut by: 74, 99, 101, 115? 120? 127?	Bedrock	Bedrock Cut just E of Reservoir Lip
B.4:195	Poss	I1	--	--	Equals: 191, 192, B.2:114B; Cut by: 275	Bedrock	Bedrock E face of Reservoir and cut edge of channel
B.4:246	Unct	I1	--	--	Equals: 191, 192; Under: 237	Bedrock	Collapsed Bedrock, once part of 194
B.4:250	Unct	I1	--	--	Equals: 168	Channel	--
B.4:277	Poss	I1	--	--	Equals: 191, 192, 195, 246; Seals against: 282	Bedrock	Bedrock S face of Reservoir
C.5:228	Poss	I1	--	--	Under: 212; Over: Bedrock	Cistern	Cistern S of Wall 200, E of Wall 90, Unexcavated
D.4:65	Prob	I1	--	--	Under: 57; Sealed Against by: 63, 74, 75; Abuts: 67, 73	Wall	E Wall of subterranean room
D.4:66	Prob	I1	--	--	Under: 57; Cuts: 132, 134, 138?; Sealed Against by: 63, 74, 75	Wall	W Wall of subterranean room
D.4:73	Prob	I1	--	--	Under: part of 25; Seals Against: 65, 66; Sealed Against by: 63, 74, 75; Abuts: 65, 66	Wall	N Wall of subterranean room
D.4:75	Prob	I1	--	--	Under: 74; Over: 81; Seals Over: 81; Seals Against: 65, 66, 67, 73	Cobsurf	Cobble Surface in subterranean room
D.4:136	Prob	I1	He!?	I1A	Under: 121; Seals Against: 66; Sealed by: 121; Cuts: 132, 134, 138	FTrench	Foundation Trench for Wall 66

Stage B

Locus	Cert				Relationships	Type	Description
C.1:124	Cert	I1	I1B	I1A	Under: 123B, 127; Over: 131, 132; Cut by: 51	Dump	Soil layer on slope below Settlement
C.1:126	Cert	I1	I1B	I1A	Under: 127; Over: 124; Cut by: 51	Dump	Soil layer on slope below Settlement

C.1:127	Cert	II	IIB	IIB	Under: 123B; Over: 126, 130	Dump	Soil layer on slope below Settlement
C.1:128	Cert	II	IIB	IIA	Under: 126; Over: 131	Dump	Soil layer on slope below Settlement
C.1:129	Cert	II	--	--	Under: 126; Over: 131	Dump	Soil layer on slope below Settlement
C.1:130	Cert	II	IIB	IIB	Under: 127; Over: 126	Dump	Soil layer on slope below Settlement
C.1:131	Cert	II	IIB	IIA	Under: 126, 128, 129, 130; Over: 134; Cut by: 51	Dump	Soil layer on slope below Settlement
C.1:132	Cert	II	IIB	IIA	Equals: 124, C.5:1947; Under: 127; Over: 131; Cut by: 51	Dump	Soil layer on slope below Settlement
C.1:133	Cert	II	IIB	IIA	Under: 130, 131; Over: 136	Dump	Soil layer on slope below Settlement
C.1:134	Cert	II	IIA	IIA	Under: 131; Over: 123B, 135, 136	Dump	Soil layer on slope below Settlement
C.1:135	Cert	II	IIA	IIA	Under: 134; Over: 133; Cut by: 51	Dump	Soil layer on slope below Settlement
C.1:136	Cert	II	IIB	IIA	Under: 133; Over: 137; Cut by: 51	Dump	Soil layer on slope below Settlement
C.1:137	Cert	II	IIB	IIA	Under: 136; Over: 138; Cut by: 51	Dump	Soil layer on slope below Settlement
C.1:138	Cert	II	IIB	IIA	Under: 137; Over: 139	Dump	Soil layer on slope below Settlement
C.1:139	Cert	II	IIB	IIA	Under: 138; Over: 140; Cut by: 51	Dump	Soil layer on slope below Settlement
C.1:140	Cert	II	IIB	IIA	Under: 139; Over: 141	Dump	Soil layer on slope below Settlement
C.1:141	Cert	II	IIB	IIA	Under: 140; Over: 142	Dump	Soil layer on slope below Settlement
C.5:171	Prob	II	IIB	IIB	Under: 163; Over: 172	Dump	Soil layer on slope below Settlement
C.5:172	Prob	II	IIB	IIA	Under: 163, 171; Over: 182; Cut by: 62B	Dump	Soil layer on slope below Settlement
C.5:182	Cert	II	IIB	IIA	Under: 172; Over: 183; Cut by: 62B	Dump	Soil layer on slope below Settlement
C.5:183	Cert	II	IIB	IIA	Under: 182; Over: 194; Cut by: 136	Dump	Soil layer on slope below Settlement
C.5:193	Prob	II	IIC	IIB	Under: 192; Over: 196, 205, 206; Cut by: 82	Dump	Soil layer on slope below Settlement
C.5:194	Cert	II	IIC	IIA	Equals: C.1:132? Under: 183; Over: Unexcavated; Cut by: 136	Dump	Soil layer on slope below Settlement
C.5:196	Prob	I2	I2A	IIB	Under: 193, 206; Over: 218; Cut by: 82	Dump	Soil layer on slope below Settlement
C.5:205	Prob	I1/2	I2	II	Under: 193; Over: 206	Dump	Soil layer on slope below Settlement
C.5:206	Prob	I1/2	I2A	IIB	Under: 193, 205; Over: 196, 218; Cut by: 82	Dump	Soil layer on slope below Settlement
C.5:218	Prob	I1/2	I2A	IIB	Under: 196; Over: Unexcavated; Cut by: 82	Dump	Soil layer on slope below Settlement
C.5:227B	Poss	I1/2	ER3	IIA	Under: 225, 226; Over: Bedrock	Soillay	Soil layer, Series of arbitrary peels--note pails 540-543

Locus					Relationships	Type	Description
D.4:63	Prob	I1	Hel?	LB?	Under: 62; Over: 74; Seals Against: 65, 66, 73	Soillay	Soil layer in subterranean room
D.4:74	Prob	I1	Hel?	II	Under: 63; Over: 75; Seals Over: 75; Seals Against: 65, 66, 67, 73	Soilsur	Soil layer above cobbled surface in subterranean room
D.4:81	Prob	I1	IIC	IIA	Under: 75; Over: 82; Seals Against: 66, 73	Fill	Soil layer in Bedrock Trench Fill
D.4:82	Prob	I1	IIC	IIA	Under: 81; Over: Unexcavated; Seals Against 66, 73	Fill	Soil layer in Bedrock Trench Fill

Stage A

D.4:115	Cert.	II	IIC	IIA	Under: 107; Over: 124; Seals Against: 25; Cut by: 122	Fill	Soil layer in Bedrock Trench Fill

Stratum 17
Stage C

B.1:146	Poss	I2	--	--	Equals: 150; Under: 145; Over: 147	Plaslin	Plaster Lining in Reservoir
B.1:150	Poss	I2	Iron	Iron	Equals: 146; Under: 149; Over: 152	Plaslin	Plaster Lining in Reservoir
B.2:113B	Poss	I2	--	--	Equals: B.4:190B; Under: 113A; Over: 113C	Plaslin	Plaster Lining in Reservoir E face
B.4:190B	Poss	I2	--	--	Equals: B.2:113B; Under: 190A; Over: 190C	Plaslin	Plaster Lining in Reservoir E face
B.4:275A	Poss	I2	--	--	Cuts: 194, 195, 246	Channel	Bedrock Channel for Reservoir
B.4:275B	Poss	I2	--	--	Cuts: 194, 195, 246	Channel	Bedrock Channel for Reservoir
B.4:275C	Poss	I2	--	--	Cuts: 194, 195, 246	Channel	Bedrock Channel for Reservoir

Stage B

C.1:118	Prob	I2	I2	I1	Under: 105; Over: 123; Cut by: 51	Dump	Soil layer on slope below Settlement
C.1:123B	Prob	I2	I2B	IIA	Under: 118; Over 124, 127; Cut by: 51	Dump	Soil layer on slope below Settlement
C.2:73	Prob	I2	I2	I1	Under: 44, 48; Over: 86; Cut by: 90	Dump	Soil layer on slope below Settlement
C.2:86	Prob	I2	A/M	I1?	Equals: 92, 93, 94, 95, 96, 97; Under: 63, 73, 83; Over: Bedrock	Dump	Soil layer on slope below Settlement

Locus	Reliability	Period	Phase	Phase	Stratigraphic Relationships	Category	Description
C.2:89	Prob	I2	I2	I2	Equals: 86, 95; Under: 52; Over: Bedrock	Dump	Soil layer on slope below Settlement
C.2:95	Unct	I2	I2	I1	Equals: 86, 92, 93, 94; Under: 55; Over: 96	Subbalk	Subsidiary balk
C.2:97	Unct	I2	I1	I1	Equals: 55, 92, 93, 94, 96	Subbalk	Subsidiary balk
C.5:130	Unct	I2	I2	I1	Under: 124, 135; Over 173, 178	Dump	Soil layer on slope below Settlement
C.5:147	Prob	I2	I2	I1	Under: 131; Over: 163	Dump	Soil layer on slope below Settlement
C.5:152	Prob	I2	IIC	IIB	Equals: 147, 155; Under: 131; Over: 163	Dump	Soil layer on slope below Settlement
C.5:155	Prob	I2	I2	I1	Equals: 147, 152; Under: 131; Over: 163; Cut by 62B	Dump	Soil layer on slope below Settlement
C.5:159	Prob	I2	IIB	IIB	Equals: 163?; Under: 141; Over: 193; Cut by 141	Dump	Soil layer on slope below Settlement
C.5:163	Prob	I2	I2	I1	Equals: 159?; Under: 147, 152, 155; Over: 171, 172; Cut by 62B	Dump	Soil layer on slope below Settlement
C.5:173	Prob	I2	IIB	IIA	Equals: 175?; Under: 130, 179; Over: 184; Cut by 82, 130?	Dump	Soil layer on slope below Settlement
C.5:175	Prob	I2	IIB	IIA	Equals: 173? Under: 164, 170; Over: 180; Cut by 82, 141	Dump	Soil layer on slope below Settlement
C.5:180	Prob	I2	IIB	IIA	Equals: 184?; Under: 175; Over: 189; Cut by 82, 141	Dump	Soil layer on slope below Settlement
C.5:184	Prob	I2	IIA	IIA	Equals: 180; Under: 173; Over: 185; Cut by 82, 130?	Dump	Soil layer on slope below Settlement
C.5:185	Prob	I2	IIB	IIA	Under: 184; Over: 187; Cut by 130?	Dump	Soil layer on slope below Settlement
C.5:187	Prob	I2	I2	I1	Under: 185; Over: Unexcavated	Dump	Soil layer on slope below Settlement
C.5:189	Prob	I2	I1	I1	Equals: 147?, 152?, 155?; Under: 180; Over: 159, 192; Cut by 82, 141	Dump	Soil layer on slope below Settlement
C.5:192	Prob	I2	IIC	IIA	Equals: 159; Under: 189; Over: 193; Cut by 82	Dump	Soil layer on slope below Settlement

Stratum 16
Stage C

Locus	Reliability	Period	Phase	Phase	Stratigraphic Relationships	Category	Description
B.1:121	Poss	I2/P	Iron	Iron	Equals:144; Under:119=143; Over:145, 149	Plaslin	Plaster Lining of Reservoir, Surface of
B.1:128	Poss	I2/P	–	–	Equals: 121, 144A; Under:119=143; Over 145, 149	Plaslin	Cupmarks in Plaster Lining of Reservoir
B.1:144	Poss	I2/P	–	–	Equals: 121; Under:119=143; Over 145, 149	Plaslin	Surface of Plaster Lining at Bottom of Reservoir
B.1:144A	Poss	I2/P	–	–	Equals: 121 128; Under:119=143; Over 145, 149	Plaslin	Cupmarks in Plaster Lining of Reservoir
B.1:145	Poss	I2/P	Iron	Iron	Equals: 149; Under:121=144; Over 146	Plaslin	Plaster Lining of Reservoir

Locus	Cert	Per	Per	Per	Relations	Type	Description
B.1:149	Poss	I2/P	-		Equals: 145; Under:121=144; Over 150	Plaslin	Plaster Lining of Reservoir
B.2:113A	Poss	I2/P	-		Equals: B.4:190A; Over 113B; Sealed by: Reservoir Fill Layers	Plaslin	Plaster Lining of Reservoir
B.2:138	Poss	I2/P	-		Equals: B.1:145=149, B.2:113A; Under: 137	Plaslin	Plaster Lining of Reservoir
B.4:190A	Poss	I2/P	-		Equals: B2:113A; Under 147: Over: 190B	Plaslin	Plaster Lining of Reservoir E Face
B.4:234	Unct	I2/P	-		Under: 249, 260, 263, 271; Seals Against: 135, 265, Bedrock; Sealed by: 228, 229, 249	Plaslin	Plaster Lining of Bedrock Pool 265
B.4:242	Poss	I2	Iron		Under: 231; Cuts: 191	Channel	Plastered Channel in Bedrock
B.4:244	Poss	I2	I2/P		Equals: 242?; Under 231; Cuts: 191, 194, 195	Channel	Bedrock Channel
B.4:245	Poss	I2	Hel		Under 186; Over: Bedrock; Cuts: 191, Bedrock	Channel	Water Channel leading to Channel 242
B.4:265	Unct	I2/P	-		Under: 249; Over: Bedrock; Sealed by: 234; Contains: 228, 229, 249, 264, 271	Reservr	Circular Reservoir cut in Underground Bedrock Opening
B.4:282	Poss	I2	-		Equals: 190; Seals Against: 277	Plaslin	Plaster Lining of Reservoir
C.1:90	Cert	I2/P	I2/P	I1	Equals: C.2:52=90; Under: 84, 89; Over: 91; Cuts: 95, 97, 98, 99, 100; Cut by: 88? 89?	Wall	Probable Foundation Wall
C.2:49	Prob	I2/P	Hel?	I1	Under: 31=34; Over: 73; Sealed Against by: 44	RetWall	Wall Retaing Layer 44 as a Terrace
C.2:52	Cert	I2/P	I2/P	I2/P	Equals: 90; C1:90; Under: 50; Cuts: 54, 55, 73, 86, 92, 93, 94, 96, 98, 99; Cut by: 37?	Wall	Foundation Wall for Terrace or Structure
C.2:88	Cert	I2/P	I2/P	I2	Over: 52	Soillay	Soil between two stones in top course of Wall 52
C.2:90	Cert	I2/P	I2/P	I2	Equals: 52	Wall	Foundation Wall for Terrace or Structure
C.3:26A	Poss	I2/P	-	-	Equals: C.7:44A; Under: 23; Over Bedrock	Wall	NS Wall at South Balk
C.3:32	Cert	I2/P	I2/P	I1	Under: 26, 38; Over 43; Seals Over: 43; Sealed by: 38; Cut by: 34?	Wall	Foundation Wall
C.3:34	Cert	I2/P	I2/P	I2/P	Equals: 26A; C.7:44A; Under 27, 31; Over: Bedrock	Wall	Foundation Wall
C.3:43	Prob	I2/P	-	-	Under: 32, 41; Over: Bedrock; Sealed by: 32	Wall	Probable Wall in Bedrock Shelf Corner
C.7:44A	Poss	I2/P	-	-	Equals: C.3:26A; Under 43; Over: Bedrock; Sealed by: 60, 69; Contains 100	Wall	NS Wall in line with C.3:26
C.7:74	Prob	I2/P	Iron	Iron	Under: 44? 69; Over: Bedrock	Soillay	Soil layer W of and under? 1st Course of Wall 44
C.7:97	Prob	I2/P	Iron	Iron	Under: 44, 96; Over: Bedrock	Soillay	Soil layer under 1st Course of Wall 44

Stage B

Locus	Cert	Per	Per	Per	Relations	Type	Description
A.3:56	Prob	I2/P	I2/P		Under: 55; Over: Bedrock	Soillay	Soil layer in Bedrock Pocket

Locus					Relationships	Type	Description
B.4:159	Prob	12/P	12/P	11	Under: 157; Over: 164	Soillay	Soil layer above Reservoir Drains
B.4:164	Prob	12/P	--	--	Under: 159; Over: Bedrock	Soillay	Soil layer in Bedrock Pocket
B.4:271	Unct	12/P	12/P	12/P	Under: 249; Over: 234; Within: 265	Soillay	Soil layer somewhat mixed with Locus 249 in Pool 265
C.2:44	Cert	12/P	12/P	11	Equals: C.3:40? 41? Under: 41; Over: 51, Bedrock; Seals Against: 49; Cut by: 31=34	Soillay	Soil layer on slope below Settlement
C.2:51	Cert	12/P	12/P	12/P	Under: 31=34, 44; Over: 73? Bedrock; Seals Against: 49?	Soillay	Soil layer retained by Wall 49 and in Bedrock Cavity
C.2:56	Cert	12/P	12/P	11?	Equals: 64; Under: 47; Over: 57	Dump	Soil layer on slope below Settlement
C.2:57	Cert	12/P	12/P	11?	Equals: 65; Under: 56; Over: 58	Dump	Soil layer on slope below Settlement
C.2:58	Cert	12/P	A/M	12/P	Equals: 66; Under: 57; Over: 59	Dump	Soil layer on slope below Settlement
C.2:59	Cert	12/P	12/P	12/P	Equals: 67; Under: 58; Over: 60	Dump	Soil layer on slope below Settlement
C.2:60	Cert	12/P	12/P	12	Equals: 68; Under: 59; Over: 61	Dump	Soil layer on slope below Settlement
C.2:61	Cert	12/P	12	12	Equals: 72; Under: 60; Over: 62	Dump	Soil layer on slope below Settlement
C.2:62	Cert	12/P	12	11	Equals: 82; Under: 61; Over: 63	Dump	Soil layer on slope below Settlement
C.2:63	Cert	12/P	12/P	11?	Equals: 83; Under: 62; Over: 86	Dump	Soil layer on slope below Settlement
C.2:64	Cert	12/P	12	12	Equals: 56; Under: 47; Over: 65	Dump	Soil layer on slope below Settlement
C.2:65	Cert	12/P	12/P	12/P	Equals: 57; Under: 64; Over: 66	Dump	Soil layer on slope below Settlement
C.2:66	Cert	12/P	12/P	12/P	Equals: 58; Under: 65; Over: 67	Dump	Soil layer on slope below Settlement
C.2:67	Cert	12/P	12/P	12/P	Equals: 59; Under: 66; Over: 68	Dump	Soil layer on slope below Settlement
C.2:68	Cert	12/P	12/P	12/P	Equals: 60; Under: 67; Over: 72	Dump	Soil layer on slope below Settlement
C.2:72	Cert	12/P	ER	12/P	Equals: 61; Under: 68; Over: 62	Dump	Soil layer on slope below Settlement
C.2:82	Cert	12/P	12	12	Equals: 62; Under: 81; Over: 83	Dump	Soil layer on slope below Settlement
C.2:83	Cert	12/P	ER	12/P	Equals: 63; Under: 82; Over: 86	Dump	Soil layer on slope below Settlement
C.2:101	Cert	12/P	12/P	11	Under: 51; Over: Bedrock	Dump	Soil layer on slope below Settlement
C.3:39	Cert	12/P	12/P	11	Under: 38; Over: Bedrock; Seals Against: 32?	Soillay	Soil layer over Bedrock
C.3:40	Cert	12/P	12/P	11	Under: 38; Over: 41; Seals Against: 32	Soillay	Soil layer N of Wall 32
C.3:41	Cert	12/P	12/P	11	Under: 40; Over: 44? Seals Against: 32	Soillay	Soil layer W of Bedrock Shelf

C.5:86	Poss	I2/P	A/M	IIC	Equals: C.1:103; Under: 52; Over: 105; Cut by: 62	Soillay	Soil layer under Locus 52 in NE Corner
C.5:105	Poss	I2/P	I2/P	I2/P	Under: 86; Over: 107; Cut by: 62, 77, 136	Soillay	Soil layer N of Wall 60 and W of Wall 77
C.5:107	Poss	I2/P	ER	I2/P	Under: 105; Over: 109; Cut by: 62, 136	Soillay	Soil layer in NE Corner
C.5:109	Poss	I2/P	I2	I2	Under: 107; Over: 110; Cut by: 62, 136	Soillay	Soil layer in NE Corner
C.5:110	Poss	I2/P	I2/P	I2/P	Under: 109; Over: 112, 118; Cut by: 62, 136	Soillay	Soil layer in NE Corner
C.5:112	Poss	I2/P	I2/P	I2/P	Under: 110; Over: 117, 129; Cut by: 62, 136	Soillay	Soil layer in NE Corner
C.5:114	Poss	I2/P	I2/P	I2/P	Under: 88; Over: 119	Stair	Row of 5 stones; Poss Wall or Step
C.5:117	Poss	I2/P	--	--	Under: 112; Over: 118, 119, 129	Soilsur	Soil Surface in the NE Corner
C.5:119	Poss	I2/P	I2	I2/P	Under: 114, 118; Over: 131	Soillay	Soil layer in NE Corner, N of Wall 60
C.5:129	Poss	I2/P	I2	I2	Under: 112, 117; Over: 131; Cut by: 62, 136	Soillay	Soil layer in NE Corner, N of Wall 60
C.5:131	Poss	I2/P	ER	II	Under: 119, 129; Over: 147, 150, 152, 155; Cut by: 62, 136	Soillay	Soil layer N of Wall 60
C.5:168	Poss	I2/P	IIB	IIB	Under: 164, 165; Over: 170	Soillay	Soil layer along W Balk, N of Wall 82
C.5:170	Poss	I2/P	IIC	IIB	Equals: 164; Under: 168; Over: 175	Soillay	Soil layer along W Balk
C.5:178	Poss	I2/P	Byz	II	Under: 127, 135; Over: 179; Seals Against: 82	Soillay	Soil layer at W Balk, S of Wall 82
C.5:179	Poss	I2/P	ER	Iron	Under: 135, 178; Over: 173	Soillay	Soil layer at W Balk, S of Wall 82

Stage A

B.1:119	Prob	I2/P	I2/P	I2/P	Equals: 143, B.2:137; Under: 118=142; Over: 121=144	Fill	Soil layer at bottom of Reservoir
B.1:143	Prob	I2/P	I2/P	II	Equals: 119, B.2:137; Under: 118=142; Over: 121=144	Fill	Soil layer at bottom of Reservoir
B.2:137	Prob	I2/P	I2/P	I2/P	Equals: B.1:119=143; Under: 136; Over: 138; Seals Against: 113	Fill	Soil layer at bottom of Reservoir
C.2:41	Cert	I2/P	I2/P	II	Equals: C.3:38; Under: 25; Over: 44; Cut by: 31=34	Soillay	Soil layer on slope below Settlement
C.2:50	Cert	I2/P	I2/P	II?	Equals: 100?; Under: 37; Over: 52, 86, 102; Seals Over: 52	Soillay	Soil layer running up to Wall 52
C.2:100	Cert	I2/P	I2/P	II?	Equals: 50; Under: 91; Cut by: 52=90	Soillay	Soil layer South of Wall 52
C.3:38	Cert	I2/P	I2/P	II?	Under: 37; Over: 32, 40; Seals Over: 32; Seals Against: 32	Soillay	Soil layer over Wall 32

Unassigned

C.2:75	Poss	I2/P	A/M	I1	Under: 40, 49; Over: 76	Huwlay	Huwwar layer in SE Corner
C.2:76	Poss	I2/P	I2/P	I1	Under: 75; Over: 77	Huwlay	Huwwar layer in SE Corner
C.2:77	Poss	I2/P	A/M	I1	Under: 76; Over: 78	Huwlay	Huwwar layer in SE Corner
C.2:78	Poss	I2/P	LR	I1	Under: 77; Over: 79	Huwlay	Huwwar layer in SE Corner
C.2:79	Poss	I2/P	I2/P	I2/P	Under: 78; Over: 80	Huwlay	Huwwar layer in SE Corner
C.2:80	Prob	I2/P	I2/P	I1	Under: 79; Over: 81	Huwlay	Huwwar layer in SE Corner
C.2:81	Prob	I2/P	Abd	I1	Under: 80; Over: 82	Huwlay	Huwwar layer in SE Corner
C.2:91	Poss	I2/P	ER	I2/P	Under: 90; Over: 90	Huwlay	Huwwar layer at S Balk

Stratum 15
Stage C (Stratum 16 Fill)

B.1:14C	Poss	Hel	I2/P	I2/P	Under: 14B; Over: 18; Cut by: 57	Fill	Soil Fill layer at top of Reservoir Fill
B.1:15B	Poss	Hel	I2	I2	Equals: B.2:70=72; Under: 15A; Over: 19; Cut by: 57	Fill	Soil Fill layer at top of Reservoir Fill
B.1:18	Poss	Hel	Hel	I2	Equals: 24; Under: 14B, 14C; Over: 26, 36; Cut by: 10, 57	Fill	Soil layer in Reservoir Fill
B.1:19	Prob	Hel	I2	I2	Equals: B.2:73=74; Under: 15A, 15B; Over: 24; Cut by: 57	Fill	Soil layer in Reservoir Fill
B.1:23B	Poss	I2/P	I2/P	I2/P	Equals: 33; Under: 21, 22, 23A, 25, 34, 35; Over: 30; Cut by: 17, 21, 27, 28	Fill	Soil layer in Reservoir Fill
B.1:24	Prob	Hel	Hel	I2	Equals: 18, B.2:73=74; Under: 19; Over: 31; Cut by: 17, 29, 57	Fill	Soil layer in Reservoir Fill
B.1:26	Prob	Hel	I2	I2	Under: 18; Over: 36	Fill	Soil layer in Reservoir Fill
B.1:30	Prob	Hel	Hel	I2	Under: 23B; Over: 32; Cut by: 17, 27	Fill	Soil layer in Reservoir Fill
B.1:31	Prob	Hel	I2/P	I2	Equals: B.2:73=74, 79; Under: 24; Over: 37, 41, 42; Cut by: 17, 29, 57	Fill	Soil layer in Reservoir Fill
B.1:32	Prob	Hel	Hel	I2	Under: 30; Over: 50; Cut by: 17, 27	Fill	Soil layer in Reservoir Fill
B.1:33	Poss	I2/P	--	--	Equals: 23B	Fill	Soil layer in Reservoir Fill
B.1:34	Prob	Hel	I2/P	I2/P	Under: 20; Over: 23B; Cut by: 17, 25, 28	Fill	Soil layer in Reservoir Fill
B.1:36	Prob	Hel	I2/P	I2/P	Under: 18, 26; Over: 38, 39, 40; Cut by: 40, 57	Fill	Soil layer in Reservoir Fill

B.1:37	Prob	Hel	L2/P	L2	Under: 31; Over: 42; Cut by: 29	Fill	Soil layer in Reservoir Fill
B.1:38	Prob	Hel	L2/P	L2	Under: 36; Over: 39; Cut by: 40	Fill	Soil layer in Reservoir Fill
B.1:39	Prob	Hel	L2/P	L2	Under: 36, 38; Over: 44; Cut by: 40, 57	Fill	Soil layer in Reservoir Fill
B.1:41	Prob	Hel	L2/P	L2/P	Under: 31; Over: 42; Cut by: 57	Fill	Soil and Rock layer in Reservoir Fill
B.1:42	Prob	Hel	L2/P	L2	Equals: 43, B.2:80, 81; Under: 31, 37, 41; Over: 45A; Cut by: 29, 57	Fill	Soil layer in Reservoir Fill
B.1:43	Prob	Hel	L2/P	L2	Equals: 42, B.2:80, 81; Under: 42; Over: 45A; Cut by: 29, 57	Fill	Soil layer in Reservoir Fill
B.1:44	Prob	Hel	L2/P	L2	Equals: 85; Under: 39, 45B; Over: 47, 85; Cut by: 40, 57	Fill	Soil layer in Reservoir Fill
B.1:45A	Prob	Hel	L2/P	L2	Equals: B.2:83; Under: 42=43; Over: 45B=63; Cut by: 40, 57	Fill	Soil layer in Reservoir Fill
B.1:45B	Prob	Hel	L2/P	L2	Equals: 63, B.2:83; Under: 45A; Over: 44=64; Cut by: 40, 57	Fill	Soil layer in Reservoir Fill
B.1:47	Prob	Hel	L2/P	L2	Equals: 67, 68, 69; Under: 44=66; Over: 48=75, 49=76, 52=78, 84; Cut by: 40, 57	Fill	Soil layer in Reservoir Fill
B.1:48	Prob	Hel	L2/P	L2	Equals: 75; Under: 47; Over: 49=76; Cut by: 40	Fill	Soil layer in Reservoir Fill
B.1:49	Prob	Hel	L2/P	L2	Equals: 76; Under: 47, 48=75; Over: 51=77, 52=78; Cut by: 40	Fill	Soil layer in Reservoir Fill
B.1:50	Prob	Hel	L2/P	L2	Under: 32; Over: 54; Cut by: 17, 27	Fill	Soil layer in Reservoir Fill
B.1:51	Prob	Hel	L2/P	L2/P	Equals: 77; Under: 49=76; Over: 52=78; Cut by: 40	Fill	Soil layer in Reservoir Fill
B.1:52	Prob	Hel	L2/P	L2/P	Equals: 78, 79, 81, 82, 88, 90; Under: 42, 49=76, 51=77; Over: 53=91; Cut by: 40	Fill	Soil layer in Reservoir Fill
B.1:53	Prob	Hel	L2/P	L2	Equals: 91; Under: 52=90; Over: 55=92; Cut by: 40	Fill	Soil layer in Reservoir Fill
B.1:54	Prob	Hel	L2/P	L2	Under: 50; Cut by: 17, 27	Fill	Soil layer in Reservoir Fill
B.1:55	Prob	Hel	L2/P	L2	Equals: 92, 93, 95, 96; Under: 53=90, 91; Over: 94; Cut by: 40	Fill	Soil layer in Reservoir Fill
B.1:56	Prob	Hel	--	--	Equals: 45? B.2:94; Under: 45; Cut by: 29?	Soillay	Rock and Soil layer in Reservoir Fill
B.1:63	Prob	Hel	L2/P	L2	Equals: 45B	Fill	Soil layer in Reservoir Fill
B.1:64	Prob	Hel	L2/P	L2	Equals: 44	Fill	Soil layer in Reservoir Fill
B.1:65	Prob	Hel	L2/P	L2	Equals: 44	Fill	Soil layer in Reservoir Fill
B.1:66	Prob	Hel	L2/P	L2	Equals: 44	Fill	Soil layer in Reservoir Fill
B.1:67	Prob	Hel	L2/P	L2	Equals: 47	Fill	Soil layer in Reservoir Fill
B.1:68	Prob	Hel	L2/P	L2	Equals: 47	Fill	Soil layer in Reservoir Fill
B.1:69	Prob	Hel	L2/P	L2	Equals: 47	Fill	Soil layer in Reservoir Fill

Locus					Relationships		Description
B.1:75	Prob	Hel	I2/P	I2/P	Equals: 48; Over: 76; Cut by: 40	Fill	Soil layer in Reservoir Fill
B.1:76	Prob	Hel	I2/P	I2/P	Equals: 49; Under: 48=75; Over: 51=77, 52=78; Cut by: 40	Fill	Soil layer in Reservoir Fill
B.1:77	Prob	Hel	I2/P	I2/P	Equals: 51; Under: 49=76; Over: 52=78; Cut by: 40	Fill	Soil layer in Reservoir Fill
B.1:78	Prob	Hel	I2/P	I2/P	Equals: 52; Under: 47, 49=76, 51=77; Over: 52=78; Cut by: 40	Fill	Soil layer in Reservoir Fill
B.1:79	Prob	Hel	I2/P	I2/P	Equals: 52, 81; Under: 52=78; Over: 52=82, 80; Cut by: 40	Fill	Soil layer in Reservoir Fill
B.1:80	Prob	Hel	I2/P	I2/P	Equals: 87; Under: 79=81=82, 84, 52=82; Over: 52=88, 92; Cut by: 40	Fill	Soil layer in Reservoir Fill
B.1:81	Prob	Hel	I2/P	I2/P	Equals: 52=79	Fill	Soil layer in Reservoir Fill
B.1:82	Prob	Hel	I2/P	I2/P	Equals: 52; Under: 52=79; Over: 52=88=90, 80; Cut by: 40	Fill	Soil layer in Reservoir Fill
B.1:83	Prob	Hel	--	--	Under: 56; Over: 100	Fill	Large Rock in Reservoir Fill
B.1:84	Prob	Hel	I2/P	I2/P	Equals: B.2:94; Under: 44, 47, 64, 65, 66, 67, 68, 69, 85; Over: 80=87	Fill	Soil layer in Reservoir Fill
B.1:85	Prob	Hel	I2/P	I2/P	Equals: 44, 64; Under: 44, 86; Over: 84	Fill	Soil layer in Reservoir Fill
B.1:86	Prob	Hel	I2/P	I2/P	Equals: B.2:94; Under: 85	Fill	Soil layer in Reservoir Fill
B.1:87	Prob	Hel	I2/P	I2/P	Equals: 80, B.2:94; Under: 84; Over: 92	Fill	Soil layer in Reservoir Fill
B.1:88	Prob	Hel	I2/P	I2/P	Equals: 52; Under: 52=82, 80; Over: 52=90, 92; Cut by: 40	Fill	Soil layer in Reservoir Fill
B.1:89	Prob	Hel	I2/P	I2/P	Equals: B.2:94; Under: 92; Over: 97	Fill	Soil layer in Reservoir Fill
B.1:90	Prob	Hel	I2/P	I2/P	Equals: 52, 92; Under: 52=82=88; Over: 53=91, 55=92; Cut by: 40	Fill	Soil layer in Reservoir Fill
B.1:91	Prob	Hel	I2/P	I2/P	Equals: 53; Under: 52=90; Over: 55=92; Cut by: 40	Fill	Soil layer in Reservoir Fill
B.1:92	Prob	Hel	I2/P	I2/P	Equals: 55, 90, B.2:94; Under: 53=91, 80=87, 88; Over: 89, 93, 94, 95, 99, 55=96; Cut by: 40	Fill	Rock Tumble in Reservoir Fill
B.1:93	Prob	Hel	I2/P	I2/P	Equals: 55; Under: 92; Over: 94; Cut by: 40	Fill	Soil layer in Reservoir Fill
B.1:94	Prob	Hel	I2/P	I2/P	Equals: 92? Under: 55=96, 92, 93; Over: 106, 108, 118=126=142; Cut by: 40	Fill	Rock layer in Reservoir Fill
B.1:95	Prob	Hel	I2/P	I2/P	Equals: 55; Under: 55=92; Over: 55=96	Fill	Soil layer in Reservoir Fill
B.1:96	Prob	Hel	I2/P	I2/P	Equals: 55; Under: 55=92=95; Over: 94	Fill	Soil layer in Reservoir Fill
B.1:97	Prob	Hel	I2/P	I2/P	Equals: 129; Under: 89, 99; Over: 98, 105; Cut by: 40	Fill	Soil layer in Reservoir Fill
B.1:98	Prob	Hel	I2/P	I2/P	Under: 97; Over: 105, 130	Fill	Soil layer in Reservoir Fill
B.1:99	Prob	Hel	--	--	Under: 92; Over: 97; Cut by: 40	Fill	Soil layer in Reservoir Fill

Locus					Relations	Type	Description
B.1:100	Prob	Hel	12/P	12/P	Under: 83; 99?	Fill	Soil layer in Reservoir Fill
B.1:101	Prob	Hel	12/P	12/P	--	Fill	Subsidiary Balk running from 83 to N Balk in Reservoir Fill
B.1:102	Prob	Hel	12/P	12/P	--	Fill	E-W Subsidiary Balk running along foundation trench 40
B.1:104	Prob	Hel	12/P	12/P	Equals: 102	Fill	E-W Subsidiary Balk running along foundation trench 40
B.1:105	Prob	Hel	12/P	12/P	Equals: 130, B.2:94; Under: 97, 98; Over: 106=131, 107=133, 112; Cut by: 40	Fill	Soil layer in Reservoir Fill
B.1:106	Prob	Hel	12/P	12/P	Equals: 131, B.2:94; Under: 94, 105=130; Over: 107=133	Fill	Soil layer in Reservoir Fill
B.1:107	Prob	Hel	12/P	12/P	Equals: 133, B.2:94; Under: 105, 106=131, 112, 113, 114; Over: 118=134; Cut by: 40	Fill	Soil layer in Reservoir Fill
B.1:108	Prob	Hel	12/P	12/P	Equals: 134, B.2:94; Under: 94, 107=133, 113; Over: 109, 110=136=137, 115=125=141; Cut by: 40	Fill	Soil layer in Reservoir Fill
B.1:109	Prob	Hel	12/P	12/P	Equals: 135, B.2:107; Under: 108=134; Over: 110=136=137	Fill	Soil layer in Reservoir Fill
B.1:110	Prob	Hel	12/P	12/P	Equals: 136, 137, B.2:111=118; Under: 108=134, 109=135; Over: 111=122=138, 115=125=141, 118, 123=139; Cut by: 40	Fill	Soil layer in Reservoir Fill
B.1:111	Prob	Hel	12/P	12/P	Equals: 122	Fill	Soil layer in Reservoir Fill
B.1:112	Prob	Hel	12/P	12/P	Equals: 130; Under: 105; Over: 107=133, 113; Cut by: 40	Fill	Soil layer in Reservoir Fill
B.1:113	Prob	Hel	12/P	12/P	Under: 112; Over: 107=133, 108=134, 114; Cut by: 40	Fill	Soil layer in Reservoir Fill
B.1:114	Prob	Hel	12/P	12/P	Under: 113; Over: 107=133	Fill	Soil layer in Reservoir Fill
B.1:115	Prob	Hel	12/P	12/P	Equals: 125, 141, B.2:124; Under: 108=134, 110=136=137, 124=140; Over: 116, 118=126=142	Fill	Soil layer in Reservoir Fill
B.1:116	Prob	Hel	12/P	12/P	Under: 115=125=141; Over: 118=126=142	Fill	Soil layer in Reservoir Fill
B.1:118	Prob	Hel	12/P	12/P	Equals: 126, 142, B.2:125, 126, 128-136; Under: 94, 110=136=137, 115=125=141, 116; Over: 119=143	Fill	Soil layer in Reservoir Fill
B.1:122	Prob	Hel	12/P	12/P	Equals: 111, 138, B.2:111, 118; Under: 110=136=137; Over: 124=140	Fill	Soil layer in Reservoir Fill
B.1:123	Prob	Hel	12/P	12/P	Under: 111=122=138; Over: 124=140	Fill	Soil layer in Reservoir Fill
B.1:124	Prob	Hel	12/P	12/P	Equals: 140, B.2:120; Under: 111=122=138, 123=139; Over: 115=125=141	Fill	Soil layer in Reservoir Fill
B.1:125	Prob	Hel	12/P	12/P	Equals: 115, 141, B.2:124; Under: 124=140; Over: 118=126=142	Fill	Soil layer in Reservoir Fill
B.1:126	Prob	Hel	12/P	12/P	Equals: 118, 142, B.2:125	Fill	Soil layer in Reservoir Fill
B.1:129	Prob	Hel	12/P	12/P	Equals: 92, 97, B.2:94; Under: 127; Over: 130; Cut by: 40	Fill	Soil layer in Reservoir Fill

Locus						
B.1:130	Prob	Hel	I2/P	Equals: 105, 112, B.2:94; Under: 97=129, 98; Cut by: 40	Fill	Soil layer in Reservoir Fill
B.1:131	Prob	Hel	11	Equals: 106, B.2:94; Under: 105=130; Over: 107=133, 132; Cut by: 40	Fill	Soil layer in Reservoir Fill
B.1:132	Prob	Hel	I2/P	Under: 106=131; Over: 107=133	Fill	Soil layer in Reservoir Fill
B.1:133	Prob	Hel	I2/P	Equals: 107, B.2:94; Under: 106=131, 105=130, 112, 113, 132; Over: 108=134; Cut by: 40	Fill	Soil layer in Reservoir Fill
B.1:134	Prob	Hel	I2/P	Equals: 108, B.2:94; Under: 107=133, 113; Over: 109=135, 110=136=137, 115=125=141; Cut by: 40	Fill	Soil layer in Reservoir Fill
B.1:135	Prob	Hel	11	Equals: 109, B.2:107; Under: 108=134; Over: 110=136=137	Fill	Soil layer in Reservoir Fill
B.1:136	Prob	Hel	I2/P	Equals: 110, 137, B.2:111, 118; Under: 108=134, 135; Over: 111=122=138, 123=139; Cut by: 40	Fill	Soil layer in Reservoir Fill
B.1:137	Prob	Hel	I2/P	Equals: 110, 136, B.2:111, 118; Under: 108=134, 135; Over: 111=122=138, 123=139; Cut by: 40	Fill	Soil layer in Reservoir Fill
B.1:138	Prob	Hel	I2/P	Equals: 111, 122, B.2:111, 118; Under: 110=136=137; Over: 123=139; Cut by: 40	Fill	Soil layer in Reservoir Fill
B.1:139	Prob	Hel	11	Equals: 123, B.2:111, 118; Under: 111=122=138, 110=136=137; Over: 124=140; Cut by: 40	Fill	Soil layer in Reservoir Fill
B.1:140	Prob	Hel	I2/P	Equals: 124, B.2:120; Under: 123=139; Over: 115=125=141	Fill	Soil layer in Reservoir Fill
B.1:141	Prob	Hel	I2/P	Equals: 115, 125, B.2:124; Under: 115=125=141, 124=140; Over: 118=126=142	Fill	Soil layer in Reservoir Fill
B.1:142	Prob	Hel	11	Equals: 118, 126, B.2:125, 126, 128, 129, 131, 132, 133, 134, 135, 136; Under: 94, 115=125=141; Over: 123=139	Fill	Soil layer in Reservoir Fill
B.2:35B	Prob	Hel	I2/P	Equals: part of B.1:15B; Under: 33; Over: 36, 42	Fill	Soil layer in Reservoir Fill
B.2:36	Prob	Hel	I2/P	Equals: part of B.1:15B; Under: 35B; Over: 37	Fill	Soil layer in Reservoir Fill
B.2:37	Prob	Hel	I2/P	Equals: part of B.1:15B; Under: 36; Over: 38, 41, 42	Fill	Soil layer in Reservoir Fill
B.2:38	Prob	Hel	ER	Equals: part of B.1:15B; Under: 31, 37; Over: 39, 41; Cut by: 69	Fill	Soil layer in Reservoir Fill
B.2:39	Prob	Hel	I2/P	Equals: part of B.1:15B; Under: 38, 41, 42; Over: 40, 65	Fill	Soil layer in Reservoir Fill
B.2:40	Prob	Hel	I2/P	Equals: 65, part of B.1:15B; Under: 39, 57; Over: 67, 68, 70; Cut by: 69	Fill	Soil layer in Reservoir Fill
B.2:41	Prob	Hel	--	Equals: part of B.1:15B; Under: 37, 38; Over: 39	Fill	Soil layer in Reservoir Fill
B.2:42	Prob	Hel	I2/P	Under: 35B, 37; Over: 39; Cut by: 69	Fill	Soil layer in Reservoir Fill
B.2:56	Prob	Hel	I2/P	Under: 48; Over: 72; Cut by: 69	Fill	Soil layer in Reservoir Fill
B.2:57	Prob	Hel	ER	Under: 48; Over: 40=65, 66; Cut by: 69	Fill	Soil layer in Reservoir Fill

Locus					Relationships		
B.2:58	Prob	Hel	L2/P	L2/P	Under: 53; Over: 59	Fill	Soil layer in Reservoir Fill
B.2:59	Prob	Hel	ER	L2/P	Under: 58; Over: 60	Fill	Soil layer in Reservoir Fill
B.2:60	Prob	Hel	L2/P	L2/P	Under: 51, 59; Over: 61	Fill	Soil layer in Reservoir Fill
B.2:61	Prob	Hel	L2/P	L2/P	Under: 60; Over: 72	Fill	Soil layer in Reservoir Fill
B.2:65	Prob	Hel	L2/P	L2/P	Equals: 40, part of B.1:15B; Under: 39, 57; Over: 67, 68, 70; Cut by: 69	Fill	Soil layer in Reservoir Fill
B.2:66	Prob	Hel	L2/P	L2/P	Under: 57; Over: 72; Cut by: 69	Fill	Soil layer in Reservoir Fill
B.2:67	Prob	Hel	L2/P	L2/P	Equals: part of B.1:15B; Under: 40=65; Over: 68, 72	Fill	Soil layer in Reservoir Fill
B.2:68	Prob	Hel	L2/P	L2/P	Equals: part of B.1:15B; Under: 40, 65, 67; Over: 70=72; Cut by: 69	Fill	Soil layer in Reservoir Fill
B.2:70	Prob	Hel	L2/P	L2/P	Equals: 72, B.1:15B; Under: 40, 65, 68	Fill	Soil layer in Reservoir Fill
B.2:72	Prob	Hel	L2/P	L2/P	Equals: 70, B.1:15B; Under: 56, 61, 66, 67, 68; Over: 73, 79; Cut by: 69	Fill	Soil layer in Reservoir Fill
B.2:73	Prob	Hel	Hel	L2/P	Equals: 74, B.1:19, 24, 31; Under: 64, 72; Over: 79, 81	Fill	Soil layer in Reservoir Fill
B.2:74	Prob	Hel	LR	L2/P	Equals: 73, B.1:19, 24, 31	Fill	Soil layer in Reservoir Fill
B.2:79	Prob	Hel	L2/P	II	Equals: B.1:31; Under: 72, 73; Over: 80, 81, 83; Cut by: 69	Fill	Soil layer in Reservoir Fill
B.2:80	Prob	Hel	L2/P	L2/P	Equals: 81, B.1:41, 42, 43; Under: 79; Over: 83; Cut by: 69	Fill	Soil layer in Reservoir Fill
B.2:81	Prob	Hel	L2/P	L2/P	Equals: 80, B.1:41, 42, 43; Under: 73, 79; Over 83	Fill	Soil layer in Reservoir Fill
B.2:83	Prob	Hel	Hel	L2/P	Equals: 91, B.1:45A; Under: 79, 80, 81; Over: 94	Fill	Soil layer in Reservoir Fill
B.2:91	Prob	Hel	--	--	Equals: 83	Fill	Soil layer in Reservoir Fill
B.2:94	Prob	Hel	ER	L2/P	Equals: B.1:56, 84, 86, 87, 89, 92, 97=129, 105, 106, 107, 108, 130, 133, 134, B.4:202=205, 203, 207; Under: 62, 83; Over: 107; Seals Against: 113A; Cut by: 69	Fill	Soil layer in Reservoir Fill
B.2:100	Prob	Hel	L2/P	L2/P	--	Fill	Soil layer in Reservoir Fill
B.2:107	Prob	Hel	L2/P	II	Equals: B.1:109=135; Under: 94; Over: 111	Fill	Soil layer in Reservoir Fill
B.2:111	Prob	Hel	L2/P	L2/P	Equals: 118, B.1:111=122, 123=139, 136, 137, 138; Under: 107; Over: 120; Seals Against: 113A	Fill	Soil layer in Reservoir Fill
B.2:118	Prob	Hel	ER	II	Equals: 111, B.1:136, 138, 139; Over: 119	Fill	Soil layer in Reservoir Fill
B.2:119	Prob	Hel	L2/P	II	Under: 118; Over: 120; Seals Against: 113A	Fill	Soil layer in Reservoir Fill
B.1:120	Prob	Hel	ER	II	Equals: B.1:24=140; Under: 111=118, 119; Over: 121, 124: Seals Against: 84, 113A	Fill	Soil layer in Reservoir Fill
B.2:121	Prob	Hel	--	--	Under: 120; Seals Against: 84	Fill	Soil layer in Reservoir Fill

Locus					Relationships	Type	Description
B.2:122	Prob	Hel	I2/P	I2/P	Under: 62, 108, 117; Over: 94	Fill	Soil layer in Reservoir Fill
B.2:124	Prob	Hel	I2/P	II	Equals: B.1:115=125=141; Under: 120; Over: 125; Seals Against: 84, 113	Fill	Soil layer in Reservoir Fill
B.2:125	Prob	Hel	I2/P	I2/P	Equals: B.1:118=126=142; Under: 124; Over: 126; Seals Against: 84, 113A	Fill	Soil layer in Reservoir Fill
B.2:126	Prob	Hel	I2/P	I2/P	Equals: B.1:118=126=142; Under: 125; Over: 128; Seals Against: 113A	Fill	Soil layer in Reservoir Fill
B.2:128	Prob	Hel	I2/P	II	Equals: B.1:118=126=142; Under: 126; Over: 129	Fill	Soil layer in Reservoir Fill
B.2:129	Prob	Hel	I2/P	I2/P	Equals: B.1:118=126=142; Under: 128; Over: 130, 131; Seals Against: 113	Fill	Soil layer in Reservoir Fill
B.2:130	Prob	Hel	--	--	Under: 129; Over: 131	Fill	Soil layer in Reservoir Fill
B.2:131	Prob	Hel	I2/P	II	Equals: B.1:118=126=142; Under: 129, 130; Over: 132; Seals Against: 113A	Fill	Soil layer in Reservoir Fill
B.2:132	Prob	Hel	I2/P	I2/P	Equals: B.1:118=126=142; Under: 131; Over: 133; Seals Against: 113A	Fill	Soil layer in Reservoir Fill
B.2:133	Prob	Hel	I2/P	II	Equals: B.1:118=126=142; Under: 132; Over: 134, 135, 136: Seals Against: 113A	Fill	Soil layer in Reservoir Fill
B.2:134	Prob	Hel	I2/P	I2/P	Equals: B.1:118=126=142; Under: 133; Over: 135, 136: Seals Against: 113A	Fill	Soil layer in Reservoir Fill
B.2:135	Prob	Hel	I2/P	I2/P	Equals: B.1:118=126=142; Under: 133, 134; Over: 136: Seals Against: 113A	Fill	Soil layer in Reservoir Fill
B.2:136	Prob	Hel	I2/P	I2/P	Equals: B.1:118=126=142; Under: 133, 134, 135; Over: 137; Seals Against: 113A	Fill	Soil layer in Reservoir Fill
B.4:202	Prob	Hel	I2/P	II	Equals: 205, B.2:94; Under: 173, 201 (Cleanup); Over: 203=205, 221; Cut by: 204, 233? 236? 239?	Fill	Soil layer in Reservoir Fill
B.4:203	Prob	Hel	I2/P	I2/P	Equals: 205, B.9:94; Under: 202=205; Over: 205=218; Cut by: 204, 221	Fill	Soil layer in Reservoir Fill
B.4:205	Prob	Hel	ER	II	Equals: 202, 203, 218, 219, 220 224, B.2:94: Under: 173, 199 (Cleanup) 200 (Cleanup), 201 (Cleanup), 202, 203; Over: 207=215=216; Seals Against: 190, 191; Cut by: 204, 225, 231, 233, 236, 255, 268, 269	Fill	Soil layer in Reservoir Fill
B.4:207	Prob	Hel	I2/P	I2/P	Equals: 215, 216, B.2:94: Under: 205=224; Over: 272, Seals Against: 190, 191; Cut by: 209, 225, 231, 255, 268, 269	Fill	Soil layer in Reservoir Fill
B.4:215	Prob	Hel	I2/P	I2/P	Equals: 207	Fill	Soil layer in Reservoir Fill
B.4:216	Prob	Hel	--	--	Equals: 207	Fill	Soil layer in Reservoir Fill
B.4:218	Prob	Hel	--	--	Equals: 205: Under: 221	Fill	Soil layer in Reservoir Fill
B.4:219	Prob	Hel	I2/P	I2/P	Equals: 205	Fill	Soil layer in Reservoir Fill
B.4:220	Prob	Hel	I2/P	I2/P	Equals: 205	Fill	Soil layer in Reservoir Fill
B.4:224	Prob	Hel	I2/P	I2/P	Equals: 205	Fill	Soil layer in Reservoir Fill
B.4:272	Prob	Hel	I2/P	I2/P	Under: 207; Over: 273; Cut by: 255, 269, 280	Fill	Soil layer in Reservoir Fill

Locus						Description	Type
B.4:273	Prob	Hel	12/P	12/P	Under: 272; Over: 274	Soil layer in Reservoir Fill	Fill
B.4:274	Prob	Hel	12/P	12/P	Under: 264, 269, 270, 273; Over: Unexcavated	Soil layer in Reservoir Fill	Fill
B.7:39	Prob	Hel	12/P	12/P	Equals: B.2:47: Under: 33, 37 (Bedrock)	Soil layer in Reservoir Fill	Fill

Iron Age
Unassigned

Locus						Description	Type
A.2:11	Unct	Iron	A/M	Hel	Under: 1; Cuts Through: 49	Cistern	Cistern
A.5:61	Poss	Iron	—	—	Under: 33; Over: Unexcavated; Cut by: 87, 89; Contains: 62A-62F	Store Silo connected to Silos 62 and 79	Storesilo
A.5:62	Poss	Iron	—	—	Equals: 63; Under: 33; Over: 62B; Within 61, 62, 79	Store Silo connected to Silos 62 and 79	Storesilo
A.5:79	Poss	Iron	—	—	Under: 10B, 80; Contains: 62A, 62B, 62C, 62D, 62E, 62F	Store Silo in Bedrock, in SW corner connected to 61, 62	Storesilo
A.5:90	Poss	Iron	—	—	Under: 51; Over: Bedrock; Contains: 90A, 90B, 90C, 90D, 90E	Store Silo connected to Silo 61	Storesilo
B.3:47	Poss	Iron	—	—	Under: 44, 46; Over: Bedrock; Contains: 50, 51, 52, 69	Store Silo dug in floor of Bedrock Cave 100	Storesilo
B.3:59	Poss	Iron	—	—	Under: 57; Over: Bedrock; Contains: 58, 60, 61, 62, 63, 66	Store Silo dug in floor of Bedrock Cave 100, E of Silo 47	Storesilo
B.3:64	Poss	Iron	—	—	Under: 70; Over: Bedrock; Contains: 67, 68	Store Silo dug in floor of Bedrock Cave 100, N of Silos 57 and 59	Storesilo
B.4:188	Poss	Iron	—	—	Under: 144; Contains: 184, 187, 189, 232, 240, 241, 243, 252 (Bedrock)	Store Silo dug in Bedrock Floor of Cave 74	Storesilo
D.2:77	Poss	Iron	—	—	Under: 82, 86; Sealed by: 82; Sealed Over by: 76; Contains: 77A, 77B	Store Silo centered on E Balk line	Storesilo
D.2:80	Poss	Iron	—	—	Under: 43; Contains: 80A (Cleanup), 80B, 80C, 80D, 80E	Store Silo in NW	Storesilo
D.2:95	Poss	Iron	—	—	Under: 73, 88; Contains: 95A, 95B, 95C, 95D, 95E	Store Silo in N Center of Square	Storesilo
D.3:57	Poss	Iron	—	—	Under: 43, 63; Contains: 57A, 57B, 57C, 57D, 57E, 57F	Store Silo under fill for stairway	Storesilo
D.6:47	Poss	Iron	A/M	12/P	Under: 43, 45; Over: Bedrock	Store Silo in corner of Walls 3 and 19	Storesilo
D.6:48	Poss	Iron	A/M	12/P	Under: 45; Over: Bedrock	Store Silo in E fourth of Square	Storesilo
G.1:47	Poss	Iron	Hel	—	Under: 42, 46; Over: 48; Contains: 48	Cistern (poss Store Silo) in center of Square	Cistern

Appendix B

TELL HESBAN OBJECTS
FOR STRATA 21-16

Appendix B

Tell Hesban Objects for Strata 21-16

Locus	Object No.	Material	Description	Period	Allocation
Stratum 21					
C.1:96B:758	1623	Bone	Spindle Whorl	I1A	HAM73.0314
C.1:142:979	2935	Ceramic	Spindle Whorl Fragment	I1A	HAM76.0671
C.1:143:982	2928	Ceramic	Spindle Whorl Fragment?	I1A	HAM76.0664
C.1:143:984	2929	Ceramic	Spindle Whorl Fragment	I1A	HAM76.0665
C.2:94:575	1817	Chert	Slingstone	I1A	HAM74.0155
Stratum 20					
B.3:93:153	1708	Limestone	Mortar	Iron	HAM74.Storage
D.4:138:292	2796	Ceramic	Spindle Whorl Fragment	Iron	HAM76.0546
D.4:138:292	2797	Ceramic	Spindle Whorl Fragment	Iron	HAM76.0547
D.4:142:302	2927	Ceramic	Spindle Whorl	Iron	HAM76.0663
D.4:142:302	2948	Limestone	Door Socket	Iron	HAM76.Storage
D.4:142:308	2845	Ceramic	Spindle Whorl	Iron	HAM76.0588
D.4:142:308	2846	Ceramic	Pottery Disc	Iron	HAM76.0589
D.4:142:308	2847	Ceramic	Pottery Disc	Iron	HAM76.0590
D.4:142:308	2848	Ceramic	Pottery Disc	Iron	HAM76.0591
D.4:142:308	2849	Ceramic	Pottery Disc	Iron	HAM76.0592
D.4:142:308	2850	Ceramic	Pottery Disc	Iron	HAM76.0593

Stratum 18

C.1:124:885	2306	Limestone	Weight	Iron	HAM76.0123
C.1:124:889	2432	Ceramic	Spindle Whorl Fragment	Iron	HAM76.0228
C.1:124:889	2433	Ceramic	Spindle Whorl Fragment	Iron	HAM76.0229
C.1:124:889	2434	Ceramic	Spindle Whorl Fragment	Iron	HAM76.0230
C.1:124:889	2435	Ceramic	Spindle Whorl	Iron	HAM76.0231
C.1:124:889	2437	Ceramic	Pottery Disc	Iron	HAM76.0233
C.1:124:896	2419	Limestone	Weight	Iron	HAM76.0215
C.1:124:896	2431	Ceramic	Spindle Whorl Fragment	Iron	HAM76.0227
C.1:124:899	2445	Limestone	Door Socket Fragment	Iron	HAM76.Storage
C.1:124:899	2512	Ceramic	Spindle Whorl Fragment	Iron	HAM76.0297
C.1:124:901	2482	Ceramic	Spindle Whorl Fragment	Iron	HAM76.0272
C.1:126:897	2428	Carnelian	Bead	Iron	HAM76.0224
C.1:126:905	2452	Sandstone	Seal	Iron	DAJ
C.1:126:905	2501	Ceramic	Spindle Whorl Fragment	Iron	HAM76.0289
C.1:126:905	2511	Ceramic	Spindle Whorl Fragment	Iron	HAM76.0296
C.1:126:908	2459	Limestone	Unfinished Seal	Iron	HAM76.0251
C.1:126:908	2574	Ceramic	Spindle Whorl Fragment	Iron	HAM76.0350
C.1:126:918	2575	Ceramic	Spindle Whorl Fragment	Iron	HAM76.0351
C.1:127:903	2484	Ceramic	Spindle Whorl Fragment	Iron	HAM76.0274
C.1:127:906	2513	Ceramic	Spindle Whorl Fragment	Iron	HAM76.0298
C.1:129:916	2573	Ceramic	Spindle Whorl Fragment	Iron	HAM76.0349
C.1:131:920	2576	Ceramic	Spindle Whorl Fragment	Iron	HAM76.0352
C.1:131:920	2577	Ceramic	Spindle Whorl Fragment	Iron	HAM76.0353
C.1:131:924	2701	Ceramic	Spindle Whorl Fragment	Iron	HAM76.0463
C.1:131:925	2708	Ceramic	Spindle Whorl Fragment	Iron	HAM76.0470
C.1:131:928	2723	Ceramic	Spindle Whorl Fragment	Iron	HAM76.0482
C.1:131:928	2728	Ceramic	Spindle Whorl Fragment	Iron	HAM76.0487
C.1:132:923	2596	Limestone	Muller	Iron	HAM76.0370
C.1:133:935	2652	Limestone	Weight	Iron	HAM76.0422
C.1:133:937	2706	Ceramic	Spindle Whorl Fragment	Iron	HAM76.0468

C.1:133:937	2707	Ceramic	Spindle Whorl Fragment	Iron	HAM76.0469
C.1:133:937	2710	Ceramic	Spindle Whorl Fragment	Iron	HAM76.0472
C.1:133:938	2703	Ceramic	Spindle Whorl Fragment	Iron	HAM76.0465
C.1:133:938	2705	Ceramic	Spindle Whorl Fragment	Iron	HAM76.0467
C.1:133:938	2709	Ceramic	Spindle Whorl Fragment	Iron	HAM76.0471
C.1:133:939	2660	Ceramic	Spindle Whorl Fragment	Iron	DAJ
C.1:133:939	2702	Ceramic	Spindle Whorl Fragment	Iron	HAM76.0464
C.1:133:944	2724	Ceramic	Spindle Whorl Fragment	Iron	HAM76.0483
C.1:133:945	2766	Ceramic	Spindle Whorl	Iron	HAM76.0521
C.1:133:945	2770	Ceramic	Spindle Whorl Fragment ?	Iron	HAM76.0525
C.1:133:948	2767	Ceramic	Spindle Whorl Fragment	Iron	HAM76.0522
C.1:134:929	2730	Ceramic	Spindle Whorl Fragment	Iron	HAM76.0489
C.1:135:932	2711	Ceramic	Spindle Whorl Fragment	Iron	HAM76.0473
C.1:136:94	2725	Ceramic	Spindle Whorl Fragment	Iron	HAM76.0484
C.1:136:943	2726	Ceramic	Spindle Whorl Fragment ?	Iron	HAM76.0485
C.1:136:943	2727	Ceramic	Spindle Whorl Fragment	Iron	HAM76.0486
C.1:136:947	2771	Ceramic	Spindle Whorl Fragment	Iron	DAJ
C.1:137:950	2768	Ceramic	Spindle Whorl Fragment	Iron	HAM76.0523
C.1:137:951	2772	Ceramic	Spindle Whorl Fragment	Iron	HAM76.0526
C.1:138:955	2842	Ceramic	Pottery Disc	Iron	HAM76.0585
C.1:138:957	2780	Chert	Slingstone	Iron	HAM76.0532
C.1:138:959	2834	Ceramic	Spindle Whorl Fragment	Iron	HAM76.0577
C.1:138:960	2831	Ceramic	Spindle Whorl Fragment	Iron	HAM76.0574
C.1:138:963	2836	Ceramic	Spindle Whorl Fragment	Iron	HAM76.0579
C.1:138:966	2838	Ceramic	Spindle Whorl Fragment ?	Iron	HAM76.0581
C.1:138:966	2839	Ceramic	Spindle Whorl Fragment	Iron	HAM76.0582
C.1:138:967	2806	Glass	Inset of Ring	Iron	HAM76.0553
C.1:138:967	2837	Ceramic	Spindle Whorl Fragment	Iron	HAM76.0580
C.1:138:967	2840	Ceramic	Spindle Whorl Fragment	Iron	HAM76.0583
C.1:138:971	2932	Ceramic	Spindle Whorl Fragment	Iron	HAM76.0668
C.1:139:958	2830	Ceramic	Spindle Whorl Fragment	Iron	HAM76.0573
C.1:139:964	2833	Ceramic	Spindle Whorl Fragment	Iron	HAM76.0576

C.1:139:964	2841	Ceramic	Pottery Disc	Iron	HAM76.0584
C.1:139:965	2823	Basalt	Stone Bowl Fragment	Iron	HAM76.0569
C.1:139:965	2832	Ceramic	Spindle Whorl Fragment	Iron	HAM76.0675
C.1:139:968	2835	Ceramic	Spindle Whorl Fragment	Iron	HAM76.0578
C.1:139:972	2931	Ceramic	Spindle Whorl Fragment	Iron	HAM76.0667
C.1:139:972	2934	Ceramic	Spindle Whorl Fragment	Iron	HAM76.0670
C.1:141:976	2930	Ceramic	Spindle Whorl Fragment	Iron	HAM76.0666
C.5:183:450	2828	Ceramic	Pottery Disc	Iron	DAJ
C.5:194:491	2826	Ceramic	Figurine	I1	DAJ

Stratum 17

C.1:123B:883	2261	Ceramic	Spindle Whorl Fragment	Iron	HAM76.0083
C.1:123B:886	2399	Ceramic	Spindle Rest/Pottery Disc	Iron	HAM76.0198
C.1:123B:886	2400	Ceramic	Spindle Whorl Fragment	Iron	HAM76.0199
C.1:123B:886	2402	Ceramic	Spindle Whorl Fragment	Iron	HAM76.0201
C.1:123B:886	2403	Ceramic	Spindle Whorl Fragment	Iron	HAM76.0202
C.1:123B:886	2404	Ceramic	Spindle Whorl Fragment	Iron	HAM76.0203
C.1:123B:886	2405	Ceramic	Spindle Whorl	Iron	HAM76.0204
C.1:123B:893	2385	Bronze	Ring	Iron	HAM76.0186
C.1:123B:898	2439	Limestone	Weight	Iron	HAM76.0235
C.1:123B:898	2440	Obsidian	Bead	Iron	HAM76.0236
C.1:123B:900	2481	Ceramic	Spindle Whorl Fragment	Iron	HAM76.0271
C.1:123B:900	2483	Ceramic	Spindle Whorl Fragment	Iron	HAM76.0273

Stratum 16

B.1:119:318	1329	Iron	Blade Point	Iron	HAM73.0076
B.1:119:318	1392	Ceramic	Lamp Fragments	Iron	HAM73.0126
B.1:143:376	1631	Ceramic	Figurine	I2/P	DAJ
B.1:143:378	1561	Ceramic	Possible Ostracon	Iron	HAM73.0271
B.1:143:386	1547	Iron	Arrowhead	Iron	HAM73.0258
B.1:143:395	1576	Ceramic	Horse Head Figurine	I2/P	DAJ

B.1:143:402	1657	Ceramic	Ostracon	I2/P	DAJ
C.2:44:471	1633	Ceramic	Incised Pottery Fragment	Iron	HAM73.0321
C.2:44:503	1676	Ceramic	Incised Vessel Fragment/Ostracon	I2/P	DAJ
C.2:44:503	1681	Ceramic	Horse Head figurine	I2/P	HAM73.0352
C.2:51:513	1672	Chert	Slingstone	Iron	HAM73.0345
C.2:51:513	1673	Chert	Slingstone	Iron	HAM73.0346
C.2:51:513	1674	Basalt	Rubbing Stone	Iron	HAM73.0347
C.2:51:514	1669	Bone	Weaving Pattern Spatula	Iron	DAJ
C.2:58:588	1789	Chert	Slingstone	Iron	HAM74.0130
C.2:76:557	1850	Stone	Spindle Rest?	Iron	HAM74.Storage
C.3:41:228	1600	Chert	Slingstone	Iron	HAM73.0295

Stratum 15 (Stratum 16 Fill)

B.1:15B:78	0152	Frit	Egyptian God "Bes"	Iron	DAJ
B.1:18:88	0184	Ceramic	Loom Weight	Iron	HAM68.0180
B.1:18:97	0186	Copper	Probable Armor Scale	Iron	HAM68.0184
B.1:32:168	0283	Ceramic	Pottery Disc	Iron	HAM68.0053
B.1:32:171	0300	Basalt	Stone Vessel Fragment	Iron	HAM68.Storage
B.1:38:129	0240	Bronze	Pin/Hook?	Iron	DAJ
B.1:39:140	0245	Hematite	Weight	Iron	HAM68.0051
B.1:42:136	0237	Bone	Weaving Pattern Spatula	Iron	HAM68.0208
B.1:42:136	0239	Bronze	Pin/Hook?	Iron	DAJ
B.1:44:147	0260	Stone	Spindle Whorl	Iron	HAM68.0128
B.1:44:177	0310	Limestone	Mortar	Iron	HAM68.Storage
B.1:47:185	0302	Copper	Fibula Spring	Iron	HAM68.0238
B.1:52:187	0309	Ceramic	Ostracon	I2/P	DAJ
B.1:53:199	0299	Bone	Bead	Iron	DAJ
B.1:75:215	0566	Limestone	Whetstone Fragment	Iron	HAM71.0135
B.1:76:220	0567	Chert	Slingstone	Iron	HAM71.0136
B.1:77:226	1044	Ceramic	Lamp Fragment	Iron	HAM71.0407
B.1:78:227	0651	Ceramic	Figurine Fragment	I2/P	HAM71.0194
B.1:84:229	0652	Bronze	Spatula	Iron	HAM71.0195

B.1:84:229	0769	Basalt	Stone Object	Iron	HAM71.Storage
B.1:90:243	0803	Ceramic	Ostracon	I2/P	DAJ
B.1:91:246	0767	Chert	Slingstone	Iron	HAM71.0237
B.1:91:246	0768	Bone	Awl	Iron	HAM71.0238
B.1:91:248	0804	Limestone	Rubbing Stone	Iron	HAM71.0263
B.1:91:249	0805	Lead	Weight	Iron	HAM71.0264
B.1:91:249	0806	Alabaster	Stone Cup Fragment	Iron	HAM71.0265
B.1:92:251	0814	Stone	Stone Rim Fragment	Iron	HAM71.Storage
B.1:92:251	0815	Chert	Slingstone	Iron	HAM71.0272
B.1:94:256	0820	Shell	Clam Shell Fragment	Iron	HAM71.0276
B.1:97:274	0877	Soapstone	Whetstone Fragment	Iron	HAM71.0425
B.2:38:106	1117	Bronze	Brace	Iron	HAM71.0442
B.2:42:84	1045	Bronze	Fibula Spring	Iron	HAM71.0427
B.2:47:110	1184	Ceramic	Possible Ostracon	Iron	HAM71.0491
B.2:60:117	1228	Bone	Pendant	Iron	HAM71.0529
B.2:72:130	1313	Basalt	Stone Bowl Fragment	Iron	HAM73.Storage
B.2:72:130	1317	Basalt	Rubbing Stone	Iron	HAM73.0065
B.2:72:130	1318	Chert	Slingstone	Iron	HAM73.0066
B.2:72:130	1658	Ceramic	Ostracon	Iron	DAJ
B.2:72:130	1659	Ceramic	Ostracon	Iron	DAJ
B.2:72:140	1343	Bronze	Fibula	Iron	HAM73.0089
B.2:73:133	1319	Basalt	Rubbing Stone	Iron	HAM73.0067
B.2:73:133	1320	Chert	Slingstone	Iron	HAM73.0068
B.2:74:137	1324	Copper	Bar	Iron	HAM73.0072
B.2:80:150	1538	Bronze	Coin: Roman A.D. 2nd-4th Centuries	LR/BZ	HAM.73.0249
B.2:81:153	1396	Basalt	Weight	Iron	HAM73.0130
B.2:83:154	1401	Stone	Spindle Whorl	Iron	HAM73.0135
B.2:83:154	1404	Chert	Slingstone	Iron	HAM73.0138
B.2:83:155	1431	Chert	Slingstone	Iron	HAM73.0161
B.2:94:222	1656	Ceramic	Ostracon	I2/P	DAJ
B.2:94:237	1625	Stone	Scarab	Iron	HAM73.0315
B.2:118:261	1727	Bone	Weaving Pattern Spatula	Iron	HAM74.0075

B.2:124:300	2034	Bronze	Button	Iron	HAM74.0349
B.2:125:304	2071	Bone	Weaving Pattern Spatula	Iron	HAM74.0383
B.2:126:311	2092	Ceramic	Ostracon	I2/P	HAM74.0400
B.2:133:321	2275	Ivory	Inlay	Iron	HAM76.0096
B.2:135:328	2531	Ceramic	Juglet Fragment	Iron	HAM76.0315
B.2:135:330	2309	Basalt	Stone Bowl Fragment	Iron	HAM76.0125
B.2:137:337	2581	Ceramic	Figurine	I2/P	HAM76.0357
B.4:202:366	1757	Bronze	Needle	Iron	HAM74.0101
B.4:205:372	1728	Shell	Shell, Pierced Hole	Iron	HAM74.0076
B.4:205:373A	1827	Ivory	Inlay	Iron	HAM74.0165
B.4:205:373B	1704	Stone	Worked Flints	Iron	HAM74.0055
B.4:205:376	2103	Limestone	Stone Vessel Fragment	Iron	HAM74.0410
B.4:205:403	1793	Ceramic	Horse Head Figurine	I2/P	HAM74.0134

Appendix C

FAUNA SUMMARY LIST
FOR STRATA 21-16

Appendix C
Fauna Summary List for Strata 21-16

Bones were saved and processed during each of the five seasons of the Heshbon Expedition. This was done under the direction of Robert Little in the 1968 season and under Øystein LaBianca during the remainder of the seasons. In-depth study of the bones from the 1968 season was unfortunately never carried out and the only account of them remains the preliminary report (Little 1969: 232-39).

Quantitative analysis was only able to be done however, on the bones from the 1976 season in that it was only during this season that every fragment was saved. In all previous seasons the very tiny unidentifiable fragments were discarded as "scrap" (Boessneck and von den Driesch 1978: 260-61; LaBianca 1995a: 12; von den Driesch and Boessneck 1995: 67).

This appendix contains information on the find spots of bones of the more significant domestic and wild animals found within the Iron Age strata. Due to the incompleteness of the data mentioned above, generalizations can be made only from the bones of the 1976 season. Information on the bones from the 1971-1974 seasons have been added in order to round out the data only and should not be considered in the same light as those from the 1976 season. In order to make a differentiation, the season/year has been included.

Information on the bones from the 1976 season was taken from the detailed quantitative information found in the Heshbon Expedition Archives. Although a detailed analysis is available on the bones of the 1971 season (LaBianca 1995a: 8-9), since the "scrap" was not saved, this information remains incomplete. Detailed analysis was begun on the bones from the 1974 season, but was never finished, and also suffers from the incompleteness of data mentioned above. The information that appears here was taken from the data which appears on the locus sheets. The same is true for the bones from the 1973 season.

Locus	Year	Cattle	Sheep/Goat	Sheep	Goat	Pig	Camel	Horse	Donkey	Chicken	Fish	Gazelle	Fallow Deer	Wild Sheep/Goat	Wild Sheep	Wild Goat	Wild Pig
Stratum 21																	
C.1:95	73	--	4	--	--	--	--	--	--	--	--	--	--	--	--	--	--
C.1:95	76	--	1	--	--	--	--	--	--	--	--	--	--	--	--	--	--
C.1:96B	73	2	14	--	--	--	--	--	--	--	--	--	--	--	--	--	--
C.1:99	73	1	8	--	--	--	--	--	--	--	--	--	--	--	--	--	--
C.1:142	76	2	10	3	1	2	--	--	--	--	--	--	--	--	--	--	--
C.1:143	76	5	21	3	2	1	--	--	--	--	--	--	--	--	--	--	--
C.2:54	74	--	--	--	--	--	--	--	--	--	--	2	--	--	--	--	--
C.2:55	74	--	3	--	--	--	--	--	--	--	--	--	--	--	--	--	--
C.2:92	74	1	4	--	--	--	--	--	--	--	--	--	--	--	--	--	--
C.2:94	74	--	2	--	--	--	--	--	--	--	--	2	--	--	--	--	--
Total	--	11	67	6	3	3	0	0	0	0	0	4	0	0	0	0	0
Stratum 20																	
B.3:76	73	--	--	--	--	1	--	--	--	--	--	--	--	--	--	--	--
B.3:77	73	--	45	--	--	1	--	5	2	2	--	--	--	--	--	--	--
B.3:81	73	1	2	--	--	--	--	--	--	--	--	--	--	--	--	--	--
B.3:82	73	2	4	--	--	--	--	--	--	--	--	--	--	--	--	--	--
B.3:89	74	--	4	--	--	--	--	--	--	--	--	--	--	--	--	--	--
B.3:91	74	2	9	--	--	--	--	--	--	--	--	--	--	--	--	--	--
B.3:92	74	1	4	--	--	--	--	--	--	--	--	--	--	--	--	--	--
B.3:93	74	1	5	--	--	--	--	--	--	--	--	--	--	--	--	--	--
B.3:94	74	3	3	--	--	1	--	--	--	--	--	--	--	--	--	--	--

	B.3:95	B.3:96	D.4:67	D.4:124	D.4:125	D.4:126	D.4:128	D.4:129	D.4:131	D.4:132	D.4:134	D.4:135	D.4:138	D.4:139	D.4:140	D.4:141	D.4:142	D.4:143	D.4:144	D.4:146	D.4:147	D.4:148	D.4:150	Total
	–	–	–	–	–	–	–	–	–	–	–	–	–	–	–	–	–	–	–	–	–	–	–	0
	–	–	–	–	–	–	–	–	–	–	–	–	–	–	–	–	–	–	–	–	–	–	–	0
	–	–	–	–	–	–	–	–	–	–	–	–	–	–	–	–	–	–	–	–	–	–	–	0
	–	–	–	–	–	–	–	–	–	–	–	–	–	–	–	–	–	–	–	–	–	–	–	0
	–	–	–	–	–	–	–	–	–	–	–	–	–	–	–	–	–	–	–	–	–	–	–	0
	–	–	–	–	–	–	–	1	–	–	–	–	1	–	2	–	–	–	–	–	–	–	–	4
	–	–	–	–	–	–	–	–	–	–	–	1	1	–	–	–	–	–	–	–	–	–	–	2
	–	–	–	–	–	–	–	–	–	–	–	–	–	–	–	–	–	–	–	–	–	–	–	2
	–	–	–	–	–	–	–	–	–	–	–	–	–	–	–	–	–	–	–	–	–	–	–	2
	–	–	–	–	–	–	–	–	–	–	–	–	–	–	–	–	–	–	–	–	–	–	–	5
	–	–	–	–	–	–	–	–	–	–	–	–	–	1	–	–	2	–	–	–	–	–	–	3
	–	–	1	–	–	–	–	1	–	–	3	2	–	3	1	15	1	–	–	–	–	–	–	27
	–	–	–	1	–	1	3	–	–	–	3	4	–	3	6	1	–	2	1	–	–	–	–	22
	–	–	–	1	–	–	–	1	1	–	3	6	2	1	3	10	1	1	1	–	–	–	–	25
	–	1	1	11	10	9	3	–	–	22	1	44	49	4	60	56	53	8	10	1	1	1	3	393
	2	–	–	2	–	2	2	1	–	3	–	6	5	–	2	38	58	3	10	2	–	–	1	140
	74	74	76	76	76	76	76	76	76	76	76	76	76	76	76	76	76	76	76	76	76	76	76	–
Total																								

Stratum 18

Locus	N															
B.2:84	73	–	–	–	–	–	–	–	–	–	–	–	1	–	–	–
C.1:124	76	35	144	9	7	1	2	–	–	1	1	–	–	–	–	–
C.1:126	76	13	77	13	5	6	1	–	–	–	2	–	–	–	–	–
C.1:127	76	9	60	6	2	–	–	–	–	–	–	–	1	–	–	–
C.1:128	76	8	31	4	–	4	–	–	–	–	–	–	–	–	–	–
C.1:129	76	–	25	1	–	1	–	–	–	–	–	–	–	–	–	–
C.1:130	76	–	2	–	1	1	–	–	–	–	–	–	–	–	–	–
C.1:131	76	35	164	13	11	25	–	–	–	–	–	–	–	–	–	–
C.1:132	76	3	13	–	3	1	–	–	–	–	–	–	–	–	–	–
C.1:133	76	47	84	9	6	6	–	1	–	–	–	1	–	–	–	–
C.1:134	76	24	92	10	14	32	1	–	–	–	1	–	–	–	–	–
C.1:135	76	2	8	1	–	–	–	–	–	–	–	–	–	–	–	–
C.1:136	76	5	92	5	5	–	–	–	–	–	–	1	–	–	–	–
C.1:137	76	6	43	6	1	2	–	1	–	3	1	–	–	–	1	1
C.1:138	76	6	110	16	7	4	–	–	–	–	1	1	–	1	–	–
C.1:139	76	13	50	14	3	1	–	–	–	–	–	–	–	–	–	–
C.1:140	76	4	22	4	–	–	–	–	–	–	–	1	–	–	–	–
C.1:141	76	1	11	1	1	–	–	–	–	–	–	–	–	–	–	–
C.5:182	76	1	3	1	1	1	–	–	–	–	–	–	–	–	–	–
C.5:183	76	3	5	–	–	–	–	–	–	–	–	–	–	–	–	–
C.5:193	76	3	20	1	2	–	–	1	–	–	–	–	–	–	–	–
C.5:194	76	–	7	–	–	–	–	–	–	–	–	–	–	–	–	–
C.5:196	76	12	40	7	1	4	–	–	–	–	–	–	–	–	–	–
C.5:205	76	1	2	–	–	–	–	–	–	–	–	–	–	–	–	–

Context																	
C.5:206	76	—	—	—	—	3	—	—	—	—	—	—	—	—	—	—	—
D.4:63	74	—	1	—	—	—	—	—	—	—	—	—	—	—	—	—	—
D.4:136	76	3	14	1	1	1	—	—	—	—	—	—	—	—	—	—	—
Total	—	234	1120	121	70	95	4	5	3	0	6	7	3	3	1	1	1

Stratum 17

Context																	
C.1:118	74	1	31	—	—	—	—	—	—	—	—	—	—	—	—	—	—
C.1:123B	76	40	112	23	16	7	—	—	—	—	2	—	—	—	—	1	—
C.2:89	74	—	2	—	—	—	—	—	—	—	—	—	—	—	—	—	—
C.5:147	76	—	2	—	4	—	—	—	—	—	—	—	—	—	—	—	—
C.5:152	76	3	13	2	1	—	—	—	—	—	—	—	—	—	—	—	—
C.5:163	76	—	1	—	—	—	—	—	—	—	—	—	—	—	—	—	—
C.5:173	76	1	11	2	—	—	—	—	—	—	—	—	—	—	—	—	—
C.5:175	76	—	1	—	—	—	—	—	—	—	1	—	—	—	—	—	—
C.5:180	76	1	1	—	2	—	—	—	—	—	—	—	—	—	—	—	—
C.5:184	76	—	—	—	—	—	—	—	—	—	—	—	—	—	—	—	—
C.5:187	76	—	2	—	—	—	—	—	—	—	—	—	—	—	—	—	—
C.5:189	76	14	25	5	5	—	—	—	—	—	—	—	—	—	—	—	—
C.5:192	76	1	—	—	—	—	—	—	—	—	—	—	—	—	—	—	—
Total	—	61	201	32	28	7	0	0	0	0	3	0	0	0	0	1	0

Stratum 16

Context																	
B.1:119	73	9	72	—	—	—	1	—	1	—	—	—	—	—	—	—	—
B.1:143	73	22	143	—	—	—	—	—	1	—	—	1	—	—	—	—	—
B.2:137	76	5	17	8	2	—	1	—	—	—	—	—	1	—	—	—	—

	B.2:138	C.2:41	C.2:44	C.2:50	C.2:56	C.2:57	C.2:58	C.2:59	C.2:60	C.2:61	C.2:62	C.2:64	C.2:66	C.2:75	C.2:76	C.2:77	C.2:78	C.2:79	C.2:80	C.2:81	C.2:82	C.2:88	C.2:101	C.3:32	C.3:40	C.3:41
	–	–	–	–	–	–	–	–	–	–	–	–	–	–	–	–	–	–	–	–	–	–	–	–	–	–
	–	–	–	–	–	–	–	–	–	–	–	–	–	–	–	–	–	–	–	–	–	–	–	–	–	–
	–	–	–	–	–	–	–	–	–	–	–	–	–	–	–	–	–	–	–	–	–	–	–	–	–	–
	–	–	–	–	–	–	–	–	–	–	–	–	–	–	–	–	–	–	–	–	–	–	–	–	–	–
	–	–	–	–	–	–	–	–	–	–	–	–	–	–	–	–	–	–	–	–	–	–	–	–	–	–
	–	–	–	–	–	–	–	–	–	–	–	–	–	–	–	–	–	–	–	–	–	–	–	–	–	–
	–	–	–	–	–	–	–	–	–	–	–	–	–	–	–	–	–	–	–	–	–	–	–	–	–	–
	–	–	–	–	–	–	–	–	–	–	1	–	–	–	–	–	–	–	–	–	–	1	–	–	–	–
	–	2	–	–	–	–	–	–	–	–	–	–	–	–	–	–	–	–	–	–	–	–	–	–	1	–
	–	–	–	–	–	–	–	–	–	–	–	–	–	–	–	–	–	–	–	–	–	–	–	–	–	–
	–	–	–	–	–	–	–	–	–	–	–	–	–	–	–	–	–	–	–	–	–	–	–	–	–	–
	–	–	–	–	1	–	–	–	–	–	–	–	–	–	–	–	–	–	–	–	–	–	3	–	–	–
	–	–	–	–	–	–	–	–	–	–	–	–	–	–	–	–	–	–	–	–	–	–	–	–	–	–
	–	–	–	–	–	–	–	–	–	–	–	–	–	–	–	–	–	–	–	–	–	–	–	–	–	–
	4	25	31	1	32	5	6	3	1	1	3	5	4	2	5	4	3	1	2	2	1	2	–	1	1	1
	–	2	–	–	10	–	3	–	–	–	–	1	–	2	1	–	–	1	1	–	–	3	–	–	–	–
	76	73	73	76	74	74	74	74	74	74	74	74	74	74	74	74	74	74	74	74	74	74	74	73	73	73

C.3:43	76	–	1	–	–	–	–	–	–	–	–	–	–	–	–	–	–
C.5:86	76	5	8	–	–	–	–	–	–	–	–	–	–	–	–	–	–
C.5:105	76	–	1	–	–	–	–	–	–	–	–	–	–	–	–	–	–
C.5:109	76	–	2	1	–	–	–	–	–	–	–	–	–	–	–	–	–
C.5:110	76	–	3	1	–	–	–	–	–	–	–	–	–	–	–	–	–
C.5:112	76	–	1	–	–	–	–	–	–	–	–	–	–	–	–	–	–
C.5:114	76	1	1	–	–	–	–	–	–	–	–	–	–	–	–	–	–
C.5:119	76	–	2	–	–	–	–	–	–	–	–	–	–	–	–	–	–
C.5:129	76	–	4	–	–	–	–	–	–	–	–	–	–	–	–	–	–
C.5:131	76	1	3	2	–	–	–	–	–	–	–	–	–	–	–	–	–
C.5:168	76	1	–	–	–	–	–	–	–	–	–	–	–	–	–	–	–
C.5:170	76	8	9	1	–	–	–	–	–	–	–	–	–	–	–	–	–
C.7:97	76	–	2	–	–	–	–	–	–	–	–	–	–	–	–	–	–
Total	–	76	415	13	2	4	2	0	5	2	0	1	0	1	0	0	0

Stratum 15 (Stratum 16 Fill)

B.1:19	76	–	–	–	–	1	–	–	–	–	–	–	–	–	–	–	–
B.1:30	71	–	1	–	–	–	–	–	–	–	–	–	–	–	–	–	–
B.1:33	71	1	1	–	–	–	–	–	–	–	–	–	–	–	–	–	–
B.1:34	71	–	1	–	–	–	–	–	–	–	–	–	–	–	–	–	–
B.1:44	71	2	13	–	–	–	–	–	2	–	–	–	–	–	–	–	–
B.1:167	71	–	1	–	–	–	–	–	–	–	–	–	–	–	–	–	–
B.1:75	71	–	11	–	–	–	–	–	–	–	–	–	–	–	–	–	–
B.1:76	71	1	11	–	–	–	–	–	–	–	–	–	–	–	–	–	–
B.1:77	71	–	1	–	–	–	–	–	–	–	–	–	–	–	–	–	–

	B.1:78	B.1:80	B.1:81	B.1:82	B.1:84	B.1:85	B.1:86	B.1:87	B.1:88	B.1:89	B.1:90	B.1:91	B.1:92	B.1:93	B.1:94	B.1:96	B.1:97	B.1:100	B.1:101	B.1:102	B.1:103	B.1:104	B.1:105	B.1:107	B.1:108	B.1:109
										1					13	8	4	6			1					
															1		1	16			1					
	17	3	1	6	27	5	2	20	29	4	13	17	14	1	51	6	49	17	2	3	11	24	31	3	14	1
	1				7	3			3	5	1		1		2		6	1				1	2		3	
	71	71	71	71	71	71	71	71	71	71	71	71	71	71	71	71	71	71	71	71	71	71	71	71	71	71

B.1:110	B.1:111	B.1:112	B.1:113	B.1:115	B.1:116	B.1:118	B.1:122	B.1:123	B.1:124	B.1:125	B.1:126	B.1:127	B.1:130	B.1:131	B.1:133	B.1:134	B.1:135	B.1:136	B.1:137	B.1:138	B.1:139	B.1:140	B.1:141	B.1:142	B.2:35B
–	–	–	–	–	–	–	–	–	–	–	–	–	–	–	–	–	–	–	–	–	–	–	–	–	–
–	–	–	–	–	–	–	–	–	–	–	–	–	–	–	–	–	–	–	–	–	–	–	–	–	–
–	–	–	–	–	–	–	–	–	–	–	–	–	–	–	–	–	–	–	–	–	–	–	–	–	–
–	–	–	–	–	–	–	–	–	–	–	–	–	–	–	–	–	–	–	–	–	–	–	–	–	–
–	–	–	–	–	–	–	–	–	–	–	–	–	–	–	–	–	–	–	–	–	–	–	–	–	–
–	–	–	–	–	1	2	–	–	–	–	–	–	–	–	–	–	–	–	–	–	–	1	–	–	–
–	–	–	–	–	–	–	–	–	–	–	–	–	–	–	–	–	–	–	–	–	–	–	1	–	–
–	–	–	–	–	–	–	–	4	–	2	–	–	–	–	–	–	–	–	–	–	–	–	–	–	–
–	–	–	–	–	–	–	–	–	–	–	–	–	–	–	–	–	–	–	–	–	–	–	–	–	–
–	–	–	–	–	–	–	–	–	–	–	–	–	–	–	–	–	–	–	–	–	–	–	–	–	–
–	–	–	–	–	–	–	–	–	–	3	–	–	–	–	–	–	–	–	–	–	–	–	–	–	–
–	–	–	–	–	–	–	–	–	–	–	–	–	–	–	–	–	–	–	–	–	–	–	–	–	–
–	–	–	–	–	–	–	–	–	–	–	–	–	–	–	–	–	–	–	–	–	–	–	–	–	–
3	1	10	2	8	20	43	14	76	30	35	3	21	53	98	21	5	28	37	46	6	80	37	37	163	1
–	–	–	–	–	3	5	–	3	–	–	–	–	–	6	–	–	–	1	–	–	2	–	3	5	–
71	71	71	71	71	71	73	73	73	73	73	73	73	73	73	73	73	73	73	73	73	73	73	73	73	71

	B.2:38	B.2:72	B.2:73	B.2:79	B.2:80	B.2:83	B.2:94	B.2:118	B.2:119	B.2:120	B.2:122	B.2:124	B.2:125	B.2:126	B.2:128	B.2:129	B.2:130	B.2:131	B.2:132	B.2:133	B.2:134	B.2:135	B.2:136	B.4:202	B.4:205
															3		3	1		2		6			
				1											4					5	1	3			
		1	1				1	5		1	1	1													9
											1												1		
																									1
											1									12		1			
											5														
															22		2	5		7	7	8	12		
															29	1	2	8	1	22	7	25	18		
	8	51	28	66	52	127	33	184	30	11	72	83	36	15	178	6	21	73		72	45	90	61	12	163
	1		1	3	5	15	1	5	4		2	4	1	3	28			5		15	9	31	15		1
	71	73	73	73	73	73	74	74	74	74	74	74	74	74	76	76	76	76	76	76	76	76	76	74	74

	B.4:219	B.4:220	B.4:224	B.4:272	B.4:274	Total
	:	:	:	:	:	0
	:	:	:	:	:	0
	:	:	:	:	:	0
	:	:	:	:	:	1
	:	:	:	:	:	15
	:	:	:	:	:	18
	:	:	:	:	:	1
	1	:	:	:	:	27
	:	:	1	:	:	38
	:	:	:	:	:	1
	:	:	:	:	:	34
	:	:	:	:	:	9
	:	:	:	:	:	63
	:	:	:	:	:	113
	11	5	29	7	8	2865
	:	:	1	:	1	219
	74	74	74	74	74	--

References

References

Abu Dayyah, A. S.; Green, J. A.; Hassan, I. H.; and Suleiman, E.
1991 Archaeological Survey of Greater Amman, Phase 1: Final Report. *Annual of the Department of Antiquities of Jordan* 35: 361-95.

Adams, R. M. C.
1974 The Mesopotamian Social Landscape: A View from the Frontier. Pp. 1-11 in *Reconstructing Complex Societies*, ed. C. B. Moore. Bulletin of the American Schools of Oriental Research Supplement 20.

Aharoni, Y.
1973a Remarks on the "Israeli" Method of Excavation. Pp. 48-53 in *Eretz-Israel* 11 (Dunayevsky volume) (Hebrew; English summary, p. 23*).

1973b *Beer-Sheba I: Excavations at Tel Beer-Sheba 1969-1971 Seasons.* Tel Aviv: Tel Aviv University.

Al-Eisawi, D. M.
1985 Vegetation in Jordan. Pp. 45-57 in *Studies in the History and Archaeology of Jordan II*, ed. A. Hadidi. Amman: Department of Antiquities.

Albright, W. F.
1924 Researches of the School in Western Judea. *Bulletin of the American Schools of Oriental Research* 15: 2-11.

1932a The Excavation of Tell Beit Mirsim, 1: The Pottery of the First Three Campaigns. *Annual of the American Schools of Oriental Research* 12. New Haven, CT: American Schools of Oriental Research.

1932b *The Archaeology of Palestine and the Bible.* London: Revell.

1933 In Memoriam: Melvin Grove Kyle. *Bulletin of the American Schools of Oriental Research* 51: 5-7.

1934 New Books by Officers of the Schools. *Bulletin of the American Schools of Oriental Research* 54: 27-28.

1938 The Present State of Syro-Palestinian Archaeology. Pp. 1-46 in *The Harverford Symposium on Archaeology and the Bible,* ed. E. Grant. New Haven: CT: American Schools of Oriental Research.

1943 The Excavation of Tell Beit Mirsim, 3. *Annual of the American Schools of Oriental Research* 21-22. New Haven, CT: American Schools of Oriental Research.

1969 The Impact of Archaeology on Biblical Research. Pp. 1-14 in *New Directions in Biblical Archaeology*, eds. D. N. Freedman and J. Greenfield. Garden City, NY: Doubleday.

1971 *The Archaeology of Palestine.* Glouster, MA: Peter Smith.

Albright, W. F., and Kelso, J. L.
1968 *The Excavation of Bethel (1934-1960). Annual of the American Schools of Oriental Research* 39. Cambridge, MA: American Schools of Oriental Research.

Aldred, C.
1987 *The Egyptians.* Revised ed. New York: Thames and Hudson.

Americans to Dig for Bible City. *New York Times,* 5 April 1971.

Amiran, R.
1969 *Ancient Pottery of the Holy Land.* Jerusalem: Massada.

Andrews University Heshbon Expedition.
1977 Outline of Final Publication Procedures for the Tell Hesban Excavations: The Period Reports (Adopted by Geraty et al. November 18, 1977). Unpublished study.

ANET = Pritchard, J. B.
1969 *Ancient Near Eastern Texts Relating to the Old Testament.* 3rd ed. Princeton: Princeton University.

Atkinson, K.
1994 Diggers From Paid Peasants to Eager Volunteers. *Biblical Archaeology Review* 20.1: 66-71, 80.

Aufrecht, W. E.
1989 *A Corpus of Ammonite Inscriptions.* Lewiston, NY: Edwin Mellen.

Avigad, N.
1980 *Discovering Jerusalem.* Nashville, TN: Thomas Nelson.

Bade, W. F.
1934 *A Manual of Excavation in the Near East: Methods of Digging and Recording of the Tell en-Nasbeh Expedition in Palestine.* Berkeley: University of California.

Barakat, G.
1973 *The Archaeological Heritage of Jordan: The Archaeological Periods and Sites (East Bank).* Amman: Department of Antiquities.

Barkay, G.
1992 The Iron Age II-III. Pp. 302-73 in *The Archaeology of Ancient Israel,* ed. A. Ben-Tor. New Haven, CT: Yale University.

1993 The Redefining of Archaeological Periods: Does the Date 588/586 B.C.E. Indeed Mark the End of the Iron Age Culture? Pp. 106-9 in *Biblical Archaeology Today,* 1990, eds. A. Biran and J. Aviram. Jerusalem: Israel Exploration Society.

Barth, F.
1961 *Nomads of South Persia: The Basseri Tribe of the Khamseh Confederacy.* Boston: Little, Brown and Company.

Battenfield, J. R.
1991 Field C: The Northern Suburb. Pp. 53-73 in *Madaba Plains Project 2: The 1987 Season at Tell el-ᶜUmeiri and Vicinity and Subsequent Studies,* eds. L. G. Herr et al. Berrien Springs, MI: Andrews University/Institute of Archaeology.

Battenfield, J. R., and Herr, L. G.
1989 Field C: The Northern Suburb. Pp. 258-81 in *Madaba Plains Project 1: The 1984 Season at Tell el-ᶜUmeiri and Vicinity and Subsequent Studies,* eds. L. T. Geraty et al. Berrien Springs, MI: Andrews University/Institute of Archaeology.

Beegle, D. M.
1969 Area B. *Andrews University Seminary Studies* 7.2: 118-26.

1975 Soundings Area G. *Andrews University Seminary Studies* 13.2: 213-15.

Beit-Arieh, I., and Cresson, B. C.
1991 Ḥorvat ᶜUza: A Fortified Outpost on the Eastern Negev Border. *Biblical Archaeologist* 54: 126-35.

Bender, F.
1974 *Geology of Jordan.* Contributions to the Regional Geology of the Earth, ed. H. J. Martini. Supplementary Edition of vol. 7. Berlin: Gebuder Bortraeger.

Ben-Tor, A.
1995 Tel Hazor, 1994. *Israel Exploration Journal* 45: 65-68.

2000a Hazor and the Chronology of Northern Israel: A Reply to Israel Finkelstein. *Bulletin of the American Schools of Oriental Research* 317: 9-15.

2000b Tell Hazor, 2000. *Israel Exploration Journal* 50: 243-49.

Ben-Tor, A., and Ben-Ami, D.
1998 Hazor and the Archaeology of the Tenth Century B.C.E. *Israel Exploration Journal* 48: 1-37.

Bennett, C.
1972 Review of *Heshbon 1968: The First Campaign at Tell Hesban*, by R. S. Boraas and S. H. Horn. *Palestine Exploration Quarterly* 104: 161.

1975 Excavations at the Citadel, Amman, 1975. *Annual of the Department of Antiquities of Jordan* 20: 131-42.

1979a Excavations at the Citadel (al Qalᶜa) Amman, 1977. *Annual of the Department of Antiquities of Jordan* 23: 151-59.

1979b Excavations on the Citadel (al Qalᶜa), Amman, 1978. Fourth Preliminary Report. *Annual of the Department of Antiquities of Jordan* 23: 61-170.

Berlin, A. M.
1997 Between Large Forces: Palestine in the Hellenistic Period. *Biblical Archaeologist* 60: 2-51.

Bienkowski, P.
1989 Prosperity and Decline in LBA Canaan: A Reply to Liebowitz and Knapp. *Bulletin of the American Schools of Oriental Research* 275: 59-63.

1992 The Beginning of the Iron Age in Southern Jordan: A Framework. Pp. 1-12 in *Early Edom and Moab: The Beginning of the Iron Age in Southern Jordan*, ed. P. Bienkowski. Sheffield Archaeological Monographs 7. Sheffield: J. R. Collis.

1995 The Small Finds. Pp. 79-92 in *Excavations at Tawilan in Southern Jordan*, eds. C. M. Bennett and P. Bienkowski. British Academy Monographs in Archaeology 8. British Institute at Amman for Archaeology and History: Oxford University.

Bikai, P. M.
1993 Khirbet Salameh 1992. *Annual of the Department of Antiquities of Jordan* 37: 521-32.

Binford, L. R.
1962 Archaeology as Anthropology. *American Antiquity* 28: 217-25.

1968 Archaeological Perspectives. Pp. 5-32 in *New Perspectives in Archaeology*. eds. S. R. and L. R. Binford. Chicago: Aldine.

Blakely, J. A.
1993 Frederick Jones Bliss: Father of Palestinian Archaeology. *Biblical Archaeologist* 56: 110-15.

Bliss, F. J., and Macalister, R. A. S.
1902 *Excavations in Palestine During the Years 1898-1900*. London: Palestine Exploration Fund.

Boessneck, J., and von den Driesch, A.
1978 Preliminary Analysis of the Animal Bones From Tell Hesban. *Andrews University Seminary Studies* 16.1: 259-87.

Boling, R. G.
1969 Bronze Age Buildings at the Shechem High Place: ASOR Excavations at Tananir. *Biblical Archaeologist* 32: 82-103.

1988 *The Biblical Community in Transjordan*. Sheffield: Almond.

1989 Site Survey in the el-ᶜUmeiri Region. Pp. 98-188 in *Madaba Plains Project 1: The 1984 Season at Tell el-ᶜUmeiri and Vicinity and subsequent Studies*. eds. L. T. Geraty et al. Berrien Springs, MI: Andrews University/Institute of Archaeology.

Boraas, R. S.
1968 Letter to Staff.

1974a Notes and News. *Palestine Exploration Quarterly* 106: 5-6.

1974b Circular Letter No. 3.

1984 Some Aspects of Archaeology—Tactics and Strategy. Pp. 39-50 in *The Answers Lie Below: Essays in Honor of Lawrence Edmund Toombs*, ed. H. O. Thompson. Lanham, MD: University Press of America.

1986 Iron IA Ceramics at Tell Balatah: A Preliminary Examination. Pp. 249-63 in *The Archaeology of Jordan and Other Studies*, eds. L. T. Geraty and L. G. Herr. Berrien Springs, MI: Andrews University.

1988 Publication of Archaeological Reports. Pp. 325-33 in *Benchmarks in Time and Culture: An Introduction to Palestinian Archaeology*, eds. J. F. Drinkard, G. L. Mattingly and J. M. Miller. Atlanta: Scholars.

1994 Hesban and Field Method How We Dug and Why. Pp. 15-23 in *Hesban After 25 Years*, eds. D. Merling and L.T. Geraty. Berrien Springs, MI: Institute of Archaeology/Horn Archaeological Museum.

Boraas, R. S., and Geraty, L. T.
1976 Andrews University Heshbon Expedition, The Fourth Campaign at Tell Hesban (1974): A Preliminary Report. *Andrews University Seminary Studies* 14.1: 1-16.

1978 Andrews University Heshbon Expedition, The Fifth Campaign at Tell Hesban (1976): A Preliminary Report. *Andrews University Seminary Studies* 16.1: 1-17.

Boraas, R. S., and Horn, S. H.
1969a Andrews University Heshbon Expedition: The First Campaign at Tell Hesban (1968). *Andrews University Seminary Studies* 7.2: 97-17.

1969b The Results of the First Season's Work. *Andrews University Seminary Studies* 7.2: 217-22.

1973 Andrews University Heshbon Expedition: The Second Campaign at Tell Hesban (1971). *Andrews University*

Seminary Studies 11.1: 1-16.

1975 Andrews University Heshbon Expedition: The Third Campaign at Tell Hesban (1973). *Andrews University Seminary Studies* 13.2: 101-16.

Borowski, O.
1987 *Agriculture in Iron Age Israel*. Winona Lake: Eisenbrauns.

1998 *Every Living Thing: Daily Use of Animals in Ancient Israel*. Walnut Creek, CA: AltaMira.

Brandfon, F.
1987 The Limits of Evidence: Archaeology and Objectivity. *Maarav* 4: 5-43.

Braudel, F.
1972 *The Mediterranean and the Mediterranean World in the Age of Phillip II*, vol. 1 (trans. Siân Reynolds). New York: Harper & Row.

Broshi, M.
1995 Review of *Sedentarization and Nomadization: Food System Cycles at Hesban and Vicinity in Transjordan*, by Ø. S. LaBianca. *Israel Exploration Journal* 45: 205-6.

Brower, J. K.; LaBianca, Ø. S.; and Mitchel, L. A.
1980 Stages in the Development of an Archaeological Data Base: Goals Envisioned, Work Done, and Lessons Learned in an Effort to Computerize Stratigraphic and Typological Data from the Excavations at Tell Hesban, Jordan. Unpublished manuscript. Andrews University, Institute of Archaeology.

Brower, J. K., and Storfjell, J. B.
1982 The Value of Coins as a Primary Basis for Findspot Dating. Unpublished manuscript. Andrews University, Institute of Archaeology.

Bruins, H. J.
1994 Comparative Chronology of Climate and Human History in the Southern Levant

from the Late Chalcolithic to the Early Arab Period. Pp. 301-14 in *Late Quaternary Chronology and Paleoclimates of the Eastern Mediterranean*, eds. O, Bar-Yosef and R. S. Kra. Radiocarbon.

Buhl, M.-L., and Holm-Nielsen, S.
1969 *Shiloh: The Danish Excavations at Tall Sailun, Palestine, in 1926, 1929, 1932 and 1963.* Copenhagen: The National Museum of Denmark.

Bullard, R. G.
1972 Geological Study of the Heshbon Area. *Andrews University Seminary Studies* 10.2: 129-41.

Bunimovitz, S.
1995a How Mute Stones Speak: Interpreting What We Dig. *Biblical Archaeology Review* 21.2: 58-67, 96-100.

1995b On the Edge of Empires Late Bronze Age (1500-1200 BCE). Pp. 321-31, 581-83 in *The Archaeology of Society in the Holy Land*, ed. T. E. Levy. London: Leicester University.

Bunimovitz, S., and Lederman, Z.
1997 Beth-Shemesh: Culture Conflict on Judah's Frontier. *Biblical Archaeology Review* 23.1: 42-49, 75-77.

Carcasson, R. H.
1977 *A Field Guide to the Coral Reef Fishes of the Indian and West Pacific Oceans.* London: Collins.

Christopherson, G. L.
1991 Limekins from the Regional Survey. Pp. 343-52 in *Madaba Plains Project 2: The 1987 Season at Tell el-ᶜUmeiri and Vicinity and Subsequent Studies*, eds. L. G. Herr et al. Berrien Springs, MI: Andrews University/Institute of Archaeology.

1994 In Pursuit of the Long Durée: Environmental Models and Cycles of Intensification and Abatement from the ᶜUmeiri Survey. Unpublished manuscript. Andrews University, Institute of Archaeology.

1997a The 1989 Random Square Survey in the Tall al-ᶜUmayri Region. Pp. 250-90 in *Madaba Plains Project 3: The 1989 Season at Tell el-ᶜUmeiri and Vicinity and Subsequent Studies*, eds. L. G. Herr et al. Berrien Springs, MI: Andrews University/Institute of Archaeology.

1997b Madaba Plains Project: Regional Survey Sites, 1989. Pp. 291-302 in *Madaba Plains Project 3: The 1989 Season at Tell el-ᶜUmeiri and Vicinity and Subsequent Studies*, eds. L. G. Herr et al. Berrien Springs, MI: Andrews University/Institute of Archaeology.

1997c A Regional Approach to Archaeology on the Madaba Plain: Random Survey and Settlement Patterns. Paper Presented at the Annual Meeting of the American Schools of Oriental Research. November 17, 1997, Napa, California. Http://nexus.srnr.arizona.edu/~garych/hrs1_report/hrs1.html.

Christopherson, G. L., and Dabrowski, B.
1997 Using a Geographic Information System to Create Probability Models for Sites with Tombs from the al-ᶜUmayri Regional Survey. Pp. 39-45 in *Studies in the History and Archaeology of Jordan VI*, eds. G. Bisheh, M. Zaghloul and I. Kehrberg. Amman: Department of Antiquities.

Christopherson, G. L., and Guertin, D. P.
1995 Soil Erosion, Agriculture Intensification, and Iron Age Settlement in the Region of Tall al-ᶜUmayri, Jordan. Paper presented at the Annual Meeting of the American Schools of Oriental Research. November 1995, Philadelphia. Http://nexus.srnr.arizona.edu/~garych/Um_erosion/erosion_pap.html.

1996 Visibility Analysis and Ancient Settlement Strategies in the Region of Tall al-ᶜUmayri, Jordan. Paper presented at the Annual Meeting of the American Schools of Oriental Research. November 1996, New Orleans. Http://nexus.srnr.arzona.edu/~garych/viewshed/vspaper.htm.

Christopherson, G. L.; Guertin, D. P.; and Borstad, K. A.
1996 GIS and Archaeology: Using Arc/Info to Increase our Understanding of Ancient Jordan. Paper presented at the Annual Meeting of the American Schools of Oriental Research. November 1996, New Orleans. Http://www.esri.com/base/common/userconf/proc96/T0150/PAP119/P119.htm.

Christopherson, G. L., and Herr, L. G.
1994 The Madaba Plains Project: Jalul Regional Survey Manual. Unpublished manuscript. Andrews University, Institute of Archaeology.

Christopherson, G. L.; Boling, R. G.; Cole, J. A.; Hopkins, D. C.; Mattingly, G. L.; Schnurrenberger, D. W.; and Younker, R. W.
1997 Summary Descriptions of Archaeological Sites from the Survey at Tall al-ᶜUmayri, Jordan. Http://nexus.srnr.arizona.edu/~garych/umsites/umsite_start.html.

Clark, D. R.
1991 Field B: The Western Defensive System. Pp. 53-73 in *Madaba Plains Project 2: The 1987 Season at Tell el-ᶜUmeiri and Vicinity and Subsequent Studies*, eds. L. G. Herr et al. Berrien Springs, MI: Andrews University/Institute of Archaeology.

1994 The Iron 1 Western Defense System at Tell El-ᶜUmeiri, Jordan. *Biblical Archaeologist* 57: 138-48.

1997 Field B: The Western Defensive System. Pp. 53-98 in *Madaba Plains Project 3: The 1989 Season at Tell el-ᶜUmeiri and Vicinity and Subsequent Studies*, eds. L. G. Herr et al. Berrien Springs, MI: Andrews University/Institute of Archaeology.

Clark, D. R.; Cole, J. A.; and Sandness, G. A.
1997 Landscape Resources and Human Occupation of Ancient Jordan: A Perspective from Subsurface Mapping Techniques Utilized by the Madaba Plains Project. Pp. 31-38 in *Studies in the History and Archaeology of Jordan VI*, eds. G. Bisheh, M. Zaghloul and I. Kehrberg. Amman: Department of Antiquities.

Cole, D. P.
1984 *Shechem I: The Middle Bronze II B Pottery*. Winona Lake: Eisenbrauns.

Cole, J. A.
1989a Available Water Resources and Use in the Tell el-ᶜUmeiri Region. Pp. 41-50 in *Madaba Plains Project 1: The 1984 Season at Tell el-ᶜUmeiri and Vicinity and Subsequent Studies*, eds. L. T. Geraty et al. Berrien Springs, MI: Andrews University/Institute of Archaeology.

1989b Random Square Survey in the el-ᶜUmeiri Region. Pp. 51-97 in *Madaba Plains Project 1: The 1984 Season at Tell el-ᶜUmeiri and Vicinity and Subsequent Studies*, eds. L. T. Geraty et al. Berrien Springs, MI: Andrews University/Institute of Archaeology.

Conder, C. R.
1882 Lieutenant Conder's Report No. IX: Heshbon and Its Cromlechs. *Palestine Exploration Fund Quarterly Statement* 14: 7-15.

1892 *Heth and Moab*. London: Alexander P. Watt.

Corbo, V., and Loffreda, S.
1981 Nuove scoperte alla Fortezza di Macheronte. *Liber Annuus* 31: 257-86.

Crawford, P.
1976a Botany and Ethnobotany: Proposed Research. Unpublished manuscript. Andrews University, Institute of Archaeology.

1976b Excavation of the Control Square: Proposed Research. Unpublished manuscript. Andrews University, Institute of

Archaeology.

1976c The Mollusca of Tell Hesban. *Andrews University Seminary Studies* 14.2: 171-75.

1986 Flora of Tell Hesban and Area, Jordan. Pp. 75-98 in *Environmental Foundations: Studies of Climatical, Geological, Hydrological and Phytological Conditions in Hesban and Vicinity*, eds. Ø. S. LaBianca and L. Lacelle. *Hesban 2.* Berrien Springs, MI: Andrews University.

Cribb, R.
1991 *Nomads in Archaeology.* Cambridge: Cambridge University.

Cross, F. M.
1969 An Ostracon From Heshbon. *Andrews University Seminary Studies* 7.2: 223-29.

1973 W. F. Albright's View on Biblical Archaeology and Its Methodology. *Biblical Archaeologist* 36: 2-5.

1975 Ammonite Ostraca from Heshbon: Ostraca IV-VIII. *Andrews University Seminary Studies* 13.1: 1-20.

1982 Alphabets and Pots: Reflections on Typological Method in the Dating of Human Artifacts. *Maarav* 3: 121-36.

1993 Ammonite Ostraca from Tell Hesban. Unpublished manuscript. Andrews University, Institute of Archaeology.

Cross, F. M., and Geraty, L. T.
1994 The Ammonite Ostraca from Tell Hesban. Pp. 169-74 in *Hesban After 25 Years*, eds. D. Merling and L. T. Geraty. Berrien Springs, MI: Institute of Archaeology/Horn Archaeological Museum.

Crowfoot, J. W.; Kenyon, K. M.; and Sukenik, E. L.
1942 *Samaria-Sebaste I: The Buildings.* London: Palestine Exploration Fund.

Dabrowski, B.
1993 Terracotta Figurines from Tell Hesban and Vicinity (1968-1976). Unpublished manuscript. Andrews University, Institute of Archaeology.

Dajani, R. W.
1966a An Iron Age Tomb from Amman. *Annual of the Department of Antiquities of Jordan* 11: 41-47.

1966b Jabal Nuzha Tomb at Amman. *Annual of the Department of Antiquities of Jordan* 11: 48-52.

1970 A Late Bronze-Iron Age Tomb Excavated at Sahab, 1968. *Annual of the Department of Antiquities of Jordan* 15: 29-34.

Dalman, G.
1928- *Arbeit und Sitte in Palästina*, 7 vols.
1942 Schriften des Deutschen Palästina-Instituts 3-10. Gütersloh: Bertelsmann.

Danin, A.
1995 Man and the Natural Environment. Pp. 24-39, 351-52 in *The Archaeology of Society in the Holy Land*, ed. T. E. Levy. London: Leicester University.

Daviau, P. M.
1992 Preliminary Report of the Excavations at Tell Jawa in the Madaba Plains (1991). *Annual of the Department of Antiquities of Jordan* 36: 145-62.

1994 Excavations at Tell Jawa, Jordan (1993): Preliminary Report. *Annual of the Department of Antiquities of Jordan* 38: 173-93.

1995 Iron Age II Pithoi from Tell Jāwa, Jordan: Construction Techniques and Typology. Pp. 607-16 in *Studies in the History and Archaeology of Jordan V*, ed. K. ꜥAmr, F. Zayadine and M. Zaghloul. Amman: Department of Antiquities.

1996 The Fifth Season of Excavations at Tall

Jawa (1994): A Preliminary Report. *Annual of the Department of Antiquities of Jordan* 40: 83-100.

1997 Moab's Northern Border: Khirbat al-Mudayna on the Wadi ath-Thamad. *Biblical Archaeologist* 60: 222-28.

1998 Canadian Team Finishes First Season of Excavations at Khirbat al-Mudayna. Http://info.wlu.ca/~wwwarch/jordan/stairway.html.

Davies, G. I.
1988 British Archaeologists. Pp. 37-62 in *Benchmarks in Time and Culture: An Introduction to Palestinian Archaeology*, eds. J. F. Drinkard, G. L. Mattingly and J. M. Miller. Atlanta: Scholars.

Davis, T. W.
1993 Faith and Archaeology: A Brief History to the Present. *Biblical Archaeology Review* 19.2: 54-59.

1995 Albright & Archaeology: The Search for Realia. *Archaeology in the Biblical World* 3.1: 42-50.

Dearman, J. A.
1989 Historical Reconstruction and the Mesha^C Inscription. Pp. 155-210 in *Studies in the Mesha Inscription and Moab*, ed. A. Dearman. Atlanta: Scholars.

1992 Settlement Patterns and the Beginning of the Iron Age in Moab. Pp. 65-75 in *Early Edom and Moab: The Beginning of the Iron Age in Southern Jordan*, ed. P. Bienkowski. Sheffield Archaeological Monographs 7. Sheffield: J. R. Collis.

1997 Roads and Settlements in Moab. *Biblical Archaeologist* 60: 205-13.

Dever, W. G.
1973 Two Approaches to Archaeological Method—the Architectural and the Stratigraphic. *Eretz Israel* 11 (Dunayevsky volume): 1*-8*.

1974 *Archaeology and Biblical Studies: Retrospects and Prospects*. The Winston Lectures, Seabury-Western Evangelical Theological Seminary, 1972. Evanston: Seabury-Western.

1980a Archaeological Method in Israel: A Continuing Revolution. *Biblical Archaeologist* 43: 41-48.

1980b Biblical Theology and Biblical Archaeology: An Appreciation of G. Ernest Wright. *Harvard Theological Review* 73: 1-15.

1981 The Impact of the "New Archaeology" on Syro-Palestinian Archaeology. *Bulletin of the American Schools of Oriental Research* 242: 15-29.

1982 Retrospects and Prospects in Biblical and Syro-Palestinian Archaeology. *Biblical Archaeologist* 45: 103-7.

1984 The Relationship Between Bible, Oriental Studies, and Archaeology from the Perspective of an Archaeologist. Pp. 31-45 in *A Symposium on the Relationship Between Bible, Oriental Studies, and Archaeology*, ed. L. T. Geraty. Occasional Papers of the Horn Archaeological Museum No. 3. Berrien Springs, MI: Andrews University/Horn Archaeological Museum.

1985 Syro-Palestinian and Biblical Archaeology. Pp. 31-74 in *The Hebrew Bible and Its Modern Interpreters*, eds. D. A. Knight and G. M. Tucker. Vol. 1 of The Bible and Its Modern Interpreters. Chico: Scholars.

1986 *Gezer IV: The 1969-71 Seasons in Field VI, the "Acropolis."* Annual of the Hebrew Union College Biblical and Archaeological School in Jerusalem IV. Jerusalem: Hebrew Union College-Jewish Institute of Religion.

1988 Impact of the "New Archaeology." Pp. 337-52 in *Benchmarks in Time and Culture: An Introduction to Palestinian Archaeology*, eds. J. F. Drinkard, G. L.

Mattingly and J. M. Miller. Atlanta: Scholars.

1990 *Recent Archaeological Discoveries and Biblical Research.* Seattle: University of Washington.

1992 Archaeology, Syro-Palestinian and Biblical. Pp. 354-67 in *The Anchor Bible Dictionary*, vol. 1, ed. D. N. Freedman. New York: Doubleday.

1993a Biblical Archaeology: Death and Rebirth. Pp. 706-22 in *Biblical Archaeology Today, 1990*, eds. A. Biran and J. Aviram. Jerusalem: Israel Exploration Society.

1993b What Remains of the House that Albright Built? *Biblical Archaeologist* 56: 25-35.

1993c Further Evidence on the Date of the Outer Wall at Gezer. *Bulletin of the American Schools of Oriental Research* 289: 33-54.

1993d Syro-Palestinian Archaeology "Comes of Age": The Inaugural Volume of the Hesban Series A Review Article. *Bulletin of the American Schools of Oriental Research* 290-91: 127-30.

1993e Gezer. Pp. 496-506 in *The New Encyclopedia of Archaeological Excavations in the Holy Land*, vol. 2, ed. E. Stern. Jerusalem: Israel Exploration Society.

1994 Archaeology, Texts, and History-Writing: Toward an Epistemology. Pp. 105-17 in *Uncovering Ancient Stones: Essays in Memory of H. Niel Richardson*, ed. L. M. Hopfe. Winona Lake, IN: Eisenbrauns.

1995 The Death of a Discipline. *Biblical Archaeology Review* 21.5: 50-55, 70.

1996 The Tell: Microcosm of Cultural Process. Pp. 37-45 in *Retrieving the Past: Essays on Archaeological Research and Methodology in Honor of Gus W. Van Beek*, ed. J. Seger. Winona Lake, IN: Eisenbrauns.

1997 Gezer. Pp. 396-400 in *The Oxford Encyclopedia of Archaeology in the Near East*, vol. 2, ed. E. M. Meyers. Oxford: Oxford University.

1998 Archaeology, Ideology, and the Quest for an "Ancient" or "Biblical Israel." *Near Eastern Archaeology (formerly Biblical Archaeologist)* 61: 39-52.

Dever, W. G., and Lance, H. D., eds.
1978 *A Manual for Field Archaeologists.* Cincinnati: Hebrew Union College.

Dever, W. G., and Younker, R. W.
1991 Tel Gezer, 1990. *Israel Exploration Journal* 41: 282-86.

Dever, W. G.; Lance, H. D.; and Wright, G. E.
1970 *Gezer I: Preliminary Report of the 1966-67 Seasons*. Annual of the Hebrew Union College Biblical and Archaeological School in Jerusalem I. Jerusalem: Hebrew Union College-Jewish Institute of Religion.

Dever, W. G.; Lance, H. D.; Bullard, R. G.; Cole, D. P.; and Seger, J. D.
1974 *Gezer II: Report of the 1967-70 Seasons in Fields I and II*. Annual of the Hebrew Union College Biblical and Archaeological School in Jerusalem II. Jerusalem: Hebrew Union College-Jewish Institute of Religion.

Dimbleby, G. W.
1967 *Plants and Archaeology.* London: Humanities.

Dornemann, R. H.
1983 *The Archaeology of the Transjordan in the Bronze and Iron Ages.* Milwaukee: Milwaukee Public Museum.

1990 Preliminary Comments on the Pottery Traditions at Tell Nimrin, Illustrated from the 1989 Season of Excavations. *Annual of the Department of Antiquities of Jordan* 34: 153-81.

Dothan, T.
1982 *The Philistines and Their Material*

Culture. Jerusalem: Israel Exploration Society.

Eickelman, D. F.
1981 *The Middle East: An Anthropological Approach.* Englewood Cliffs, NJ: Prentice Hall.

Eph᷂al, I.
1982 *The Ancient Arabs: Nomads on the Boarders of the Fertile Crescent 9th-5th Centuries B.C.* Jerusalem: Magnes.

Falconer, S. E.
1987 Heartland of Villages: Reconsidering Early Urbanism in the Southern Levant. Unpublished Ph.D. Dissertation, University of Arizona.

1992 Review of *Sedentarization and Nomadization: Food System Cycles at Tell Hesban and Vicinity in Transjordan,* by Ø. S. LaBianca. *American Anthropologist* 94.3: 760-761.

Final Publication Archives.
Records of the Final Excavation Reports Process of the Heshbon Expedition. Berrien Springs, MI: Andrews University/Institute of Archaeology.

Finkelstein, I.
1984 The Iron Age "Fortresses" of the Negev Highlands: Sedentarization of the Nomads. *Tel Aviv* 11: 189-209.

1988 *The Archaeology of Israelite Settlement.* Jerusalem: Israel Exploration Society.

1990 Excavations at Khirbet ed-Dawwara: An Iron Age Site Northeast of Jerusalem. *Tel Aviv* 17: 163-208.

1992 Pastoralism in the Highlands of Canaan in the Third and Second Millennia B.C.E. Pp. 133-42 in *Pastoralism in the Levant: Archaeological Materials in Anthropological Perspectives.* Monographs in World Archaeology No. 10, eds. O. Bar-Yosef and A. Khazanov. Madison, WI: Prehistory.

1993a Review of Hesban I (LaBianca) and Hesban 5 (Ibach). *Biblical Archaeology Review* 19.4: 6, 76.

1993b *Shiloh: The Archaeology of a Biblical Site,* ed. I. Finkelstein. Tel Aviv: Institute of Archaeology.

1995a *Living on the Fringe: The Archaeology and History of the Negev, Sinai and Neighboring Regions in the Bronze and Iron Ages.* Monographs in Mediterranean Archaeology 6. Sheffield: Sheffield Academic.

1995b The Date of the Settlement of the Philistines in Canaan. *Tel Aviv* 22: 213-39.

1996a Ethnicity and Origin of the Iron I Settlers of the Highlands of Canaan: Can the Real Israel Stand Up? *Biblical Archaeologist* 59: 198-212.

1996b The Archaeology of the United Monarchy: An Alternative View. *Levant* 28: 177-87.

1998a From Sherds to History: Review Article. *Israel Exploration Journal* 48: 120-31.

1998b Biblical Archaeology or Archaeology in the Iron Age? A Rejoinder. *Levant* 30: 167-74.

1998c Philistine Chronology: High, Middle or Low? Pp. 140-47 in *Mediterranean Peoples in Transition: Thirteenth to Early Tenth Centuries BCE,* eds. S. Gitin, A. Mazar and E. Stern. Jerusalem: Israel Exploration Society.

1998d Notes of the Stratigraphy and Chronology of Iron Age Ta᷂anach. *Tel Aviv* 25: 208-18.

1999a Hazor and the North in the Late Iron Age: A Low Chronology Perspective. *Bulletin of the American Schools of Oriental Research* 314: 55-70.

1999b State Formation in Israel and Judah: A

Contrast in Context, A Contrast in Trajectory. *Near Eastern Archaeology* 62: 35-52.

Finkelstein, I., and Perevolotsky, A.
1990 Processes of Sedentarization and Nomadization in the History of Sinai and the Negev. *Bulletin of the American Schools of Oriental Research* 279: 67-88.

FFB = Committee on Translations.
1980 *Fauna and Flora of the Bible.* 2nd ed. New York: United Bible Societies.

Fischer, D. H.
1970 *Historians' Fallacies: Toward a Logic of Historical Thought.* New York: Harper and Row.

Fisher, J. R.
1994 Hesban and the Ammonites During the Iron Age. Pp. 81-95 in *Hesban After 25 Years*, eds. D. Merling and L. T. Geraty. Berrien Springs, MI: Institute of Archaeology/Horn Archaeological Museum.

Flannery, K. V.
1967 Culture History vs. Cultural Process: A Debate in American Archaeology. *Scientific American* 217: 119-22.

1973 Archaeology With a Capital S. Pp. 47-53 in *Research and Theory in Current Archaeology*, ed. C. Redman. New York: Wiley.

Franken, H. J.
1969 *Excavations at Deir ᶜAlla I: A Stratigraphical and Analytical Study of the Iron Age Pottery.* Leiden: Brill.

1992 *Excavations at Tell Deir ᶜAlla: The Late Bronze Age Sanctuary.* Louvain: Peeters.

Frick, F. S.
1985 *The Formation of the State in Ancient Israel.* Sheffield: Almond.

Friend, G.
1998 *Tell Taannek: The Loom Weights.* Birzeit: Palestinian Institute of Archaeology, Birzeit University.

Furumark, A.
1941a *Mycenaean Pottery I: Analysis and Classification.* Stockholm: Svenska Institutet I Athen.

1941b *Mycenaean Pottery II: Chronology.* Stockholm: Svenska Institutet I Athen.

Geraty, L. T.
1972 Heshbon: A Case of Biblical Confirmation or Confutation? *Spectrum* 4.2: 29-36.

1973 Heshbon 1971: Area D. *Andrews University Seminary Studies* 11.1: 89-112.

1974 The Excavations at Tell Hesban, 1974. *American Schools of Oriental Research Newsletter* 5: 1-8.

1975a The 1974 Season of Excavations at Tell Hesban. *Annual of the Department of Antiquities of Jordan* 20: 47-56.

1975b Hesban (Heshbon). *Revue Biblique* 82: 576-86.

1975c Excavating Biblical Heshbon, 1974—2: The Anatomy of the Heshbon "Dig." *Review and Herald* September, 25: 4-6.

1975d Excavating Biblical Heshbon, 1974—3: A Visit to Ancient Heshbon. *Review and Herald* October, 2: 9-11.

1976 The 1976 Season of Excavations at Tell Hesban. *Annual of the Department of Antiquities of Jordan* 21: 41-53.

1977a Excavations at Tell Hesban, 1976. *American Schools of Oriental Research Newsletter* 8: 1-15.

1977b Hesban (Heshbon). *Revue Biblique* 84: 404-8.

1977c Five Seasons at Heshbon—3: Results of the 1976 "Dig." *Review and Herald* July, 14: 7-9.

1980 Tell Hesban (1976). *Archiv für Orientforschung* 27.1: 251-55.

1981 Heshbon Exhibit and Lectures. *Biblical Archaeologist* 44: 247.

1982 Heshbon. Pp. 699-702 in *The International Standard Bible Encyclopedia*, vol.2, ed. G. W. Bromiley. Grand Rapids: Eerdmans.

1983 Heshbon: The First Casualty in the Israelite Quest for the Kingdom of God. Pp. 239-48 in *The Quest for the Kingdom of God: Essays in Honor of George E. Mendenhall*, eds. H. B. Huffmon, F. A. Spina and A. R. W. Green. Winona Lake, IN: Eisenbrauns.

1985 The Andrews University Madaba Plains Project: A Preliminary Report on the First Season at Tell el-ᶜUmeiri (June 18-August 8, 1984). *Andrews University Seminary Studies* 23: 85-110.

1990 Preface. Pp. xv-xvi in *Sedentarization and Nomadization: Food System Cycles at Hesban and Vicinity in Transjordan*, by Ø. S. LaBianca. *Hesban 1*. Berrien Springs, MI: Andrews University.

1992 Heshbon. Pp. 181-84 in *The Anchor Bible Dictionary*, vol. 3, ed. D. N. Freedman. New York: Doubleday.

1993 Heshbon. Pp. 626-30 in *The New Encyclopedia of Archaeological Excavations in the Holy Land*, vol. 2, ed. E. Stern. Jerusalem: Israel Exploration Society.

1994 Why We Dug at Tell Hesban. Pp. 39-52 in *Hesban After 25 Years*, eds. D. Merling and L. T. Geraty. Berrien Springs, MI: Institute of Archaeology/Horn Archaeological Museum.

1997 Ḥesban. Pp. 19-22 in *The Oxford Encyclopedia of Archaeology in the Near East*, vol. 3, ed. E. M. Meyers. Oxford: Oxford University.

Geraty, L. T., and House, C. L.
1984 The Archaeological Field Grid: A Discussion of Its Attributes and Use. Pp.

97-112 in *The Answers Lie Below: Essays in Honor of Lawrence Edmund Toombs*, ed. H. O. Thompson. Lanham, MD: University Press of America.

Geraty, L. T., and LaBianca, Ø. S.
1985 The Local Environment and Food Procuring Strategies in Jordan: The Case of Tell Hesban and Its Surrounding Region. Pp. 323-30 in *Studies in the History and Archaeology of Jordan II*, ed. A. Hadidi. Amman: Department of Antiquities.

Geraty, L. T., and Running, L. G., eds.
1989 *Historical Foundations: Studies of Literary References to Hesban and Vicinity. Hesban 3*. Berrien Springs, MI: Andrews University.

Geraty, L. T., and Willis, L.
1986 The History of Archaeological Research in Transjordan. Pp. 3-72 in *The Archaeology of Jordan and Other Studies*, eds. L. T. Geraty and L. G. Herr. Berrien Springs, MI: Andrews University.

Geraty, L. T.; Herr, L. G.; and LaBianca, Ø. S.
1987 The Madaba Plains Project: A Preliminary Report on the First Season at Tell el-ᶜUmeiri and Vicinity. *Annual of the Department of Antiquities of Jordan* 31: 187-99.

1988 The Joint Madaba Plains Project: A Preliminary Report on the Second Season at Tell el-ᶜUmeiri and Vicinity (June 18-August 6, 1987). *Andrews University Seminary Studies* 26: 217-52.

1989 Madaba Plains Project: The 1987 Season at Tell el-ᶜUmeiri and Vicinity. *Annual of the Department of Antiquities of Jordan* 33: 145-76.

Geraty, L. T.; Herr, L. G.; LaBianca, Ø. S; Battenfield, J. R.; Boling, R. G.; Clark, D. R.; Lawlor, J. I.; Mitchel, L. A.; and Younker, R. W.
1986 Madaba Plains Project: A Preliminary Report of the 1984 Season at Tell el-ᶜUmeiri and Vicinity. *Bulletin of the*

American Schools of Oriental Research Supplement No. 24: 117-44.

Geraty, L. T.; Herr, L. G.; Labianca, Ø. S.; and Younker, R. W.
1989a *Madaba Plains Project 1: The 1984 Season at Tell el-ᶜUmeiri and Vicinity and Subsequent Studies.* Berrien Springs, MI: Andrews University/Institute of Archaeology.

1989b An Overview of Goals, Methods and Findings. Pp. 3-19 in *Madaba Plains Project 1: The 1984 Season at Tell el-ᶜUmeiri and Vicinity and Subsequent Studies*, eds. L. T. Geraty et al. Berrien Springs, MI: Andrews University/Institute of Archaeology.

Geraty, L. T.; Herr, L. G.; Labianca, Ø. S.; Battenfield, J. R.; Christopherson, G. L.; Clark, D. R.; Cole, J. A.; Daviau, P. M; Hubbard, L. E.; Lawlor, J. I; Low, R.; and Younker, R. W.
1990 Madaba Plains Project: A Preliminary Report of the 1987 Season at Tell el-ᶜUmeiri and Vicinity. *Bulletin of the American Schools of Oriental Research Supplement* No. 26: 59-88.

Gill, D.
1994 How They Met: Geology Solves Mystery of Hezekiah's Tunnelers. *Biblical Archaeology Review* 20.4: 20-33; 64.

Gilliland, D.
1986 Paleoethnobotany and Paleoenvironment. Pp. 122-42 in *Environmental Foundations: Studies of Climatical, Geological, Hydrological and Phytological Conditions in Hesban and Vicinity*, eds. Ø. S. LaBianca and L. Lacelle. *Hesban 2.* Berrien Springs, MI: Andrews University.

Gitin, S.
1990 *Gezer III: A Ceramic Typology of the Late Iron II, Persian and Hellenistic Periods at Tell Gezer.* Jerusalem: Hebrew Union College-Jewish Institute of Religion.

Giveon, R.
1971 *Les Bédouins Shosou des Documents*

Égyptiens. Leiden: Brill.

Glock, A. E.
1983 The Use of Ethnography in an Archaeological Research Design. Pp. 171-79 in *The Quest for the Kingdom of God: Studies in Honor of G. E. Mendenhall*, eds. H. B. Huffman, F. A. Spina and A. R. W. Green. Winona Lake: Eisenbrauns.

1985 Tradition and Change in Two Archaeologies. *American Antiquity* 50: 464-77.

Glueck, N.
1934 Explorations in Eastern Palestine, I. *Annual of the American Schools of Oriental Research* 14. New Haven: American Schools of Oriental Research.

1935 Explorations in Eastern Palestine, II. *Annual of the American Schools of Oriental Research* 15. New Haven: American Schools of Oriental Research.

1939 Explorations in Eastern Palestine, III. *Annual of the American Schools of Oriental Research* 18-19. New Haven: American Schools of Oriental Research.

1940 *The Other Side of the Jordan.* New Haven: American Schools of Oriental Research.

1946 *The River Jordan.* Philadelphia: Westminster.

1951 Explorations in Eastern Palestine, IV. *Annual of the American Schools of Oriental Research* 25-28. New Haven: American Schools of Oriental Research.

1970 *The Other Side of the Jordan.* 2nd ed. New Haven: American Schools of Oriental Research.

Gonen, R.
1984 Urban Canaan in the Late Bronze Period. *Bulletin of the American Schools of Oriental Research* 253: 61-73.

Gordon, R. L., and Knauf, E. A.
1987 Er-Rumman Survey 1985. *Annual of the*

Department of Antiquities of Jordan 31: 289-98.

Gordon, R. L., and Villiers, L. E.
1983 Telul Edh Dhahab and Its Environs Surveys of 1980 and 1982: A Preliminary Report. *Annual of the Department of Antiquities of Jordan* 22: 275-89.

Grant, E.
1921 *The People of Palestine: An Enlarged Edition of "The Peasantry of Palestine, Life, Manners and Customs of the Village Life."* Philadelphia: J. B. Lippincott.

1931 *Ain Shems Excavations I-II.* Haverford: Haverford College.

Hadidi, A.
1974 The Excavations of the Roman Forum at Amman (Philadelphia), 1964-1967. *Annual of the department of Antiquities of Jordan* 19: 71-91.

Hallo, W. W., and Simpson, W. K.
1971 *The Ancient Near East: A History.* San Diego: Harcourt Brace Jovanovich.

Halpern, B.
1998 Research Design in Archaeology: The Interdisciplinary Perspective. *Near Eastern Archaeology (formerly Biblical Archaeologist)* 61: 53-65.

Haltenorth, T.
1959 Beitrag zur Kenntnis des Mesopotamischen Damhirsches Cervus (Dama) mesopotamicus Brooke, 1875 - und zur Stammes- und Verbreitungsgeschichte der Damhirsche allgemein. *Säugetierkundliche Mitteilungen* 7: 1-89.

Hamilton, R. W.
1935 Excavations at Tell Abu Hawam. *Quarterly of the Department of Antiquities in Palestine* 4: 1-69.

Hankey, V.
1974 The Late Bronze Age Temple at Amman: I. The Aegean Pottery. *Levant* 6: 131-59.

Harding, G. L.
1945 Two Iron Age Tombs, Amman. *Quarterly of the Department of Antiquities in Palestine* 11: 67-74.

1951 Two Iron Age Tombs in Amman. *Annual of the Department of Antiquities of Jordan* 1: 37-40.

Harding, G. L., and Isserlin, B. S.
1953a A Middle Bronze Age Tomb at Amman. Pp. 14-26 in *Four Tomb Groups From Jordan.* Palestine Exploration Fund Annual VI, by G. L. Harding. London: Palestine Exploration Fund.

1953b An Early Iron Age Tomb at Madaba. Pp. 27-47 in *Four Tomb Groups From Jordan.* Palestine Exploration Fund Annual VI, by G. L. Harding. London: Palestine Exploration Fund.

Harding, G. L., and Tufnell, O.
1953 The Tomb of Adoni Nur in Amman. Pp. 48-72 in *Four Tomb Groups from Jordan.* Palestine Exploration Fund Annual VI, by G. L. Harding. London: Palestine Exploration Fund.

Harrison, T. P.
1996 Tell Madaba Archaeological Project. Paper Presented at the Annual Meeting of the American Schools of Oriental Research. November 1996, New Orleans. Http://www.cobb.msstate.edu/asordigs/madaba.html.

Harvey, D.
1973 Heshbon 1971: Area A. *Andrews University Seminary Studies* 11.1: 17-34.

Hennessy, J. B.
1966 Excavations of a Late Bronze Age Temple at Amman. *Palestine Exploration Quarterly* 98: 155-62.

Herr, L. G.
1976 Heshbon 1974: Area D. *Andrews University Seminary Studies* 14.1: 79-99.

1978a Heshbon 1976: Area D. *Andrews University Seminary Studies* 16.1: 109-28.

1978b *The Scripts of Ancient Northwest Semitic Seals*. Missoula: Scholars.

1979a Introduction to the Iron Age at Tell Hesban. Unpublished manuscript. Andrews University, Institute of Archaeology.

1979b Iron Age Hesban. Paper presented at the American Schools of Oriental Research Symposium on Heshbon, 1979. Andrews University.

1980 The Formal Scripts of Iron Age Transjordan. *Bulletin of the American Schools of Oriental Research* 238: 21-34.

1983a *The Amman Airport Excavations, 1976*. Annual of the American Schools of Oriental Research, vol. 48. Winona Lake, IN: Eisenbrauns.

1983b The Amman Airport Structure and the Geopolitics of Ancient Transjordan. *Biblical Archaeologist* 46: 223-29.

1989a Organization and Procedures of Excavation. Pp. 213-215 in *Madaba Plains Project 1: The 1984 Season at Tell el-ᶜUmeiri and Vicinity and Subsequent Studies*, eds. L. T. Geraty et al. Berrien Springs, MI: Andrews University/Institute of Archaeology.

1989b The Random Surface Survey. Pp. 216-32 in *Madaba Plains Project 1: The 1984 Season at Tell el-ᶜUmeiri and Vicinity and Subsequent Studies*, eds. L. T. Geraty et al. Berrien Springs, MI: Andrews University/Institute of Archaeology.

1989c The Pottery. Pp. 299-354 in *Madaba Plains Project 1: The 1984 Season at Tell el-ᶜUmeiri and Vicinity and Subsequent Studies*, eds. L. T. Geraty et al. Berrien Springs, MI: Andrews University/Institute of Archaeology.

1991 Pottery Typology and Chronology. Pp. 232-45 in *Madaba Plains Project 2: The 1987 Season at Tell el-ᶜUmeiri and Vicinity and Subsequent Studies*, eds. L.

G. Herr et al. Berrien Springs, MI: Andrews University/Institute of Archaeology.

1992 Shifts in Settlement Patterns of Late Bronze and Iron Age Ammon. Pp. 175-77 in *Studies in the History and Archaeology of Jordan IV*, eds. S. Tell et al. Amman: Department of Antiquities.

1993a Whatever Happened to the Ammonites? *Biblical Archaeology Review* 19.6: 26-35, 68.

1993b The Search for Biblical Heshbon. *Biblical Archaeology Review* 19.6: 36-37, 68.

1995a Wine Production in the Hills of Southern Ammon and the Founding of Tall al-ᶜUmayri in the Sixth Century B.C. *Annual of the Department of Antiquities of Jordan* 39: 121-25.

1995b The Late Iron II-Persian Ceramic Horizon at Tall al-ᶜUmayri. Pp. 617-19 in *Studies in the History and Archaeology of Jordan V*, eds. K. ᶜAmr, F. Zayadine and M. Zaghloul. Amman: Department of Antiquities.

1997a Ammon. Pp. 103-5 in *The Oxford Encyclopedia of Archaeology in the Near East*, vol. 1, ed. E. M. Meyers. Oxford: Oxford University.

1997b Organization of the Excavation and Summary of Results at Tall al-ᶜUmayri. Pp. 7-20 in *Madaba Plains Project 3: The 1989 Season at Tell el-ᶜUmeiri and Vicinity and Subsequent Studies*, eds. L. G. Herr et al. Berrien Springs, MI: Andrews University/Institute of Archaeology.

1997c The Pottery. Pp. 228-49 in *Madaba Plains Project 3: The 1989 Season at Tell el-ᶜUmeiri and Vicinity and Subsequent Studies*, eds. L. G. Herr et al. Berrien Springs, MI: Andrews University/Institute of Archaeology.

1997d The Iron Age II Period: Emerging Nations. *Biblical Archaeologist* 60: 114-83.

1998   Tell al-ᶜUmayri and the Madaba Plains Region during the Late Bronze-Iron Age I Transition. Pp. 251-64 in *Mediterranean Peoples in Transition: Thirteenth to Early Tenth Centuries BCE*, eds. S. Gitin, A. Mazar and E. Stern. Jerusalem: Israel Exploration Society.

1999a Tall al-ᶜUmayri and the Reubenite Hypothesis. Pp. 64*-77* in *Eretz-Israel* 26 (Cross volume).

1999b The Ammonites in the Late Iron Age and Persian Period. Pp. 219-37 in *Ancient Ammon*, eds. B. MacDonald and R. W. Younker. Leiden: Brill.

2000   The Settlement and Fortification of Tall al-ᶜUmayri in Jordan during the LB/Iron I Transition. Pp. 167-79 in *The Archaeology of Jordan and Beyond: Essays in Honor of James A. Sauer*, eds. L. E. Stager, J. A. Green and M. D. Coogan. Winona Lake, IN: Eisenbrauns.

In press a Urbanism at Tall al-ᶜUmayri During the LB/Iron I Transition. Urbanism, ed. W. Aufrecht.

In press b The History of the Collared Pithos at Tell el-ᶜUmeiri, Jordan. Doug Esse Memorial Volume, ed. S. Wolff.

Herr, L. G., and Christopherson, G. L.
1998   *Excavation Manual: Madaba Plains Project* (rev. ed). Berrien Springs, MI: Madaba Plains Project/Institute of Archaeology.

Herr, L. G., and Clark, D. R.
2001   Excavating the Tribe of Reuben. *Biblical Archaeology Review* 27.2: 36-47, 64, 66.

Herr, L. G., and Younker, R. W.
1994   *Excavation Manual: Madaba Plains Project* (rev. ed.). Berrien Springs, MI: Madaba Plains Project/Institute of Archaeology.

Herr, L. G.; Geraty, L. T.; LaBianca, Ø. S.; and Younker, R. W.
1991a *Madaba Plains Project 2: The 1987 Season at Tell el-ᶜUmeiri and Vicinity and Subsequent Studies*. Berrien Springs, MI: Andrews University/Institute of Archaeology.

1991b Madaba Plains Project: The 1989 Excavations at Tell el-ᶜUmeiri and Vicinity. *Annual of the Department of Antiquities of Jordan* 35: 155-79.

1994   Madaba Plains Project: The 1992 Excavations at Tell el-ᶜUmeiri, Tell Jalul, and Vicinity. *Annual of the Department of Antiquities of Jordan* 38: 147-72.

Herr, L. G.; Geraty, L. T.; LaBianca, Ø. S.; Younker, R. W.; and Clark, D. R.
1996   Madaba Plains Project 1994: Excavations at Tall al-ᶜUmayri, Tall Jalul and Vicinity. *Annual of the Department of Antiquities of Jordan* 40: 63-81.

1997a *Madaba Plains Project 3: The 1989 Season at Tell el-ᶜUmeiri and Vicinity and Subsequent Studies*. Berrien Springs, MI: Andrews University/Institute of Archaeology.

1997b Madaba Plains Project 1996: Excavations at Tall al-ᶜUmayri, Tall Jalul and Vicinity. *Annual of the Department of Antiquities of Jordan* 41: 145-67.

Herr, L. G.; Clark, D. R.; Geraty, L. T.; Younker, R. W.; and LaBianca, Ø. S.
2000a *Madaba Plains Project — ᶜUmayri 4: The 1992 Season at Tell al-ᶜUmayri and Subsequent Studies*. Berrien Springs, MI: Andrews University/Institute of Archaeology.

Herr, L. G.; Clark, D. R.; Geraty, L. T.; and LaBianca, Ø. S.
2000b Madaba Plains Project: Tall Al-ᶜUmayri 4, 1998. *Andrews University Seminary Studies* 38.1: 29-44.

Herzog, Z.

1984 *Beer-Sheba II: The Early Iron Age Settlements*. Tel Aviv: Tel Aviv University.

1992 Settlement and Fortification Planning in the Iron Age. Pp. 231-74 in *The Architecture of Ancient Israel*, eds. A. Kempinski and R. Reich. Jerusalem: Israel Exploration Society.

Hesban. *Jordan: A Quarterly Magazine of Tourism and Cultural Interest*, 1971: 3.2.

1970 Heshbon Expedition Abandoned. *Student Movement*, 15 October 1970.

Heshbon Exhibit Featured by Horn Museum. *Student Movement*, 1 April 1981.

Heshbon Expedition Archives. Records of the 1968-1976 Seasons. Berrien Springs, MI: Andrews University/Institute of Archaeology.

Hesse, B.

1986 Animal Use at Tell Miqne-Ekron in the Bronze Age and Iron Age. *Bulletin of the American Schools of Oriental Research* 264: 17-27.

Hodder, I.

1992 *Theory and Practice in Archaeology*. London: Routledge.

Holladay, J. S.

1990 Red Slip, Burnish, and the Solomonic Gateway at Gezer. *Bulletin of the American Schools of Oriental Research* 277/278: 23-70.

Homès-Fredericq, D.

1989 Lehun. Pp. 349-59 in *Archaeology of Jordan: Field Reports, Surveys and Sites L-Z*, eds. D. Homès-Fredericq and J. B. Hennessy. Leuven: Peeters.

1992 Late Bronze and Iron Age Evidence from Lehun in Moab. Pp. 187-202 in *Early Edom and Moab: The Beginning of the Iron Age in Southern Jordan*, ed. P. Bienkowski. Sheffield Archaeological

Monographs 7. Sheffield: J. R. Collis.

1995 Stamp and Cylinder Seal Techniques in Jordan. Pp. 469-77 in *Studies in the History and Archaeology of Jordan V*, eds. K. ᶜAmr, F. Zayadine and M. Zaghloul. Amman: Department of Antiquities.

Hopkins, D. C.

1993 Pastoralists in Late Bronze Age Palestine: Which Way Did They Go? *Biblical Archaeologist* 56: 200-211.

Horn, S. H.

1967 Circular Letter No. 1.

1968- The First Season of Excavations at Hesh-
1969 bon, Jordan. *American Schools of Oriental Research Newsletter* No. 3.2: 1-5.

1969a The 1968 Heshbon Expedition. *Biblical Archaeologist* 32: 26-41.

1969b History of Andrews University's First Archaeological Expedition—I: Choosing the Site for the Church's First Archaeological Dig. *Review and Herald* 146.1: 2-5.

1969c Die Ausgrabung des biblischen Hesbon im Jahre 1968—I: Geschichte der ersten Expedition nach Hesbon, unternommen von der Andrews-Universität. *Der Adventbote* 68.4: 66-68.

1969d Excavating Biblical Heshbon in 1968— 5: First Season's Accomplishments. *Review and Herald* 146.5: 4-7.

1969e Die Ausgrabung des biblischen Hesbon im Jahre 1968—V: Die Ergebnisse der ersten Grabeperiode. *Der Adventbote* 68.8: 144-46.

1969f Heshbon (Jordanie). *Revue Biblique* 76: 395-98, Plates 10-11a.

1970- Archaeological Activities in Jordan.
1971 *American Schools of Oriental Research Newsletter* No. 7: 2-4.

1971 Three Seals from Sahab Tomb "C."

Annual of the Department of Antiquities of Jordan 16: 103-6.

1971- The Second Season of Excavations at
1972   Heshbon. *American Schools of Oriental Research Newsletter* No. 4: 1-4.

1972a The 1971 Season of Excavations at Tell Hesban. *Annual of the Department of Antiquities of Jordan* 17: 15-22, 111-15.

1972b Heshbon (Jordanie). *Revue Biblique* 79: 422-26, Plates 41-42a.

1972c Excavating Biblical Heshbon in 1971— 3: Archaeology Is a Science. *Review and Herald* 149.2: 11-12.

1972d Excavating Biblical Heshbon in 1971— 4: Results of the 1971 Expedition. *Review and Herald* 149.3: 9-11.

1973- The Excavations at Tell Hesban 1973.
1974   *American Schools of Oriental Research Newsletter* No. 2: 1-4.

1974   The 1973 Season of Excavations at Tell Hesban. *Annual of the Department of Antiquities of Jordan* 19: 151-56.

1975   Tell Hesban. *Revue Biblique* 82: 100-105.

1976   Heshbon. Pp. 410-11 in *The Interpreter's Dictionary of the Bible, Supplementary Volume*, ed. K. Crim. Nashville: Abingdon.

1982   *Heshbon in the Bible and Archaeology.* Occasional Papers of the Horn Archaeological Museum, Andrews University 2. Berrien Springs, MI: Horn Archaeological Museum.

1994   My Life in Archaeology and the Early History of the Heshbon Archaeology Expedition. Pp. 1-13 in *Hesban After 25 Years*, eds. D. Merling and L. T. Geraty. Berrien Springs, MI: Institute of Archaeology/Horn Archaeological Museum.

Horn, S. H., and Geraty, L. T.
1974   The Excavations at Biblical Heshbon, 1973. *Ministry* 47.1: 12-14.

Horn, S. H., and Platt, E. E.
1990   Scarabs from Tell Hesban. Unpublished manuscript. Andrews University, Institute of Archaeology.

Hübner, U.
1992   *Die Ammoniter.* Abhandlung des deutschen Palästina-Vereins 16. Wiesbaden: Harrassowitz.

Hughes, G. R., and Nims, C. P.
1954   *Reliefs and Inscriptions at Karnak III: The Bubastite Portal.* Chicago: University of Chicago.

Ibach, R.
1976a Area G.8 (Umm es-Sarab). *Andrews University Seminary Studies* 14: 113-17.

1976b Archaeological Survey of the Hesban Region. *Andrews University Seminary Studies* 14: 119-26.

1978a Expanded Archaeological Survey of the Hesban Region. *Andrews University Seminary Studies* 16: 201-14.

1978b An Intensive Surface Survey at Jalul. *Andrews University Seminary Studies* 16: 215-22.

1987   *Archaeological Survey of the Hesban Region. Hesban 5.* Berrien Springs, MI: Andrews University.

1994   Two Roads Lead to Esbus. Pp. 65-79 in *Hesban After 25 Years*, eds. D. Merling and L. T. Geraty. Berrien Springs, MI: Institute of Archaeology/Horn Archaeological Museum.

Ibrahim, M. M.
1972   Archaeological Excavations at Sahab, 1972. *Annual of the Department of Antiquities of Jordan* 17: 23-36.

1974   Second Season of Excavation at Sahab,

1973. *Annual of the Department of Antiquities of Jordan* 19: 55-61.

1975 Third Season of Excavation at Sahab, 1975. *Annual of the Department of Antiquities of Jordan* 20: 69-82.

1987 Sahab and its Foreign Relations. Pp. 73-81 in *Studies in the History and Archaeology of Jordan III*, ed. A. Hadidi. Amman: Department of Antiquities.

JADIS = Palumbo, G., ed.
1994 *The Jordan Antiquities Database and Information System*. Amman: Department of Antiquities of Jordan/American Center of Oriental Research.

Ji, C. C.
1995 Iron Age I in Central and Northern Transjordan: An Interim Summary of Archaeological Data. *Palestine Exploration Quarterly* 127: 122-40.

1997a The East Jordan Valley During Iron Age I. *Palestine Exploration Quarterly* 129: 17-37.

1997b A Note on the Iron Age Four-room House in Palestine. *Orientalia* 66: 387-413.

1998 Archaeological Survey and Settlement Patterns in the Region of ᶜIraq al-ᶜAmir, 1996: A Preliminary Report. *Annual of the Department of Antiquities of Jordan* 42: 587-608.

Ji, C. C., and ᶜAttiyat, T.
1997 Archaeological Survey of the Dhbn Plateau: A Preliminary Report. *Annual of the Department of Antiquities of Jordan* 41: 115-28.

Ji, C. C., and Lee, J.-K.
1998 Preliminary Report on the Survey of the Dhībān Plateau, 1997. *Annual of the Department of Antiquities of Jordan* 42: 549-71.

Joffe, A. H.
1997 New Archaeology. Pp. 134-38 in *The Oxford Encyclopedia of Archaeology in*

the *Near East*, vol. 4, ed. E. M. Meyers. Oxford: Oxford University.

Jordan Dig Is Postponed. *Student Movement*, 12 January 1983.

Kallai, Z.
1986 *Historical Geography of the Bible: The Tribal Territories of Israel*. Leiden: E. J. Brill.

Kamp, K. A., and Yoffee, N.
1980 Ethnicity in Ancient Western Asia During the Early Second Millennium B.C.: Archaeological Assessments of Ethno-archaeological Prospectives. *Bulletin of the American Schools of Oriental Research* 237: 85-104.

Kenyon, K.
1952 *Beginning in Archaeology*. New York: Praeger.

King, P.
1983 *American Archaeology in the Mideast: A History of the American Schools of Oriental Research*. Philadelphia: American Schools of Oriental Research.

1987 The Influence of Ernest G. Wright on the Archaeology of Palestine. Pp. 15-29 in *Archaeology and Biblical Interpretation*, eds. L. G. Purdue, L. E. Toombs and G. L. Johnson. Atlanta: John Knox.

1988 American Archaeologists. Pp. 15-35 in *Benchmarks in Time and Culture: An Introduction to Palestinian Archaeology*, eds. J. F. Drinkard, G. L. Mattingly and J. M. Miller. Atlanta: Scholars.

Kitchen, K. A.
1964 Some New Light on the Asiatic Wars of Ramesses II. *Journal of Egyptian Archaeology* 50: 47-70.

1973 *The Third Intermediate Period in Egypt*. Warminster: Aris and Phillips.

1992 The Egyptian Evidence on Ancient Jordan. Pp. 21-34 in *Early Edom and Moab: The Beginning of the Iron Age in*

Southern Jordan, ed. P. Bienkowski. Sheffield Archaeological Monographs 7. Sheffield: J. R. Collis.

1993 New Directions in Biblical Archaeology: Historical and Biblical Aspects. Pp. 34-52 in *Biblical Archaeology Today, 1990*, eds. A. Biran and J. Aviram. Jerusalem: Israel Exploration Society.

Kletter, R.
1991 The Rujm El-Malfuf Buildings and the Assyrian Vassal State of Amman. *Bulletin of the American Schools of Oriental Research* 284: 33-50.

Kloner, A.
1997 Underground Metropolis—The Subterranean World of Maresha. *Biblical Archaeology Review* 23.2: 24-35; 67.

Know Your Country: Tell Hesban and the Archaeological Excavations. *Al Ra^C i*, 10 September 1971.

Köhler-Rollefson, I.
1987 Ethnoarchaeological Research into the Origins of Pastoralism. *Annual of the Department of Antiquities of Jordan* 31: 535-39.

1992 A Model for the Development of Nomadic Pastoralism on the Transjordanian Plateau. Pp. 11-18 in *Pastoralism in the Levant: Archaeological Materials in Anthropological Perspectives*. Monographs in World Archaeology No. 10, eds. O. Bar-Yosef and A. Khazanov. Madison, WI: Prehistory.

Kotter, W. R.
1979 Objects of Stone, Clay, Bone and Ivory from the Heshbon Excavations. Unpublished manuscript. Andrews University, Institute of Archaeology.

Krug, H. P.
1991 The Necropolis at Tell el-^CUmeiri (East). Pp. 356-69 in *Madaba Plains Project 2: The 1987 Season at Tell el-^CUmeiri and Vicinity and Subsequent Studies*, eds. L. G. Herr et al. Berrien Springs, MI:

Andrews University/Institute of Archaeology.

Kuhn, T. S.
1970 *The Structure of Scientific Revolutions* (rev. ed.). Chicago: University of Chicago.

LaBianca, Ø. S.
1973a Tell Hesban 1971: The Zooarchaeological Remains. *Andrews University Seminary Studies* 11: 133-44.

1973b Research Design for the Analysis and Interpretation of Multiple Assembleges of Zooarchaeological Remains from Tell Hesban, Jordan. Unpublished manuscript. Andrews University, Institute of Archaeology.

1974 A Preliminary Research Design for Ethnographic Studies at Hesban in Jordan. Unpublished manuscript. Andrews University, Institute of Archaeology.

1975 Pertinence and Procedures for Knowing Bones. *American Schools of Oriental Research Newsletter* 1: 1-6.

1976a Tell Hesban 1974: The Village of Hesban: An Ethnographic Preliminary Report. *Andrews University Seminary Studies* 14: 189-200.

1976b The Cultural Ecology of Sheep and Goat Exploitation at Hesban, Proposed Research: Heshbon Anthropology Group (March, 1976). Unpublished manuscript. Andrews University, Institute of Archaeology.

1976c An Ethnographic Study of the Management of Sheep and Goat Herds and the Utilization of Their Products and By-Products by Sedentary Pastorlists at Hesban (May, 1976). Unpublished manuscript. Andrews University, Institute of Archaeology.

1977 Local Habitat and Modes of Livelihood at Hesban Through Time: A Summary of Methods and Emerging Conclusions.

Paper presented at the Annual Meeting of ASOR. Symposium on Heshbon. December 29, San Francisco.

1978 Man, Animals, and Habitat at Hesban: An Integrated Overview. *Andrews University Seminary Studies* 16: 229-52.

1980 Taphonomy: The Study of the Processes of Destruction and Deposition of Animal Remains. Paper presented at the American Center of Oriental Research. November 11, Amman.

1984 Objectives, Procedures, and Findings of Ethnoarchaeological Research in the Vicinity of Hesban in Jordan. *Annual of the Department of Antiquities of Jordan* 28: 269-87.

1985 The Return of the Nomad: An Analysis of the Process of Nomadization in Jordan. *Annual of the Department of Antiquities of Jordan* 29: 251-54.

1986a Food System Transitions and Mechanisms of Abatement. Unpublished manuscript. Andrews University, Institute of Archaeology.

1986b The Diachronic Study of Animal Exploitation at Hesban: The Evolution of a Research Project. Pp. 167-81 in *The Archaeology of Jordan and Other Studies*, eds. L. T. Geraty and L. G. Herr. Berrien Springs, MI: Andrews University.

1988 Sociocultural Anthropology and Syro-Palestinian Archaeology. Pp. 369-87 in *Benchmarks in Time and Culture: An Introduction to Palestinian Archaeology*, eds. J. F. Drinkard, G. L. Mattingly and J. M. Miller. Atlanta: Scholars.

1989a Intensification of the Food System in Central Transjordan During the Ammonite Period. *Andrews University Seminary Studies* 27: 126-78.

1989b Hesban. Pp. 261-69 in *Archaeology of Jordan: Field Reports, Surveys and Sites*

A-K, eds. D. Homès-Fredericq and J. B. Hennessy. Leuven: Peeters.

1990 *Sedentarization and Nomadization: Food System Cycles at Hesban and Vicinity in Transjordan. Hesban 1.* Berrien Springs, MI: Andrews University.

1991 A Note on Seasonally Occupied Cave Villages. Pp. 353-55 in *Madaba Plains Project 2: The 1987 Season at Tell el-ᶜUmeiri and Vicinity and Subsequent Studies*, eds. L. G. Herr et al. Berrien Springs, MI: Andrews University/ Institute of Archaeology.

1994a The Journey from Heshbon to Hesban: An Account of the Evolution of the Heshbon Expedition's Scope of Research. Pp. 25-37 in *Hesban After 25 Years*, eds. D. Merling and L. T. Geraty. Berrien Springs, MI: Institute of Archaeology/Horn Archaeological Museum.

1994b Everyday Life at Hesban through the Centuries. Pp. 197-209 in *Hesban After 25 Years*, eds. D. Merling and L. T. Geraty. Berrien Springs, MI: Institute of Archaeology/Horn Archaeological Museum.

1995a The Development of the Bone Work on the Heshbon Expedition. Pp. 1-14 in *Faunal Remains: Taphonomical and Zooarchaeological Studies of the Animal Remains From Tell Hesban and Vicinity*, eds. Ø. S. LaBianca and A. von den Driesch. *Hesban 13.* Berrien Springs, MI: Institute of Archaeology/Andrews University.

1995b Ethonarchaeological and Taphonomical Investigations in the Village of Hesban. Pp. 15-32 in *Faunal Remains: Taphonomical and Zooarchaeological Studies of the Animal Remains From Tell Hesban and Vicinity*, eds. Ø. S. LaBianca and A. von den Driesch. *Hesban 13.* Berrien Springs, MI: Institute of Archaeology/ Andrews University.

1997 Pastoral Nomadism. Pp. 253-56 in *The Oxford Encyclopedia of Archaeology in the Near East*, vol. 4, ed. E. M. Meyers. Oxford: Oxford University.

1998 A Forest That Refuses to Disappear: Cycles of Environmental Degeneration and Regeneration in Jordan. Unpublished manuscript. Andrews University, Institute of Archaeology.

LaBianca, Ø. S., and Geraty, L. T.
1994 The Heshbon Expedition: Retrospects and Prospects. Pp. 301-12 in *Hesban After 25 Years*, eds. D. Merling and L. T. Geraty. Berrien Springs, MI: Institute of Archaeology/Horn Archaeological Museum.

LaBianca, Ø. S., and LaBianca, A. S.
1975 Tell Hesban 1973: The Anthropological Work. *Andrews University Seminary Studies* 13: 235-47.

LaBianca, Ø. S., and Lacelle, L., eds.
1986 *Environmental Foundations: Studies of Climatical, Geological, Hydrological and Phytological Conditions in Hesban and Vicinity,* eds. Ø. S. LaBianca and L. Lacelle. *Hesban 2.* Berrien Springs, MI: Andrews University.

LaBianca, Ø. S., and Ray, P. J.
1998 Preliminary Report of the 1997 Excavations and Restoration Work at Tall Hisban (June 18 to July 11, 1997). *Andrews University Seminary Studies* 36: 245-57.

1999 Madaba Plains Project 1997: Excavations and Restoration Work At Tall Hisban and Vicinity. *Annual of the Department of Antiquities of Jordan* 43: 115-25.

LaBianca, Ø. S.; Ray, P. J.; and Walker, B.
2000 Madaba Plains Project: Tall Hesban 1998. *Andrews University Seminary Studies* 38.1: 9-21.

LaBianca, Ø. S., and von den Driesch, A. eds.
1995 *Faunal Remains: Taphonomical and Zooarchaeological Studies of the Animal Remains From Tell Hesban and Vicinity. Hesban 13.* Berrien Springs, MI: Institute of Archaeology/Andrews University.

LaBianca, Ø. S., and Younker, R. W.
1995 The Kingdoms of Ammon, Moab and Edom: The Archaeology of Society in Late Bronze/Iron Age Transjordan (ca. 1400-500 BCE). Pp. 399-415, 590-94 in *The Archaeology of Society in the Holy Land*, ed. T. E. Levy. London: Leicester University.

LaBianca, Ø. S.; Herr, L. G.; Younker, R. W.; Geraty, L. T,; Clark, D. R.; Christopherson, G.; Cole, J. A.; Daviau, P. M.; Fisher, J. R.; Lawlor, J. I.; Harrison, T. P.; Hubbard, L. E.; London, G. A.; Low, R; and Schnurrenberger, D.
1995 Madaba Plains Project: A Preliminary Report on the 1989 Season at Tell El-ᶜUmeiri and Hinterland. Pp. 93-119 in Preliminary Excavation Reports: Sardis, Bir Umm Fawakhir, Tell El-ᶜUmeiri, The Combined Caesarea Expeditions, and Tell Dothan, ed. W. G. Dever. *Annual of the American Schools of Oriental Research* 52. Atlanta: American Schools of Oriental Research.

Lacelle, L.
1986 Ecology of the Flora of Tell Hesban and Area, Jordan. Pp. 99-119 in *Environmental Foundations: Studies of Climatical, Geological, Hydrological and Phytological Conditions in Hesban and Vicinity*, eds. Ø. S. LaBianca and L. Lacelle. *Hesban 2.* Berrien Springs, MI: Andrews University.

Lamon, R. S.
1935 *The Megiddo Water System.* Chicago: University of Chicago.

Lapp, N. L.
1981 The Third Campaign at Tell el-Ful: The Excavations of 1964. *Annual of the American Schools of Oriental Research,* vol. 45. Cambridge, MA: American Schools of Oriental Research.

1983 The Excavations at Araq el-Emir. *Annual*

of the American Schools of Oriental Research, vol. 47. Winona Lake, IN: Eisenbrauns.

Lapp, P. W., and Lapp, N. L.
1993 ᶜIraq el-Emir. Pp. 646-49 in *The New Encyclopedia of Archaeological Excavations in the Holy Land*, vol. 2, ed. E. Stern. Jerusalem: Israel Exploration Society.

Lawlor, J. L.
1980 The Excavation of the North Church at Hesban, Jordan: A Preliminary Report. *Andrews University Seminary Studies*. 18: 65-76.

1991 Field A: The Ammonite Citadel. Pp. 15-52 in *Madaba Plains Project 2: The 1987 Season at Tell el-ᶜUmeiri and Vicinity and Subsequent Studies*, eds. L. G. Herr et al. Berrien Springs, MI: Andrews University/Institute of Archaeology.

1997 Field A: The Ammonite Citadel. Pp. 21-52 in *Madaba Plains Project 3: The 1989 Season at Tell el-ᶜUmeiri and Vicinity and Subsequent Studies*, eds. L. G. Herr et al. Berrien Springs, MI: Andrews University/Institute of Archaeology.

Leonard, A.
1987 The Significance of the Mycenaean Pottery Found East of the Jordan River. Pp. 261-66 in *Studies in the History and Archaeology of Jordan III*, ed. A. Hadidi. Amman: Department of Antiquities.

Lepiksaar, J.
1995 Fish Remains From Tell Hesban, Jordan. Pp. 169-210 in *Faunal Remains: Taphonomical and Zooarchaeological Studies of the Animal Remains From Tell Hesban and Vicinity*, eds. Ø. S. LaBianca and A. von den Driesch. *Hesban 13*. Berrien Springs, MI: Institute of Archaeology/Andrews University.

Levy, T. E.
1995 From Camels to Computers: A Short History of Archaeological Method. *Biblical Archaeology Review* 21.4: 44-51; 64-65.

Little, R. M.
1969 An Anthropological Preliminary Note on the First Season at Tell Hesban. *Andrews University Seminary Studies* 7.2: 232-39.

Loffreda, S.
1980 Alcuni vasi ben datati della Fortezza di Macheronte. *Liber Annuus* 30: 377-402.

1992 Machaerus. Pp. 457-58 in *The Anchor Bible Dictionary,* vol. 4, ed. D. N. Freedman. New York: Doubleday.

London, B. D.
1981 The Metallurgy of Archaeological Samples from Tell Hesban. Unpublished manuscript. Andrews University, Institute of Archaeology.

London, G. A.
1991 Aspects of Early Bronze and Late Iron Age Ceramic Technology at Tell el-ᶜUmeiri. Pp. 383-419 in *Madaba Plains Project 2: The 1987 Season at Tell el-ᶜUmeiri and Vicinity and Subsequent Studies*, eds. L. G. Herr et al. Berrien Springs, MI: Andrews University/Institute of Archaeology.

1992 Tells: City Center or Home? *Eretz-Israel* 23 (the Biran volume): 71*-79*.

London, G. A., and Clark, D. R.
1997 *Ancient Ammonites & Modern Arabs: 5000 Years in the Madaba Plains of Jordan.* Amman: American Center of Oriental Research.

London, G. A., and Sinclair, M.
1991 An Ethnoarchaeological Survey of Potters of Jordan. Pp. 420-28 in *Madaba Plains Project 2: The 1987 Season at Tell el-ᶜUmeiri and Vicinity and Subsequent Studies*, eds. L. G. Herr et al. Berrien Springs, MI: Andrews University/Institute of Archaeology.

London, G. A.; Plint, H.; and Smith, J.
1991 Preliminary Petrographic Analysis of Pottery from Tell el-ᶜUmeiri and

Hinterland Sites, 1987. Pp. 429-39 in *Madaba Plains Project 2: The 1987 Season at Tell el-ᶜUmeiri and Vicinity and Subsequent Studies*, eds. L. G. Herr et al. Berrien Springs, MI: Andrews University/Institute of Archaeology.

Long, B. O.
1993 Mythic Trope in the Autobiography of William Foxwell Albright. *Biblical Archaeologist* 56: 36-45.

Loud, G.
1948 *Megiddo II.* Chicago: University of Chicago.

Low, R. D.
1991 Field F: The Eastern Shelf. Pp. 170-231 in *Madaba Plains Project 2: The 1987 Season at Tell el-ᶜUmeiri and Vicinity and Subsequent Studies*, eds. L. G. Herr et al. Berrien Springs, MI: Andrews University/Institute of Archaeology.

1997 Field F: The Eastern Shelf. Pp. 188-221 in *Madaba Plains Project 3: The 1989 Season at Tell el-ᶜUmeiri and Vicinity and Subsequent Studies*, eds. L. G. Herr et al. Berrien Springs, MI: Andrews University/Institute of Archaeology.

Low, R. D., and Schnurrenberger, D. W.
1997 Preliminary Observations on the Lithic Collection. Pp. 350-51 in *Madaba Plains Project 3: The 1989 Season at Tell el-ᶜUmeiri and Vicinity and Subsequent Studies*, eds. L. G. Herr et al. Berrien Springs, MI: Andrews University/ Institute of Archaeology.

Lugenbeal, E. N., and Sauer, J. A.
1972 Seventh-sixth Century B.C. Pottery from Area B at Heshbon. *Andrews University Seminary Studies* 10: 21-69.

MacDonald, B.
1994 *Ammon, Moab and Edom: Early States/Nations of Jordan in the Biblical Period (end of the 2nd and During the 1st Millennium B.C.).* Amman, Al Kutba.

Mare, W. H.
1976 Heshbon 1974: Area C. *Andrews University Seminary Studies* 14.1: 63-78.

1978 Heshbon 1976: Area C.1, 2, 3, 5, 7 *Andrews University Seminary Studies* 16.1: 51-70.

Marks, J. H.
1967- Spring in Jordanian Jerusalem. *American*
1968 *Schools of Oriental Research Newsletter* No. 2: 1-7.

Marquet-Krause, J.
1949 *Les Fouilles de ᶜAy (Et-Tell) 1933-1935.* Paris: Librairie Orientaliste Paul Geuthner.

Marx, E.
1977 The Tribe as a Unit of Subsistence: Nomadic Pastoralism in the Middle East. *American Anthropologist* 79: 343-63.

1992 Are there Pastoral Nomads in the Middle East? Pp. 255-60 in *Pastoralism in the Levant: Archaeological Materials in Anthropological Perspectives.* Monographs in World Archaeology No. 10, eds. O. Bar-Yosef and A. Khazanov. Madison, WI: Prehistory.

Master, D. M.
2001 State Formation Theory and the Kingdom of Ancient Israel. *Journal of Near Eastern Studies* 60: 117-31.

Mattingly, G. L.
1992 Mesha. P. 707 in *The Anchor Bible Dictionary*, vol. 4, ed. D. N. Freedman. New York: Doubleday.

1994 Moabites. Pp. 317-33 in *Peoples of the Old Testament World*, eds. A. J. Hoerth, G. L. Mattingly and E. M. Yamauchi. Grand Rapids, MI: Baker.

1995 Searching for Benchmarks in the Biblical World: The Development of Joseph A. Callaway as Field Archaeologist. *Biblical Archaeologist* 58: 14-25.

1996 Al-Karak Resources Project 1995: A Preliminary Report of the Pilot Season. *Annual of the Department of Antiquities of Jordan* 40: 349-68.

1997 A New Agenda for Research on Ancient Moab. *Biblical Archaeologist* 60: 214-21.

Mazar, A.
1981 Giloh: An Early Israelite Settlement Near Jerusalem. *Israel Exploration Journal* 31: 1-36.

1985 The Emergence of the Philistines Material Culture. *Israel Exploration Journal* 35: 95-107.

1997 Iron Age Chronology: A Reply to Finkelstein. *Levant* 29: 157-67.

1998 On the Appearance of Red Slip in the Iron Age I period in Israel. Pp. 368-78 *in Mediterranean Peoples in Transition: Thirteenth to Early Tenth Centuries BCE*, eds. S. Gitin, A. Mazar and E. Stern. Jerusalem: Israel Exploration Society.

Mazar, A., and Camp, J.
2000 Will Tel Rehov Save the United Monarchy? *Biblical Archaeology Review* 26.2: 38-48; 50-51; 75.

McGovern, P. E.
1980 Explorations in the Umm Ad-Dananir Region of the Baqᶜah Valley 1977-1978. *Annual of the Department of Antiquities of Jordan* 24: 55-67.

1983 Test Soundings of Archaeological and Resistivity Survey Results at Rujm Al-Henu. *Annual of the Department of Antiquities of Jordan* 27: 105-41.

1986 *The Late Bronze and Early Iron Ages of Central Transjordan: The Baqᶜah Valley Project, 1977-1981.* University Museum Monograph. Philadelphia: University Museum.

1987 Central Transjordan in the Late Bronze and Early Iron Ages: An Alternative Hypothesis of the Socio-Economic Transformation and Collapse. Pp. 267-73 in *Studies in the History and Archaeology of Jordan III*, ed. A. Hadidi. Amman: Department of Antiquities.

1989 The Baqᶜah Valley Project 1987: Khirbet Umm Ad-Dananir and Al-Qesir. *Annual of the Department of Antiquities of Jordan* 33: 123-36.

1992 Settlement Pattern of the Late Bronze and Iron Ages in the Greater Amman Area. Pp. 179-83 in *Studies in the History and Archaeology of Jordan IV*, eds. S. Tell et al. Amman: Department of Antiquities.

McNicoll, A.; Smith, R. H.; and Hennessy, B.
1982 *Pella in Jordan 1: Plates and Illustrations.* Canberra: Australian National Gallery.

Meadow, R. H.
1983 The Study of Faunal Remains from Archaeological Sites. *Biblical Archaeologist* 46: 49-53.

Merling, D.
1991 Heshbon: A Lost City of the Bible. *Archaeology in the Biblical World* 1.2: 10-16, 48.

1994 The "Pools of Heshbon": As Discovered by the Heshbon Expedition. Pp. 211-23 in *Hesban After 25 Years*, eds. D. Merling and L. T. Geraty. Berrien Springs, MI: Institute of Archaeology/Horn Archaeological Museum.

1996 *The Book of Joshua: Its Theme and Role in Archaeological Discussions.* Berrien Springs, MI: Andrews University.

2001 The Book of Joshua, Part I: Its Evaluation by Nonevidence. *Andrews University Seminary Studies* 39: 61-72.

Merling, D., and Geraty, L. T., eds.
1994 *Hesban After 25 Years.* Berrien Springs, MI: Institute of Archaeology/Horn Archaeological Museum.

Michigan Scholar Digs in Near East For Exodus Secret. *Detroit Free Press*, 27 October 1973.

Miller, J. E.
1991   The Bronze Ptolemaic Coin of Rujm Selim. Pp. 381-82 in *Madaba Plains Project 2: The 1987 Season at Tell el-ᶜUmeiri and Vicinity and Subsequent Studies*, eds. L. G. Herr et al. Berrien Springs, MI: Andrews University/ Institute of Archaeology.

Miller, J. M.
1992   Moab. Pp. 882-93 in *The Anchor Bible Dictionary*, vol. 4, ed. D. N. Freedman. New York: Doubleday.

Miller, J. M., ed.
1991   *Archaeological Survey of the Kerak Plateau*. Atlanta: Scholars.

Mitchel, L. A.
1992   *Hellenistic and Roman Strata. Hesban 7*. Berrien Springs, MI: Andrews University.

1994   Caves, Storage Facilities, and Life at Hellenistic and Early Roman Hesban. Pp. 97-106 in *Hesban After 25 Years*, eds. D. Merling and L. T. Geraty. Berrien Springs, MI: Institute of Archaeology/ Horn Archaeological Museum.

Moorey, P.R.S.
1991   *A Century of Biblical Archaeology*. Louisville: Westminster/John Knox.

Morton, W. H.
1989   A Summary of the 1955, 1956 and 1965 Excavations at Dhiban. Pp. 239-46 in *Studies in the Mesha Inscription and Moab*, ed. A. Dearman. Atlanta: Scholars.

Muhly, J. D.
1980   The Bronze Age Setting. Pp. 25-67 in *The Coming of the Iron Age*, eds. T. A. Wertime and J. D. Muhly. New Haven: Yale University.

1982   How Iron Technology Changed the Ancient World. *Biblical Archaeology Review* 8: 42-54.

Musil, A.
1907   *Arabia Petraea*. Part I. Wein: Kaiserliche Akademie der Wissenschaften.

Naᵓaman, N.
1997   King Mesha and the Foundation of the Moabite Monarchy. *Israel Exploration Journal* 47: 83-92.

Negbi, O.
1991   Were There Sea Peoples in the Central Jordan Valley at the Transition from the Bronze Age to the Iron Age? *Tel Aviv* 18.2: 205-43.

Netzer, E.
1999   Floating in the Desert: Jordan's Pleasure Palace. *Archaeological Odyssey* 2.1: 46-55.

Neumann, J., and Parpola, S.
1987   Climatic Change and the Eleventh - Tenth Century Eclipse of Assyria and Babylonia. *Journal of Near Eastern Studies* 46: 161-82.

Noth, M.
1958   *The History of Israel*. New York: Harper and Brothers.

Olavarri, E.
1965   Sondages a ᶜAroᶜer sur L'Arnon. *Revue Biblique* 72: 77-94.

1983   La Campagne de Fouilles 1982 a Khirbet Medeinet al-Muᶜarradjeh pres de Smakieh (Kerak). *Annual of the Department of Antiquities of Jordan* 27: 165-78.

1993   Aroer (in Moab). Pp. 92-93 in *The New Encyclopedia of Archaeological Excavations in the Holy Land*, vol. 1, ed. E. Stern. New York: Simon and Schuster.

Olmstead, A. T.
1948   *History of the Persian Empire*. Chicago: University of Chicago.

Oredsson, D.
2000 *Moats in Ancient Palestine.* Stockholm: Almqvist and Wiksell International.

Osborne, G. R.
1991 *The Hermeneutical Spiral: A Comprehensive Introduction to Biblical Interpretation.* Downers Grove, IL: InterVarsity.

Parker, S. T.
1976 Archaeological Survey of the *Limes Arabicus*: A Preliminary Report. *Annual of the Department of Antiquities of Jordan* 21: 19-31.

Parrot, A.
1971 Review of *Heshbon 1968: The First Campaign at Tell Hesban*, by R. S. Boraas and S. H. Horn. *Syria* 48: 503-4.

Plan Fourth Trip to Jordan. *Berrien Springs (MI) Journal Era*, 24 October 1973.

Platt, E. E.
1983 Textile Tools. Unpublished manuscript. Andrews University, Institute of Archaeology.

1989 ᶜUmeiri Objects. Pp. 355-66 in *Madaba Plains Project 1: The 1984 Season at Tell el- ᶜUmeiri and Vicinity and Subsequent Studies*, eds. L. T. Geraty et al. Berrien Springs, MI: Andrews University/ Institute of Archaeology.

1992 Jewelry, Ancient Israelite. Pp. 823-34 in *The Anchor Bible Dictionary*, vol. 3, ed. D. N. Freedman. New York: Doubleday.

Portugali, Y.
1982 A Field Methodology for Regional Archaeology (the Jezreel Valley Survey, 1981). *Tel Aviv* 9: 170-88.

Prag, K.
1991 A Walk in the Wadi Hesban. *Palestine Exploration Quarterly* 123: 48-61.

1992 Bronze Age Settlement Patterns in the South Jordan Valley: Archaeology Environment and Ethnology. Pp. 155-60

in *Studies in the History and Archaeology of Jordan IV*, ed. S. Tell. Amman: Department of Antiquities.

Pritchard, J. B.
1962 *Gibeon Where the Sun Stood Still.* Princeton: Princeton University.

1964 *Winery, Defenses, and Soundings at Gibeon.* Philadelphia: University of Pennsylvania.

1985 *Tell Es-Saᶜidiyeh: Excavations on the Tell, 1964-1966.* Philadelphia University of Pennsylvania.

Rasmussen, C. G.
1986 The Economic Importance of Caravan Trade for the Solomonic Empire. Pp. 153-66 in *A Tribute to Gleason Archer: Essays on the Old Testament*, eds. W. C. Kaiser and R. F. Youngblood. Chicago: Moody.

Rast, W. E.
1974 Review of *Heshbon Pottery 1971: A Preliminary Report on the Pottery of the 1971 Excavations at Tell Hesban*, by J. A. Sauer. *American Journal of Archaeology* 78: 434-35.

1978 *Taanach I. Studies in the Iron Age Pottery*, ed. A. E. Glock. Cambridge, MA: American Schools of Oriental Research.

1992 *Through the Ages in Palestinian Archaeology: An Introductory Handbook.* Philadelphia: Trinity.

Ray, P. J.
1993 The Great Controversy: The "Outer Wall" at Gezer. *Near East Archaeological Society Bulletin* 38: 39-52.

1995 The Iron Age Fortresses of the Negev Highlands: Another Look. Unpublished manuscript. Andrews University, Institute of Archaeology.

1997 Dibon: Its Archaeological and Historical Setting in Old Testament Times. Unpublished manuscript. Andrews University, Institute of Archaeology.

2000a Kedemoth. P. 761 in *Eerdmans Dictionary of the Bible*, ed. D. N. Freedman. Grand Rapids, MI: Eerdmans.

2000b Nebo. Pp. 952-53 in *Eerdmans Dictionary of the Bible*, ed. D. N. Freedman. Grand Rapids, MI: Eerdmans.

Redford, D. B.
1982a Contact Between Egypt and Jordan in the New Kingdom: Some Comments on Sources. Pp. 115-19 in *Studies in the History and Archaeology of Jordan I*, ed. A. Hadidi. Amman: Department of Antiquities.

1982b A Bronze Age Itinerary in Transjordan. *Journal for the Society for the Study of Egyptian Antiquities* 12: 55-74.

1992 *Egypt, Canaan, and Israel in Ancient Times*. Princeton: Princeton University.

Reich, R.
1992 Building Materials and Architectural Elements in Ancient Israel. Pp. 1-16 in *The Architecture of Ancient Israel*, eds. A. Kempinski and R. Reich. Jerusalem: Israel Exploration Society.

Reich, R., and Shukron, E.
1999 Light at the End of the Tunnel. *Biblical Archaeology Review* 25.1: 22-33, 72.

Renfrew, C., and Bahn, P.
1991 *Archaeology: Theories, Methods and Practice*. London: Thames and Hudson.

Rosen, A. M.
1986 *Cities of Clay: The Geoarchaeology of Tells*. Chicago: University of Chicago.

Rosen, B.
1994 Subsistence Economy in Iron Age I. Pp. 339-51 in *From Nomadism to Monarchy: Archaeological and Historical Aspects of Early Israel*, eds. I. Finkelstein and N. Naaman. Jerusalem: Israel Exploration Society.

Rosen, S. A.
1988 Finding Evidence of Ancient Nomads. *Biblical Archaeology Review* 14.5: 46-53.

1992 Nomads in Archaeology: A Response to Finkelstein and Perevolotsky. *Bulletin of the American Schools of Oriental Research* 287: 75-85.

Rosen, S. A., and Avni, G.
1993 The Edge of the Empire: The Archaeology of Pastoral Nomads in the Southern Negev Highlands in Late Antiquity. *Biblical Archaeologist* 56: 189-99.

Routledge, C.
1995 Pillared Buildings in Iron Age Moab. *Biblical Archaeologist* 58: 236.

2000 Seeing through Walls: Interpreting Iron Age I Architecture at Khirbat al-Mudayna al-ᶜAliya. *Bulletin of the American Schools of Oriental Research* 319: 37-70.

Rowton, M. B.
1974 Enclosed Nomadism. *Journal of the Economy and Social History of the Orient* 17: 1-30.

1976 Dimorphic Structure and Typology. *Oriens Antiques* 15: 2-31.

1977 Dimorphic Structure and the Parsocial Element. *Journal of Near Eastern Studies* 36: 181-98.

Saller, S. J.
1966 Iron Age Tombs at Nebo, Jordan. *Liber Annuus* 16: 165-298.

Saller, S. J., and Bagatti, B.
1949 *The Town of Nebo (Khirbet el-Mekhayyat)*. Jerusalem: Franciscan.

Sasson, J. A.
1993 Albright as an Orientalist. *Biblical Archaeologist* 56: 3-7.

Sauer, J. A.
1973 *Heshbon Pottery 1971: A Preliminary*

Report on the Pottery from the 1971 Excavations at Tell Hesban. Berrien Springs, MI: Andrews University.

1975a Heshbon 1973: Area B and Square D.4. *Andrews University Seminary Studies* 13.2: 133-67.

1975b Review of the Excavations at Dibon (Dhiban) in Moab: The Third Campaign 1952-1953. *Annual of the Department of Antiquities of Jordan* 20: 103-9.

1976 Heshbon 1974: Area B and Square D.4. *Andrews University Seminary Studies* 14.1: 29-62.

1978 Heshbon 1976: Area B and Square D.4. *Andrews University Seminary Studies* 16.1: 31-49.

1982 Prospects for Archaeology in Jordan and Syria. *Biblical Archaeologist* 45: 73-84.

1986 Transjordan in the Bronze and Iron Ages: A Critique of Glueck's Synthesis. *Bulletin of the American Schools of Oriental Research* 263: 1-26.

1994 The Pottery at Hesban and Its Relationships to the History of Jordan: An Interim Hesban Pottery Report, 1993. Pp. 225-81 in *Hesban After 25 Years*, eds. D. Merling and L. T. Geraty. Berrien Springs, MI: Institute of Archaeology/Horn Archaeological Museum.

Sauer, J. A., and Herr, L. G.
1997 Transjordan: Transjordan in the Bronze and Iron Ages. Pp. 231-35 in *The Oxford Encyclopedia of Archaeology in the Near East*, vol. 5, ed. E. M. Meyers. Oxford: Oxford University.

Forth- *Ceramic Finds. Hesban 11.* Berrien
coming Springs, MI: Andrews University.

Sclater, P. L., and Thomas, O.
1897- *The Book of Antelopes*, vols. 3 and 4.
1898 London: R. H. Porter.

Schnurrenberger, D. W.
1991 Preliminary Comments on the Geology of the Tell el-ᶜUmeiri Region. Pp. 370-76 in *Madaba Plains Project 2: The 1987 Season at Tell el-ᶜUmeiri and Vicinity and Subsequent Studies*, eds. L. G. Herr et al. Berrien Springs, MI: Andrews University/Institute of Archaeology.

1997a A Preliminary Report on Basalt Sources in Central and Northern Jordan. Pp. 308-10 in *Madaba Plains Project 3: The 1989 Season at Tell el-ᶜUmeiri and Vicinity and Subsequent Studies*, eds. L. G. Herr et al. Berrien Springs, MI: Andrews University/Institute of Archaeology.

1997b Geological Background to the Tall al-ᶜUmayri Region. Pp. 311-19 in *Madaba Plains Project 3: The 1989 Season at Tell el-ᶜUmeiri and Vicinity and Subsequent Studies*, eds. L. G. Herr et al. Berrien Springs, MI: Andrews University/Institute of Archaeology.

1997c Locating Intact Archaeological Sites in the Tall al-ᶜUmayri Region. Pp. 320-22 in *Madaba Plains Project 3: The 1989 Season at Tell el-ᶜUmeiri and Vicinity and Subsequent Studies*, eds. L. G. Herr et al. Berrien Springs, MI: Andrews University/Institute of Archaeology.

Service, E.
1962 *Primitive Social Organization.* New York: Random House.

Shafer, E.
1969 An Expedition from Berrien Springs to Heshbon Jordan. *South Bend Tribune Magazine*, 1 June 1969.

Shanks, H.
1983 Tom Croster Has Found the Ark of the Covenant—Or Has He: False Report of Ark Sighting Results in Cancellation of Important American Excavation. *Biblical Archaeology Review* 9.3: 66-69.

Shea, W. H.
1979 Heshbon in Iron Age History. Paper presented at the American Schools of

Oriental Research Symposium on Heshbon, 1979. Andrews University.

Shiloh, Y.
1984 *Excavations at the City of David, I 1978-1982: Interim Report of the First Five Seasons*. Jerusalem: Israel Exploration Society.

Stager, L. E.
1985 The Archaeology of the Family in Ancient Israel. *Bulletin of the American Schools of Oriental Research* 260: 1-35.

1995 The Impact of the Sea Peoples in Canaan (1185-1050 BCE). Pp. 332-48; 583-85 in *The Archaeology of Society in the Holy Land*, ed. T. E. Levy. London: Leicester University.

Steiner, M.
1997 The Popular Cult Sites of Ancient Palestine: Cave 1 in Jerusalem and E 207 in Samaria. *Scandinavian Journal of the Old Testament* 11.1:16-28.

Stern, E.
1982 *Material Culture of the Land of the Bible in the Persian Period 538-332 B.C.* Warminster: Aris & Phillips.

2001 Archaeology of the Land of the Bible: The Assyrian, Babylonian, and Persian Periods (732-332 BCE). New York: Doubleday.

Steward, J. H.
1955 *Theory of Culture Change*. Urbana: University of Illinois.

Storfjell, J. B.
1983 The Stratigraphy of Tell Hesban, Jordan in the Byzantine Period. Unpublished Ph.D. Dissertation, Andrews University.

Strange, J. F.
1988 Computers and Archaeological Research. Pp. 307-24 in *Benchmarks in Time and Culture: An Introduction to Palestinian Archaeology*, eds. J. F. Drinkard, G. L. Mattingly and J. M. Miller. Atlanta: Scholars.

Stronach, D.
1959 The Development of the Fibula in the Near East. *Iraq* 21: 181-206.

Swidler, W.
1973 Adaptive Processes Regulating Nomad-Sedentary Interaction in the Middle East. Pp. 23-42 in *The Desert and the Sown: Nomads in the Wider Society*, ed. C. Nelson. Institute of International Studies, Research Series 21. Berkeley: University of California.

Thompson, H. O.
1972 The 1972 Excavation of Khirbet al-Hajjar. *Annual of the Department of Antiquities of Jordan* 17: 47-72.

1973a The Excavations of Tell Siran (1972). *Annual of the Department of Antiquities of Jordan* 18: 5-14, 89-98.

1973b Rujm al-Malfuf South. *Annual of the Department of Antiquities of Jordan* 18: 47-50, 117-19.

1975 Heshbon 1973: Area C. *Andrews University Seminary Studies* 13.2: 169-81.

1984 The Excavation of Rujm el-Mekheizin. *Annual of the Department of Antiquities of Jordan* 28: 31-38.

1986 An Iron Age Tomb at Madaba. Pp. 331-63 in *The Archaeology of Jordan and Other Studies*, eds. L. T. Geraty and L. G. Herr. Berrien Springs, MI: Andrews University.

Tompkins, P. H.
1983 Adventist Raiders of the Lost Ark. *Spectrum* 13.4: 49-54.

Toombs, L. E.
1982 The Development of Palestinian Archaeology as a Discipline. *Biblical Archaeologist* 45: 89-91.

Tortonese, E.
1975 *Fauna d'Italia*, vol. 11. *Osteichthyes.* Bologna: Calderini.

Trapped by Fighting in Jordan. Benton Harbor News Palladium, 30 June 1967.

Tubb, J. N.
1988 Tell es-Sa^cidiyeh: Preliminary Report of the First Three Seasons of Renewed Excavations. *Levant* 20: 23-88.

Tufnell, O.
1953 *Lachiah III (Tell ed-Duweir) The Iron Age.* London: Oxford University.

Tushingham, A. D.
1972 The Excavations at Dibon (Dhbân) in Moab. *Annual of the American Schools of Oriental Research,* vol. 40. New Haven: American Schools of Oriental Research.

1990 Dhībân Reconsidered: King Mesha and His Works. *Annual of the Department of Antiquities of Jordan* 34: 183-92.

U.N. Food and Agriculture Organization.
1973 *FAO Species Identification Sheets for Fishery Purposes. Mediterranean and Black Sea (Fishing Area 37),* vols. 1 and 2. Rome.

van der Steen, E. J.
1995 Aspects of Nomadism and Settlement in the Central Jordan Valley. *Palestine Exploration Quarterly* 127: 141-58.

1996 The Central East Jordan Valley in the Late Bronze and Early Iron Ages. *Bulletin of the American Schools of Oriental Research* 302: 51-74.

Van Elderen, B.
1970- The Week of June 7-13. *American
1971 Schools of Oriental Research Newsletter* No. 2: 2-4.

1976 Heshbon 1974: Area A. *Andrews University Seminary Studies* 14.1: 17-28.

Van Zyl, A. H.
1960 *The Moabites.* Leiden: Brill.

de Vaux, R.
1970 On Right and Wrong Uses of Archaeology. Pp. 64-80 in *Near Eastern Archaeology in the Twentieth Century: Essays in Honor of Nelson Glueck,* ed. J. A. Sanders. Garden City: Doubleday.

Vinogradov, B. S.; Novikova, G. A.; and Portenko, L. A.
1953 *Atlas of Game and Economic Birds and Mammals of USSR,* vol. 2: *Mammals.* Moscow: Izdvo. Akademii Nauk.

von den Driesch, A, and Boessneck, J.
1995 Final Report on the Zooarchaeological Investigation of Animal Bone Finds from Tell Hesban, Jordan. Pp. 65-108 in *Faunal Remains: Taphonomical and Zooarchaeological Studies of the Animal Remains from Tell Hesban and Vicinity,* eds. Ø. S. LaBianca and A. von den Driesch. *Hesban 13.* Berrien Springs, MI: Institute of Archaeology/Andrews University.

Vyhmeister, W. K.
1968 The History of Heshbon from the Literary Sources. *Andrews University Seminary Studies* 6.2: 158-77.

1989a The History of Heshbon from the Literary Sources. Pp. 1-23 in *Historical Foundations: Studies of Literary References to Hesban and Vicinity,* eds. L. T. Geraty and L. G. Running. *Hesban 3.* Berrien Springs, MI: Andrews University.

1989b Hesban in the Literary Sources Since 1806. Pp. 65-72 in *Historical Foundations: Studies of Literary References to Hesban and Vicinity,* eds. L. T. Geraty and L. G. Running. *Hesban 3.* Berrien Springs, MI: Andrews University.

Waldbaum, J. C.
1978 *From Bronze to Iron: The Transition from the Bronze Age to the Iron Age in the Eastern Mediterranean.* Studies in Mediterranean Archaeology 54. Gothenburg: P. Åströms.

1980   The First Archaeological Appearance of Iron and the Transition to the Iron Age. Pp. 69-98 in *The Coming of the Iron Age*, eds. T. A. Wertime and J. D. Muhly. New Haven: Yale University.

1991   Two Attic Sherds.   P. 243 in *Madaba Plains Project 2: The 1987 Season at Tell el-ᶜUmeiri and Vicinity and Subsequent Studies*, eds. L. G. Herr et al. Berrien Springs, MI: Andrews University/ Institute of Archaeology.

Wampler, J. C.
1947   *Tell en-Nasbeh. The Pottery*. Berkeley, CA: The Palestine Institute of Pacific School of Religion.

Ward, W. A.
1966   Scarabs' Seals and Cylinders From Two Tombs at Amman. *Annual of the Department of Antiquities of Jordan* 11: 5-16.

1972   The Shasu Bedouin: Notes on a Recent Publication. *Journal of the Economic and Social History of the Orient* 15: 35-60.

Waterhouse, S. D, and Ibach, R.
1975   Heshbon 1973: The Topographical Survey. *Andrews University Seminary Studies* 13.2: 217-33.

Waterhouse, S. D., ed.
1998   *The Necropolis of Hesban: A Catalogue of Tombs and Their Contents. Hesban 10*. Berrien Springs, MI: Andrews University.

Weinstein, J. M.
1981   The Egyptian Empire in Palestine: A Reassessment. *Bulletin of the American Schools of Oriental Research* 241: 1-28.

1998   Egyptian Relations with the Eastern Mediterranean World at the end of the Second Millennium BCE. Pp. 188-96 in *Mediterranean Peoples in Transition: Thirteenth to Early Tenth Centuries BCE*, eds. S. Gitin, A. Mazar and E. Stern. Jerusalem: Israel Exploration Society.

Weippert, M.
1974   Semitische Nomaden des 2. Jahrtausends. *Biblica* 55: 265-80.

Weippert, M., and Weippert, H.
1988   German Archaeologists. Pp. 87-108 in *Benchmarks in Time and Culture: An Introduction to Palestinian Archaeology*, eds. J. F. Drinkard, G. L. Mattingly and J. M. Miller. Atlanta: Scholars.

Wente, E. F., and Van Siclen, C. C.
1976   A Chronology of the New Kingdom. Pp. 217-61 in *Studies in Hornor of George R. Hughes*, ed. by J. H. Johnson and E. F. Wente. Chicago: Oriental Institute.

Willey, G. R., and Sabloff, J. A.
1974   *A History of American Archaeology*. San Francisco: Freeman.

1980   *A History of American Archaeology*. Revised ed. San Francisco: Freeman.

Wimmer, D. H.
1987a Tell Safut Excavations, 1982-1985 Preliminary Report. *Annual of the Department of Antiquities of Jordan* 31: 159-74.

1987b The Excavations at Safut. Pp. 179-282 in *Studies in the History and Archaeology of Jordan III*, ed. A. Hadidi. Amman: Department of Antiquities.

1989   Safut (Tell). Pp. 512-15 in *Archaeology of Jordan: Field Reports, Surveys and Sites L-Z*, eds. D. Homès-Fredericq and J. B. Hennessy. Leuven: Peeters.

Winnett, F. V., and Reed, W. L.
1964   *The Excavations at Dibon (Dhībân) in Moab. Annual of the American Schools of Oriental Research*, vol. 36-37. New Haven: American Schools of Oriental Research.

Wood, B. G.
1990   *The Sociology of Pottery in Ancient Palestine: The Ceramic Industry and Diffusion of Ceramic Style in the Bronze and Iron Ages*. JSOT Supplement Series

103. JSOT/ASOR Monographs 4. Sheffield: JSOT.

Worschech, U.
1997 Egypt and Moab. *Biblical Archaeologist* 60: 229-34.

Wright, G. E.
1952 *The God Who Acts: Biblical Theology as Recital.* London: SCM.

1957 *Biblical Archaeology.* Philadelphia: Westminster.

1958a Archaeology and Old Testament Studies. *Journal of Biblical Literature* 77: 39-51.

1958b Comments on Yadin's Dating of the Shechem Temple. *Bulletin of the American Schools of Oriental Research* 150: 34-35.

1959 Samaria. *Biblical Archaeologist* 22: 67-78.

1962 Archaeological Fills and Strata. *Biblical Archaeologist* 25: 34-40.

1969 Biblical Archaeology Today. Pp. 149-65 in *New Directions in Biblical Archaeology*, eds. D. N. Freedman and J. Greenfield. Garden City, NY: Doubleday.

1970- Amman. *American Schools of Oriental Research Newsletter* No. 8: 2-3.
1971

1971 What Archaeology Can and Cannot Do. *Biblical Archaeologist* 34: 70-76.

1974 The Tell: Basic Unit for Reconstructing Complex Societies in the Near East. Pp. 123-43 in *Reconstructing Complex Societies*, ed. C. B. Moore. Bulletin of the American Schools of Oriental Research Supplement 20.

1975 The "New" Archaeology. *Biblical Archaeologist* 38: 104-15.

Wright, K.; Schick, R.; and Brown, B.
1989 Report on a Preliminary Survey of the Wadi Shuᶜeib. *Annual of the Department*

of Antiquities of Jordan 33: 345-50.

Yadin, Y.
1958 A Note on Dating the Shechem Temple. *Bulletin of the American Schools of Oriental Research* 150: 34.

1975 *Hazor: The Rediscovery of a Great Citadel of the Bible.* New York: Random House.

Yadin, Y.; Aharoni, Y; Amiran, R; Dothan, T.; Dothan, M.; Dunayevsky, I.; and Perrot. J.
1961 *Hazor III-IV: An Account of the Third and Fourth Seasons of Excavation, 1957-1958 (Plates).* Jerusalem: Israel Exploration Society.

Yadin, Y.; Aharoni, Y; Amiran, R; Ben-Tor, A; Dothan, M.; Dothan, T.; Dunayevsky, I.; Shulamit, G; and Stern, E.
1989 *Hazor III-IV: An Account of the Third and Fourth Seasons of Excavation, 1957-1958 (Text).* Jerusalem: Israel Exploration Society.

Yamauchi, E.
1996 *Persia and the Bible.* Grand Rapids, MI: Baker.

Yassine, K.
1975 Anthropoid Coffins from Raghdan Royal Palace Tomb in Amman. *Annual of the Department of Antiquities of Jordan* 20: 57-68, 165-68.

Yassine, K., ed.
1988 *Archaeology of Jordan: Essays and Reports.* Amman: University of Jordan.

Yassine, K.; Ibrahim, M.; and Sauer, J. A.
1988 The East Jordan Valley Survey, 1976. Pp. 189-207 in *Archaeology of Jordan: Essays and Reports*, ed. K. Yassine. Amman: University of Jordan.

Younker, R. W.
1989a Present and Past Plant Communities of the Tell el-ᶜUmeiri Region. Pp. 32-40 in *Madaba Plains Project 1: The 1984 Season at Tell el-ᶜUmeiri and Vicinity and Subsequent Studies*, eds. L. T. Geraty

et al. Berrien Springs, MI: Andrews University/Institute of Archaeology.

1989b "Towers" in the Region Surrounding Tell el-ᶜUmeiri. Pp. 195-98 in *Madaba Plains Project 1: The 1984 Season at Tell el-ᶜUmeiri and Vicinity and Subsequent Studies*, eds. L. T. Geraty et al. Berrien Springs, MI: Andrews University/ Institute of Archaeology.

1991a The Judgment Survey. Pp. 269-334 in *Madaba Plains Project 2: The 1987 Season at Tell el-ᶜUmeiri and Vicinity and Subsequent Studies*, eds. L. G. Herr et al. Berrien Springs, MI: Andrews University/Institute of Archaeology.

1991b Architectural Remains from the Hinterland Survey. Pp. 335-41 in *Madaba Plains Project 2: The 1987 Season at Tell el-ᶜUmeiri and Vicinity and Subsequent Studies*, eds. L. G. Herr et al. Berrien Springs, MI: Andrews University/Institute of Archaeology.

1991c A Preliminary Report of the 1990 Season at Tel Gezer: Excavations of the "Outer Wall" and the "Solomonic" Gateway (July 2 to August 10, 1990). *Andrews University Seminary Studies* 29: 19-60.

1993 Some Thoughts on the Identity of Tell Jalul, Jordan. Unpublished manuscript. Andrews University, Institute of Archaeology.

1994a Ammonites. Pp. 293-316 in *Peoples of the Old Testament World*, eds. A. J. Hoerth, G. L. Mattingly and E. M. Yamauchi. Grand Rapids: Baker.

1994b Hesban: Its Geographical Setting. Pp. 55-63 in *Hesban After 25 Years*, eds. D. Merling and L. T. Geraty. Berrien Springs, MI: Institute of Archaeology/ Horn Archaeological Museum.

1995 Balanophagy and the Bedrock Industries of Ancient Jordan. Pp. 685-91 in *Studies in the History and Archaeology of Jordan V*, ed. K. ᶜAmr, F. Zayadine and M.

Zaghloul. Amman: Department of Antiquities.

1997a Moabite Social Structure. *Biblical Archaeologist* 60: 237-48.

1997b The Emergence of the Ammonites: Sociocultural Transformation on the Transjordan Plateau During the Late Bronze/Iron Age Transition. Unpublished Dissertation. Andrews University, Institute of Archaeology.

1999 The Emergence of the Ammonites. Pp. 189-218 in *Ancient Ammon*, eds. B. MacDonald and R. W. Younker. Leiden: Brill.

Younker, R. W., and Daviau, P. M.
1993 Is Mefaᶜat to Be Found at Tell Jawa (South)? *Israel Exploration Journal* 43: 23-28.

Younker, R. W., and Merling, D.
2000 Madaba Plains Project: Tall Jalul 1999. *Andrews University Seminary Studies* 38.1: 45-58.

Younker, R. W.; Geraty, L. T.; Herr, L. G.; and LaBianca, Ø. S.
1990 The Joint Madaba Plains Project: A Preliminary Report of the 1989 Season, Including the Regional Survey and Excavations at El-Dreijat, Tell Jawa and Tell el-ᶜUmeiri (June 19 to August 8, 1989). *Andrews University Seminary Studies* 28: 5-52.

1993 The Joint Madaba Plains Project: A Preliminary Report of the 1992 Season, Including the Regional Survey and Excavations at Tell Jalul and Tell el-ᶜUmeiri (June 16-July 31, 1992). *Andrews University Seminary Studies* 31: 205-38.

Younker, R. W.; Geraty, L. T.; LaBianca, Ø. S.; Herr, L. G.; and Clark. D. R.
1996 Preliminary Report of the 1994 Season of the Madaba Plains Project: Regional Survey, Tall al-ᶜUmayri and Tall Jalul Excavations (June 15 to July 30, 1994).

Andrews University Seminary Studies 34: 65-92.

1997   Preliminary Report of the 1996 Season of the Madaba Plains Project: Regional Survey, Tall al-ᶜUmayri and Tall Jalul Excavations (June 19 to July 31, 1996). *Andrews University Seminary Studies* 35: 227-40.

Zayadine, F.
1973   Recent Excavations on the Upper Citadel of Amman (A Preliminary Report). *Annual of the Department of Antiquities of Jordan* 18: 17-35; 99-114.

1981   Recent Excavations and Restorations of the Department of Antiquities (1979-80). *Annual of the Department of Antiquities of Jordan* 31: 341-55.

Zayadine, F.; Najjar, M.; and Greene, J. A.
1987   The Excavations on the Citadel of Amman (Lower Terrace): A Preliminary Report. *Annual of the Department of Antiquities of Jordan* 31: 299-311.

Zayadine, F.; Humbert, J. B.; and Najjar, M.
1989   The 1988 Excavations on the Citadel of Amman Lower Terrace, Area A. *Annual of the Department of Antiquities of Jordan* 33: 357-63.

Zeder, M.
1996   The Role of Pigs in Near Eastern Subsistence: A View from the Southern Levant.   Pp. 297-312 in *Retrieving the Past: Essays on Archaeological Research and Methodology in Honor of Gus W. Van Beek*, ed. J. Seger.   Winona Lake, IN: Eisenbrauns.

Zertal, A.
1986-   An Early Iron Age Cultic Site on Mount
1987   Ebal: Excavation Seasons 1982-1987. *Tel Aviv* 13-14: 105-65.

1994   To the Land of the Perizzites and the Giants: On the Israelite Settlement in the Hill Country of Manasseh.   Pp. 47-69 in *From Nomadism to Monarchy: Archaeological and Historical Aspects of Early Israel*, eds. I. Finkelstein and N. Naaman. Jerusalem: Israel Exploration Society.

Zobel, H.
1979   Review of *Heshbon 1971: The Second Campaign at Tell Hesban*, by R. S. Boraas and S. H. Horn. *Theologische Literaturzeitung* 104.4: 288.

Zorn, J. R.
1997a Mizpah: Newly Discovered Stratum Reveals Judah's Other Capital. *Biblical Archaeology Review* 23.5: 28-38, 66.

1997b An Inner and Outer Gate Complex at Tell en-Nasbeh.   *Bulletin of the American Schools of Oriental Research* 307: 53-66.

Index

Index

basin 134
bats 88
bath house 26
Bath-rabbim 169
bead (s) 106, 108, 123, 139
bedouin 65
bedrock 20, 22, 25, 28-29, 57, 68, 75, 89, 98-101, 107,
    115, 130, 134, 141-142, 161, 167
bedrock features 167
bedrock shelf 121, 126, 132, 139, 142
bedrock trench 45, 80, 84, 88-93, 96, 98-100, 106-107,
    109-110, 115, 167
bedrock trough 126
Beegle, Dewey 17, 22
Beer Sheba 115
behaviorist-processualist 33
Beitin 16
Ben-Tor, Amnon 61
Bes 138
Beth Bamoth 154
Bethel 43, 49, 61, 79
Beth-Jeshimoth 93
Beth-shean 69, 80
Beth-Shemesh 32, 107, 110
Bezer 112, 125, 154
Biblical Archaeology 3, 18, 24, 36-37, 169
bichrome ware 49, 61
Binford, Lewis 32
Bird, Phyllis 18, 19
black ware 141, 144
blade point (s) 137, 146, 150
Blaine, Michael B. 27
Bliss, Frederick, J. 13, 14
Boessneck, Joachim 27
bone analysis 25
bone data 8, 22
bones 20-21, 27, 31, 34, 67, 79-80, 96, 108, 124, 138-
    139, 145, 148
Boraas, Roger 17-18, 22, 25, 27, 37
botanical remains 8, 28
bowls 99
brace 139
Braudel, Fernand 35, 37
British Archaeology 21
British Mandate 14
broad bean 148
bronze 111
Bronze Age 29
Brower, James 30
Brown, Robin 27
building (s) 15-16
Bullard, Reuben 18, 20

burclover 148
burnish 49, 53, 57, 99, 107, 109, 124, 141, 144
button 139, 146
buttress 130
Byzantine period 5, 9, 18-20, 23, 26-28, 30-31, 34, 142

C

Callaway, Joseph A. 15, 17
Calvin Theological Seminary 25, 27
camel 96, 109, 145, 148-149
caravan routes 145
caravan traffic 115, 155, 168-169
carbonized seeds 8, 25, 31, 34, 95, 109, 139, 147, 149
carburization 150
carinated bowls 43, 45, 79, 93
carnelian 108
catchment 110, 121
cattle 67, 80, 96, 108, 114, 124, 148
caves 65, 70, 161
cave installations 28
cave villages 34
cemetery (ies) 19, 21, 22-23, 26, 28, 30, 70
central hill country 43, 79, 167
central Jordanian Plateau 3
central place theory 93
central Transjordan 7, 21, 70
ceramic chronology 13
ceramic horizon (s) 106, 121
ceramic sequence 13
ceramic typology 14, 16, 24
cereal cultivation 80, 96, 148
cereal production 111-112, 124
cereals 108, 148
Chalcolithic period 26
chalice 68-69, 80, 95, 110
chalk 106
channel (s) 89, 100, 121, 132, 134, 142, 155
charcoal 108
chicken 96, 148-149
chiefdom 115, 155
chinkstones 100, 130
Christopherson, Gary L. 34
church (es) 20, 22, 28, 30
Cisjordan 43, 45, 53, 57, 61, 67-69, 79, 95, 108-109,
    115-116, 121, 124, 144, 155, 160, 167-168
cistern (s) 21, 80, 84, 88, 99, 101, 110
city 116
city wall 139
clan 80
Clark, Douglas R. 34, 91
Clarke, D. L. 22

Nebo 57, 67, 70, 112, 125, 144, 154
Nebuchadnezzar II 147
negative evidence 65
Negev 108, 142, 145, 160
Neo-Babylonian 57, 147
neo-orthodox biblical theology movement 16
New Archaeology 3, 21-22, 25, 29, 32-33, 35- 38
New World Archaeology 24
Nichol, Murray 19
nomad (s) 8, 31, 66, 111
nomadic interlude 65
nomadic-pastoral 110
nomadic-sedentary continuum 66, 70, 80, 169
nomadization   5, 33, 35, 37, 66, 169
nonevidence 65
normal science 35
normative model 33
north-south and east-west axes 18, 22, 27-28
numismatic finds 21
nuts 111, 150

O

oak 111, 150
obsidian 123
occupational features 92
occupational phase 75
occupational surfaces 160
offset-inset wall 126, 155, 168
offset-rimmed bowl 57, 144
olive (s) 148, 168
olive trees 111-112, 150
Omrides 125
organic matter 108
ornithological evidence 29
Osborne, Grant R. 36
ostracon (a) 134, 137, 139, 144-146, 167-168
Ottoman period 5, 29
overtaxation 147

P

paint 57, 124
palaeobotanists 34
Palestine 7-8, 13-16, 36, 45, 61, 93, 116, 147, 161
Palestine Exploration Fund 13
Palestine Exploration Quarterly 19
palynology 34
Papyrus Anastasi VI 65
Papyrus Harris I 65
paradigm shift 35
parallel retreat 90

Parker, Thomas 27
parrot fish 124
pastoral encampments 66
pastoral nomads 65
pastoralism 66
pastoralists 8, 124, 126, 168
pastoral-nomadic 150
pastoral-nomadism 70
pasture 150
pea 96
Pella 17, 57, 69
pendant (s) 108, 139, 146
Penuel 114, 121
percussion instrument 108
perimeter wall 68, 139, 159
Perkins, Paul 27
Persia 150, 168
Persian period 57, 61, 75, 147, 154
Persians 155, 168
pestles 155, 162
Petrie, Flinders 13, 14
Philadelphia-Amman 160-162, 169
Philistia 53
Philistines 45, 49, 126, 146
Phoenicia 145
Phoenician 107
photography 35
pig (s) (swine) 79-80, 96, 108-109, 115, 148-149
pigweed 148
pin 138
pistachio 111, 150
pit 15, 67, 93, 101, 106, 130, 160
Pitt-Rivers, Augustus Lane-Fox 13, 15
plant remains 22
plaque figurine 108
plaster 89, 100, 107, 121, 126, 132, 134, 137-138, 142, 155
plaster surface 121
plastered floor 23
plastered pool 134
plateau 150, 151, 154
pluralism 36
political history 14
pollen 25, 29
pool (s) 162, 169
Portugali, Yuval 93
positivism 14
post-modern 36
post-processual archaeology 36, 37
post-structualist 36
pottery disc (s) 88, 96, 106, 108, 138, 146
poultices 96, 148

seismic refraction 34
Seleucids 160, 162
Sellin, Ernst 14
semi-hewn boulders 96
semi-nomads 70
settled population 93
settlement pattern 3, 161, 168
settlement strategy 95
Shea, William H. 89
Shechem 15-17, 43, 49, 79
sheep 67, 80, 96, 108, 114, 124, 148-149, 167
shell ornaments 139
shelved tell structures 93
Shephelah 160
Sheshonq (Shishak) 53, 121
Shiloh 49, 61
shrine 80, 88, 95, 110
shrines 70
Sibmah 144
significance 36
Sihon 18, 21-24, 27, 29, 31, 34, 37-38, 169
silos (s) 99, 137, 142, 155, 160, 168
silt 84, 89, 137
silt layer 26
site formation processes 15
site hierarchy 116, 155, 162
Six-Day War 16, 19
slingstone (s) 75, 106, 134, 138, 146, 155, 159, 162
slip 53, 109
slope decline 90
slope evolution studies 90
small finds 27, 31
Smith, Eli 13
social organization 3, 24, 115
social science 33
soil 88, 96, 111, 141, 150, 153, 159-160
soil creep 90
soil layer (s) 75, 79, 84, 93, 95, 101, 106-107, 123, 126, 130, 134, 137-139, 160
soil samples 25
soil/debris layers 3, 5
Solomon 53, 107, 110, 114, 121, 155, 167, 169
spatula 139
specialist (s) 16-20, 22, 25-27, 29,-31, 169
specialist reports 21
specialist studies 27, 32
spindle rest 88, 123, 137
spindle whorl (s) 75, 80, 88, 96, 106, 123, 138
spinning 80
Stager, Lawrence E. 37
state 110
steep side (tell) 93

steep slope (tell) 90
steppe zone 111, 150
Steward, Julian 29
Stirling, James H. 25, 27
stone bass 95, 145
stone bowl (s) 106, 108, 145
stone vessels 146, 148
stoppers 142
storage silo 137
Storfjell, Bjørnar 65
strainer-spouted jugs 45
stratigraphy 13-14, 24
subsistence agriculture 160
subsistence economy 8, 80, 96, 115, 148, 168
subsistence patterns 110
subsistence strategy (ies) 3, 109, 148, 150, 168
subterranean cave complexes 161
subterranean habitation 88
subterranean room 100, 106-107
Succoth 121
surfaces 160
survey (s) 3, 5, 7-9, 14, 20-22, 25-27, 29, 30-31, 34, 66-67, 111-112, 116, 144, 151, 154, 160-162
sweat pea 148
symbiotic relationship 65
symposia 30
synchronic 36
Syria 19, 69
Syro-Palestinian archaeology 13, 24, 31-33, 35-36, 38
systems theory 24, 32

T

Taanach 43, 53
tabun 26
Tananir 67
taphonomical studies 22
tares 96, 148
Tel el-Ful 144
Tell Abu Hawam 53, 69
Tell el-ᶜUmeiri 3, 29, 34, 43, 57, 66, 68, 70, 79, 89, 91, 93, 111-112, 114, 151, 154, 160-161
Tell el-Ful 49, 53
Tell el-Hesi 13
Tell el-Kafrein 151, 153, 161
Tell en-Nasbeh 43, 49, 53
Tell er-Rameh 112, 151, 161
Tell es-Saᶜidiyeh 57, 69
Tell es-Sawwan 115
tell formation model 93, 115
Tell Ghreimu 66

DATE DUE
